GERMAN MARXISM AND
RUSSIAN COMMUNISM

GERMAN MARXISM AND RUSSIAN COMMUNISM

by
JOHN PLAMENATZ

GREENWOOD PRESS, PUBLISHERS
WESTPORT, CONNECTICUT

Library of Congress Cataloging in Publication Data

Plamenatz, John Petrov.
    German Marxism and Russian communism.

    Reprint of the 1954 ed. published by Longmans, Green,
London.
    Includes index.
    1. Communism--Germany. 2. Communism--Russia.
I. Title.
HX273.P45 1975   335.4'09   75-1135
ISBN 0-8371-7986-6

Originally published in 1954 by Longman, London

Reprinted with the permission of Longman Group Limited

Reprinted in 1975 by Greenwood Press,
a division of Williamhouse-Regency Inc.

Library of Congress Catalog Card Number 75-1135

ISBN 0-8371-7986-6

Printed in the United States of America

PREFACE

THIS book is not a criticism of the Communists but an account of their doctrines. If they have done any good in the world, that good stands to their credit, however false their theories. Arguments different from the ones used in this book would be needed to condemn their policies. There is more than a little error in all social and political theories, and it cannot greatly matter whether their adherents are consistent. We condemn men for their actions rather than their opinions, and for their opinions only because they use them to excuse their actions. Inconsistency is a minor fault in practical men dealing with vast affairs whose complexity they only half understand.

What better evidence of the immaturity of the Communists than the great pride they take in their own consistency, or of their inhumanity than their thinking it more important to have 'correct' opinions about doubtful matters than to be mild and just? But it is not to establish these conclusions that the author has written nearly one hundred and forty thousand words. Men's actions are affected by their opinions; and when they have power, it is important to discover what those opinions are and how they came by them. The modern Communists, puerile thinkers though they sometimes are, have taken many of their opinions from the social and political theories of Karl Marx—a remarkably confused but also truly great and original thinker. This book attempts to expound and criticize those theories, and then to explain how the Russian Communist or Bolshevik doctrines arose out of them.

The author is grateful to his wife for reading carefully through the manuscript of the book and helping him to express his meaning more clearly and concisely than he would otherwise have done. He has also to thank Mr. Isaiah Berlin, who has read part of the book in manuscript, for valuable criticisms and suggestions.

J.P.

April 1953

CONTENTS

		Page
PREFACE		v
INTRODUCTION		xi

PART ONE: GERMAN MARXISM

Chapter One		REVOLUTIONARY MARXISM	3
	I	The Five Exponents of 'Marxism'	5
	II	The Unimportance of Dialectical Materialism	8
Chapter Two		HISTORICAL MATERIALISM	18
	I	The Relations of Production	21
	II	Economic Contradictions and the Class Struggle	28
Chapter Three		IDEOLOGY AND THE CLASS STRUGGLE	36
Chapter Four		THE FACTS ALLEGED BY MARX AND ENGELS IN SUPPORT OF THEIR THEORY	55
Chapter Five		THE MARXIAN CONCEPTION OF SOCIETY AND ITS PROGRESS	74
	I	Society as an Organic Whole Developing According to the Law of its Kind	76
	II	Fundamentalism	81
Chapter Six		THE MARXIAN ANALYSIS OF CAPITALISM	88
Chapter Seven		THE POLITICS OF MARX AND ENGELS	115
	I	Marx Compared with the Other Socialists	115
	II	The Proletariat and Other Classes	121
		(i) The Communist Manifesto	121
		(ii) The Address to the Communist League	127

Page

III   The Marxian Theory of the State   135
       (i) The State as an Instrument of Class
              Oppression   135
       (ii) The State as a Parasite on Society   144
       (iii) The Disappearance of the State   151
IV   The Dictatorship of the Proletariat   155
V   Engels and Reformism   164

Chapter Eight   THE DECAY OF GERMAN MARXISM   168

PART TWO: RUSSIAN COMMUNISM

Chapter Nine   RUSSIA AND THE BOLSHEVIK
                   REVOLUTION   191
I   Peasants and Landlords   192
II   The Russian State   197
III   Ideologies before Marxism   200
IV   Marxism   203
V   The Fall of Tsardom   205
VI   The Triumph of the Bolsheviks   209

Chapter Ten   BOLSHEVISM BEFORE THE REVOLUTION   217
I   Marxism in a Backward Society   217
II   The Party of the Proletariat   222
III   The Uninterrupted Revolution   227
IV   The Proletarian 'Half-State'   240

Chapter Eleven   BOLSHEVISM AFTER THE REVOLUTION 250
I   The Fight for Power after the Revo-
          lution   252
II   Leninism after the Revolution   261
III   Stalinism   266

Chapter Twelve   TROTSKYISM   281

Chapter Thirteen   MARXISM AND COMMUNISM   306
I   The Marxian Legacy of Ideas   306
II   Bolshevism   317
III   Bolshevism and the World   329

INDEX   353

On peut de plus poser pour maxime générale
que toute révolution prévue n'arrivera jamais.

MONTESQUIEU

INTRODUCTION

WHEN Montesquieu published *The Persian Letters*, they were universally admired; but his first critics warned the public that, admirable though the *Letters* might be, their author knew almost nothing about Persians. He had met none, and for his little knowledge about them had to rely on travellers' tales. His Persians were Frenchmen dressed up to look like foreigners, that their surprise at the absurdities of ordinary French life might seem the more natural. Two hundred and thirty years ago Europe was still culturally separate from the rest of the world; she had her own civilization and was affected by others as little as she affected them. The English, the Spaniards, the French, the Dutch, and the Portuguese had possessions outside Europe, but they were mostly islands or small coastal territories. Only in America, the emptiest of the continents, had they penetrated even a hundred miles into the interior. The world was already beginning to feel the power of the Europeans. But only a little, and not yet nearly enough to make them seem admirable or worth imitating. The Europeans were either unknown or despised,[1] and were not even objects of curiosity. Indeed, they were more curious about other peoples than the others about them.

In 1721, when *The Persian Letters* were published, Paris and London were the intellectual capitals of Europe; and Europe, under the cultural hegemony of the English and the French, was more civilized than she had been since the fall of the Roman Empire. Her kings made war on one another, but they made it

[1] Of all the Asiatic peoples, the Turks knew the Europeans best, and most heartily despised them. This apparently ineradicable contempt survived innumerable Turkish defeats. When Marashli Ali Pasha, Vizir of Belgrade, crossed the Danube in 1816, at the Sultan's order, to pay his respects to the Austrian Emperor Francis, who was then visiting Zemun, he invited Francis to sit down in his presence. The interpreter, probably a Greek, took care not to translate what the Vizir had said. To Marashli it had seemed a matter of course that a Moslem who was also the Sultan's representative should take precedence over a Christian emperor.

in the service of similar ambitions. The common language of Europe was no longer dead Latin but living French, no longer a survival from another world clumsily used by pedants, but something altogether more fresh, vigorous, and subtle, and only recently brought to perfection by the most scrupulous, pure, and delicate of European writers. The wars of religion were over, respect for truth and freedom greater than ever before, and scepticism much more the scourge of pretentious ignorance than a refuge for the timid. In those days doubt itself was ardent because it was the symptom of a thirst for knowledge. It was an age when despots valued the opinions of clever men and sometimes feared their wit. The intellectual unity of Europe had never been greater, not even in the Middle Ages, and her hopes for this world were much stronger. It was then that faith in 'progress' was born, and the future began to look better than the past.

Since 1721 the power of the Europeans has become overwhelming. Their influence is felt everywhere, it is no longer possible to ignore them, and they are more hated than despised. No people can have independence and respect except at the price of adapting themselves to European ways; they must either imitate the Europeans or else become subject to them. The most successful imitators of all were the only Asiatic people to achieve in modern times the status of a Great Power. It used to be said as a compliment to the Japanese that they had consented to becoming superficially European the better to remain essentially Japanese. But life offers no such easy compromise. The imitators may not become like what they imitate, except superficially, but they do cease to be what they were before. The civilized European peoples have been very little affected except by one another, and by the Mediterranean society whose heirs they consider themselves to be; and the barbarians of Europe, though they have been exposed to external and disruptive influences, have at least felt them to come from people like themselves. Whereas the Asiatics and Africans, civilized or barbarous, have felt the European influence as a thing alien to themselves, as all-pervasive as it is irresistible. Whether they like it or not, they must come to terms with it. They can have independence only if they break with the past, and provide themselves with armies, industries, and administrations on the European model.

The Europeans were never stronger than today. The centres of their power have shifted to North America and to the far east of Europe, but that power is incomparably greater than it was in Montesquieu's time. The military and economic resources of the United States alone are several times larger than those of all the non-European peoples put together; and the strength of the Soviet Union, though smaller, is also, when compared with any but European power, overwhelming. The world will continue to be made 'European' not less but more quickly than before. The last, foolish Emperors of Germany and Russia, whose little understanding of the world lost them their thrones, might talk of a Yellow Peril, but the real Peril is White. Greed and ferocity are not dangerous unless jaws are strong and teeth sharp. Among the peoples of the world only the Europeans are dangerous both to others and to themselves. There are several wars now in progress in Asia, where most of the killed are Asians and nearly all their weapons European. Whether their governors are aliens or natives, the peoples of Asia are now ruled or driven in the service of European ideals; they are made to work and to fight either for democracy or for Communism. The vast majority of them probably care nothing for either system, but the minorities whom they serve are excited by them. Understood or misunderstood, preserved in their purity or distorted and debased, all ideals deemed worth fighting and dying for in the modern world are European. It is a pity this should be so, and mankind are already the poorer for it. There are no doubt many excellent things not dreamt of in our European philosophies, and if the peoples of Asia are now abandoning them, it is more because they are impressed by our wealth and power than by our wisdom, taste, and virtue.

Montesquieu's Europe, touching the outside world at many points, affected it but little. It was culturally united; while our Europe, which quite overwhelms the outside world and deprives it of all that it once lived by, is deeply divided against itself. The Europeans have two political faiths or ideologies they think worth fighting for, and the rest of mankind none at all except reflections of these two. Both ideologies are worldly; the rewards they promise are to be enjoyed in this life and not in another. They are not philosophies of resignation; they preach not patience but endeavour; and those who hold to them always seek to change their environments. Though transplantation has greatly changed one of them, the origins of both go back to the civilized Europe of the eighteenth century, the secular Europe of Locke, Montesquieu, and Rousseau, the Europe whose political and social philosophies were fashioned by the preferences and prejudices of the English and the French. Their origins were therefore, in the wide sense of the word, liberal; and their avowed object is so to change society that men's lives in it may be enriched, made happier, and more free.

If we mean by liberalism the doctrine that society should, as far as possible, be so organized as to enable every man to live his own life in his own way, provided he respects the right of others to do likewise, then not only democracy, but almost all the varieties of socialism, including even Marxism, derive from the same liberal principle. There are illiberal elements in the systems of Rousseau and Saint-Simon, the two men who, together with Marx, contributed most of the ideas going to make up continental radicalism and socialism, but neither was a totalitarian, though both have been called by that name. Rousseau's sovereign was an assembly of equals, where every man had as much as any other the right to speak his mind freely; and he expressly forbade the existence of any organized majority or minority likely to impose their will on the community. He believed that justice cannot long be maintained in any community unless all its members have the right to take a free and equal part in the management of their common affairs. The decisions of the assembly cannot be sovereign—that is, binding on all—unless every man in it has the right to express his own opinion, no matter what the opinions of others. Should this condition not be fulfilled the social contract is broken and the citizen retains his natural right to resist all oppressors. Saint-Simon believed neither in political democracy nor in equality, but that those persons in society should have the greatest influence who contribute most to the common good. His ideas were vague, and it is often difficult to know what he was attacking and what he meant to defend; but he did hold fast to two opinions: that the administrators of the ideal society must provide every member of it with the opportunity to make the best of his talents, and that they must never use force to oblige anyone to do what he does not want. Saint-Simon was in several ways less liberal than Rousseau, but in at least one more so; he believed in hierarchy but not in enforced discipline. Marx, with whom this book is more particularly concerned, remained all his life in principle a believer in extreme democracy;[1] and he denounced what the liberals called democracy only because he believed it to be a sham. His ideal society, which he called communist and in whose inevitable coming he believed, would be a society of equals, where none could use force to impose his will on another. Whatever he may have been by temperament, Marx was not by doctrine illiberal; he believed that every man in the classless society would be as free as social institutions could make him, and merely denied that, while society remained divided into classes, this freedom was possible. Marx's avowed purpose was to work for the coming of the classless society, the only society where the rights of man dear to the liberals would not be the privilege of a minority.

My purpose in this book is to describe one of the two European ideologies that divide not only the Europeans but all the peoples of the world against one another. Since both are in origin liberal, what has set them so far apart that men who owe allegiance to the one regard adherents of the other as enemies? Are they as different as they seem? What are the differences between them, and how have they arisen? This book does not offer a

---

[1] Marxists sometimes deny that Marx was a democrat. Democracy, they say, is a form of government, and all government involves the use of force. But in the communist society whose coming Marx predicted, force would not be used. There would be administration but not government, and therefore, strictly speaking, no democracy. This 'strictness of speech,' however, is a peculiarity of the Marxists, and does not conform to common usage. Administration by consent of the administered is, to all intents and purposes, the same thing as democracy.

Critics of Marxism also sometimes deny that Marx was a democrat. If the denial is meant to suggest that he did not think it important that governments should be truly responsible to the governed, it is unjust. But if it means no more than that he did not understand what institutions are essential for the proper working of democracy in the modern world, then there is a good deal of force to it. The Marxian attack on bourgeois democracy, to the extent that it denounced institutions necessary to democracy, whether bourgeois or not, was in fact dangerous to political freedom. Not only Marx and Engels but several other nineteenth-century socialists noticed and exaggerated the defects of parliamentary democracy, using them to condemn that system of government as a sham. They did not inquire whether those defects might be remedied, nor consider the possibility that the irremediable among them might be inherent in any institutions designed to make the governments of large states responsible to the governed.

complete answer to these questions, but seeks rather to put the reader in the way of answering them for himself.

Marxism, like the other varieties of socialism, is a product of the French and the industrial revolutions. The ends it approves of are those recommended by the liberal and radical philosophers of the eighteenth century. About those ends there is nothing specifically German. Indeed, the Germans did not adopt them until they had been popular for some considerable time in both England and France. The early socialists added nothing to them; they wanted for mankind nothing that Locke or Montesquieu or Rousseau or Paine had not wanted. Their ideal was that of the American and French revolutionaries: that every man should be free to make the best use of his life according to his own notions of what is good. They differed from the older philosophers in the means they recommended but not in the ends they approved. The Englishmen, Frenchmen, and Americans who were the first champions of freedom in the modern world had hoped that private property and government by consent would together suffice to give men as much freedom as they could reasonably expect in any society. The socialists who came after them believed that, while some men remained much richer than others and could engross all natural wealth and important instruments of production, the others could not be free. There could be freedom for the great majority only if the material resources of the community were deliberately controlled for the common good by persons responsible to the community. The early socialists, who were English and French, had widely different opinions about how that control should be exercised, what should remain private, and what become public property, and the proper size of the productive unit; but what made them socialists was the belief that, without some such control, the rich would exploit the poor and make it impossible for them, whatever the legal rights granted to them, to lead the full and free life that the philosophers had said ought to be secured to them. These early socialists were improving on what Rousseau had said before them: that men cannot be free while some are much richer than others, and that therefore every just society will take it upon itself to ensure that inequalities of wealth are never great enough to endanger freedom. Rousseau was sometimes, almost as much as the socialists, an opponent of 'laissez-faire'; he differed from them most in wanting every man the possessor of his own instruments of production. He lived before the industrial revolution, at a time when production was still on so small a scale that the ideal of a democratic society of independent producers did not seem impossible of attainment.

Though Marxism was, until the Russians got hold of it, an essentially western social and political theory, it was also in important respects different from the earlier varieties of socialism. Not in being scientific, for that it never was. Nor yet in being tied to a 'philosophy of history' predicting the inevitable coming of what to its inventors seemed the perfect society. Saint-Simon imagined just such another 'philosophy,' and Marx borrowed heavily from him. The greater part of what belongs to the properly social and political side of Marx's doctrine can be found in the writings of Frenchmen or Englishmen who died before the world had heard of Marx. No more than the general philosophy that the Marxian social theory is supposed to rest on is peculiarly German. But, as I shall try to show later, the theory does not in fact rest on the philosophy, which serves only to provide it with a vocabulary it would be better without. The intellectual ancestry of Marx the social and political theorist is predominantly not German; and much that he did borrow from German writers, he could have got as easily from French ones. I do not say this to impugn the originality of Marx; like most system builders, he got his materials from many sources, though the way he put them together was his own. Of all schools of socialism, his has proved by a long way the most important.

The peculiarity of the Marxian social theory, and what makes it to the English, the French, and the Americans an alien creed, lies not so much in the doctrines embodied in it, nor even in the manner of their embodiment, as in the emotions that find utterance through it. It is something altogether vaster, more elaborate, harsher, and less accommodating than any French or English brand of socialism; it is more demanding, arrogant, and contemptuous; it thrusts aside with disdain whatever does not suit it, as if facts were not worth noticing unless they bore it out. It is a German theory, overwhelming in its profuseness, like a broad river in full spate carrying everything before it. How gentle the French and English socialists seem—even those among them who preached revolution—when we compare them with Marx! How quiet their voices and how circumscribed their arguments! They were not less original or intelligent or ingenious than he was, but they were less exciting and less formidable. The important difference between Marxism and the theories of the English and French socialists is aesthetic; it lies in the different quality of the impact it makes on the mind of the convert to it. There is a power often uncontrolled by reason in the roar and clatter of the long German sentences as they make their heavy way regardless of obstacles irresistibly towards the 'Truth.' Marx believed that in the communist society men would be freer than they had ever been; he believed that proletarian democracy would be more truly democratic and less oppressive than the parliamentary governments of the bourgeois; and he warned the workers against premature revolution and useless violence. Yet Marx was not mild or kind or generous; he hated oppressors more than he loved the oppressed; and he thought more of the struggle than of the victory coming after it. The ideal communities that the early socialists loved to depict and contemplate, their faith in reason and in men's being persuaded by it, even their hopes of quick and easy success, attest their humanity; they did not, like Marx, place the millennium after a long, bitter, and uncompromising struggle, and then devote all their thoughts to the fight with almost none to spare for what made it worth fighting. Though Marx called them Utopians, because they had mild and inadequate notions about how mankind were to make their way to the free and just society, the longer and more terrible road that he described no more led to it than did theirs. They hoped the way would be easy, while he—knowing no more about it than they did—was certain that it must be painful. Because he felt certain while they mostly hoped, he called himself scientific and them Utopian.

Marxism, as Marx and Engels left it to the world, has been often described and even more often criticized. Whereas its transformation by the Russians has been quite neglected. It might therefore seem best to take German Marxism almost for granted, giving only the briefest summary of it, and to devote much the longer part of the book to describing how Russian

Communism emerged out of it. Why tread painfully through two morasses when it might be enough to tread through one? I would gladly have saved myself that much trouble had I found it possible to do so; but I did not find it possible. German Marxism has been so variously and often so superficially interpreted that there exists no lucid account of it which is both adequate and just. I have therefore thought it best to come to my own conclusions about it, setting them out for the benefit of the reader as clearly as I could. I have preferred to risk making my own mistakes rather than adopt other people's. I have not considered every part of the theory, but only those parts of it that seemed important to me for one or other of two reasons: either because they have influenced the political behaviour of mankind, or because they raise for the student of society and politics questions of the first importance. Those questions I have tried to discuss to the best of my ability, and have sometimes found myself obliged to discuss them at considerable length. On the other hand, the general philosophy supposed to lie behind Marx's social theory, I have deliberately neglected. He was no philosopher[1] and I am not one, and I have thought it kinder to both of us to neglect that part of his writings. Social and political theorists who dabble in philosophy too often bring their own subject into contempt; philosophers are astonished at the naïveté and clumsiness of their philosophies, and are only too ready to conclude that their social and political theories are no better. From this there arises the unfortunate consequence that philosophers think themselves competent to pass judgment on the merits of social and political theories, sometimes even treating them as if they were minor and inferior branches of philosophy.

Plato and Aristotle, living at a time before the empirical studies were divorced from what we still call philosophy, excelled both as philosophers and social theorists, but in modern times, no one —except Hobbes and (perhaps) Hegel—who was, in our narrower contemporary sense, an important philosopher has done much to

---

[1] I am here using the word 'philosopher' in the narrower modern sense, which includes the logician, the epistemologist, and the maker of theories about what is called the 'essential nature' of the universe. Elsewhere, I have sometimes used it in the older and wider sense, which includes the social and political theorist, and even the natural scientist. The context always, I hope, makes it clear in what sense I am using the word.

enlarge our understanding of social and political phenomena. Locke, one of the greatest of philosophers, either took social facts for granted or else misunderstood them, devoting his energies, not to the study of society and government as they really are, but to explaining why it is men's duty to obey their rulers; while Hume mostly destroyed what Locke had built up. Their ingenious theories were important because they affected men's opinions and conduct, but they did not go far towards making society and politics more intelligible. The men who have in the last three centuries taught us to think about society, law, custom, government, and institutions of all kinds—and these are the proper study of the social and political theorist—in new and profitable ways, have mostly not been philosophers: I mean such men as Harrington, Montesquieu, Rousseau, Burke, Adam Smith, Saint-Simon, Tocqueville, and Durkheim. It is in their company that Marx occupies a really important place. What more can be justly said in praise of him than that, in spite of inconsistency, confusion, and obscurity, the problems he raised are among the most important and difficult that confront the social theorist? The majority of Marx's critics have ignored these problems, preferring either to praise him for what he did not say or to score easy victories over him.

I have not treated Russian Communism in the same way as German Marxism. The latter is important both to the serious student of society and to the historian, but the former to the historian alone. Had German Marxism never been adopted as the creed of any considerable political movement, it would still be worth studying. The man who made it was a great thinker, and his system, for all its defects, deserves scrupulous and severe analysis. We cannot fairly ask of a political theorist, who is also a system builder, that he should present us with anything like a true account of the phenomena he seeks to explain; the state of our knowledge about things social and political does not warrant any such demand. We ought to be grateful to him, if, when we have pulled his system to pieces, we are appreciably wiser than we were before. Nor should we blame him for having attempted the impossible; for it is ordinarily the boldest speculators who invent the most fruitful hypotheses. The accumulation of knowledge is inevitably a wasteful process, and the refuse that has to be thrown away many times more abundant than what is worth preserving. That, at least, is true of the social studies, which, if they are to make progress, require in their practitioners a fertile imagination and an acute critical sense, qualities seldom found together; and that, no doubt, is one of the reasons why the progress they have made has been small.

Russian Communism is not worth scrupulous criticism; it is enough to expound it and to explain how it arose. I have not attempted to do more. Lenin has, no doubt, often been treated as an important thinker; and I should be glad to follow this fashion, if I could do so honestly. But I find it impossible to share this common opinion. Lenin was a practical politician, a revolutionary leader, and for several years the ruler of a great country when that country was most difficult to rule. No man ever changed the world more, and more quickly, than he did. But that does not make him an important political thinker. Indeed, it would be surprising if he were one. Since the Europeans first began to speculate about politics, there has scarcely ever been a great statesman who was also an important political theorist. The apparent exceptions to this rule are mostly effects of misplaced flattery. Cicero did no more than repeat other men's theories, and deserves credit only for lucidity. Burke, who was a great thinker, was never an important member of any government. This man of genius was the club bore in an assembly that prided itself on being 'the best club in Europe.' Perhaps the only exception to this rule worth noticing is James Madison, the one truly original thinker among the three authors of *The Federalist*, and even he, as a man of affairs, is reckoned among the lesser Presidents of the United States. The truth is that men of business, be their business public or private, are seldom interested in generalities that are not widely accepted and probably also widely misunderstood. Those few among them who are interested in such things seldom do more than understand other men's less popular ideas. The active political life, more almost than any other, absorbs a man's energies, leaving him but little time to reflect to good purpose on matters of theory.

Lenin left Marxism poorer than he found it; he took little interest in what was truly profound or subtle in it, and used it mostly as a source of quotations and slogans to justify his many and not always consistent policies. He did not even understand how he had distorted it. He added nothing to it that was really his own[1] except some reflections about the peculiar character of the class struggle and the proper organization of a revolutionary Marxist party in a backward country like Russia, together with a variety of precepts about the tactics that party should adopt in order to get power sooner than Marxism, as most people then understood it, would lead one to suppose was possible. Since Marx was himself often inconsistent, and sometimes (in his impatience for action) gave advice incompatible with his own theories, Lenin could always find the quotations needed to justify his policies. His precepts are certainly important, and only a shrewd and bold man would have thought of them; but their importance is entirely practical. To the mere political and social theorist they are not interesting. Nor did Lenin ever understand how acceptance of his precepts, as soon as the attempt[2] is made to justify them theoretically, produces a corpus of doctrine in some ways profoundly different from the Marxism of Marx and Engels. Why this should be so I have also tried to explain.

This book is not a condemnation of Communist policies. A man might well believe that German Marxism, considered as a social and political theory, is almost entirely false, and that what the Russians have since made of it is even less to be defended than what they took over from the Germans, and yet he might, on quite reasonable grounds, decide to support the Communists. He might, for instance, produce good reasons for believing that what the Communists are doing in the 'backward' parts of the world urgently needs doing, and that they alone, despite the absurdities of their fundamental theory, have courage and faith enough to do it. I do not in fact share this opinion, but nothing said about the errors of Marxian theory or the doctrinal inconsistencies of Lenin can prove it false. I have wanted in this book to do two things: to discuss an important theory intended by its German authors to serve both as an explanation of the inevitable

[1] Lenin's theory about imperialism, for which he has been greatly praised, was not original; he got most of it from J. A. Hobson and Rudolf Hilferding. He also borrowed considerably from other people—Rosa Luxemburg among them; but with those elements of his theory I am not concerned, for they do not help us to understand what has made Russian Communism what it is.

[2] An attempt that he never made. Trotsky came nearer to making it, and to that extent his writings are more interesting than Lenin's to the student of society.

progress of every human society and as a general guide to the political activities of the industrial working class in economically advanced communities; and to discover what happened to that theory when it was taken over by a revolutionary party in the most backward of the great European countries.

PART ONE

GERMAN MARXISM

Chapter One

REVOLUTIONARY MARXISM

MARX was a revolutionary socialist, and the theory called Marxism, greatly though it has changed as a result of its transplantation from the West into Russia, has not ceased to be revolutionary. The western Marxists called themselves revolutionaries until after the First World War; and later on, when they began to be willing to admit that they were no longer what they had once thought themselves to be, they quietly dropped the habit of calling themselves Marxists. No doubt, they took it badly when the Bolsheviks accused them of betraying Marxism; no one likes to be called a traitor even to a cause he no longer entirely believes in. The German Social-Democrats did their best—and it was a good best, though the world took less notice of their explanations than of the achievements of Lenin—to prove that the Bolsheviks had done what Marxists ought not to have done and were not doing what Marxists ought to do; they still cared about Marxism; they still thought it useful for many purposes, and themselves better able than other people to determine what those purposes were; and they were also anxious that a German doctrine they had long adhered to and still respected and in part accepted should not be appropriated by the Slavs. They thought they had a better right than the Bolsheviks to speak for Marx, though they no longer called themselves Marxists.[1] They agreed with him about some things, and differed from him about others; they would neither deny his authority nor affect to follow it in all things.

The Bolsheviks, on the other hand, did pride themselves on their orthodox Marxism, and so too did the western socialists who broke away from their parties because those parties no longer even pretended to be revolutionary. At the invitation of Lenin,

[1] They did not mind being called Marxists, but felt the need to explain just in what sense they were so.

the Bolsheviks called themselves Communists, and their western admirers soon followed their example; they did so to make clear their breach with the main body of the socialists. The Communists claimed to have remained true to the essential doctrines of Marxism; and if they accepted what Lenin added to those doctrines, it was only, they said, because he had adapted them to situations no one could have foreseen before the twentieth century. Lenin had not betrayed the Marxian doctrine; he had merely developed it. This, said the Communists, was not only permissible but necessary; Marx and Engels had themselves in their day done it.

There is no need to inquire into the difference between 'betrayal' and 'development.' The Communists have been bolder, more truculent, and more successful than the socialists; they have created a new kind of society. That society, whether or not Marx would have approved of it, is at least very different from the capitalism he described and condemned. The socialists have been diffident, unprovocative, and self-critical; whenever they have gained power, they have used it to make what by Communist standards are mild reforms. They know that Marxism was, in Marx's time, a revolutionary doctrine, and they also know that they have ceased to be revolutionaries. They are too self-critical, too honest with themselves, to be able to pretend that they are still orthodox Marxists; they admit a great debt to Marx and believe they have a better right than the Communists to invoke his authority, but that is all. Whereas the Communists, though they have quite transformed his doctrine, still claim to be his disciples; whatever additions they have made to the Marxian doctrine are, they say, entirely in the spirit of it. The Communists are, as Marx was, revolutionary socialists; they use his vocabulary, quote freely from his writings, and never deny his authority; they are willing, in order to appear the more closely bound to him, to explain away whatever might seem to separate them from him. This, they think, is enough to put both him and them into one camp together, and all the other socialists outside it. Their tenacity and truculence have served them well; and today, when we speak of the Marxists, we refer, not to the German Social-Democrats and those who think like them, but to the Russian Bolsheviks and their Communist allies the world over.

I. THE FIVE EXPONENTS OF 'MARXISM'

We must be allowed to speak of 'Marxism' and 'Marxists'; these two words are too convenient to be dispensed with. There is no harm in using them provided we know what we are about when we do so. There never was, and certainly is not today, a consistent and fully intelligible doctrine called Marxism. Marx was exceptionally prolific and imaginative, but he had only one life to live, and so could not contradict himself as often as his many disciples have contradicted each other and him. He left behind him a stock of ideas, invented or else borrowed and re-fashioned to look Marxian, from which could be selected and arranged the foundations of several different and incompatible theories of society. Any one of the theories erected upon a selection from these ideas could properly be called Marxist by a theorist grateful enough to acknowledge himself a disciple. Nevertheless, not all such theories are admitted by the world to be Marxist, even when their makers call them so. The name has stuck to some theories but not to others, and those it has stuck to are not necessarily the more firmly erected upon their Marxian foundations. When once the name has stuck to some theories, it becomes the more difficult to attach it to others. Marxism means not all but only some of the theories inspired by the teachings of Marx. It means, more particularly, the theories of Marx himself, Engels, Lenin, Stalin, and Trotsky.[1] Orthodox Marxism or, in other words, Communism, consists of the doctrines of only the first four of these five men.

Of the four fathers of Communism only Marx is a truly original and great thinker. He is, indeed—and that though every part of his teaching has been exposed to severe and effective attack—the greatest of socialist thinkers. Only Saint-Simon is fit to be compared with him. The three others, though this is least true of Stalin, are also important, though for very different reasons. Engels is important because he worked with Marx and was his closest friend, and also because his most important contribution to the Marxian theory, *Herr Eugen Dühring's Revolution in Science*,

[1] Plekhanov in Russia and Kautsky in Germany were also important theorists, but their doctrines are not incorporated in Communism. Their theories will not be closely studied in this book, though there will be considerable mention of them.

commonly called *Anti-Dühring*, was read to the master while he was still alive and was approved by him. Indeed, one of the chapters of *Anti-Dühring*, the tenth chapter of Part II, was actually written by Marx himself. Engels not only collaborated with Marx; he also defended him against his critics, both before Marx's death and after it. In defending the theory, he interpreted it. That is the real importance of *Anti-Dühring* and also of Engels's *Socialism, Utopian and Scientific*, which is only three chapters of *Anti-Dühring*, published separately. Marx died in 1883 and Engels not until 1895. Engels had time to say quite a deal about Marxism that Marx was in no position to approve or correct; he had also to meet new criticisms and to adapt the theory to conditions Marx knew nothing of. During the last twelve years of his life Engels was therefore more than the interpreter of Marx. And yet we cannot argue that what Engels said after 1883 is not Marxism. He was Marx's closest friend and much more than his faithful disciple; he was, even while Marx lived, a minor contributor to the common doctrine; and, modest though he was whenever he compared himself with Marx, he could still, with perfect justice, refer to Marxism as 'our' doctrine. Engels is part author of Marxism, and his words, even with no Marx alive to sanction them, are still good Marxist authority.

The importance of Lenin as a theorist is easily explained. He too, like Engels, defended Marxism against a host of critics and rival interpreters. Whether his interpretations are correct and theirs false is a matter of dispute in no way affected by his extraordinary political career. Indeed, it may be that both he and his opponents have equally good authority for their opinions, since neither Marx nor Engels, to whom they all appeal, is always consistent. But the importance of Lenin as a defender and interpreter of the doctrine is not really very great. He was much less fitted for the task than Engels, for he was neither a contemporary, nor a compatriot, nor a collaborator of Marx. His importance lies much more in what he added, especially to what Marx had to say about political strategy. The two men were in important respects alike. They were both masterful, argumentative, resourceful, aggressive, and sincere. They were both by temperament doctrinaire and revolutionary. If it were merely a question of comparing texts, there would often be as much to say

for Lenin's Marxist adversaries as for Lenin himself; they were as well versed in the scriptures, as partisan as he was, and rather more subtle. But if we look at the lives of the two men, it is impossible to deny that Lenin was in some ways closer to Marx than any other great Marxist. There is something tough, indefatigable, unrelenting, sharp, and cynical about both of them; and yet they were both sincere and ardent revolutionaries, as much in love with their theories as men have ever been. They were often confused, uncritical, or absurd; they were never sloppy or weak. When we consider doctrines so charged with emotion as Marxism, similarity of temperament is always important. It may well be true that if Marx had been alive in Russia in 1917 he would have been a Bolshevik. This, however, is a judgment about a certain very peculiar person called Karl Marx; it does not imply that the Bolsheviks were in 1917 more orthodox Marxists than the Mensheviks.

Stalin is important as a Marxist thinker for a very different reason.[1] Lenin's additions to Marxism were revolutionary additions to a revolutionary creed; they were made to prepare and to justify bolder and quicker action than most contemporary Marxists thought possible; they were ideas that helped to make a revolution. Whereas Stalin's Marxism, the least lively and the least original, is little more than a selection of those texts that happen to suit his policies best. I do not mean by that to suggest that Stalin is insincere. He may be an opportunist; but then so, too, was Lenin; and, if you like, Marx as well, for he also altered his theories to suit circumstances, and quite often without knowing he had done so. Stalin, no doubt, is sincere, but he does not give the impression that Marxism inspires him. He accepts it and holds fast to it, but only because it is the one system of ideas he is at all familiar with. His mind received it in his youth and has never since let go of it. He is not, as Marx, Engels, Lenin, and Trotsky all were, a man of ideas, a man whose emotions and faith are united indissolubly and dedicated to the same cause, who cannot live happily except where doctrines and controversies flourish. He is a quiet, cool, confident Marxist, with no taste for subtlety and argument. In his writings and pronouncements, he expounds an expurgated, simplified, and soulless Marxism which avoids all difficulties and all heat. Even when he abuses his

[1] This was written before Stalin died.

enemies—and all Marxists do that—his abuse is almost perfunctory. He does not waste his hatred in insults, and his enemies have more to fear than his words. His brand of Marxism is a kind of primer for practical men who are too busy to think much about first principles. I shall not have much to say about it.

The Marxism of Trotsky is important because it is the greatest of the Marxist heresies. When I call it a heresy, I do not mean to suggest that Trotsky is less truly than Stalin the disciple of Marx and Lenin. These disputes about the loyalty of disciples to their masters' doctrines are dreary things. Who can tell which, among the many conflicting statements made by Marx, Engels, and Lenin, more truly represent their fundamental thought? What can be meant by 'fundamental thought' in such a connection? We none of us always know what we really mean, and we are all of us often inconsistent. Trotsky had perhaps as good a right to call himself a Marxist as anyone who stayed in Russia with Stalin. Yet his doctrine is important because it is a heresy, because it is an act of revolt against the persons who have successfully established an organized religion in Marx's name. Trotsky, no doubt, thought everything he wrote after he left Russia a defence of Marxism against the Stalinists; but the social significance of what he wrote is that it was an attack against an ideology supported by organized power, and an attack made in the name of teachers recognized by that power. Heresy, after all, is as much a social as an intellectual phenomenon; indeed, it is, if we take into account not what it teaches but only its heretical character, entirely a social phenomenon. Science, which is concerned with truth and error, knows nothing of either orthodoxy or heresy. A heretic challenges authority, not truth; and it is this challenge that makes him a heretic. Authority, as authority, is neither true nor probable opinion; it is opinion supported by power. The historical importance of Trotskyism is that it is a Marxist attack on the authority of Moscow; and of all such attacks it is the most plausible, the most cleverly argued, and the best sustained.

II. THE UNIMPORTANCE OF DIALECTICAL MATERIALISM

Marxism, we have often been told, is not only a theory about society; it is also an entire system of philosophy. Historical materialism, which is Marx's theory of the evolution of society, is only a part of that philosophy; it is, so we are told, the application to social phenomena of certain fundamental principles that apply to the whole universe. These principles are called dialectical materialism; so that historical materialism and dialectical materialism are not one thing but two, of which the former is merely the application of the latter to one class of phenomena.

This being so, it might seem wise to discuss first 'dialectical' and then 'historical' materialism. But this is precisely what I do not propose to do. Marx's philosophy, as distinguished from his theory of society, is not worth discussing, and that for a quite simple and, I hope, sufficient reason. Marx was not really a philosopher at all; that he appears to have been one is merely an accident of German history. It was the fashion in his day and in his country—the English and French were already beginning to learn better—for men to derive their political theories from their general views about the nature of the universe. The supreme example of this method is Hegel, whose disciple Marx in his early twenties was and, to a considerable extent, never ceased to be. Hegel, like Plato before him, believed that the universe is essentially ideal or spiritual, and, again like Plato, distinguished between a real spiritual world and a phenomenal world which is somehow not real but apparent. On the other hand, unlike Plato, Hegel conceived of the Idea, not as something unchanging and laid up in heaven apart from the world of experience which is merely its imperfect copy, but as a continual process of development. This process he called 'dialectic,' a word borrowed from Plato, who had himself given a special sense to it. The Hegelian 'dialectic' is different from the Platonic; it is not the way in which finite minds can acquire knowledge of ultimate reality, it is rather the life of the spirit or Idea, the eternal process which the spirit essentially is. For the development of the spirit is through the conflict and reconciliation of opposites, a process whereby what is gives birth to what is opposed to it, the resulting conflict ending in a reconciliation which transforms both opposites. The state or phase of the process which gives birth to its opposite, Hegel called thesis; its opposite he called antithesis; and the state or phase reached when the conflict is over and the opposites are reconciled and transformed, he called synthesis; and every synthesis, except the last, which is the Absolute, is also a thesis and gives birth to its opposite. The process, therefore, is continuous and yet has stages, of which each is 'higher' than the one before it. The whole philosophy of Hegel depends on applying logical categories to natural phenomena. Nature, as the scientists describe her, knows nothing of opposites, of theses, antitheses, and syntheses. But Hegel—because he said that reality is essentially ideal, and because ideas are involved in all thinking and assertion, and because what one man asserts can be contradicted by another (and even by himself), and because knowledge is improved by argument—because of these things, Hegel found it easy to speak of 'contradictions' in nature and to describe every natural process as an evolution from lower to higher through the conflict and reconciliation of opposites or 'contradictions.'

What I have said about Hegel's philosophy is not, and is not meant to be, intelligible, still less to be a recognizable description of the world as any of us know it. I have not tried to bring light into dark places. People supposed to be competent judges have spoken of Hegel as if he plunged philosophy into depths that no light could penetrate. I have tried to do no more than repeat some of the words and connections of ideas used by Hegel, because Marx later took them over from him, believing them necessary for an adequate description of the evolution of human societies. Marx, too, believed that all development is a process by stages from lower to higher by means of the conflict and reconciliation of opposites. He differed from Hegel in thinking matter, not mind, the ultimate reality; and he thought mind derivative from matter. It is to this difference that Marxists allude when they distinguish between the 'dialectical idealism' of Hegel and the 'dialectical materialism' of Marx.

It is best, I think, for a number of reasons, to say as little as possible about 'dialectical materialism.' In the first place, Marxists are not very interested in it. What really matters to them is 'historical materialism,' the theory of society supposed to be derived from it. Marx himself was always much more interested in law, politics, and economics than in philosophy. A good German and a former Hegelian, he was determined to be fully equipped intellectually; and he therefore acquired his theory of the universe as well as his theory of society, and, like many other German intellectuals of his day, thought it a mistake not to derive the latter from the former. A theory of society not closely bound up with a general philosophy would probably have seemed to him superficial, inadequate, and incapable of giving him the insight he needed into the matters that really interested him. Those matters were social.

Nowadays, unless we are Marxists, we seldom believe that what we still agree to call philosophy, that is to say, logic, epistemology, and (where it is still practised) metaphysics, has anything much to do with the social studies. It has nothing more to do with them than with physics, chemistry, or biology. We are therefore quite entitled, as students of society, to ignore 'dialectical materialism,' or at least to take only the most superficial notice of it; just enough notice, in fact, to make ourselves familiar with some of Marx's habits of mind and his curious vocabulary. But to try to refute 'dialectical materialism' is surely a waste of time. It is to follow Marx and Engels into regions they had no business to enter, regions where they soon lost their way. That they did not know they had lost it is no credit to them; and in any case is no reason why other students of society should go where their study does not take them.

Marx was primarily a sociologist and an economist. Though he was perhaps equally confident of his own superiority in that sphere, he usually left philosophy to Engels. The unfinished *German Ideology*, the *Holy Family*, and the few sentences entitled *Theses on Feuerbach*: these are, or contain, the more important philosophical pronouncements for which Marx was directly responsible. He must also be taken to have approved the philosophical opinions of Engels, expressed while he was alive and submitted to him. We are told that Engels read out to him, while they were still in manuscript, all the chapters, and therefore also the philosophical ones, of his *Anti-Dühring*; but we cannot know how attentively Marx listened to Engels.

It illustrates, I think, the poverty of German philosophy in their time that not only Marx and Engels but many other people as well should have believed that economic determinism—the theory that it is how men produce goods and services which determines the general character of all their social behaviour—stands or falls with materialism, with the theory that matter is prior to mind and mind derivative from matter. There is no necessary connection between the two theories. The human behaviour studied by the economist is as much mental as it is physical; and no theory about matter and mind and the relations between them can be relevant to the study of any social phenomena. Yet we find the enemies of the Marxists attacking their materialism, and the Marxists defending it, as if historical materialism somehow or other depended on its truth.

Though philosophy (by which I mean logic, epistemology, and metaphysics) has no closer rational connection with the social studies than with the natural sciences, the historical connection between them cannot be denied. As a matter of fact, political and social theorists have often derived their social and political theories from their philosophy; or rather they have so constructed their philosophical premises that certain political conclusions seemed to follow from them. This has been the habit of political theorists since Plato's time, and they have not yet broken with it. The natural sciences are now free of philosophy, but the social studies are still tainted with it. Therefore, if we want to understand a man's social theory, a passing acquaintance with his philosophy is still often necessary. Otherwise, we cannot understand why it is that certain ideas and sequences of ideas seem important to him, and how it has come about that he uses certain words in the way he does. That is why, when we study Marxism, we must not altogether ignore the Hegelian philosophy and the 'dialectical materialism' which owes so much to it; we must take a look at these things because they give us a clue to Marx's mental habits, but we need not understand or criticize them. For what the student of society ought always to do is to stick to the sphere of his competence; he ought not to allow other donkeys' carrots to tempt him off the path which it is his business to tread. Though Marx sometimes, and Engels and Lenin often, philosophized we must not do so.

Though historical materialism is supposed to be derived from dialectical, the connection between them is merely formal; if we know what dialectical materialism is and also that it was Marx's intention to apply it to the evolution of human societies, all we can infer is that that evolution will be explained as a series of epochs, proceeding from the lower to the higher by means of conflicts always resolved and always repeated. We cannot infer what the epochs will be, or the nature of the conflicts, or economic determinism, or the sense in which the later stages are higher than the earlier. Nor can we infer anything of what Marx and Engels said about social classes, ideologies, and political warfare. Only the formal structure of the Marxian social theory is an inverted Hegelianism. Historical materialism might be true though dialectical materialism were false or even meaningless; and, in any case, if historical materialism is divested of the peculiar philosophical vocabulary in which its authors express it, if it is translated into the ordinary language still used to describe social phenomena, it becomes an hypothesis that only the historian and social theorist are competent to verify.

Before I attempt to give an account of 'historical materialism', I must discuss two more ideas that Marx got from Hegel. One of them, indeed, is closely related to the theory of dialectic. The dialectic cannot be expressed as a law of the kind the natural scientist is familiar with. It does not describe a uniformity in nature. It does not say that whenever an event of a given kind occurs under such and such conditions an event of another given kind will follow. It purports, rather, to describe the way in which the behaviour of the totality of events is determined, to describe the general character of a process in which all events are involved. So, too, historical materialism does not tell us that under certain circumstances such and such social phenomena occur. It purports to describe the general character of all social evolution, to give a clue to the history of every human society. It therefore supposes that a human society is a highly integrated individual whole, with a life history whose general course can be discovered, so that it becomes possible to predict the future. Science tells us that if we put dry paper into the fire, the paper will burn, but it does not predict that we will put the paper into the fire. Science tells us the laws in accordance with which any thing of a given kind will behave in certain circumstances. But historical materialism does not describe uniformities of behaviour to which every particular of a given kind will conform under the appropriate circumstances. It describes, not uniformities of behaviour applying to particular events, but the general pattern of behaviour to which the totality of events of the kind called 'social' must conform. It therefore makes a claim for the science of society that none of the natural sciences has ever made. I have no wish to contest this claim as a matter of principle, to argue on general grounds that no such historical laws can be discovered. That is a task for the philosopher, for the student of scientific method. All I shall attempt is to prove that the Marxists have not made out a case for the particular hypothesis which is central to their whole theory, namely, for historical materialism.

Hegel believed that the evolution of society and of the state, though it forms the minds of individuals, need not be understood by them. He did not believe, as so many political theorists have done, that political and social institutions have somehow been contrived by men for the better satisfaction of their strongest and most common needs and desires; and that therefore the student of politics must begin his inquiry by considering the motives and purposes of men, especially those of their motives and aspirations that are common to them all and are the most regular in their operation. It was on certain assumptions about the psychology of individuals that Hobbes, Locke, and even Rousseau, raised their political theories. Hegel's method was quite different. As a political theorist he was interested, so far as mundane facts could detain him, in social and political phenomena. The minds of individuals are, he thought, changed by the progress of society; and it is therefore that progress which must be the first object of study. This idea, that social and political institutions are not contrivances for the satisfaction of individual needs and desires, is not original with Hegel. It is to be found, implied if not explicit, in much that Plato and Aristotle wrote; and it is the assumption on which rests the argument of perhaps the most original of modern political treatises, Rousseau's *Discourse on the Origins of Inequality Among Men*. Burke also sometimes presupposes it. But neither Rousseau nor Burke understood its theoretical importance, and they both often neglected it. Hegel, however, understood its importance and always held firmly to it; and it was from Hegel that Marx took it.

Marx expressed it in the aphorism: 'It is not the consciousness of men that determines their existence, but rather, it is their social existence that determines their consciousness.' In English ears this aphorism sounds queerly. It can be translated into a sentence more easily understood: it is not men's interests and theories that determine their institutions, but rather their institutions that determine their interests and theories. Many of Marx's commentators and admirers have drawn their readers' attention to the theoretical importance of this aphorism. They have thought it true and that its acceptance establishes the 'autonomy' of the social sciences, their existence as a separate branch of study with appropriate methods of its own.

I certainly do not wish to contest the importance of this aphorism, though I think it could be better put and in a form that is less misleading. The truth of the matter is perhaps rather different from what Marx thought, but that is something to be discussed later. I am, however, surprised that Marx should be given the credit for discovering such truth as the aphorism contains; he got the idea from Hegel, who developed it from a number of suggestions made by Rousseau; and the fact that Hegel also believed, which Marx did not, in 'the rational will' and 'the world spirit' makes no difference to the issue. For the Hegelian 'rational will' and 'world spirit,' though it is 'manifest' in them, is not the same thing as the minds of individuals. The 'rational will' finds objective expression in the laws and institutions of the state, and it is through the influence upon them of laws and institutions that the minds of individuals are formed. It does not matter what Hegel meant, if indeed he meant anything, by such expressions as 'rational will,' 'world spirit,' 'manifest,' and 'objective'; the fact remains that his theory does not treat social and political institutions as contrivances made by men for the satisfaction of their desires, interests, and aspirations. The idea, truth or half-truth (whichever we prefer to think it), is equally present in both theories. If Hegel wraps it up in more and worse nonsense than Marx, it is not the less true that he lived before Marx and that Marx was his disciple. We no longer admire Hegel and we still respect Marx. But we must not forget the great debt that Marx owed to Hegel, nor yet the fact that Hegel—and I speak now, not of his logic and metaphysics, but of his political theory—was also, in his own peculiar and sometimes unpleasant way, a great thinker. It was he who, long before Marx, understood and explained the theoretical importance of certain opinions about the relations between society and the individual first expressed in modern times by Montesquieu and Rousseau.

As a matter of fact, neither Hegel nor Marx, though they shared this idea, believed in the 'autonomy of sociology.' Hegel derived his political conclusions from logical and metaphysical premises, and he probably constructed those premises in order to arrive at the conclusions. Marx also, though less obviously, thought it wise to broad-base his social and political theory on the whole system of the universe; and, like Hegel, thought of the universe, not as an infinite whole which, though its parts may be always changing according to discoverable laws, remains essentially the same, but as a totality with a history of its own that conforms to law and is therefore in principle predictable. Like Hegel, though perhaps even less aware of his motives, he sought the alliance of the universe, seeking to prove that all things tend to what he thought good. As an American writer, Max Eastman, has said in a book called *Marxism, Is It Science?*, this attitude is essentially religious; and it is not the less so because Marx had no need of a God in his universe.

Both these ideas—that societies are integral wholes whose histories obey discoverable laws, and that social and political institutions are not means for the satisfaction of individual desires, interests, and aspirations—these ideas, and the religious attitude I have just described, Marx got from Hegel. He got them from Hegel because he was a young man in Germany when Hegel's influence was still at its height. If Marx had had the good fortune to be born a Frenchman, he might have got both ideas and the religious attitude from another and a more estimable source, from Saint-Simon. Saint-Simon was born in 1760, ten years before Hegel, and died in 1825, six years before Hegel. He arrived at his social and political theories quite independently of Hegel; and he died without ever knowing anything of the 'dialectic' and the 'ultimate reality of the Idea.' He was by birth a nobleman, and by occupation a journalist, an amateur scientist, and something of an adventurer; he was never a metaphysician. Marx, as we shall see later, learnt more than a little from him, but probably not until after he had passed under the influence and acquired the vocabulary of Hegel. These two ideas, which were perhaps Saint-Simon's before they were Hegel's, though neither got them from the other, Marx discovered and accepted in their German and metaphysical form, the form given them by Hegel. This is, I think, a misfortune, because it is much more difficult to be rid of Hegel's influence than Saint-Simon's; or, rather, since the influence of both is to some extent salutary, it is more easy to take Saint-Simon for what he is worth, without being either too strongly attracted or too strongly repelled by his theories. Hegel's theory of the universe expressed in such language as nobody had dared use before him is certainly impressive. If once we concede that the language means something, it is almost impossible to decide where that meaning ends and where the elaborate play with words begins. Confronted by the Hegelian system, we are either tempted to plunge recklessly into the midst of it, cutting adrift from common sense in the hope of attaining a deeper wisdom, or else we turn away from it in despair or disgust. Saint-Simon, on the other hand, is verbose without being overbearing; he uses ordinary language and makes ordinary mistakes. His confusions are of the kind that our teachers have often warned us against; they are easily noticed and allowed for. It may be, too, that the difference of temperament between the two men explains the different quality of their influence; Hegel was magisterial, speaking with all the authority that a professorial chair can give to a German, while Saint-Simon was an eccentric nobleman who had gone down in the world, a man excited by a vision he was trying to explain to a sceptical people, a people always more willing to be amused and interested than convinced. We must not forget the effects of national idiosyncrasies; though their originality is as great, the influence of French thinkers seems often to lie less heavily on their disciples.

Chapter Two

HISTORICAL MATERIALISM

DIALECTICAL materialism is not really a theory at all; it means very little and implies very little; it is a kind of preliminary patter to prepare the mind for historical materialism, which no more rests upon it than a ship does on its own reflection in the water. The heart of Marxism, what every part of it is connected with (though the ties are not always logical), is historical materialism.

Historical materialism is the theory of Marx and Engels about the fundamental causes of social change. They never succeeded in giving exact expression to it, though they both said a great deal about it. They felt their way to it slowly; and it was not until 1859, in the *Preface* to *The Critique of Political Economy*, that Marx attempted to set it out in a series of propositions. It would, no doubt, be possible to show that these propositions contradict other statements about historical materialism made both before and after 1859. Nevertheless, it is with these propositions that we ought to start. Marx himself said of them that they served as a guide to all his studies, and they have always, since that time, been treated as the classic formulation of historical materialism. Marx certainly believed, when he wrote them, that they gave the gist of his fundamental theory about society, his most important contribution to the sum of human wisdom; and that belief he never abandoned. It may be that he was afterwards not always of one mind about historical materialism; it may be that both he and Engels sometimes explained social change rather differently after 1859; but, if they did so, they certainly did not know it. Neither of them ever repudiated the classic formulation of the *Preface* to *The Critique of Political Economy*; whatever they said afterwards seemed to them no more than an elucidation of what Marx had there said. Therefore, not only convenience, but justice as well, requires that we should begin with the classic formulation.

When that formulation is closely scrutinized, there are two conclusions about it that impose themselves: firstly, that it gives us no clear idea of how what Marx called the 'economic basis' of society is related to what he called its 'superstructure'; and secondly, that, far from its being true that it explains the political struggle between classes as the effect of 'contradictions' within the 'economic basis' of society, it leaves both the struggle and the 'contradictions' unexplained. If we want to discover how these 'contradictions' occur, we have to look outside the classic formulation of historical materialism; and what we then find is that the 'contradictions' within the 'economic basis' are never accounted for except as consequences of the political struggle between the classes. If I am right, if it is true that Marx had no clear idea about how the 'basis' of society is connected with its 'superstructure,' and also could not explain the 'contradictions' within the 'basis' except as consequences of the class struggle, it follows that he did not himself know what he was doing, what exactly he was saying and committing himself to, when he put forward the theory called historical materialism. The theory he formulated, which both he and Engels often attempted to explain and illustrate, is in fact so obscure and confused that it is impossible to understand a great part of it. I shall hope to establish, not only that the theory, taken as a whole, is unintelligible, but also that the evidence collected by Marx and Engels to support it refutes most of the intelligible parts of it. These two men understood so little what they were doing that they put themselves to considerable trouble to undermine their own theory. This, of course, does not detract from the historical importance of that theory; on the contrary, it is precisely because the theory is obscure and confused that it has been plausibly argued of almost every major historical event that it confirms its truth.

Let me begin by quoting once again the often quoted passage from the *Preface* to *The Critique of Political Economy* which purports to give the gist of Marx's social theory.

In the social production of their material life, men enter into definite relations that are indispensable and independent of their wills; these relations of production correspond to a definite stage of the development of their material forces of production. The sum

total of these relations of production makes up the economic structure of society—the real foundation on which arises a legal and
political superstructure and to which correspond definite forms of
social consciousness. The mode of production of material life determines the social, political, and intellectual life process in general.
It is not the consciousness of men that determines their [social]
existence, but rather it is their social existence that determines their
consciousness. At a certain stage of their development, the material
forces of production in society come into conflict with the existing
relations of production or—what is but a legal expression of the
same thing—with the property relations within which they have
been at work before. From forms of development of the productive forces these relations turn into their fetters. Then begins an
epoch of social revolution. With the change of the economic
foundation the entire immense superstructure is more or less
rapidly transformed.

What is known as the 'classic formulation' of historical materialism is about twice as long as the passage I have quoted, which is
the first half of it with just one sentence that adds nothing to the
meaning left out. The second half is only a number of unconnected comments on what has gone before; the gist of the
theory, such as it is, is in the first half.

Before I comment on the passage I have just quoted, I want
first to try to put Marx's meaning rather more simply than he has
done. I take it that what he means is approximately this: whenever men co-operate to produce the means of satisfying their
essential needs, they enter into certain relations with each other,
relations that are indispensable and independent of their wills;
these are the relations of production, which vary with the way
in which men produce what satisfies their needs. The relations
of production, taken together, are the economic structure of
society, and they determine the general character of society's
laws, political institutions, and intellectual activities. The way
in which men produce what satisfies their needs determines the
way in which their social and political institutions and their
intellectual activities develop. It is not men's interests and
theories that determine their social institutions but these institutions that determine their interests and theories. As the methods
men use to produce what satisfies their needs improve, there
comes a time when further improvement is impeded by the

social relations of production between them or—to put it in another way—by the system of property which is the legal aspect of those relations. These relations, which once promoted improvement in the methods of production, now stand in the way of that improvement; and there therefore begins an epoch of social revolution. As soon as the economic structure of society changes, the laws, political institutions, and intellectual activities of the men who make up that society also change, more or less rapidly.

I have done my best in the simple rendering above to be true to Marx's meaning. Where it was impossible to make even a plausible guess, I have merely repeated his own words. I have, for instance, repeated the phrase 'the social relations of production,' a phrase which is certainly not self-explanatory; but it presents so many problems that I must comment on it later without attempting to translate it now. It is a phrase used not to express thought, but to cover up its absence, and is therefore not to be rendered into meaningful English. Where it was impossible to be certain of Marx's meaning but possible to guess at it, I have read into his words what seemed to make the best sense of his theory. Nobody can know for certain whether or not Marx, when he said that the relations of production are, at certain stages in the historical process, 'forms of development of the productive forces,' meant that these relations actually promote improvements in productive methods; but that is, I think, the most plausible interpretation of his words. Again, the word 'consciousness,' which is the literal English rendering of what Marx actually wrote in German, is not easy to understand in the sense he uses it. It has been variously interpreted by different commentators, but its most plausible meaning in this context is, I think, 'theories, current opinions, and conscious aspirations.'

I. THE RELATIONS OF PRODUCTION

Let us consider, first of all, what Marx has said in these few sentences about the 'relations of production,' because it 'through them that he connects the economic basis with the su of society. He has said that these relations are 'indis independent of men's wills,' and that men enter 'the social production of their material life.' Th means that, unless men stand in certain relations to one another, they cannot co-operate to produce what satisfies their needs. *Social* production must, of course, mean *co-operative* production; the word 'social' cannot, in this context, refer to any previously existing social relations, for the whole purpose of the theory is to explain how all social relations arise. These 'indispensable' relations in which men must stand vary with their methods of production; and they are presumably indispensable and independent of their wills because men are not free to choose their methods of production. Men find them there when they are born into society, and can modify them only slightly. By calling them 'relations of production,' Marx tells us nothing about them except that they are what must subsist between men when they are engaged in co-operative production, the implication being that, if every man produced only for himself and never exchanged his products for any other man's, no such relations would subsist between men. By telling us they are determined by prevailing methods of production and are indispensable and independent of men's wills, Marx gives us no certain clue to their identity.

What else does Marx tell us about them? That the system of property is their 'legal expression.' This cannot mean that the system of property is the same thing as these relations, for an expression and what it expresses are not one thing but two; but it does imply that the system of property is determined, at least indirectly, by prevailing methods of production. Now, this assertion—that the system of property is determined (and not merely affected) by prevailing methods of production—is not self-evident; indeed, it is not even plausible. We know, for instance, that in western Europe in the Middle Ages there were both serfs and free peasants, and that the land was cultivated in much the same way whether the former or the latter predominated.[1]

---

[1] It is not true that, agricultural methods in the Middle Ages being what they were, there had to be a lord of the manor taking for his own use a great part of the manor's produce. The social organization of the manor was mostly the effect of the need to maintain and defend the lord's supremacy—a supremacy whose causes were primarily military and administrative. Where there is an economically non-productive class taking a large share of the social produce, the demand for luxuries increases, industries arise to meet the demand, trade expands, and towns grow larger. This is what happened in medieval Europe, and it is an example of what Marxists call the 'superstructure' of society profoundly affecting its 'foundation.'

We also know that methods of production are today more alike in the Soviet Union and in the United States than, say, in the United States and Switzerland, though the systems of property of the two former countries differ more than those of the two latter. This, of course, does not prove that methods of production have no effect or only a small effect on systems of property. Marxists have no doubt produced a good deal of evidence that methods of production do affect systems of property, but not nearly enough to establish the truth of Marx's assertion. That methods of production greatly affect systems of property is a truth compatible with two others: that many other things also affect them, and that systems of property greatly affect methods of production. But the truth of these two latter assertions, for which there is also good evidence, is incompatible with historical materialism.

There is, I think, a certain air of paradox about the statement that the methods of production prevailing in any society determine its system of property. If we are to believe the historians (and among them we must include some Marxists in their more unguarded moments) there have been many societies where the persons who owned the most property did the least work or none at all. Now, what we have to believe, if historical materialism is true, is that in such societies the way people work (the instruments and methods they use) determines that those who do no work at all shall receive the lion's share of the products of labour. This is not impossible; the assertion is not self-contradictory and we have no right to decide *a priori* that it cannot be true. But it is certainly unplausible, and we are entitled, before we begin to take it seriously, to require much better evidence in its favour than the Marxists have ever produced.

It is now easy to see just how useful the phrase 'the relations of production' is to the Marxists; it is useful because it is impossible to discover its precise meaning. I do not mean that the phrase was deliberately invented to throw dust in our eyes; the inventor of 'historical materialism' was an exceptionally honest and sincere man, and he would not deceive us unless he had first deceived himself. The phrase is useful for two reasons. In the first place, it looks plausible. After all, why should there not be such things as 'relations of production'? Indeed, there certainly are: the relations, for instance, between a foreman and the men under him, between an architect and a building contractor, between every kind of manager and the workmen whose labour he directs. Now, these 'relations of production' which result inevitably from every division of labour, in whatever society they exist, do *not* find 'legal expression' in the system of property. On the contrary, they are largely independent of that system, though they, too, like the methods of production, are certainly affected by it. They cannot therefore do for Marx what he needs if the connection he speaks of between methods of production and the system of property is to be established. They vary, more or less, with changes in methods of production, whereas the 'relations of production' required to save the Marxian hypothesis must, though originally determined by these methods, be resistant to influence by them. For, otherwise, how could they ever become, to use Marx's own words, 'fetters on the forces of production'? Nevertheless, though the only 'relations of production' to be found in the real world cannot be the ones required by Marx's theory, yet their existence is useful to that theory. Because of them, the phrase 'relations of production' has a possible meaning, and sounds well even to persons who are unfamiliar with it. On the other hand, if nobody bothers to look at the phrase too closely, it can be used pretty much as its inventor wishes, without raising doubts either in his mind or in other people's. Introduced as a something nobody quite knows what between 'prevailing methods of production' and the 'relations of property,' it gives a better appearance to a statement which, in its naked simplicity, might be rather difficult to accept: that the methods of production prevailing in any society determine its system of property.

Moreover, the phrase is useful for another reason. It helps to make more plausible a distinction on which the whole Marxian theory depends, the distinction between the economic 'basis' of society and its legal, political, and cultural 'superstructure.' The fundamental social process, according to Marx, is a progressive evolution by means of the conflict and reconciliation of opposites. If economic determinism is true, if the economic factor is fundamental in some sense in which the others are not, these conflicts must happen within the basis of society. They happen, Marx tells us, between the forces (i.e. methods) and what he calls the 'relations' of production, between two things both of which can fairly be said to be economic. If he had said without more ado that they happen between the methods of production and the system of property, it would have been too easily apparent that he had abandoned economic determinism. For a system of property is more properly called a legal than an economic phenomenon, and therefore belongs to the Marxian 'superstructure' and not to the Marxian 'basis.' The owner of property, merely as such, is neither a producer nor a distributor of goods and services. His being an owner means only that he has a claim protected by society to the exclusive use of certain things, and the system of property is only the way in which such claims are distributed. Now, claims protected by society are legal rights; they are therefore something quite different from, though closely related to, the production and distribution of marketable goods and services, of what we ordinarily mean by wealth. Everyone admits that the system of property greatly affects productive and distributive processes, but that does not make it any more 'economic' than anything else having a similar effect. Science, war, religion, and government, all have a great effect on the production and distribution of wealth, but no one is therefore tempted to call them economic. Property is not economic; and this Marx admitted by implication when he called it the 'legal expression' of something else, something which, in his opinion, is economic. What he meant by 'legal expression' I cannot pretend to know.

Though we do not know what certain phrases mean, we can still estimate their utility to the persons who invent and use them. What Marx needed to make his theory look plausible was a fundamental conflict, of which he could always say that it happens within the economic 'basis,' and yet also speak of as if it happened between part of the 'basis' and part of the 'superstructure.' Let us admire the ingenuity with which he deceived himself. The really fundamental conflict is between the methods and the relations of production; and everyone must admit, if only because the word 'production' is used to describe them, that both these things are economic, that they properly belong to the 'basis.' On the other hand, the system of property is merely the 'legal expression' of the relations of production; and therefore there can never be any harm in talking of the fundamental conflict as if it were between productive methods and the system of property, as if it were not entirely within the 'basis' but between part of it and part of the 'superstructure.'

That is why neither Marx nor any Marxist has ever hesitated to speak of conflicts or contradictions between productive methods and the system of property, between what belongs to the 'basis' and what belongs to the 'superstructure.' Now this, since the fundamental process is economic and is a development by stages through the reconciliation of opposites, is an apparent inconsistency. The fundamental process, and therefore both conflicting opposites, must be economic. Otherwise, the distinction between 'basis' and 'superstructure,' of which the 'basis' alone is economic, is useless, and economic determinism is tacitly abandoned. Thanks to the two saving phrases, 'relations of production' and 'legal expression,' the Marxist can say that the inconsistency is only apparent, since the real conflict is always between the methods and the relations of production, the system of property being merely the 'legal expression' of the latter.

We see therefore how useful this mysterious phrase, the 'relations of production,' is to the Marxists. They never tell us what these relations are: they never point them out to us in the real world to which both they and we belong. They tell us only how these relations are related to other things, and not what they relate; they do not point to the terms between which these relations subsist, except only to tell us they are human beings. But then there are so many different kinds of relations that relate human beings to one another! Marx and Engels both tell us that these relations arise whenever human beings co-operate to produce what satisfies their needs; and they say that the system of property is the 'legal expression' of them. This is to tell us much less than enough to enable us to recognize them. For the only relations that seem to arise of necessity whenever men co-operate in production, whenever there is a division of labour between them, are certainly not such that we can call the system of property their 'legal expression.' A factory, for instance, can be managed either by its owner or by someone who receives a salary for his trouble; both co-operate with the workers in pretty much the same way. There are countless such 'relations of production' in this obvious, technical, and only intelligible sense, and the vast majority of them have no connection whatever, except the most indirect—such as they might have with any other social institution—with the system of property. It may be that Marx had these relations vaguely in mind when he wrote the *Preface* to his *Critique of Political Economy*, but he could not have thought much about them, for, had he done so, he could hardly have called the 'relations of property' their 'legal expression.'

We might liken the 'relations of production' to a ghost battalion closing a vital gap in the front of Marxian theory. Marx and his many disciples have believed in it, and so, too, have most of his critics. So long as no one questions that battalion's existence, the front is never attacked at one of its weakest points, the point at which a connection is established between 'basis' and 'superstructure.' That is why I have discussed the phrase 'relations of production' at considerable length; the whole doctrine of economic determinism turns upon it.

The reader may consider the criticisms so far made pedantic and unfair. None of his disciples has ever pretended that Marx was exact and scrupulous in his use of language; he was no precisian, and lacked the quality that pedants most admire. He may have used the phrase 'relations of production' in several different senses, and often embodied it in arguments that are not sound. But was he not striving to say something really important, that the minute critic may miss but that is intelligible enough to the man of good will and good sense?

There is perhaps no surer way of misunderstanding a great thinker than being too eager to discover his faults. But the purpose of my argument has not been to reckon mere ambiguities and confusions of thought against Marx. It does not greatly matter that he and Engels used the phrase 'relations of production' in different and incompatible senses; it does not matter that they never exactly defined it, nor even that the contexts of its use too often leave us without a clue to its meaning. If they had only sometimes used it in a sense that made their economic determinism intelligible, I should have attached myself to that sense and made the most of it. The brunt of my argument against them is precisely that there is no such sense, that there are no social relations between men determined (and not merely affected) by their methods of production, and which in their turn determine (and not merely affect) the system of property and the class structure of society.

II. ECONOMIC CONTRADICTIONS AND THE CLASS STRUGGLE

I have tried to show that Marx has given no real content to what ought to be one of the most important concepts of his fundamental theory, the concept of the 'social relations of production.' I now want to consider what he has to say about the contradictions that inevitably arise within what he calls the 'economic basis' of society. The process of social development is, according to Marx, 'dialectic.' That is to say, human societies proceed from stage to stage of their development in such a way that, within each stage, fundamental 'contradictions' or incompatibilities arise and, when they are resolved, society passes from one stage into another. It is therefore of the utmost importance to the Marxian theory that these 'contradictions' should be properly accounted for, and that the account should be consistent with economic determinism.

If we look at the classic formulation of historical materialism we see that the 'contradictions' or incompatibilities are merely asserted and that no cause is ascribed to them. We are merely told that the 'relations of production' become fetters on the forces of production, or, to put it more clearly, that in every society there comes a time, in each stage or epoch of its development, when the further improvement of techniques of production is prevented by what Marx calls the 'relations of production,' relations of which we know nothing more than that the system of property is their 'legal expression.' Now this, on the face of it, is an astonishing statement. Marx has already told us, at the beginning of his classic formulation of historical materialism, that the 'relations of production' are indispensable, that men enter into them, whether they like it or not, whenever they co-operate to satisfy their needs; and he has also told us that these relations correspond to the productive methods in use. The obvious inference would therefore appear to be that when these methods change so, too, do the relations corresponding to them. If these latter are, to use the Marxian phrase, 'forms of the development of the productive forces,' it is difficult to see how they can ever become 'fetters.' Since, in the first place, the 'relations of production' are determined by the 'forces of production,' we should expect every development in the latter to produce a corresponding change in the former. Marx begins his account of the theory which has served him as a guide in all his studies by using language that suggests the concomitant variation of two variables, of which only one is dependent on the other. And then, all of a sudden, without warning and without explanation, he tells us that there nevertheless arises inevitably from time to time an incompatibility between them which only social revolution can resolve. This incompatibility apparently arises because the dependent variable begins to impede the free operation of the variable on which it depends. This is an astonishing statement, and yet Marx can make it without even being aware that it requires explanation. If the 'relations' correspond to the 'material forces' of production, how can there ever be 'contradictions' between them? The classic formulation gives no clue to an answer to this question.

Let us take it for granted that the contradictions happen. How are they resolved? Is there any need that they should ever be so? Again, nothing said in the *Preface* to *The Critique of Political Economy* provides an answer to either of these questions. What, after all, is a 'contradiction,' in this peculiar German and Marxian sense of the word? I have supposed that it is an incompatibility between institutions. It ought to be that and not a conflict between classes, if historical materialism is really to be what Marx wanted it to be, a theory which explains class conflicts as effects of something more 'fundamental' than themselves. That is what 'contradictions' ought to be; and yet, if that is what they are, there is no apparent reason why they should ever be resolved. Why should not the 'relations of production,' once they have become incompatible with the forces, continue so for ever? Why should not economic progress come to a stop? Why should there not be economic and social stagnation?

The truth is that, if we want the reasons Marx gives either to account for the incompatibility or to explain how it is resolved, we must look elsewhere than in the *Preface* to *The Critique of Political Economy*. How can the 'relations of production' become 'fetters' on the 'forces of production'? Let us first attempt an answer to this question.

We know that, according to Marx, the 'relations of production' find 'legal expression' in the system of property. Just what is meant by 'finding legal expression' I do not pretend to know. Nevertheless, two inferences are, I think, permissible: that the system of property is very closely connected with the 'relations of production,' and that it is the latter which determine the former and not the other way about. We know, too—to use another word out of the Marxian vocabulary—that the system of property 'reflects' the structure of classes. It is not at all clear what is meant, in this connection, by the word 'reflects,' but part at least of its meaning must be either 'determines' or 'is determined by.' For our present purpose it does not much matter which of these two alternatives we choose. Marx and Engels sometimes speak as if the system of property determined the structure of classes, and sometimes as if it were the other way about; but what they always affirm and never deny is that the 'relations of production' ultimately determine both.

Now, according to the Marxian theory, given a society divided into classes and the system of property appropriate to that division, there is always one class, the privileged and ruling class, whose interest is to prevent change in the existing 'relations of production' and therefore in the system of property which is their 'legal expression.' Since we do not know, because Marx never tells us, what the 'relations of production' are, we cannot know what must be done to prevent them changing. But we do know what a system of property is, and we can understand what the ruling class, the class that benefit from the system, must do to maintain it. The ruling class dispose of the coercive power of society; that, indeed, is what is meant by calling them a ruling class; and this power they use to prevent whatever changes would, in their opinion, endanger their privileged position. On the other hand—and this, too, we can learn from *The Communist Manifesto*, from certain passages in Marx's *Capital*, and from other sources—the ruling class do not attempt to prevent improvements in methods of production. There is a very simple and obvious reason why they should not do so: they are the ruling class who appropriate the lion's share of the products of industry.

The greater those products, the greater the wealth that accrues to them; they have more to gain than any other class by the enrichment of society. No doubt, it is also part of the Marxian theory that technical progress must, in the long run, bring about the ruin of the ruling class; but that they need not know. It is the immediate interest of the ruling class to maintain unchanged the system of property (and therefore also the 'relations of production') on which their social supremacy depends, and it is no less their immediate interest to allow the technical progress that multiplies the wealth of which they appropriate the lion's share. Because they prevent change in the one case and allow it in the other, there eventually arise the fundamental 'contradictions' that Marx and Engels so often speak of. Marx and Engels do not, of course, offer this explanation as unambiguously as I have done,[1] but it is in fact the only plausible explanation which can be extracted from their works. To the simple question, why, since the 'forces of production' determine the 'relations of production,' need there ever arise 'contradictions' or incompatibilities between them, Marx and Engels (though they do their best to hide their theory behind the obscurity of long and barely intelligible words and phrases) have no better answer than this: because the ruling class behave as they do. It is the ruling class who, though they do not know it, produce the 'fundamental' contradictions or incompatibilities. Like all classes they are short-sighted; they can see no more than their immediate interests; they cannot foresee the remoter consequences of their behaviour.

It is, according to Marx, these 'contradictions' or fundamental incompatibilities between institutions which lead to social revolution. Now, a social revolution is not the incompatibility of some institutions with others. An incompatibility of that kind might never be resolved; the 'relations of production' might put a stop to all further improvements in the methods of production; or else these improvements, continually introduced, might lead to always greater waste and inefficiency. In other words, the 'contradictions' Marx speaks of might lead either to stagnation or to economic anarchy. What ensures that they are resolved,

---

[1] For if they did so, doubts would arise in their own and their readers' minds about historical materialism.

that the progress of society continues? For an answer to this question we must also look outside the *Preface* to *The Critique of Political Economy*, to those of Marx's writings where he treats of social classes and of the struggles between them. In the first section of *The Communist Manifesto*, the section called *Bourgeois and Proletarian*, the process is described whereby capitalist methods of production, as they arise and develop, first bring into existence, and then multiply, unite, and strengthen, a class of exploited men who own no property and live by selling their labour. This class, the proletariat, become, as the capitalist system develops, not only always stronger but always more revolutionary. They challenge the political supremacy of the bourgeois; and, though they are at first often defeated, their final victory is assured. For the capitalist system is such that the bourgeois must always be doing their best to develop and improve productive methods. By so doing they not only promote the incompatibilities we have already discussed, but also increase the size of the proletariat, who of necessity become a revolutionary class because they are the chief sufferers from these incompatibilities. In the words of the *Manifesto*: 'What the bourgeoisie therefore produces is, above all, its own grave-diggers. Its fall and the victory of the proletariat are alike inevitable.'

It is therefore the political victory of the revolutionary class which resolves the contradictions, by causing the transformation, gradual or sudden, of the 'relations of production,' which are part of the 'economic basis' of society, as well as of the whole immense 'superstructure' erected upon them. The victory of the bourgeois, when they were the revolutionary class, was not perhaps gained in quite the same way, because earlier ruling classes (if we are to believe the *Manifesto*) did not themselves promote technical improvements but at best only tolerated them. These earlier classes were therefore never, in their day, their own grave-diggers. But, though the nature of the class struggle may vary with the classes taking part in it, it is always the victory of the revolutionary class which transforms the 'relations of production.'

I shall not, at this stage of my argument, discuss more particularly what Marx has to say about class struggles. My present object is merely to establish two points: the first, that Marxism offers us no explanation of why the 'relations of production' should not change with every change in the forces of production, to which they are said to 'correspond,' except that it is the interest of a ruling class that they should not, of a class having the power to prevent their doing so; and the second, that Marxism offers us no explanation of why the resulting incompatibilities should at last be resolved except the inevitable political victory of a revolutionary class, whose interest it is to destroy the old 'relations of production' and replace them with new ones that are not fetters on economic progress. The gradual development of the forces of production and the discontinuous but more rapid changes in the 'relations of production' do not, therefore, constitute an autonomous economic process. The conservatism of the ruling class and the revolutionary activities of the exploited class are not mere effects of that process; they are quite essential to it. It is not just a question of their having some influence on it, an influence that is only secondary, for, without them, the fundamental historical process, falsely called economic by the Marxists, would not even be 'dialectical.' It is the political activities of these classes, the use of their political power by the exploiters, and the revolutionary struggle of the exploited, which both cause the contradictions between the 'forces' and 'relations of production' and resolve them. These are conclusions we cannot avoid if we take the trouble of looking a little closely at what Marx himself said. I have made no attempt to test Marx's hypothesis by considering the historical evidence; I have not been interested in what happens in the real world but only in how Marx himself stated his fundamental hypothesis, the theory he called 'historical materialism.'

He called it 'materialism,' and by giving it that name clearly meant to imply that men's economic activities are fundamental in some sense in which their other activities are not, that the tools, sources of power, and methods they use to produce and distribute goods and services determine in a general way the character of everything else they do. Unless he meant to imply at least that much, there was no point at all in making the distinction he did make between the economic 'basis' and the 'superstructure' of society. Now, the activities called 'fundamental' cannot be so in any intelligible sense unless their development is more or less autonomous, unless it can be explained without making any essential phases of it the effects of men's other than economic activities. The fundamental social process is said to be 'dialectical,' that is to say, a kind of progress whose repeated theme is the emergence and resolution of incompatibilities. If the process is to be 'dialectical' and 'material' in the Marxian senses of those words, not only must both 'contradictory' opposites belong to the economic 'basis' of society, but so, too, must the cause of their 'contradictions' and whatever brings them to an end. Unless Marx can show that these four things—the two sets of incompatible things, the cause of their incompatibility, and what ends it—are all properly included in the 'basis,' he has no right to call his theory 'historical materialism.'

What does Marx in fact show us? The 'forces of production,' one of the two sets of institutions which become incompatible with each other, are correctly assigned to the 'basis'; they are the tools, methods, and sources of power used in the production of wealth, and are therefore properly called 'economic.' The other set of institutions are given a name, and that name suggests they are economic; but their nature is never described. We do not know what they are; we know only that the system of property is their 'legal expression,' and that, though they 'correspond to' the forces of production, they also sometimes become 'fetters' upon them. As soon as we look around us and try to discover in the real world anything that the name invented by Marx could be applied to, we see only the relations that men stand in when they co-operate to produce wealth; but those relations have no very direct or clear connection with the system of property, which is very obviously not their 'legal expression.' The classic formulation of historical materialism tells us nothing at all about the cause of the incompatibilities between the forces and relations of production nor yet about what brings them to an end. For an account of how these things happen we must look elsewhere in Marx's writings, and, when we look, we can find nothing better by way of explanation than the political struggle between classes. Marx, when he called his theory 'historical materialism,' deceived both himself and his readers.

What made this deception possible? We can only guess at the answer to this question. Marx had some ideas about society that greatly excited him, ideas that gave him, so he thought, a deeper insight into the causes of social change than anyone had had before him. Those ideas he never worked out properly, though he always felt their influence upon him. He had no gift for the clear exposition of fundamentals; when he tried to set out his ideas in a series of precise statements, he failed miserably. But he never knew he had failed; his faith in his own vision, his use of a vocabulary inherited from Hegel, his German education which filled and excited his mind much more than it increased his power to control and order his thoughts: these things blinded him to his defects. He felt his own greatness and was not deceived; he was deceived only in his estimate of what he had accomplished.

Chapter Three

IDEOLOGY AND THE CLASS STRUGGLE

I T is only the first half of the famous passage so often quoted from the *Preface* to *The Critique of Political Economy* which is a more or less connected account of the gist of historical materialism. The second half is merely a series of propositions illustrating or adding to what has already been said; it is a number of unconnected observations, of which some are more important than the others.

Marx tells us, among other things, that (i) we should always distinguish 'between the material transformation of the economic conditions of production, which can be determined with the precision of natural science, and the legal, political, religious, aesthetic, or philosophic—in short, ideological forms in which men become conscious of this conflict [he means the conflict between the forces and the relations of production] and fight it out'; that (ii) 'no social order ever disappears before all the productive forces for which there is room in it have developed, and new, higher relations of production never appear before the material conditions of their existence have matured in the womb of the old society'; that (iii) 'we can, in broad outline, point to the Asiatic, the ancient, the feudal, and the modern bourgeois modes of production as so many progressive epochs in the formation of society'; and (iv) that 'the bourgeois relations of production are the last antagonistic form of the social process of production.'

The second of these four statements cannot be verified. Since what Marx calls a social order is determined by the 'relations of production' it rests on, and since we do not know, because he has not told us, what 'relations of production' are, we can never discover just how much 'room' there is for 'productive forces' in any social order. Nor can we discover the 'material condi-

36

tions of the existence of any set of 'relations of production.' We cannot verify the statement, and yet we can say that, if the intelligible part of it is true, some things are impossible. We may not know what 'relations of production' are, but we do know, more or less, what a 'social order' is. The term is admittedly vague, but it is in ordinary use, and we can suppose that Marx used it in the ordinary way. Where we find a stable social order and certain methods of production used in it, we can legitimately infer that that social order has at least room enough for those productive methods. If we afterwards discover that, in a particular country where that social order prevails and those productive methods (or others more primitive) are used, men are trying to make a revolution in order to establish a more 'advanced' type of society, we can condemn their attempt as premature and confidently predict its failure. The second of these statements therefore, though it cannot be verified, is nevertheless important. If its truth is taken for granted—and by the Marxists it is so taken—certain negative conclusions follow from it. When we come to consider the controversy between Bolsheviks and Mensheviks in Russia, we shall see just how important these negative conclusions can be.

The first of the four statements tells us that 'the material transformation of the economic conditions of production' can be 'determined with the precision of natural science.' In other words, we can, according to Marx, give as accurate an account of how an economic system works and how its character alters as we can of the laws of physics and chemistry. Marx was perhaps too greatly impressed by the efforts of statisticians, though the information they had collected by 1859 was small indeed if we compare it with what they have collected since. Though economists now dispose of a mass of statistics immensely greater than Marx knew anything of, they are almost as far as they ever were from attaining anything like the precision of natural science. Marx, when he made this statement, must have forgotten the great gulf that divides the social studies from the natural sciences. Besides, the study of what Marx calls the 'material transformation of the economic conditions of production' is not economics; it is economic history. There is not the least reason to suppose that economic history is more precise than political or any other kind of history; and historical generalizations, as even the Marxists know, are much more to be doubted than scientific laws. As a matter of fact, economic history is, except perhaps in what relates to the nineteenth and twentieth centuries, the least to be trusted of all. We know, for instance, much more about what Marx would call the 'superstructure' of Roman or Athenian society than we do about the 'basis.' Indeed, our ignorance about economic conditions and developments in most countries during much the greater part of their histories has been an immense advantage to the Marxists. How much less plausible economic determinism would seem if so much of what they choose to consider fundamental had not been left unrecorded! Marx's assertion, which is equivalent to a claim that economic history can attain 'the precision of natural science,' is in any case quite gratuitous; he had nothing to gain by making it, for it adds precisely nothing to our understanding of historical materialism, which it was his purpose to expound.

Nor would Marx have lost anything useful to his theory had he refrained from telling us that in 'broad outline, we can point to the Asiatic, the ancient, the feudal, and the modern bourgeois modes of production as so many progressive epochs in the economic formation of society.' As Karl Federn has said in his excellent book, *The Materialist Conception of History*, we can attach no meaning at all to such notions as the 'Asiatic' and the 'ancient' modes of production. There were many different types of societies in what the Europeans call the ancient world. Their economic histories, if we knew them, would perhaps reveal transformations as great as those that happened in modern Europe between the fifteenth and eighteenth centuries. As for Asiatic societies before European industrialism began to affect them, they must have differed even more than the ancient; for, not only is Asia of vast extent, but some of her peoples have existed as separate and self-sufficing civilized communities for thousands of years. To speak, therefore, of an 'Asiatic' and an 'ancient' mode of production is, however broad the outline, absurd; and it is even more absurd to speak of them, together with feudalism and capitalism, as 'so many progressive epochs in the economic formation of society.' There never was a society which was once Asiatic, and then became ancient, and then feudal, and then at last bourgeois capitalist. It is only in western Europe during the last ten centuries that we can find what might be called a single society which has lived through two of the epochs mentioned by Marx, namely the feudal and the bourgeois capitalist. Is the western Europe of after the barbarian invasions the same society as the Roman Empire? Was there ever, before the Roman Empire, anything that could be called a single Mediterranean society, whose economic system can be treated as something which emerged from conflicts between methods and relations of production in Asia? What was Marx thinking of when he said what he did about the 'progressive epochs in the economic formation of society'? Indeed, we may ask, without impertinence, was he thinking at all? This extraordinary statement, let us remember, forms part of what Marxists have called the classic formulation of historical materialism, which is the central tenet of their creed. I do not want to make too much of the absurdity of what Marx said. Social and political theorists have always been inclined to be reckless; they use a vocabulary which is not at all precise, and the phenomena they study are so varied and difficult to observe, that, if they insist on being sensible, scrupulous, and exact, they can hope to make only a little progress at the cost of prolonged effort. Marx was not afraid of hard work, but he was immoderate and avid, and wanted quick results; and so, in spite of his vast erudition, he could not resist the temptation of making statements that only a little thought and slight reading can show to be false. These lapses occur, I think, with special frequency in Germany, though her scholars are as well-read, as thorough, and as ingenious as any. They may be called the tribute that learning pays to folly.

The first of the four propositions not only tells us that 'the material transformation of the economic conditions of production' can be 'determined with the precision of natural science' but also enjoins us always to distinguish between this 'material transformation' and the 'ideological forms in which men become conscious of this conflict [between the forces and relations of production] and fight it out.' In other words, we must always distinguish between the growing incompatibility between two elements within the economic basis of society and the political and other conflicts within its superstructure occasioned by that incompatibility. I take this to be Marx's meaning, though his words do not quite bear the construction I have put on them. He speaks of a 'material transformation' and of men's becoming 'conscious of a conflict' and fighting it out in 'ideological forms.' This, if we take it literally, is an extraordinary statement. What is involved in men's becoming conscious of this conflict? Do they become aware of it? And how do they fight it out in 'ideological' forms? Do they just argue about it? If we insist on answers to these questions, we shall certainly not get them; and what is more, we shall be unfair to Marx. German thinkers, when they have something important to say, quite often do not say exactly what they mean. We must always take notice of the general character of their theory. There are certain literal interpretations of what Marx said that must be false, though his own words and the rules of grammar may seem to require them.

When Marx says that men become 'conscious' of this conflict (which is, of course, the incompatibility or 'contradiction' between the relations and the forces of production) he does not mean that they become aware of it; he only means that this incompatibility is the ultimate cause of the class struggle.[1] It is, he thinks, the interest of the ruling class that the existing 'relations of production' and the system of property which 'expresses' them should not change; and it is the interest of the exploited and revolutionary class that they should. The stability of the superstructure, and of the 'relations of production' it rests on, is the interest of the ruling class, because their position as a ruling class depends on those relations being just what they are; and it is the interest of the exploited and revolutionary class that those relations should be transformed, because they are the condition of their being exploited and of their social and political inferiority. It is not at all necessary, Marx tells us, that either the ruling or the revolutionary class should understand or even be aware of the fundamental incompatibility which is the ultimate cause of their hostility and their disputes. Neither the rulers nor the revolutionary leaders need ever have had such ideas in their heads as Marx tried to express by such phrases as

[1] We have seen that this is not so, that the incompatibility cannot be accounted for except as an effect of the class struggle. Marx was not aware of this defect in his theory, and it does not affect his account of the 'ideological' and political struggle between classes. It is this account that we now have to consider.

'productive forces' and 'relations of production.' The revolutionary leaders may not even know that it is the interest of their class that the system of property should be transformed. They may at one time, prompted by this or that grievance, desire this or that particular change; and at other times, prompted by other grievances, make other demands. They may win their inevitable victory piecemeal; or else, owing to the successful resistance of the ruling class, their demands may accumulate until only violence can satisfy them. Whatever happens, there will be struggle and resistance; and the final outcome of the victory of the revolutionary class will be the complete transformation of the 'relations of production' and of the immense superstructure erected upon them.

What of the 'ideological forms'? What is an ideology? The word was used once upon a time to mean the science or study of ideas. But Marx and his disciples have helped to give it another and a more popular meaning. By an ideology[1] we are to understand any theory or system of ideas whose social function, whatever the amount of truth in it, is to justify the aspirations and activities of some group or other of men. Marx and Engels sometimes speak as if all theories were ideologies, and at other times as if it were possible to distinguish between ideologies and scientific theories or at least between the ideological and scientific aspects of theories.

There seems to have been some confusion in their minds which they never succeeded in dispelling. Science has its history like everything else, and that history must have been influenced by men's other activities and by motives other than disinterested curiosity, the desire for knowledge for its own sake. Some sciences have progressed faster than they would otherwise have done because the knowledge they acquire is useful to men in their endeavours to produce wealth more efficiently or to make effective war on one another. Others have made little or no progress over long periods of time because they have been discouraged, lest their discoveries should upset the cherished beliefs of powerful corporations. The progress of science has affected

---

[1] This conception of 'ideology' is one of the most useful introduced by Marx into social theory. It is already present in Saint-Simon's writings, but it is vaguer there and less vigorously expressed.

and been affected by philosophy, and philosophy in its turn has affected and been affected by religion, morals, and political theory. It is notorious that men's religions, and also their moral and political beliefs, often suit their interests; and it is not less true that the social function of these beliefs is to influence their behaviour. Science and ideology, if we look at their histories, are certainly very closely related. What is more, the experimental sciences cannot make progress unless society provides the instruments and facilities they require. There are therefore not only economic and political conditions of scientific progress; there are also causes other than disinterested curiosity and the accumulation of knowledge, which determine that some sciences progress more quickly than others, while yet others are stuck fast for centuries in prejudice and nonsense. But this is only to say that the history of science is part of the history of mankind. However closely science and ideology are linked together in their growth, and though the same ideas may on occasion serve them both, they are not one but two, and the difference between them is absolute.

Marx and Engels often recognized this difference though they did not deliberately assert it. We have already seen how, in the *Preface* to *The Critique of Political Economy*, Marx invites us always to distinguish between the 'material transformation of economic conditions, which can be determined with the precision of natural science' and the 'ideological forms' in which men fight out their conflicts. The theory which purports to account for the genesis of ideologies—that is to say, Marx's own theory— must claim to be scientific. It may be, of course—and Marx believed that it was—a theory useful to the proletariat; and it may also be a theory which could only have emerged at a certain stage of the evolution of society. It may therefore serve as an ideology, a theory helping to justify the common aspirations and activities of the industrial workers as soon as they have become a politically united and revolutionary class. Marx certainly intended his theory to be useful to the proletariat. The great purpose of his life was to help prepare their victory. He was their friend, their scientist, and their philosopher; and he never pretended otherwise. His being so ought to put us on our guard against him, because a partisan is always liable to prejudice.

But it does not follow that his theory must be false because it is useful, that it is mere ideology and nothing more. It is not impossible, though it may be unlikely, that a theory of society constructed for the benefit of an exploited class should be scientific. Marx certainly did not believe that the theories of society serving the interests of classes other than the proletariat were scientific; but then, since those theories differed from his own, which he believed to be true, it was only natural that he should think as he did. There is nothing inconsistent or absurd about his doing so. It may be that before the capitalist era the social conditions for the emergence of a true science of society did not exist; and if that true science, when it emerged, should establish, as Marx apparently thought it did, that the industrial workers would challenge the political supremacy of the bourgeois and would be victorious, then that science must be in the interest of the workers. In other words, if, at a certain stage in the historical process, a true science of society emerges, it cannot be the less true because, that process being what it is, the science can also serve as the ideology of a revolutionary and inevitably victorious class. The victory of that class, when it comes, will be evidence, and most important evidence, in favour of the theory. Nor will the fact that belief in the theory was one of the causes of victory make that theory the less scientific; for the theory accounts for its own discovery and its becoming the ideology of a class. Some critics of Marxism have argued that this cannot be, that the theory, if belief in its truth by the class whose victory it foretells is a part cause of that victory, cannot be scientific. On the strength of this argument they have called Marx a pragmatist, that is, a person who believes that a doctrine is true so long as the activities inspired by it are successful. This argument is, I think, false;[1] and historical materialism cannot be called unscientific for no better reason than its being an ideology necessary to the victory of the proletariat. The truth of a doctrine is not, of course, the same thing as the success of the persons who practise it; but it does not follow that it cannot be true if it predicts this success and asserts that the condition of it is that those who succeed should believe in the doctrine.

---

[1] I do not mean to deny that Marx sometimes spoke as if he were a pragmatist; I mean only that this argument does not prove that he was one.

Marx and Engels both often spoke as if historical materialism were both science and ideology. That, indeed, is the assumption behind most of their arguments. Their attitude to what they called bourgeois 'ideology' was never: Well, that is what *they* think, but *we* think differently, and there is no way of deciding between us. On the contrary, they were continually engaged in proving that bourgeois ideologies are false, absurd, or unrelated to the facts; that, though they contain some truth, it is distorted and mixed up with mere fantasy and nonsense. They called themselves 'scientific' socialists, and all socialists before them 'Utopian.' The claim they made for their theories was of the kind made by all scientists and persons who think themselves scientists. Marx, said Engels, had done for the social studies what Darwin did for biology. They believed, of course, that their theories might be improved and corrected; they did not claim omniscience and infallibility. But they did claim to be scientific, and abated nothing of their claim because their science was useful to the proletariat. Their main purpose in life was to serve that proletariat, but they did not therefore believe that their theories were no more true than those of the 'bourgeois ideologists,' whose theories were useful to the ruling class.

Though this claim and this assumption lie behind their arguments, it does not mean that Marx and Engels were clearly aware of them. They also, following Hegel, sometimes treated all theories and all science as 'relative,' thereby implying, not only that men are liable to error and that knowledge accumulates slowly, but also that no theory, whether it is science or mere ideology, can ever be true for all men at all times. Engels, who wrote more philosophy than Marx, was the more liable of the two to speak in this way. He seems to have believed that all knowledge must be relative because it is acquired in different conditions at different times. The motives from which men acquire knowledge vary, the uses to which they put it are many, and the interests it serves are never the same. Science can be ideology, and is almost never entirely free from it; but ideologies always serve temporary and above all class interests. These considerations and his Hegelian training caused Engels to believe that even natural science is relative, as if it followed that, because scientists are always rejecting old hypotheses and constructing new ones, what is true at one time could be false at another, or that a theory could be more or less true at one time than another.

It is a pity, perhaps, that Marx and Engels should have sometimes believed in the 'relativity' of knowledge. It is a belief they got from Hegel; but it most certainly does not (though they may, when they affirmed it, have thought otherwise) follow from 'historical materialism.' Even if we suppose it true that men's economic activities determine the general character of everything else they do, and that the fundamental economic process is dialectical (that 'contradictions' are repeatedly generated within it and repeatedly 'reconciled'), it does not follow that anything that is true can become false or more or less true than it was before. The relativity of knowledge is not even required to explain the character of what Marx called 'ideological conflicts.' They may still have the causes and effects he ascribed to them, though every truth should be, what indeed it must be to be a truth, eternal.

Marx and Engels, though they sometimes implied and even asserted the 'relativity' of knowledge, nearly always wrote and spoke as if their own theory of society were true absolutely. Should it require correction later, it would do so, not because what was once true had become false, but because they, being fallible, had been mistaken. This much they assumed whenever they engaged in controversy with bourgeois writers, whose interests and aspirations were different from their own. 'Historical materialism' is not, in their eyes, merely an ideology; it is a science which can serve as an ideology because it predicts only one more social revolution, and is therefore in the interest of the class destined to make that revolution. Marx and Engels also, in practice and in spite of their Hegelian training, treated the natural sciences with the same respect as they did their own theory. Scientists may make mistakes, old hypotheses be discarded, the origins of the sciences socially determined, but their essential purpose, their proper business as scientists, is to describe the real world and not to assist or justify or challenge the exploitation of the weak by the powerful. This is what Marx and Engels in practice believed, whatever they sometimes thought their theory required them to say.

Neither their theory nor any natural science prescribes to men what they should do. It may affect their conduct, either by giving them knowledge they would otherwise not have had of how best to attain their ends, or else by causing them to reflect on the world they live in and so abandon some ends and pursue others. Though science cannot tell a man what ends he should pursue, he may, as he absorbs the knowledge it gives him, cease to desire some things and come to desire others. Historical materialism could not prescribe to Marx and Engels how they should act, but it did affect their behaviour. It told them what was coming, what the whole social process was moving towards; and since they approved that future they decided to work for it. Had they decided otherwise, had they remained loyal to the middle class they were born into, their decision would have been no less and no more rational. They might then have hoped, and with good reason, that the proletarian revolution would happen after they were dead; they might have said with Louis XV: *Après moi le déluge.*

Though historical materialism allows us to distinguish between ideology and science, it does, nevertheless, deny the absolute validity of any code of morals, and therefore of any political theory which is primarily a theory of political obligation. Moral judgments, according to Marx and Engels, are socially conditioned, not in the sense that they are truths which men could have discovered only at a certain period of history, or truths which it happens to be their interest to accept at one time rather than another, but in the sense that they are not really objective truths at all. They look like statements about what is external to men's feelings but are in fact only expressions of feeling. What men approve and disapprove, what they are proud and ashamed of, the kinds of behaviour that arouse these feelings in them vary with their interests; and these interests, in their turn, vary with the class-structure of society. In the last resort, it is the interests of the ruling class which determine the moral code prevalent in any society. The sort of behaviour that suits them is generally approved; the sort of behaviour that is against their interests is generally disapproved. Because they are powerful, they control the schools and the churches; and it is therefore what suits them that is taught in these places. They do not, of course, deliberately invent and propagate a morality suitable to the interests of their class. A code of morals grows up slowly, and the rulers who benefit from it are as much convinced of its eternal truth as are the classes they exploit by its aid. Political and economic theory, because they describe men's social behaviour, are deeply affected by this morality; and so, too, are literature and the arts. For men's tastes and aesthetic ideals are closely related to their morals.

We are nowadays very familiar with this part of the Marxian theory, though it was, at the time when its author expounded it, something of a novelty. Long before Marx, there had been people who denied the existence of a genuine moral science, who said that moral judgments merely express the feelings or preferences of those who make them, or, at least, the feelings and preferences prevalent in the society or class they belong to. Already in the sixteenth century, Montaigne had shown what very different feelings the same behaviour can arouse at different times and places. Doubts about the universal validity of any code of morals were as common among educated people in Marx's time as they are today. What was not common was his belief that the prevailing code of morals is always in the interest of the ruling class, and can be so, though neither that class nor any other are aware of the fact. This belief, whatever the truth or error in it, is certainly interesting; it is one of those valuable hypotheses which, whether they are finally rejected or greatly modified, lead to the most fruitful researches. It may well be partly true. But put in the way I have put it, which seems to me not unfair to Marx and Engels, it makes two assumptions difficult to accept: firstly, that the interests common to all the members of society are less important than the interests peculiar to the ruling class in determining the general character of moral judgments; and secondly, that interests can be so defined as not to include or imply common notions of justice, honour, and dignity. I very much doubt whether the sharp distinction between objective class interests and moral principles, which the Marxian theory requires, can in fact be made. Men have certain primitive needs which they would satisfy even if they lived in isolation. About these needs there may be nothing moral. But their 'interests' in society, though related to these needs, are something quite different in kind; they are social interests. How then can we say of any one class of social phenomena that they are determined by these interests but themselves scarcely affect them? How could Marx and Engels know *a priori* that morals 'reflect' interests but have very little power to change them? Sociology is an empirical study and no one can know what affects what, and to what extent, unless he makes a long and careful study of the phenomena he claims to describe.

Marx and Engels were not only social theorists, they were also revolutionary socialists. They offered an explanation of how men come by their moralities, but they also had their own strong preferences. When they condemned bourgeois society they did more than foretell its death; they expressed their own feelings about it. When a doctor tells his patient that he is about to die, he passes no moral judgment on him. He may, indeed, prefer him to his grandson who has fifty years to live. And if, like the communist society prophesied by Marx, that grandson should be granted immortality, the doctor might still prefer the old man to him. He might put it down to the injustice of Providence that only the last and least worthy generation should continue for ever. Immortality is not virtue, though men have called it virtue's reward. Because the grandson comes last, and never dies, and is succeeded by no one, it does not follow that he is better than his ancestors; though the doctor, for all that he once liked the old man best, might soon find it his interest to please the young one.

But neither Marx nor Engels acted from interested motives, since they never expected to see the victory of the proletariat; what few hopes they may once have had did not survive the abortive revolutions of 1848. They worked for a victory that would happen after their deaths. What sustained them was their faith that the society which would emerge after the victory would be greatly superior to the one they knew. Historical materialism taught them that one morality succeeds another and that none is eternally valid. Their feelings taught them differently: that what would come after the next and last revolution predicted by historical materialism would be better than anything known before it. These two beliefs are not consistent with one another. If Marx and Engels had merely said that what comes next is no better and no worse than what we have now but that they happened to prefer it, no one could accuse them of inconsistency. They would then have made a statement about themselves not very important to anyone except themselves and their admirers. But they said, or, rather, implied, much more than this; they often spoke as if each successive moral system were superior to the one before it, as if there were, what historical materialism denies, certain universally valid moral principles in terms of which particular moralities, past, present, and future, could be estimated.

It was only natural they should believe this, though they could not square it with their theory of society. They were revolutionary socialists; they were enemies of the society they belonged to; they were or aspired to become leaders of the proletariat. They wanted to supply that proletariat with an ideology, with a faith to sustain them in their struggle against their oppressors. They could not, involved as they were in that struggle, say to the proletariat: What you are fighting for is no better than what your exploiters want; it is just your preferences against theirs. They had to speak to, to exhort the workers in the language that all revolutionaries had used before them—in the name of an eternal justice violated by their enemies and maintained by themselves. What is more, their own theory accounts for their inconsistency. Every system of morality, according to historical materialism, claims to be universal. It cannot perform its social function unless it does so, whether that function is to preserve existing institutions in the interest of the ruling class or to subvert them in the interest of the exploited. The social theorist must take notice of this truth, but the revolutionary socialist need not do so. He is engaged in the struggle and has accepted a system of morals; and that system, like every other, claims to be universal. What, then, is this claim? It is no more than the assumption behind the behaviour of those who accept that system. Men are so made that they can fight for their class interests effectively only when they fight in the name of the whole society to which that class belongs. They cannot fight whole-heartedly unless they believe that what they are fighting for is just absolutely. Their hearts and minds are not prepared for the fight unless they can treat the enemies of their class as enemies of society. Marx and Engels were fully engaged in the fight; not only were they prepared for it both intellectually and emotionally, but their part in it was to prepare others. They were no doubt inconsistent, but that inconsistency is easily explained: they were at the same time social theorists and revolutionary socialists. Their historical importance, their effectiveness, the influence they have had in the world, they chiefly owe to this, their double capacity. They called themselves scientific socialists. The phrase, in a sense, is self-contradictory. The scientist, merely as such, has no purpose except to account for how things happen; the socialist, as a socialist, wants to make things happen the way he thinks best. A man may well be a scientist and a socialist; his being the kind of socialist he is may be partly determined by his scientific interests. He is one person, and not two persons, scientist and socialist, in one. His science will affect his socialism, and his socialism may affect his scientific interests, may make him more interested in discovering some things than others. But, whatever the relation between his science and his socialism, as parts of the life of one man, what he can never be is a scientific socialist. Not even if his science predicts the coming of what his socialism approves. 'Scientific socialism' is a logical absurdity, a myth, a revolutionary slogan, the happy inspiration of two moralists who wanted to be unlike all moralists before them.

It is often the junior partner who has the less grateful tasks thrust upon him. So it was with Engels. Three chapters of *Anti-Dühring* are devoted to an attack on those who, like Dühring, believe that there are eternal moral truths. At the end of the first of these chapters, Engels says:

> as society has hitherto moved in class antagonisms, morality was always a class morality; it has either justified the domination and the interests of the ruling class, or, as soon as the oppressed class has become powerful enough, it has represented the revolt against this domination and the future interests of the oppressed. That in this process there has, on the whole, been progress in morality, as in all other branches of human knowledge, cannot be doubted. But we have not yet really passed beyond class morality. A really human morality which transcends class antagonisms and their legacies in thought becomes possible only at a stage of society which has not only overcome class contradictions but has even forgotten them in practical life. And now we can appreciate the presumption of Herr Dühring in advancing his claim, from the midst of the old class society and on the eve of a social revolution, to impose on the future classless society an eternal morality independent of time and of changes in the real world.

Was Engels less presumptuous than Dühring? The morality of a classless society is, he says, better than any class morality, because morality progresses and that is what it is progressing towards. In what respect is it better? Engels does not tell us. He is silent where Dühring is explicit; he has nothing to say of the standard he measures all moralities by. And yet he does claim to take their measure. He does even more. He says that the best morality 'transcends' all class antagonisms. What, then, of the other moralities? Their more particular rules may not be in keeping with the morality of a classless society, the morality which Engels thinks the best. But they must, surely, have something in common with it. If Marx and Engels are right, if every system of morals claims to be universal, it surely must be so. For how otherwise can precepts taught and enforced in the interest of only one class be made to appear just absolutely? There must be some general rules, however abstract, common to the different class moralities, whose more particular precepts can then be passed off as valid universally because a show is made of deducing them from these rules.

I pass on now to the last of the four propositions taken from the second half of Marx's classic formulation of historical material-ism. It is the proposition asserting that 'the bourgeois relations of production are the last antagonistic form of the social process of production.' Putting the same thought into simpler language, we may say that, once bourgeois capitalist society has passed away, the 'relations of production' will never again impede the smooth and efficient working of prevailing methods of produc-tion. After the next social revolution, there will always be com-plete harmony between the methods and relations of production. There must, of course, in every society where men co-operate to produce what satisfies their needs, be some 'relations of produc-tion.' Marx has already told us that there can be no social (i.e. co-operative) production unless men enter into these indis-pensable relations. He now tells us that the 'relations of produc-tion' of the society which will emerge from the next revolution, and the system of property giving 'legal expression' to them, will not divide that society into classes. There will therefore be no ruling class whose interest it will be to prevent any change in the 'relations of production,' even when such change is necessary for the further improvement of productive methods. There will be no ruling class, no exploitation, and therefore no exploited and revolutionary class.

This is a strange conclusion to what has gone before. Marx, as we know, never explained exactly what he meant by 'relations of production,' nor yet how it is that they, and the system of property giving 'legal expression' to them, determine the class structure of society. He merely asserted that they do. Co-operative production necessitates diversity of function, or, if you prefer it, a division of labour. If Marx meant anything by 'the relations of production'—and he was never explicit when he spoke about them—he probably had vaguely in mind this division of labour or else something causally connected with it. Now, though, as I said.before, neither the system of property nor the class structure of a society 'corresponds' with this division of labour, Marx probably, though he never gave much thought to the matter, believed that they do. But if they do, why should society, after the next revolution, become classless? There will still be co-operative production, and therefore a division of labour, and therefore 'relations of production.' Why should diversity of economic function divide society into classes at every stage of social evolution except the last? Historical materialism gives no answer to this question.

When I say that 'historical materialism' gives no answer, I do not mean that Marx and Engels do not. There were greater resources in their minds than they put into their favourite theory. We learn from *The Communist Manifesto* that 'our epoch, the epoch of the bourgeoisie, possesses this distinctive feature: It has simplified class antagonisms. Society as a whole is more and more splitting up into two great hostile camps, into two great classes directly facing one another—bourgeois and proletariat.' We also learn that 'of all the classes that stand face to face with the bourgeoisie today, the proletariat alone is a really revolutionary class. The other classes decay and finally disappear in the face of modern industry; the proletariat is its special and essential product'; and again, that 'all previous historical movements were movements of minorities. The proletarian movement is the self-conscious, independent movement of the immense majority in the interest of the immense majority'; and lastly, that 'if the proletariat during its contest with the bourgeoisie is compelled by force of circumstances to organize itself as a class; if, by means of a revolution, it makes itself the ruling class, and, as such, sweeps away by force the old conditions of production, then it will, along with these conditions, have swept away the conditions for the existence of class antagonisms and of classes generally, and will thereby have abolished its own supremacy as a class. In place of the old bourgeois society, with its classes and class antagonisms, we shall have an association in which the free development of each is the condition for the free development of all.'

The four passages I have quoted all come from *The Communist Manifesto*, the first three from the first section, and the last from the second. They together assert that, as capitalism develops, all classes except two will disappear, and that one of these two classes, the revolutionary class whose eventual victory is inevitable, will include the immense majority of people. Marx and Engels, the joint authors of the *Manifesto*, published these assertions in February 1848, many years before Marx gave us the gist of 'historical materialism' in the *Preface* to his *Critique of Political Economy*. But neither Marx nor Engels ever withdrew or seriously modified the four statements I have just quoted, though it is easy to see that they are in no way logically connected with what they said about productive forces and the 'relations of production.' The forces of production determine the 'relations of production,' whose 'legal expression' is the system of property; and it is these same relations that determine the class structure of society. All this is good Marxian doctrine. Though we may not know what in this context 'legal expression' means, nor yet exactly how the 'relations of production' determine the class structure, we do know that these connections, whatever they may be, are repeatedly asserted by both Marx and Engels. And we also know that, as society develops (or at least as it has developed in western Europe during the last thousand years), methods of production become more and more complicated. So, presumably, do the 'relations of production,' for they are relations that men must enter into in all social (that is, co-operative) production. The statement that they are relations that men must enter into in all co-operative production suggests that they are somehow determined by the division of labour; and in fact several passages in

Marx's *Capital* and in Engels's *Anti-Dühring* are pretty good evidence that both Marx and Engels, when they came anywhere near being explicit on the subject, did believe that they are so determined. And yet they seem also to have believed that in the fully developed capitalist economy, with the division of labour greater than ever before, the class structure would somehow be drastically simplified. It may be that they had good reasons for this belief; but, if they had them, those reasons can have nothing to do with what they said about the primal and indispensable connection between the 'forces' and 'relations' of production.

In their description of the process whereby, as capitalism develops, the class structure of society is simplified, Marx and Engels quietly abandon much that is essential to historical materialism. According to that theory, the conflict between classes is the effect of a fundamental antagonism between the 'forces' and 'relations of production.' It is because these relations are resistant to change that the fundamental antagonism develops; and it is they that determine, in some manner never explained by either Marx or Engels, the class structure of society. And yet they also argue that the exacerbation of this antagonism must, at least during the capitalist epoch if not at any time before it, eventually reduce the classes to two. But the antagonism is made sharper only because the ruling class can for a time maintain 'relations of production' which have survived their social utility and have become, to use Marx's own phrase, 'fetters on the forces of production.' The contradiction is patent. On the one hand, it is asserted that the division of society into a number of social classes is determined by the 'relations of production' prevailing in it; and on the other, that the number of classes under capitalism is eventually reduced to two, as the result of a conflict which could never happen, let alone grow sharper, unless the ruling class were making (though only for a time) a successful effort to prevent those relations being changed.

Chapter Four

THE FACTS ALLEGED BY MARX AND ENGELS
IN SUPPORT OF THEIR THEORY

MARX's classic formulation of the fundamental theory that served as a guide for all his studies, the theory that Engels sometimes preferred to call 'the materialist conception of history,' is obscure, inconsistent, and inadequate. It is obscure because at least one of the important terms included in it has no discoverable meaning that would enable it to do what is required of it;[1] it is inconsistent because some of the intelligible parts of it give the lie to others; and it is inadequate because it does not explain how the 'contradictions' within the 'economic basis' of society (the 'contradictions' which give to the whole historical process its 'dialectical' character) arise and are resolved. For that explanation we must look outside Marx's formulation of his theory; we must look at what he says when he is merely being guided by it and is not expounding it; but, if we do so, we can discover nothing plausible except what is not consistent with the theory.

Both Marx and Engels wrote a great deal about history. They were not 'abstract' social theorists; they did not build up their theory by considering man 'in the abstract' and his essential needs, and then discover what institutions would satisfy him. Their interest was in man as a member of society and in the development of institutions; and they therefore studied history much more than psychology. Indeed, their social theory is above all a philosophy of history. How did that philosophy affect their study of history? Did it really serve them as a guide when they tried to explain what had happened and what was happening to the European societies they knew best? That their explanations were affected by their theory goes without saying. When men

---

[1] Which is to explain how the 'basis' determines the 'superstructure.'

are as excited by their ideas as were Marx and Engels, their studies cannot but be affected by them. What, then, did this affection, this influence, amount to? Was it guidance? It is worth while discovering how Marx and Engels, with historical materialism behind them, explained such things as the emergence of the state and the origins of capitalism.

Engels was the friend and collaborator of Marx. the favourite expositor and defender of his doctrines. The two men first met in Germany, but the close friendship between them did not begin until their second meeting, in Paris. That friendship was broken only by the death of Marx in 1883, and was for nearly forty years an exceptionally intimate and intellectually fruitful association. We cannot know how much Engels contributed to the common stock of ideas, but we do know that he stood closer to Marx and was more familiar than anyone else with the workings of his mind. Engels freely admitted the superiority of Marx, and yet had worked with him so much and for so many years that he could, without offence to his superior (who was by no means quick to do justice to other people's claims), call historical materialism his own theory as well as Marx's. It was acknowledged by them both to be the product of their joint labours, though Engels took the less important part in making it. The two men collaborated on the tacit understanding that, though one of them was a genius and the other only a man of talent, the efforts of both were needed to give form and substance to their theory. Engels was the only collaborator and intellectual companion of Marx, and therefore his opinions, especially those published while Marx was still alive, deserve to be closely studied as authoritative statements of the common doctrine.

Of all Engels's writings the most important, when we are considering historical materialism, is certainly *Anti-Dühring*, especially the second part of it, the part that deals with political economy. In the fourth chapter of that part Engels discusses the emergence of classes in society. He says:

> As men first emerged from the animal world . . . so they made their entry into history; still half animal, brutal, still helpless in face of the forces of Nature, still ignorant of their own; and consequently as poor as the animals and hardly more productive. There prevailed a certain equality in the conditions of existence [by which

Engels presumably means that nobody was much richer or poorer than any one else], and for the heads of families also a kind of equality of social position—at least an absence of social classes—which continued among the natural agricultural communities of the civilized peoples of a later period. In each such community there were from the beginning certain common interests whose protection had to be entrusted to individuals, even though under the control of the community as a whole: such [interests] were the adjudication of disputes, the repression of encroachments by individuals on the rights of others, the control of water supplies, especially in hot countries, and finally, when conditions were still absolutely primitive, religious functions. Such offices . . . are naturally endowed with a certain measure of authority and the beginnings of state power. The productive forces gradually increase; the increasing density of population creates at one point a community of interests, at another, conflicting interests between the separate communes, whose grouping into larger units brings about in time a new division of labour, the setting up of organs to safeguard common interests and to guard against conflicting interests. These organs which, for the reason that they represent the common interests of the whole group, have a special position in relation to each individual community . . . soon make themselves even more independent, partly through heredity of functions . . . and partly because they become more and more indispensable owing to the increasing number of conflicts with the other groups. It is not necessary for us to examine here how this independence of social functions in relation to society increased with time until it developed into domination over society. . . . Here we are concerned only with establishing the fact that the exercise of a social function was everywhere the basis of political supremacy.

The reader must excuse this long quotation. Anything shorter would have been unfair to Engels. As it is, I have omitted from this passage only what adds nothing to its main argument. Supposing the historical facts alleged by Engels to be true, could we find a better refutation of historical materialism than he has given? In every community, he tells us, some men have to carry out special functions in the common interest. Two of the four functions he mentions, the adjudication of disputes and the repression of encroachments, are clearly political; and only one is economic, the control of water supplies in hot countries. These offices are, he says, the beginnings of state power. They increase in authority and grow more independent of the rest of the community, partly because they become hereditary, and partly because disputes with other communities are multiplied. Engels thinks it unnecessary to show how this independence of function develops into domination over society; all he wants is to explain that the 'exercise of a social function' is everywhere the basis of political supremacy. But he conveniently forgets that the social function he has in mind is itself political. It is not the division of labour required by prevailing methods of production, nor yet any more elusive 'relations of production' connected with that division of labour, that he points to as the cause of the emergence of social classes. He talks of diversity of functions, but the distinction he has in mind is between political and economic functions, between government and production. The only dependence of the former on the latter is that government is not required except to give protection to the community of producers, to defend it against external attack, and to maintain justice within it. Government arises in the common interest, and if it later so develops that the ruling class become the exploiters of the rest of the community, this, if we are to follow Engels's own account of the matter, appears to have nothing to do with the 'development of the forces of production.' The ruling class could not, of course, devote themselves exclusively to government unless the producers produced more than enough to satisfy their own essential needs; there must be a surplus to be consumed by the ruling or administrative class. But to say that this surplus is the condition of there being a ruling class is not to say that prevailing methods of production or any 'indispensable relations' that men enter into in the course of production determine the division of society into social classes.

Their account of the communist society to come into existence some time after the last proletarian revolution shows how little either Marx or Engels understood the implications of their own theories about the origin of classes. They tell us very little about the communist society, but they do take it for granted that, inside it, there will be both administrative and judicial functions to perform. There will therefore be what Engels, in the passage just quoted, calls 'common interests' whose protection has to be entrusted to individuals. Why should not the need to protect these interests give rise to a ruling class in the society they call 'communist' as much as in any other? We have already seen that Marx and Engels, though they taught that all social production obliges men to enter into indispensable relations that divide society into classes, said that communist society would be classless. They did not deny that there would be social production in that society, but merely that it would have its usual effect. There are therefore in the writings of Marx and Engels two different accounts of the origin of social classes: the first describes them as effects of certain indispensable relations men enter into in all co-operative production, while the second says they arise because there comes a time when society must entrust the protection of its common interests to particular persons. The first account is obscure but consistent with economic determinism; the second is more lucid and plausible but inconsistent with it, and to disguise the inconsistency Engels (no doubt unconsciously) refrains from calling the protection of common interests a political function, though that is precisely what it is. The communist society, as Marx and Engels conceive it, rests on co-operative production and requires the protection of common interests; whichever of their two accounts of the origin of social classes is true, we are still left without an explanation of why communist society should be classless. And if we want an explanation, we can only find it in the Marxian account of proletarian democracy: when the industrial workers, having become the immense majority, take over government, they will so govern that the division of society into classes must soon disappear. To call the Marxian theory 'political determinism' would not be accurate and would offend the Marxists, but would not be further from the truth than to call it 'economic determinism,' a name that pleases the Marxists better.

In the paragraph immediately after the one I quoted from, Engels says:

> But alongside this development of classes another was also taking place. The natural division of labour within the family cultivating the soil made possible, at a certain level of well-being, the introduction of one or more strangers as additional labour forces. This was especially the case in countries where the old common ownership of the land had already disappeared. . . . Production had so far

developed that the labour power of a man could now produce more than was necessary for its mere maintenance: the means of maintaining additional labour forces existed, likewise the means of employing them; labour power acquired a value. But within the community . . . there were no superfluous labour forces available. On the other hand, such forces were provided by war. . . . Up to that time they had not known what to do with prisoners of war, and had therefore simply killed them. . . . But at the stage of the 'economic order' which had now been reached, the prisoners acquired a value; their captors therefore let them live and made use of their labour. . . . Slavery was invented. . . . It was slavery that first made possible the division of labour between agriculture and industry on a considerable scale and along with this, the flower of the ancient world, Hellenism. Without slavery, no Greek state, no Greek art and science; without slavery no Roman Empire. But without Hellenism and the Roman Empire as a basis, also no modern Europe. . . . In this sense we are entitled to say: Without the slavery of antiquity, no modern socialism.

The first passage I quoted from *Anti-Dühring* might have been written by a man who had never heard of historical materialism, or even by a man who, having heard of it, wanted to refute it without mentioning it by name in case he should too openly offend its author, his friend; but this second passage is a conscious attempt to explain the past in terms of that theory. There were wars, we are told, long before there was slavery, and prisoners of war were ordinarily killed by their captors; this was the universal practice until wealth had accumulated sufficiently to enable victorious communities to feed and employ supplementary persons. In former times, they had either to kill their prisoners or to send them home; had they tried to keep them, the prisoners would presumably have starved. What Engels wants to prove by this argument is that slavery is not the mere product of force, that it does not come into existence only because victors in battle are strong enough to reduce the vanquished to servitude. It cannot exist except where economic conditions are suitable, where the victors are rich enough to maintain their slaves. Had Engels not been an historical materialist he would not have argued as he did, but that does not make his argument consistent with historical materialism. It is inspired by a belief in it, but does not bear it out. For, according to this argument, the emergence of slavery alters the system of property, and therefore also the 'relations of production,' of which that system is merely the 'legal expression.' Now, Engels has not proved that this change in the 'relations of production' is itself the effect of any change or development in the forces or methods of production.[1] The man who can now afford to keep a slave, though his grandfather could not, may be using exactly the same tools and methods of production as his grandfather. He may be richer only because he, his father, and his grandfather have all been thrifty. On the other hand, as soon as he acquires slaves, he may alter his methods of production. If he does so, an innovation in the system of property and in the 'relations of production' will have made possible an improvement in methods of production, though no such improvement was required in the first place to make possible the innovation. Let no one imagine that this is a small point made against Engels, a point so small that it need not signify. Historical materialism is a theory that claims to be scientific. One of the most important statements it makes is that the 'relations of production' prevailing in any society are relations into which men necessarily enter because they are engaged in a certain type of co-operative production. It is precisely this statement that Engels denies by implication in the passage I have just quoted, a passage taken from a book that he read to Marx in manuscript and that Marx approved.

Engels wrote *Anti-Dühring* to defend Marxian socialism against one of its earlier critics. This critic, Eugen Dühring, was himself a socialist. He disliked the general philosophy of Marx and Engels, the philosophy they called dialectical materialism; but with that issue we, as students of society, are not concerned. He also disliked their economic determinism, their theory that it is men's economic activities which determine in a general way all their other social activities, or, to put the same matter in other words, that the development of economic institutions determines in a general way how all other institutions develop. By an 'institution' I mean, in this context, any mode of behaviour which is not a natural function and yet is prevalent in society. Dühring believed that the political factor is not merely as important as,

[1] This omission he made good in 1884, in *The Origin of the Family, Private Property and the State*, where he ascribed the emergence of slavery to the domestication of animals. But it is significant that Engels never noticed the omission when he was writing *Anti-Dühring*.

but even more important than, the economic. Engels, in the second part of *Anti-Dühring*, and especially in the three chapters where he discusses what he calls the 'Force Theory,' is doing his best to refute this opinion, to prove that, in spite of all Dühring's arguments, the economic factor really is fundamental. I do not want to defend Dühring. I have never read a line he wrote except the passages quoted by Engels. But in case anyone should think I have been unfair to Engels, and also to Marx who approved his book, I shall quote one more passage, this time from Chapter Two of the second part of *Anti-Dühring*:

> Even if we exclude all possibility of robbery, violence, and fraud, even if we assumed that all private property was originally based on the owner's own individual labour, and that throughout the whole subsequent process there was only exchange of equal values for equal values, the progressive evolution of production and exchange nevertheless brings us with necessity to the present capitalist mode of production, to the monopolization of the means of production and the means of subsistence in the hands of a numerically small class, to the degradation of the other class, constituting the immense majority, into propertyless proletarians, to the periodic succession of production booms and commercial crises, and to the whole of the present anarchy of production. The whole process is explained by purely economic causes; robbery, force, the state, or political interference of any kind are unnecessary at any point whatever. 'Property founded on force' [the allusion here is to a phrase of Dühring's] proves to be nothing but the phrase of a braggart intended to cover up his lack of understanding of the real course of things.

This, then, is what 'economic determinism' really meant to Engels, and also to Marx, who listened to this passage and approved it.

How can Engels reconcile this bold assertion with the other two passages quoted from *Anti-Dühring*, passages separated from it by only twenty pages of print? The question, of course, is rhetorical. Engels cannot do it. The best he can do is to say that 'all political power is originally based on an economic, social function,' as if the words 'economic' and 'social' had the same meaning. He has himself described those functions, and they are clearly not economic or, at least, most of them are not. On the other hand, they are quite clearly 'social' functions; and if the reader (and no doubt Engels himself) can be persuaded, by the quick and quiet transition from the word 'economic' to the word 'social,' that it does not much matter, when you are discussing anything as important as historical materialism, which you use, no one will think of asking any awkward questions.

Marx in the twenty-fourth chapter of the first volume of *Capital*, the chapter called 'Primary Accumulation,' describes the genesis of the capitalist system of production in England, its first home. For the capitalist system to operate, it is necessary that there should be,

> on the one hand . . . owners of money, of the means of production, and of the means of subsistence, who desire by the purchase of others' labour-power to increase the sum of the values they own. On the other hand, there must be 'free' workers, the sellers of their own labour-power, and therefore the sellers of labour. They must be 'free' workers in a double sense. First of all, they must not themselves form a direct part of the means of production, must not belong to the means of production, as do slaves and serfs, etc. Secondly, the means of production must not belong to them, as the means of production belong to peasant proprietors. Free workers are free from, unencumbered by, any means of production of their own. . . . The process which clears the way for the capitalist system, therefore, can be nothing else than the process whereby the worker is divorced from ownership of the means of labour, a process which, on the one hand, transforms the social means of subsistence and the social means of production into capital; and, on the other, transforms the actual producers into wage-workers. The so-called primary accumulation is therefore nothing other than the historical process whereby the producer is divorced from the means of production. . . . The capitalist era, properly speaking, dates from the sixteenth century. Wherever capitalism made its appearance, this occurred in regions where the abolition of serfdom had long since been effected, and where the independent and self-governing towns that were the crowning glory of the Middle Ages had for some time been falling into decay.

Marx then goes on to describe the process whereby the men who under capitalism became wage-workers were deprived of the means of production they had once owned.

> The prelude to the revolution which laid the foundation of the capitalist method of production occurred during the last third of the fifteenth century and the first decades of the sixteenth. Great

numbers of masterless proletarians were thrown on to the labour
market by the break-up of the bands of feudal retainers. . . . This
was by no means the only cause. . . . What happened was that the
great feudal lords, in defiant opposition to king and parliament,
created a still larger, a much larger proletariat by forcibly hunting
the peasant off the land . . . and by usurpation of the common lands.
The immediate impetus to this was given by the rise of the Flemish
wool manufacture, and the corresponding increase in the price of
wool. . . . A new and terrible impetus was given to the forcible
expropriation of the masses of the people during the sixteenth cen-
tuiy by the Reformation, and by its sequel, the pillaging of the
ecclesiastical domains.

Marx also tells us, in this same chapter, that 'in England, serfdom
had practically disappeared by the latter part of the fourteenth
century.'

Marx, in the passages I have quoted, argues that two things
were necessary before the 'capitalist method of production' (he
uses that very phrase) could begin to function: firstly, that some
men should have accumulated sufficient wealth to have a surplus
available for the hire of labour, and secondly, that others, having
lost whatever means of production they formerly possessed,
should have nothing to sell but their labour. He does not tell us
why the men who have accumulated wealth should want to use
it for the hire of labour on a much greater scale than before, nor
yet how it was they accumulated that wealth. He mentions no
new 'productive forces' requiring the use of more labour and
therefore increasing the demand for it. The capitalist method of
production has not yet, we must remember, begun to function.
And when Marx describes the expropriation of the peasants who
become proletarians, he ascribes three causes to it: the breaking
up of bands of feudal retainers, the rapacity of feudal lords who
wanted to convert tillage into pasture in order to grow more wool
to be sold in Flanders, and the expropriation of Church lands.
The breaking up of bands of retainers was a political act done
from political motives; the expropriation of the peasants by the
lords was done in the hope of gain by converting the land from
one use to another, of which both had been known for centuries; and the plunder of the Church, though it enriched many
and had important economic consequences, was not therefore

the less a political act. What of the woollen industry in Flanders? Was it capitalist in character? Had it adopted new methods of production? Marx does not enlighten us about these matters, for he is describing how capitalist production was made possible in England, where, according to him, it *first* appeared. Nowhere at all, in this chapter on 'Primary Accumulation,' can we find anything that looks like an account of how new forces and methods of production were introduced, of how they eventually began to press against existing 'relations of production,' until at last the pressure was too strong for these relations and they were destroyed. On the contrary, we are told that serfdom disappeared in England in the latter part of the fourteenth century, a hundred years before the period at which Marx places the first beginnings of capitalist production. But the serfs were one of the great classes of medieval society, and their place in it must, if the Marxian theory is true, have been determined by what Marx calls 'feudal relations of production.' If, then, serfdom was abolished in the fourteenth century, these relations and the 'whole immense superstructure' resting upon them must have begun to disintegrate at least a hundred years before the new capitalist system of production was born. Now this, though it seems to follow from Marx's own description of how capitalist production became possible in England, is a conclusion incompatible with the truth of historical materialism, as it is formulated in the *Preface* to *The Critique of Political Economy*.

In *The Communist Manifesto* we are given another description of how modern bourgeois society emerged from what Marx and Engels call 'the ruins of feudal society.'

> From the serfs of the Middle Ages sprang the chartered burghers of the earliest towns. From these burgesses the first elements of the bourgeoisie were developed. The discovery of America, the rounding of the Cape, opened up fresh ground for the rising bourgeoisie. The East-Indian and Chinese markets, the colonization of America, trade with the colonies, the increase in the means of exchange and in commodities generally, gave to commerce, to navigation, to industry, an impulse never before known, and thereby, to the revolutionary elements in the tottering feudal society, a rapid development. The feudal system of industry, in which industrial production was monopolized by closed guilds, now no longer

sufficed for the growing wants of the new markets. The manufacturing system took its place. The guild masters were pushed aside by the manufacturing middle class; division of labour between different corporate guilds vanished in the face of the division of labour in each single workshop. Meanwhile the markets continued to grow, and demand to rise. Even manufacture no longer sufficed. Thereupon, steam and machinery revolutionized industrial production. The place of manufacture was taken by the giant, modern industry, the place of the industrial middle class by industrial millionaires, the leaders of whole industrial armies, the modern bourgeois. . . . We see, therefore, how the modern bourgeoisie is the product of a long course of development, of a series of revolutions in the modes of production and of exchange.

The last sentence quoted proves that the authors of the *Manifesto* believed that great changes (what they called 'revolutions') in methods of production and exchange had been the ultimate cause of the emergence and rise of the bourgeoisie. And yet, what immediately precedes that sentence does not bear it out. The burghers of the medieval towns, so long as industrial production was confined to the guilds, were, according to Marx and Engels, just as much a class belonging to feudal society as any other. For the guild system of industry is expressly called 'feudal'[1] by them. The burghers became 'bourgeois' only when the manufacturing system, which is a different mode of production from the guild system, began to develop. The manufacturing system emerged, they say, because of the discovery of new markets. But the discovery of new markets cannot properly be called a 'revolution' in either the mode of production or exchange. It is merely an increase of the area within which exchanges occur. It is very likely, if the increase is both great and rapid, to cause a revolution in methods of production and exchange, but is not itself any such revolution. It ought to be noticed that the *Manifesto* has not a word to say about the cause of these voyages of discovery which resulted in the opening up of new markets. Indeed, the *Manifesto* is never more obscure than at this point of the argument. The discovery of America and the rounding of the Cape created, we are told, new opportunities for the rising

---

[1] It is possible to take exception to the use of the word 'feudal' in this connection. When Saint-Simon first so used it, it was a misuse; but since that time it has become established usage.

bourgeoisie. We must therefore assume that the bourgeoisie had begun to arise before these events; and yet we are also told that it was these events (and others like them) which opened up the new markets that the 'feudal' or guild system of industry could not satisfy, so that the manufacturing system had gradually to take its place. In other words, the bourgeoisie arose before the bourgeois system of production. Now this, according to historical materialism, is an impossible event. A class cannot exist before the emergence of the 'relations of production' that create it, and these relations cannot exist until men have begun to use the instruments and methods appropriate to them.

Mr. Sidney Hook, in his book *Towards the Understanding of Karl Marx*, denies that historical materialism means what I have said it means. He admits that 'Marx often said that the development of technology could serve as an index of the development of society'; but he goes on to argue that

> that is altogether a different thing from saying that we must look to the development of technology as the cause or independent variable of social change. For Marx, technique was only one of three components of the productive process. The other two were nature and the social activity of man. . . . The social relations of production (which are synonymous with the expressions 'the property relations' and the 'economic foundations of culture') cannot therefore be regarded as the automatic reflection of technology. On the contrary, the development of technology is itself often dependent upon the system of social relationships in which it is found. The direction that technical invention takes is determined by needs which are not themselves narrowly technical but economic or social.

I quote this passage from Sidney Hook because I want to guard against possible misunderstanding. Mr. Hook is no doubt talking very good sense when he says that 'the development of technology is itself often dependent on the system of social relationships in which it is found.'[1] He is talking sense; but he is not, though he says the contrary, interpreting Marx, who, in

[1] Plekhanov, in *Fundamental Problems of Marxism* (English edition, London, 1929, pp. 55–7), attempted a similar defence of Marx and Engels, maintaining—on the strength of quotations from two letters written by Engels—that they both meant us to understand that the superstructure can affect the economic foundation, though the latter's influence is fundamental. He rebuked Bernstein for objecting that Engels, by the admissions made in those letters, had virtually abandoned historical materialism. In one of the letters Engels had written: 'economic relations, however great the influence on them of other relations of a political or ideological

his classic formulation of historical materialism, quite deliberately
tells us that the 'relations of production' are what men enter
into, whether they like it or not, in the course of production.
Because they produce what they need co-operatively and in the
way they do, they enter into these indispensable relations. That
is what Marx said, clumsily perhaps, but not the less deliberately
for that; and there is no other reasonable interpretation of his
words. What these 'relations of production' are may be difficult to discover. If they are merely another word for the division
of labour, it is clear that the system of property (or, to use the
phrase preferred by Marx' 'property relations') is not their 'legal
expression.' On the other hand, if that system is their 'legal
expression,' it is not easy to see what they are nor how they are
determined by prevailing methods of production. This is a point
I have already elaborated, and I wish to say no more about it.
But what is, I think, abundantly clear, is that Marx meant us to
understand that the 'relations of production' are determined by
the 'forces of production' and at the same time find 'legal expression' in the system of property.[1] Indeed, unless he meant at
least that much, he would not have been, what he undoubtedly
was, an economic determinist. For if the 'relations of production'
are not determined by the 'forces of production,' why call them
relations of *production*? If they are only partly determined by those
'forces,' then they must also depend on other causes, causes that are
not economic; and if they themselves, being partly determined by
non-economic causes, in their turn affect methods of production,
what becomes of economic determinism? What becomes of the
Marxian distinction between the 'basis' and the 'superstructure'?

Though Sidney Hook is not, I believe, a Marxist, he is certainly
well acquainted with what Marx wrote and very much disposed

order, are those whose action is ultimately decisive.' But this, as Plekhanov did not
and as Bernstein apparently did see, is to let something drop out of one hand while
appearing to hold on to it with the other. If A, B, and C are factors acting on one
another, it is plain nonsense to say that A, *however great* the action of B and C on it,
is ultimately decisive. Engels's two letters, from which Plekhanov quotes with
approval, were written towards the end of his life, when he was aware that his fundamental doctrine required qualification but did not know how far he could go in
qualifying it without abandoning it altogether.

[1] Mr. Hook is, I think, mistaken when he says that the phrases 'social relations
of production' and 'relations of property' are synonymous, though it is true that
Marx and Engels sometimes used them as if they were. If we assume, with Mr.
Hook, that they are synonymous, the Marxian theory only becomes the more
apparently absurd.

to admire him. He looks at what Marx wrote with the eyes of an admirer, turning faults into virtues. If Marx had meant what Sidney Hook wants him to have meant, he would have talked sense only at the cost of abandoning what is the very heart and pith of his doctrine. He would have made a sacrifice seldom made by a man who spends the better part of his life elaborating a theory that he calls the 'guiding thread' of all his studies; he would have rejected the proposition on whose truth that whole theory rests. When intellectuals burn their boats, they are usually boats inherited from others: the ones they have built themselves at the cost of great labour they most jealously preserve. So it was with Marx; and that is why he could, without knowing what he was about, put forward in favour of his theory arguments that are really destructive of it. No wonder, then, that Sidney Hook, anxious to admire him, was easily deceived. He has looked at some of Marx's arguments and seen where they tend, and he cannot believe that what he sees clearly was invisible to Marx. His conclusion is more charitable than just. Marx, no doubt, was as clever a man as any of his critics, but he had what they had not—a strong desire that his philosophy should be true. He had painfully acquired a number of opinions which he thought important, and could not bear to see them ruined; he therefore, guided by the instinct[1] that makes all men defend their own, tried to accommodate to his theory the facts brought to his notice by the historians. His own rare talent and the use of a vocabulary made, above all others, for the confusion of mankind, gave him and his admirers the illusion of success.

[1] This instinct is part of the economy of nature. What man would have the courage to make a theory if he could see, as soon as it came within range of his understanding, the bearing of every fact which was evidence against it? When men speculate they fall into error much more often than they find truth; but consciousness of error is depressing, whereas speculation requires hope and energy. We must therefore accept with a good grace the division of intellectual labour that makes some men build systems and others bring them down. Truth is found among the ruins; the builder discovers it and makes it part of his building, but does not know how much more valuable it is than all the rest. Not until the building is brought down is the valuable part of it known for what it is. Because his energy is limited and his imagination weak, man must blind himself to the greater part of what falls within the narrow range of his vision; and to understand a little must neglect a great deal. It is in this sense that there is no profitable activity without renunciation. But a full understanding is impossible while anything relevant is neglected, and there must therefore be in the intellectual sphere an immense division of labour. If a philosophy is worthy of respect, it is worth criticism, and if it is worth criticism, it must be criticized ruthlessly.

In the third volume of *Capital*, in a chapter entitled 'The Conditions of Distribution and Production,' Marx says that 'the relation between wage labour and capital determines the entire character of the [capitalist] mode of production'; and again, three pages later, that 'the form of labour, as wage labour, determines the shape of the entire process and specific mode of production'; and lastly, on the next page, that profit 'is a prerequisite for the new creation of means of production by means of capitalist production.' All this, we may be tempted to think, amounts to saying that the 'relations of production' determine the way in which men produce goods and services. That is surely the natural interpretation to be put on these three quotations; but, natural or not, it does not prevent Marx from adding, in the next paragraph but one, that 'the so-called conditions of distribution [by which he means the claims of labourers, capitalists and landlords to their respective shares of the social product] correspond to and arise from historically determined and specifically social forms of the process of production and of the conditions into which human beings enter in the process whereby they reproduce their lives.' The 'historically determined and specifically social forms' and the 'conditions' that Marx here speaks of are, of course, what he elsewhere calls 'relations of production.' They are 'forms of the process of production' and 'conditions into which men enter in the process whereby they reproduce their lives'; that is, in plain English, they are relations that must subsist between men when they co-operate to produce what they need to keep them alive. They determine the shares of the three great classes in the social product, and they are also 'forms of the process of production,' that is, relations men necessarily enter into in the course of production. To prove the causal connection on which his whole theory depends, to prove that the forces or methods of production determine men's social relations, Marx has nothing better to offer than examples of how these social relations determine the 'capitalist mode of production.' What can a man do with such arguments as these, when, like Mr. Sidney Hook, he has made up his mind beforehand to admire their author? For what Marx has done is to produce evidence for the opposite of what he wanted to prove.

Mr. Hook's attempt to accommodate Marxism to common

sense at the cost of abandoning its most essential doctrine will not bear examination. In the third part of *Anti-Dühring*, in one of the chapters later separately published under the title *Socialism, Utopian and Scientific*, Engels says that 'the materialist conception of history starts from the principle that production, and with production the exchange of its products, is the basis of every social order; that in every society which has appeared in history the distribution of the products and with it the division of society into classes or estates, is determined by what is produced and how it is produced, and how the product is exchanged. According to this conception, the ultimate causes of all social changes and political revolutions are to be sought, not in the minds of men, in their increasing insight into eternal truth and justice, but in changes in the mode of production and exchange; they are to be sought not in the philosophy but in the economics of the epoch concerned.' Could a statement be clearer than this? It was read out by Engels to Marx, who never told him to strike it out. Later on, when Marx was dead and Engels had to defend the common doctrine alone, he did what he could, faced as he was by critics unknown to Marx, to modify this statement, to dress it up to look more plausible. Nobody can now guess quite what he meant to concede to his critics. His intention, no doubt, was to pacify them, to subdue his own doubts and to keep firm hold of the old doctrine; and men with intentions like these rarely know exactly what they mean. They speak, not to bring light where there was darkness, but to avoid arguments that might press them too closely. The concessions made by Engels after Marx's death were made by a man who did not know, and indeed could not afford to know, just how much he was giving away. They do not interpret Marx's thought. But this quotation from the second chapter of the third part of *Anti-Dühring* most certainly does so; and that is why it has been so often quoted by Marxists the world over.

The passages I have quoted and discussed do not come from the lesser-known writings of Marx and Engels. They are taken from the acknowledged masterpieces of Marxist literature. They are taken from *The Communist Manifesto*, from two of the most often read and discussed chapters of the first and third volumes of *Capital*, and from the second and third chapters of *Anti-Dühring*, chapters specially written to defend historical materialism against one of its earlier critics who wrote before Marx died. To establish my conclusion—which is that neither Marx nor Engels understood the real implications of the intelligible part of their own theory—it was necessary to take several passages, every one of them from the most famous Marxian classics and from chapters deliberately written to expound and illustrate the theory. I have done my best to be fair to Marx and Engels by selecting a representative sample of their most often quoted arguments—arguments quoted not by their critics to confound them but by their admirers to uphold them. I am aware that great injustice can easily be done to a theorist when a critic fastens upon his less important utterances, for probably no one, however clear-headed and cautious, has ever propounded a theory which he has not occasionally denied. The charge made against Marx and Engels in this chapter is not that they occasionally denied the intelligible part of the theory that 'served them as a guide in all their studies,' but that they never denied it more consistently than when they were engaged in what they imagined was its defence.

Every historian knows that there is a great deal of evidence in favour of economic determinism, and also a great deal against it. When a man knows exactly what he wants to prove, it is usually easy enough for him to collect the evidence he needs and turn a blind eye to what he would rather not see. Marx need not, in the famous chapter on 'Primary Accumulation,' have put the disappearance of serfdom before the rise of capitalism in England; he could have discovered several economic causes of that disappearance and have plausibly argued that they were the beginnings of capitalist methods of production. He could easily have made a much better case for economic determinism than he in fact did make.

The truth is that Marx and Engels had some vague and important ideas in their minds—ideas for which all students of society are greatly indebted to them—but never succeeded in formulating them precisely or in constructing out of them a single and fairly consistent theory. Historical materialism is not what its authors honestly believed it to be. I do not mean that it is a false hypothesis, one that the facts do not bear out. What I mean is that it is not really an hypothesis at all. It is, taken as a whole, not sufficiently intelligible and self-consistent to be capable of verification. What I have tried to do is, not to show that the evidence is against its truth, but to argue that its authors, when they collected evidence for it, did not really know what it was they were trying to prove. I have cited no facts except those produced by Marx and Engels, and for the purpose of my argument it was not necessary to question any of them. Let the events have been what Marx and Engels said they were, they still do not establish the truth of historical materialism. That theory, indeed, cannot be true because it is partly self-contradictory and partly unintelligible. And the truth of that part of it that is intelligible was never established by either Marx or Engels.

In saying this I do not deny the importance of the theory. Some of the ideas contained in it or closely associated with it by its authors are plausible, original, and stimulating. Serious consideration of the theory does direct our attention to some of the most important problems that face the student of society. We understand social phenomena very little, and we have not yet evolved a vocabulary making it possible for us to discuss them precisely. During some of his excursions Marx penetrated deep into this uncharted territory. The trouble with him was that he thought he had mapped it. This illusion was not an effect of arrogance. Many had shared it before him, for it is the illusion which has made political theory possible. It is only now that we are beginning to learn that this territory, like every other, needs to be explored before we can make maps of it. And the exploration must be long and difficult; it must be the work of many, of whom even the most gifted can add only a little to the common stock of knowledge. It is slow work to be done on foot, painfully and with circumspection; whereas the great political theorists of the past imagined they could take to their wings and like eagles survey a vast territory. It was only in their dreams that they flew.

Chapter Five

THE MARXIAN CONCEPTION OF SOCIETY
AND ITS PROGRESS

HISTORICAL materialism is a theory of a type not uncommon in the nineteenth century. It is a kind of 'fundamentalism'; it is a theory which assumes that men's social activities can be divided into a number of classes or factors, one of which is more or less independent of the others and yet determines the general character of their development. It is also an example of the organic theory of society, the theory which assumes that society is an organized whole whose parts depend on one another in some way in which they do not depend on what is external to the whole. This theory takes it for granted that we can distinguish between a society and its environment in much the same way as we can distinguish between a plant and the climate, soil, air, and water that its life depends on. If we think of society in that way we quite naturally assume that its history is a kind of growth, that how it develops is determined by its structure.

Most socialists before Marx, with one great exception, had not been either fundamentalists or believers in the organic character of society. They had mostly derived their socialism from what they called the absolute principles of justice and the laws of human nature—in other words, from morals and psychology. The great exception was Saint-Simon. He, like Marx after him, believed that society develops according to a discoverable law, and that the general course of its development is determined by its internal structure. Because it is what it is, it must grow as it does. And its growth, being so determined, must be independent of men's wills. Men can, of course, discover the law of that growth, but, when they have discovered it, the best they can do, if they are wise enough not to kick against the pricks, is to follow with a good grace the course prescribed by the law 'instead of being pushed blindly onward by it.'

Saint-Simon was also, very probably though not quite as certainly as Marx, a 'fundamentalist.' He, too, probably believed that among men's social activities one kind is more important than the others in determining the course of history. He did not, however, treat the 'economic factor' as fundamental, being more inclined to believe that the accumulation of knowledge determines the general character of human progress. We cannot know for certain what he believed, because, like Marx, he often found it difficult to say exactly what he meant. He sometimes implied one thing and at other times another, but the assumption that suits his theory best is that the accumulation of knowledge is the ultimate cause of human progress. The economic 'factor' he thought more important than the political, at least during the later stages of social development; but behind them both was this other cause, the growth of science. The 'fundamentalism' of Saint-Simon is perhaps more plausible than that of Marx. It is not easy to see how what Marx calls the 'forces of production' could develop as an autonomous factor. Instruments and methods of production must be improved by men, and they cannot be improved unless men apply their knowledge to them. In some communities, the same instruments and methods have been used unchanged for centuries; in others they have been continually improved. The desire for wealth is strong in all communities but is not itself a sufficient condition of economic progress. Wealth is no less desired in economically stagnant than in economically progressive communities. It is when men begin to try out new methods of production that an economy becomes progressive, but they cannot try out new methods unless knowledge accumulates. There is little evidence that knowledge accumulates primarily because men are anxious to find more efficient means of producing wealth. On the contrary, what evidence we have suggests that the growth of science has affected economic progress more than it has been affected by it; it suggests that Saint-Simon was closer to the truth than was Marx. But it would be foolish to choose between them, for sociology can dispense with both their hypotheses.

I. SOCIETY AS AN ORGANIC WHOLE DEVELOPING ACCORDING TO THE LAW OF ITS KIND

Let us consider, first of all, the conception of society common to Saint-Simon and Marx. It is also, as we have seen (though with a difference), the conception of Hegel and even of Rousseau. But Saint-Simon and Marx, unlike Hegel and Rousseau, do not speak of society as if it had a mind or will of its own. They are both of them interested only in the welfare of individuals, and no two men ever existed who were less worshippers of the state. This is a fact we do well to remember before we consider their conception of society.

Though Marx did not call society 'organic,' his theory assumes that it is so; he treats society as an integral whole, a whole whose parts depend on one another in some way in which they do not depend on what is outside it, a something whose development is determined by its own nature, its internal structure. This is what we assume when we say that society has a life of its own, when we declare it to be something like what biologists call an 'organism.' When we use this biological simile to explain social phenomena, we must also assume that the interdependent parts whose activities determine the development of society as a whole are not individual men and women but social institutions. For whether a society is simple or complex, 'primitive' or 'advanced,' the men and women who make it up, taken apart from the influence of society on them, are always pretty much the same. That is to say, however many and great the differences between them, those differences are natural; they are the same kinds of differences at one stage of the society's history as at another. European man, considered as an animal and not as a member of society, is no different today from what he was two thousand years ago; and yet, though every society consists only of men, the social institutions of Europe are now immensely different from what they were in the first century before Christ. Nature still makes men just as she has always done in historic times, with pretty much the same kinds of hereditary differences between them. Society works on the human material that nature provides, and works on it differently at every stage of the historical process. It does so because, though it could not exist without that human material, the laws of its development are not determined by human nature. Society is therefore an organism whose growth is autonomous, that is to say, governed by laws proper to its nature.

This view of society seems to me mistaken. It may well be true that social institutions are not mere contrivances made by men to satisfy their needs; it may also be true that social phenomena obey laws that are peculiar to them, laws which cannot be wholly explained even in terms of the unconscious desires of men. It is admitted by everyone that the minds of individuals, and therefore also their specific needs and desires, conscious and unconscious, are formed by the society they live in. Such things as hunger, thirst, and sexual desire they get from nature, but not the immense number of preferences and aversions into which society converts these primitive appetites. What nature gives to man may therefore be only the condition and not the cause of social development; but it does not follow that societies are separate wholes having lives of their own.

A real organism, an animal or a plant, is a thing easily distinguished from all other things. A plant, though it is stationary and has roots, is easily detached from the ground. It cannot live without earth, air, and water, but it is something different from them all. Its limits, its shape, its colour, all its peculiar qualities are easily distinguished. Every plant and every animal is a separate whole; no part of one is at the same time part of another. But no society is individual in this same sense; no society is separate from every other. Many societies have no discoverable limits. Nor is it possible to distinguish the way in which the institutions of a society depend on one another from the way in which they depend on what is outside it. It is often quite impossible to say where a society ends and its environment begins. Even states—and there are many other kinds of societies—are not independent of each other in the way that plants are. Though all trees grow in much the same way, the growth of one tree does not affect another. An agency external to them both may affect both in the same way, as when the same wind brings them down or the same disease destroys them; but if only one tree is diseased or brought down, its sickness or fall has no effect on the other. But this is not the way in which human societies are related to each other. Suppose for instance—and this is a proper use of the word—

that we call France and England 'societies.' Have they, like any two plants, developed independently of one another though according to the same laws? Is there not, rather, a real and important sense in which, say, the French revolution is an event in English history, an event which helped to form the minds of Englishmen and to mould their institutions? But what happens in one organism is never, in this sense, an event in the history of another. If one man's heart stops beating another's is not affected, unless, of course, they are both victims of the separate actions of similar causes. On the other hand, if one man's behaviour directly affects another's, it is because they both have minds and can take account of each other's actions, because there exist between them relations quite different in kind from those that bind together the parts of an organism in a common life.

If we speak of society as if it were a living thing and of social institutions as if they were the organs whose ceaseless and inter-dependent activities maintain its life, we must, if we are true to the analogy we have chosen, liken the members of society, indi-vidual men and women, to the particles that pass in and out of an organic whole. They are absorbed into it and pass out of it, but its life continues; and it is the same organism it was years before though all the particles that now make it up are different. In the vegetable and animal kingdoms, no particle belonging to one organism can belong at the same time to another. Two plants may have similar organs and be made up of similar particles, but nothing that participates in the life of one can participate in the life of the other. With societies the case is different. A man may belong to many different societies. The Roman church is inter-national, and every nation has many churches. The various societies that any one man or woman belongs to need have nothing in common except that one member. When we speak of 'society' we do not refer to anything that is in the least like an organism, anything that is individual and separate from all other individuals, anything that in any intelligible sense enjoys a life of its own. The history of England is not the biography of England, the record of what England has done; it is the record of what has happened in England.

Institutions are maintained, sometimes quite unchanged, from generation to generation; and we therefore speak of them as if they had lives of their own. They are not contrivances made by individuals to satisfy their needs and desires, but are established modes of behaviour that individuals, whether they like it or not, have to conform to; and it is this need to conform that makes them civilized. They must conform because they are dependent on one another and can serve one another only while each behaves as the others expect. This conformity creates in men needs, desires and preferences they would not know without it, and so attaches them to their institutions. All men are born savages, but their neighbours' hope is that they will, by the time they are grown up, have become civilized according to the standards of the society they belong to. Institutions affect men in ways they know nothing of until they begin to study them; and this influence, when they first become aware of it, they find impressive and difficult to describe. They resort to metaphors and out of them construct philosophies with which they presently fall in love, so that they no longer see the world as it is but only as they describe it.

Because institutions survive from generation to generation, because men mostly do not understand them and are yet civilized by their influence, because they are not altered 'according to plan' but change in ways that men almost never foresee, it does not follow that a group of men among whom certain institutions prevail form a social whole having a law of development determined by its internal structure. How we group men will depend upon the institutions we are studying. These groups affect one another in very different ways, and there is not one of them which includes the others as an animal or plant includes the organs and cells that make it up. There is no good reason to believe that the institutions prevailing in any group sustain each other, that they form, when taken together, a 'social structure' reacting to its environment in the ways that best preserve its character. Men are conservative, creatures of custom, and could not live comfortably together unless they were so. They therefore tend to preserve whatever institutions exist. But that does not mean that it is possible to find among them groups whose institutions sustain one another in such a way as to form a self-maintaining social structure.

Both Marx and Saint-Simon were perhaps uneasily aware of

some of the points I have tried to make. Marx saw that if he wanted a society which looked as if it had a distinct and individual life of its own, a society whose development might plausibly be likened to the growth of a single whole, he must choose something much larger than a nation or a state. So he usually chose about half of Europe, adding to and subtracting from it according to the needs of his argument. The half of Europe he chose excluded the areas inhabited by the Slavs, and seemed to have a civilization of its own distinct from all others; and the history of that civilization Marx treated as the evolution of a single society. But a society so large has limits even more difficult to define than those of smaller societies. Had Marx been asked to define them he could have done no more than draw a rough map of the area where certain institutions seemed to prevail.

Marx had also to distinguish between several parts of western Europe, some of which seemed to him more 'bourgeois' or more 'feudal' than others. Whenever he found it convenient to distinguish between these parts, he treated them as separate societies. He no doubt felt that if a society is something with a life of its own, a single whole passing from phase to phase in a definite order, it is scarcely possible for one part of it to be, as it were, further on in life than another. Historical materialism is not meant to be an ordinary sociological law, a statement telling us how men usually behave when certain conditions hold good. It is supposed to describe the general law of development of every human society, to tell us what phases it must pass through and in what order. It therefore presupposes that every human society is an integrated whole, whose every part passes through each phase of the life of the whole at the same time as the other parts. Now, if that is what human societies are, it ought to be easy to distinguish them from one another, to locate in the real world the things whose law of development historical materialism purports to be. And yet we find that Marx, when he spoke of the European society whose development he thought he was describing, now meant one part of Europe and now another, and that what he meant at one time was part of what he meant at another. We find that he could not help using the word 'society', as we all use it, to mean any group of people among whom the institutions he happened to be speaking of prevailed. Because society is not what he thought it—an organized whole developing after the law of its kind—he often found it impossible to speak of it as if it were. He was often obliged, though he might not know it, to use the word 'society' to refer to whatever group the institutions he happened to have in mind belonged to. Even when he was trying to apply historical materialism, he could not avoid using this word to refer to something to which that theory could not apply.

This, of course, does not mean that there are no sociological laws. Social phenomena are to be studied like any other part of the natural world. The study of 'society' means only the study of social institutions, of common or established modes of behaviour. The word 'society' is neither superfluous nor likely to mislead anyone who uses it as it is used in ordinary conversation by people who have not in mind the requirements of any social or political theory. 'Society' is a useful word just because it can be used for many purposes. It is only when we insist on using it as the Marxian theory requires us to do that we no longer speak of the real world. The more consistently we so use it, the worse the errors we fall into. Fortunately, it is difficult to misuse words consistently, and we usually relapse into their proper uses in spite of the good resolutions made in honour of our favourite theories.

II. FUNDAMENTALISM

There are people who, while they reject both historical materialism and the concept of society it assumes, are yet inclined to believe that economic determinism, the Marxist variant of 'fundamentalism,' is true. They are not much impressed by what the Marxists say about conflicts between the 'forces' and 'relations' of production; they admit that neither of these phrases has been clearly defined by the people whose whole theory turns on them; and yet they believe that the 'economic factor' is somehow 'fundamental,' that the way people produce and distribute what satisfies their needs determines the general character of the society they live in. It is not, they say, the only factor that matters. Men's political behaviour, their religion, and their culture also affect their economic activities, but it is these activities that 'ultimately' determine the course of history. 'Fundamentalism' is still highly respectable in intellectual circles where historical materialism is not taken seriously; and the most popular kind of fundamentalism is still economic determinism. There are some people who prefer to believe, with Saint-Simon, that the progress of science is what really matters, but they are a small minority. Most fundamentalists, if they follow Marx in nothing else, follow him in this, repeating after him that it is how men produce and distribute goods and services which explains, in the last analysis, how they live.

Fundamentalism is, I think, an error, though in practice not often a dangerous one. The historian who is a fundamentalist will attend first to the factor he considers fundamental; he will stress its importance and apply adjectives to it that he does not apply to the others. But he need not therefore neglect the others. He will, if he is a good historian, give as accurate an account as he can of what really happened; and his prejudice will be revealed only by the special way in which he speaks of what he considers the fundamental factor. If, instead of speaking in this way, he used Latin words or red ink every time he referred to things fundamental, he would achieve the same purpose. It would make no difference to the story he had to tell but would be very much to the purpose of his feelings. An historian who is a fundamentalist need know nothing of the implications of the theory he believes in. His mental condition may be that of a person who likes to draw thick lines under some of the statements he makes. That is why it is possible to be a good historian and also a fundamentalist. Suppose, for instance, that the historian's task is to account for the French revolution. Among its causes he will find events, economic, political, and cultural. Whichever he chooses to call fundamental, he will get into no difficulties provided he does not deny that the others, too, were important. Only if he argues that the economic factor alone was important, that it determined the general character of the other factors but was not itself affected by them; only if he is as extreme and explicit, as imprudent and unprofessional as that, will it be easy to prove him wrong. If he refrains from statements so precise and provocative, he will have said nothing that anyone need take strong exception to. Those who share his prejudices will like

the adjectives he uses, and they will think he does well in starting his book with an account of the developments which they
and he consider fundamental. Those who do not share his
prejudices will think he might have put things differently, that
the emphasis is in the wrong place. And he, if he bothers to
answer their criticisms, will not deny that what they consider
important is so; he will say: 'Yes, of course, that too played an
indispensable part in bringing conflicts to a head in France, in
causing the great revolution; I would be a fool to deny it, and I
do not deny it. But, though important, it is a factor of secondary
importance.' The argument between them, if it continues, will
be as inconclusive as it is harmless, because the chances are that
none of them knows what he means by such phrases as 'of
secondary importance,' 'fundamental,' and 'decisive.' The argument, indeed, if it is between good scholars and honest persons,
is likely to be useful. The antagonists will look more closely at
the facts and they will look for fresh evidence. It is a pleasant
thought that the study of history can profit from the arguments
of people who do not quite know what it is they are arguing
about.

Though 'fundamentalism' is not a dangerous error, though
belief in it need not spoil a good historian any more than deaf-
ness spoils a man's sight, it is not even plausible. No one has
ever produced a good reason for believing it true; and, what is
more, no adherent of it has known what sort of evidence would
be required to prove it. Fundamentalism assumes much greater
knowledge than anyone possesses; and it also assumes that
certain distinctions can and indeed already have been made. It
assumes, in the first place, that men's activities recorded by the
historian have been properly classified, that they have been
divided into a number of mutually exclusive classes or 'factors.'
It assumes, in the second place, that the activities called fundamental change their character more or less independently of the
others. And, lastly, it assumes that changes in the character of
the activities called fundamental produce, directly or indirectly,
corresponding changes in the characters of all the other activities,
whatever the class they belong to. These assumptions are compatible with a kind of mutual dependence between the factors.
It may, for instance, be true—and it probably is true—that the

activities called fundamental could not happen without the others; for example, that men could not produce and distribute goods and services in the way they do unless there were laws, governments, and science. The fundamentalist need not say that the activities he calls fundamental could happen independently of the others, that the others are not necessary conditions of their happening as they do; all that he need say is that *changes* in the character of the activities called fundamental always or nearly always produce changes in the character of the other activities, while these others either do not change independently of changes in the fundamental factor or, if they do, then those changes have no effect or only a slight effect on that factor. Economic determinism therefore assumes—and, indeed, must assume, if it is to be a theory, a genuine hypothesis about how things happen in the world, and not merely a habit of putting emphasis on some things and not on others—that changes in men's economic behaviour are more or less independent of changes in their other behaviour, and yet always (or nearly always) alter the character of that other behaviour. Men need government no less than they need to produce and distribute what satisfies their wants; they are intellectual, artistic, and political animals as well as producers of food, clothing, and shelter; and, unless they were these other things as well, economic progress would be impossible. The economic determinist need not deny this; indeed, he would be unwise if he did so. But he must assert—if his economic determinism is to be more than an empty phrase—that, though all men's social activities are equally parts of their lives, changes in the character of one class of them determine changes in the characters of the others much more than they are determined by them. That, I think, is the least that fundamentalism must mean if it is to mean anything at all, if it is to be an intellectual position capable of defence and worth attacking.

The Marxists have not yet done the first things that must be done before their kind of fundamentalism can be proved. Are they even agreed what phenomena ought to be called economic? The Marxists often speak of property as if it were something economic, though it is not a method of production or exchange, nor yet a way in which goods and services are distributed among the persons who demand them. It is a way in which rights are distributed; it is a legal phenomenon. This the Marxists do not deny, because Marx himself (and they are his echoes) called it the 'legal expression' of something else, that mysterious something which he called 'relations of production.' But the Marxists— and not only they but Marx himself—also speak of property as if it were economic. This they think themselves entitled to do because their theory asserts that the system of property is ultimately determined by the general character of men's economic activities, by prevailing methods of production and exchange, or, rather, by the methods that prevailed at the time the system of property emerged, for it may since then have become a 'fetter on the forces of production.' Thus the Marxists, when they treat property as if it were an economic phenomenon on the ground that it is the 'legal expression' of something economic, are doing what is only excusable if their theory is true. Most of them never trouble to inquire into its truth; and, when the theory is challenged, they always defend it with arguments which assume that property is 'virtually' (that is, can for nearly all theoretical purposes be treated as if it were) an economic phenomenon. They do that the more easily because no one has yet bothered to define just what an economic phenomenon is.

For ordinary purposes, this lack of a definition does not matter. Property is often treated, by non-Marxists as well as Marxists, as if it were an economic phenomenon. It partly determines the distribution of wealth; and the production and distribution of wealth is generally agreed to be the subject-matter of the study called economics. But property is not the way in which goods and services are distributed, the methods whereby they are brought to the persons who buy them. It is a system of rights; and it is the exercise of these rights by their possessors which partly determines how goods and services will be distributed and produced. Property determines the pattern of effective demand, what sorts of goods and services, and in what quantities, will be required by the people able to pay for them; and this will have its appropriate and considerable effect on methods of distribution and production. Property is none the less a thing different in kind from the activities studied by the economist. If, when we call it economic, we wish only to draw attention to its close connection with these activities, no harm is done. But if we want to do more than this, if we want to suggest that it is so completely determined by these activities, that statements about property can be treated as equivalent to certain kinds of statements about economic relations, we assume what we have no right to assume. It is only in a very loose sense of the word 'economic' that property is an economic phenomenon. It is neither the production nor the distribution of goods and services; it is merely a system of rights of which we cannot, in the present state of our knowledge, say that it affects methods of production and distribution less than it is affected by them.

It is all very well, if we are not economic determinists, to use the word 'economic' in the ordinary, loose way. We then have no theoretical axe to grind. But if what we want is to prove that one class of men's social activities is fundamental in some sense in which the others are not, we must first either define that class or else, by our consistent use of the name we give it, make it clear to other people exactly what activities we have in mind. Because men sometimes speak of property, which is a system of rights, as if it were an economic phenomenon, it does not follow that we, being economic determinists, have the right to do so. For property, as everyone knows and Marx admits, is something legal. If then our theory asserts that there exists a class of social activities whose development determines the general character of social progress, including all really important changes in the system of law, we must not put anything legal into that class. On the contrary, we must so define it, and so speak of it, that it clearly excludes all phenomena belonging to the other classes. The classes or, if you like, the 'factors' into which we divide men's social activities must be so constructed that the class called 'fundamental' is exclusive of the others, having no member in common with them. The other classes need not be mutually exclusive but they must exclude the fundamental class. This must be so because fundamentalism asserts a causal connection of a peculiar kind; it does not describe the relations between different *aspects* of the same activities, but the peculiar influence that some of men's activities have on the general character of everything else they do.

Neither Marx nor any of his disciples ever understood what

their theory required of them, what it was they had to do before they could establish its truth. Far from applying the word 'economic' to only one class of phenomena, they used it as loosely as anyone, and, as often as not, applied it to what, on their own account of the social process, ought properly to belong to some other class. The boundary between 'basis' and 'superstructure' has always been shifted to suit their own convenience, and these repeated changes have enabled them to prove, to their own satisfaction, many different and incompatible things. Since they do not really know where the boundary ought to run and are imperfectly acquainted with the territory it runs through, they can, while taking every advantage of its mobility, believe that it never moves. It is an advantage useful to the controversialist as long as neither he nor his opponent knows that he possesses it. But, while he uses it undetected, the controversy between them is barren, and there is a waste of energy which could be employed in profitable argument.[1] Economic determinism is an hypothesis much better forgotten while those who support it have nothing more to say in its favour than what the Marxists have said.

[1] The argument may, as I said earlier, be indirectly profitable to historians, but for sociologists it is barren.

Chapter Six

THE MARXIAN ANALYSIS OF CAPITALISM

MARX invented a law which he believed must apply to the whole of history, but was not therefore interested in all history. Had he been so, he might have had doubts about his law; he might have discovered that civilizations decay, that men relapse into barbarism, that the Roman Empire was economically more primitive in its later than its earlier centuries, that in the Middle Ages neither agriculture nor industry was more efficient than it had been in ancient Greece and Rome. A prolonged and serious study of the remoter past he never attempted; he only glanced at it from time to time when he thought he could find evidence in favour of his theory. That theory was not suggested to him by the study of history; it was the child of his abstract speculations, his interest in contemporary problems, and his revolutionary and prophetic temper. What he really cared about was the present, the immediate past, and the immediate future, the epoch he called capitalist and the revolution that would bring it to an end. France had her greatest revolution not long before he was born, and England had already become the industrial and commercial centre of the world; the social and political institutions of the two most civilized and powerful nations in Europe were quickly changing. The expansion of trade, the use of new sources of power and methods of production, the decay of religion, the emergence of liberalism, radicalism and, at last, socialism: these were, to the thoughtful, stupendous developments, and it could not escape their notice that they were closely connected. Europeans had never before done as much to change their world as during the two or three centuries before Marx began to reflect on social problems. There had never been so much technical progress and so vast an accumulation of knowledge in so short a time, and that time was also a period of great social and political instability. Many people had noticed these things before Marx and some had tried to explain them, but Marx was perhaps the first to produce a vast and impressive theory to account for them and for the connections between them.[1] This was a remarkable achievement. His theory was not entirely original; no such theory ever is. But it was more convincing (though not necessarily better argued), more comprehensive, and put with greater power than any other. Marx spoke with authority. He was shrewd, sincere, persistent, aggressive, and immensely well-read. When we read him, we are, in spite of his clumsy style, his halting logic, his frequent repetitions, often impressed and sometimes excited. He was on occasion profound, not seldom ingenious, and always sincere. His utterances, unattractive though his manner is, have an undeniable air of authority. Not, perhaps, when he philosophizes or defines 'value,' 'surplus value,' and the other concepts he needs to develop his theory of capitalist exploitation, but when he describes that exploitation, comments on historical events, gives political advice, and predicts the future.

His most remarkable achievements are his analysis of contemporary society, his lessons in political strategy and tactics for the benefit of the proletariat, and his prophetic utterances. Though his analysis is not often correct, nor his advice always good, nor his prophecies true, it is as a critic of capitalism, as a counsellor of the proletariat, and as a prophet that he best displays his powers. Marx the interpreter of world history, the 'father of sociology,' the inventor of a new kind of economics: Marx, as any one of these, cuts a not very impressive figure, in spite of all the praise lavished on him. Historical materialism is pretentious, obscure, and confused; it is variously interpreted by its authors and their disciples; and, when all they have said is sifted, not much remains. Its one great merit—and it is indeed a great one—is that criticism of it leads the critic to consider problems of capital importance to the social theorist. Marx's idea of society is as false, though for quite different reasons, as the one it was intended to replace, the idea common to the political philosophers of

[1] I say 'perhaps' because Saint-Simon took notice of these same events and tried to explain them, but was less systematic and not nearly as comprehensive as Marx. He had many good ideas, but went only a little way towards building them up into an elaborate and impressive theory.

England and France of the seventeenth and eighteenth centuries.[1]
His famous epigram about its not being men's consciousness that
determines their existence but their social existence that determines their consciousness, is a clumsy half-truth. If part of its
meaning is that men's theories and 'ideologies' are merely the
effects, and not also among the important causes, of their economic and other behaviour, then that part is false. If it also
means that men's social institutions are not contrivances for the
satisfaction of their desires and aspirations, but are the important
influence forming their habits, settled purposes, and ideals, it is
partly true; but it then only repeats what others said—not in a
thoughtless moment but often and deliberately—before Marx was
born. Marx, the theoretical economist, is the not very happily
inspired disciple of Ricardo, using obsolescent ideas to formulate a theory of exploitation which could have been better and
more simply put without them. But Marx the critic of capitalism, the denouncer of the moral platitudes solemnly repeated to
excuse the horrors of industrialism, the prophet and political
strategist of revolution, the theorist of the class war, the com-
mentator on current events—that Marx is a man altogether more
formidable and persuasive. This Proteus of debate, whatever his
disguise, was often mistaken, but he sometimes saw further and
more clearly than other men. When the matter is important, to
be sometimes right when everyone else is wrong, is a great
distinction.

The characteristic of capitalist society, as Marx described it,
is that, while a few men own all the means of production, the
others, though they are free because they are neither slaves nor
serfs, have nothing to sell but their labour. The capitalists, the
owners of the means of production, do not control and use them
for the common benefit of their class; each of them controls his
own part separately and competes with the others to sell his
products, his purpose being to make as big a profit as he can.
This competition, while it accelerates technical progress, obliges
the capitalists to exploit their workers to the limits of their
endurance; it creates chronic unemployment (what Marx called
'the industrial reserve army'); it concentrates capital in fewer

[1] Nevertheless, it is, on the whole, more useful to the social studies that new
mistakes should be made than old ones repeated.

and fewer hands; it reduces all intermediate classes to the level of the proletariat. At the same time, it increases the size of the proletariat, their social discipline, and political experience, until they become at last strong enough to seize control of the state and dispossess the capitalists. The process described by Marx is as simple in its general outline as it is complicated in detail. Given the system of property and the constancy of technical progress, this, said Marx, is what must happen. In the words of the *Manifesto*:

> Modern bourgeois society, with its relations of production, of exchange, and of property, a society which has conjured up such gigantic means of production and exchange, is like the sorcerer no longer able to control the powers of the underworld summoned by his own spells. For many a decade past the history of industry and commerce has been the history of the revolt of modern productive forces against modern conditions of production, against the property relations on which depend the existence of the bourgeoisie and its rule. It is enough to mention the commercial crises that from time to time threaten the existence of bourgeois society, each time more dangerously. During these crises a great part, not only of what is currently produced, but also of previously created productive forces is destroyed, and there breaks out what would have appeared absurd in all earlier epochs, an epidemic of overproduction. . . . The conditions of bourgeois society are too narrow to contain the wealth created by them. And how does the bourgeoisie surmount these crises? On the one hand, by the enforced destruction of a mass of productive forces; on the other, by the conquest of new markets, and by the more thorough exploitation of the old ones. That is to say, by preparing the way for more extensive and more destructive crises, and by reducing the means of preventing them.

This analysis is not clear in all its details,[1] but the gist of it is obvious. The conditions under which they produce commodities for a competitive market are such that the capitalists cannot help behaving in ways that will destroy the system their own predominance rests on. The authors of *The Communist Manifesto* do not attempt to prove their case; they merely give a short account of it and point to a few facts in support of it. The real

---

[1] Why, for instance, should the destruction of productive forces and the conquest of new markets prepare the way for worse crises? They may not prevent their recurrence but can hardly hasten it. Neither Marx nor Engels could resist a touch of this kind, even at the cost of good sense.

proof, the 'preuve en règle,' is reserved for Marx's greatest work, *Capital*.

It is a peculiarity of the capitalist system, according to Marx, that nearly all the goods it produces are for the market. There were, of course, markets before there was capitalism. Wherever there are regular exchanges, regular purchases and sales, there, in the language of the economists, is a market. Before the capitalist epoch most things were consumed by the people who made them; and many others were sold because their producers needed what they got in exchange for them. Most men produced either what they needed or what could quickly be exchanged for what they needed. Even the owner of slaves or serfs forced them to work that he might enjoy the fruits of their labour. But where the capitalist system predominates, not only are few things consumed by their producers, but labour itself is a marketable commodity. Another peculiarity of the capitalist system is that the persons who control production are less interested in increasing the quantity of what they can consume than in getting the largest profit. Or, to put it in Marxian language, what the capitalist, as a capitalist, most wants is to appropriate surplus value. The satisfaction of human needs, his own or other people's, is not his first object as a controller of production. Competition with other capitalists in a limited market obliges him to lower his costs of production as much as he can; his eye is always on the market, and his constant anxiety that the return on his outlay should be as great as possible. The owner of an almost self-supporting estate, having slaves or serfs to work for him, is also an exploiter; but he is an exploiter different in kind from the capitalist. He has his eye on an entire economy, and his business is to see that everyone gets a share, though his own is much the largest. He is not a competitor, he is not a producer for the market, or is so only to a limited extent. If he is inefficient, if he neglects his interest, he is merely worse off than other members of his class. Whereas capitalists compete fiercely for a limited market, and must therefore force the pace of technical progress and also increase the pressure of exploitation. They must produce more, and that more cheaply, on pain of total ruin. They do not, like the members of former ruling classes, exploit the labouring poor separately, each on his own domain. They compete in exploitation, and the penalty for those who fail is the loss of their capital, the loss of just what puts them in the class they belong to.

How do capitalists exploit the proletariat? To explain the process Marx took over the theory of value of the English classical economists and added to it certain refinements of his own. The value of anything, its exchange value and not its utility, is, he says, equivalent to the amount of work needed to produce it. Only useful things have a value, because they alone are brought to the market, but the rates at which they are exchanged for each other or for money are determined in the long run by the average amounts of time required to produce them. Some kinds of labour are more skilled than others, and the value of what is produced in a certain time by skilled labour is greater than the value of what is produced in the same time by unskilled labour. But this, according to those who believe in it, does not affect the truth of the labour theory of value. Skill takes time to acquire; it is either taught or gained by experience, and is therefore itself a product of labour. Marx believed that every kind of labour could in principle (though not, perhaps, in practice) be estimated in terms of an abstract, uniform kind of labour, so many hours of each being reckoned as equivalent to one hour of this abstract labour. There are strong objections to almost every part of this labour theory of value, but they have been so often put that there is no need to repeat them. My immediate purpose is to explain Marx's theory of capitalist competition and exploitation.

Market fluctuations apart, commodities sell at prices corresponding to the average amounts of abstract uniform labour required to produce them. If the productivity of labour rises, the value of the goods produced by it decreases, and so, too, does their price, unless, of course, the quantity of money in circulation has increased. But if goods are exchanged in the long run in accordance with their values, and those values are determined by the average amounts of abstract labour required to produce them, how do the capitalists as a class live? Whence come their profits? Goods may sometimes sell above their values, and their producers therefore get more for them than corresponds to the labour put into them; but these gains are temporary, and are offset by similar losses; they cannot explain how the capitalists as a class get their share of the social product.

The capitalists buy two kinds of commodities to be used in production. They buy capital equipment and raw materials, and these, or the money paid for them, Marx called 'constant capital'; and they also hire workers, and the money spent for this purpose he called 'variable capital.' Marx made a distinction, which he thought important, between labour and labour-power. Labour, he said, being the source of all value, can itself have no value. What the capitalist buys when he hires workers is not labour but labour-power, which is man's capacity to work. His equipment, machinery, and raw materials, the capitalist pays for at prices that correspond to their values; and the same is true of labour-power. The capitalist pays no more for it than it cost to produce, and that cost is also a labour cost, a real value. The value of labour-power corresponds to the average amount of abstract labour required to produce what is needed to maintain a worker and his family at the standard of living prevailing among his class. The capitalist therefore buys his equipment, raw materials, and labour-power—his productive resources—at their real values; and he also sells his products at their real values. How then does he make his profit? How is exploitation possible?

There is exploitation, Marx said, whenever the workers hired by the capitalist work longer than the time required to produce what is needed to maintain them and their families. In other words, the exertion of labour-power produces a value greater than the value of that labour-power. If, in the interest of simplicity, we neglect Marx's distinction between labour and labour-power, we may say that it is the peculiarity of labour that it can produce a greater value than it possesses. The difference between the value of labour and the value produced by labour, Marx called 'surplus value.' The total amount of surplus value created in any society within a year represents the real annual income of the capitalist and exploiting class in that society; and it is out of that surplus value that all unearned incomes are paid. The work done during that part of the labourers' working time which is equivalent to the time required to produce their means of subsistence, Marx called 'necessary labour'; and the work they do during the remainder of the working day, he called 'surplus labour.' The rate of exploitation, or of 'surplus value,' is the ratio between surplus and necessary labour, or, if you like, between surplus value and variable capital. These two ratios are always equivalent, being merely different ways of saying the same thing. The object of the capitalist is to ensure that the rate of surplus value is as high as possible. This need not mean that, as capitalism develops, the workers become poorer. The rate of exploitation may rise and the standard of living with it. This follows quite simply from Marx's own premises. Technical progress increases the productivity of each unit of abstract labour, but it cannot, by Marxian definition, increase the value of what that labour produces. On the other hand, it will diminish the time required to produce what the labourer and his family need to maintain life; that is, it will diminish necessary labour time but not the quantity of goods and services the labourer buys with his wages. Indeed, the rate of exploitation might increase, though the average length of the working day were reduced and the standard of living considerably raised. There is nothing in Marx's theory of value, surplus value, and exploitation that excludes this event, though he seems to have believed, for other reasons, that it was unlikely to happen.

The capitalist's grand object is to make as great a profit as he can. But the profit he can make does not depend merely on the rate of surplus value; it depends more particularly on how much what he sells his goods for exceeds what it cost him to produce them. Among these costs is his constant capital (his factories, machines, and raw materials), themselves the products of past labour. They, unlike labour, do not create a greater value than they possess. The goods made out of them, or by their use, acquire from them only the value they themselves possess and no more. If, for instance, the value of a machine is equivalent to a hundred hours of abstract labour and it produces a thousand articles before it wears out, it must pass on to each of these articles only one-tenth of a unit of value, no more and no less. And yet, though constant capital produces no surplus value, it does not follow that the capitalist has nothing to gain by using it. On the contrary, it is his constant capital that determines the productivity of his labour. The capitalist, by installing a new machine, may produce ten articles a worker every working day instead of only six. Though the new machine should cost him no more, for each unit of its value, than the old one, and must therefore pass on value to its products at the same rate, it is still his interest to instal it. It will enable him to undersell his competitors and gain a temporary advantage over them, until they, too, have installed similar machines; and they, of course, cannot afford not to instal them, because without them they can no longer hope to sell their goods on the market.

Competition therefore obliges the capitalists continually to increase their constant capital, to use always more machinery for each worker they employ. The inevitable result, according to Marx, is that the average rate of profit falls. For the rate of profit is the ratio between surplus value and constant plus variable capital. It is something different from the rate of exploitation, which is the ratio between surplus value and variable capital alone. Thus, as the capitalist system develops, two things happen simultaneously: the rate of profit falls and the rate of exploitation increases. This is the inevitable result of every capitalist spending an always greater proportion of his resources on constant capital and an always smaller proportion on variable. The ratio of constant to variable capital, Marx called the 'organic composition of capital.' The more constant capital is used in production for each unit of variable, the higher that organic composition; the less constant capital is used for each unit of variable, the lower that composition. The general law governing capitalist production is that the organic composition of capital and the rate of exploitation rise continually while the rate of profit falls.

We can easily discover, if we accept Marx's hypotheses and suppose that his theory of value has some relevance to the facts, how it is that capitalists come to behave in the way he described. They are competitors with one another. Though the average rate of profit is determined by the ratio in industry as a whole of surplus value to constant plus variable capital, the actual profits that any particular capitalist can hope to make depend on how much he can sell at a remunerative price. What he wants is to increase productivity, that is, to lay out his capital in such a way that the labour and machinery he buys produce as much as possible for every pound spent on them. He is interested in productivity per unit of capital; and, while that is as great as he can make it, he is satisfied. If, then, he can increase productivity by spending relatively more on machinery and relatively less on labour, he will certainly do so. It is only when his competitors have followed his example that he loses the temporary advantage gained by underselling them. Though the average rate of profit is determined by the organic composition of capital over the whole of industry, the profit made by any one capitalist depends on his costs of production and his share of the market. It is the use of machinery that increases the productivity of capital, constant and variable; and it is the separate interest of every capitalist to increase productivity more quickly than his competitors. Every capitalist wants to use new and more efficient machinery as soon as he can afford to get it. In other words, competition drives him to take his part in raising the organic composition of capital over the whole of industry.

As the rate of profit falls, capitalists are more than ever determined to raise the rate of exploitation. This they can do in any of three ways: by not allowing the workers to benefit from increased productivity, by lengthening the working day, or by increasing the intensity of labour. The rise of productivity enables less labour to be spent on producing the workers' means of subsistence. The real value, in terms of abstract labour, of the food, clothing and shelter that workers and their families need therefore falls. If, then, the standard of living of the workers is prevented from rising, or is made to rise more slowly than productivity, the proportion of the working day spent on necessary labour is diminished. This is equivalent to a rise in the rate of exploitation. Of the other two expedients, the first is the less probable. The length of the working day is fixed by tradition and is difficult to alter. The intensity of labour can, however, be increased more easily. The more machinery is introduced, the more the worker becomes a mere tender of machinery. If the machine is made to work more quickly, the worker is obliged to keep pace with it. Since human endurance is limited, it might even pay the capitalists to reduce the length of the working day so as to get more out of the workers during each hour of their work.

How is it that the workers are unable to prevent their masters increasing the rate of exploitation? Whatever the amount of machinery used, it cannot be operated without labour. Labour is therefore always indispensable to production; the capitalist must hire it or else go out of business. Marx's answer was that capitalist production creates chronic unemployment or, as he put it, an 'industrial reserve army.' The unemployed are always trying to find employment, and their need of it enables the capitalists to buy labour cheap. When business is good, the industrial reserve army is at their disposal, and the increased demand for labour raises wages only a little; and when business is poor, fear of unemployment keeps the worker obedient to his master. Nothing, then, could matter more to Marx than the proof that capitalist production necessarily creates this industrial reserve army; and yet there is no step in his argument less firmly established. Indeed, he took almost no trouble with it; he merely declared that it must be so, that constant capital increases more quickly than variable, and that the latter's increase is not quick enough to keep pace with the natural increase in the working population. Why this should be so he never troubled to explain, though it is one of the matters that stand most in need of explanation if his theory about the inevitable decline of capitalism is to seem plausible.

Marx thought it enough to assert, in the twenty-third chapter of the first volume of *Capital*, that:

> With the growth of total capital, its variable constituent does also increase, but in a constantly diminishing proportion. . . . An accelerated accumulation of total capital (accelerated in geometrical progression) is needed to absorb an additional number of workers, or even . . . to keep in employment those already at work. . . . This accelerated relative decline in the variable constituent, a decline that accompanies the accelerated increase in the total capital and *proceeds more rapidly than this increase*, takes the inverse form, at the other pole, of an apparently absolute increase in the working population, an increase always proceeding more rapidly than the increase in variable capital. . . . It is capitalist accumulation itself that constantly produces . . . a population larger than suffices for the average needs of the self-expansion of capital—in short a surplus population.

Marx called this assertion 'the law of the progressive decline in the relative magnitude of variable capital.'

To put Marx's law more simply: As capital accumulates, the

proportion of it spent on the hire of labour diminishes continually, and does so more quickly than capital accumulates. In the meantime population is increasing and with it the number of people who need work, so that the proportion of capital spent on wages does not suffice to give employment to all who seek it, and the supply of labour exceeds the demand for it. Temporary influences may from time to time offset the operation of this law, but it represents an inherent tendency of capitalism. The law assumes that total capital will not accumulate so rapidly as to ensure that expenditure on wages, though an always diminishing proportion of total capital expenditure, will nevertheless increase sufficiently to keep pace with the increase in the number of persons in search of employment. Now, at the time when Marx wrote *Capital*, though it was known at what rate the population of Great Britain had increased since 1801, there was no reliable information about the accumulation of capital, the increase of total expenditure on wages, or the number of the unemployed. It was therefore quite impossible for Marx to produce any evidence in favour of his law; he could do no more than assert it, and then, in default of evidence, fill his pages with comments on it. His ignorance, after all, could place him at no disadvantage with the apologists of capitalism, whose methods were as *a priori* as his own. Indeed, he borrowed heavily from them, delighting to use their arguments, whenever he could, to reach conclusions distasteful to them.

Marx therefore proclaimed his law boldly, invented a mathematical formula for it, and then repeated it again and again, as if he hoped to lend authority to it by sheer weight of words. The device was worthy of a classical economist, and Malthus had used it before him to persuade the world that population tends to grow more quickly than the means of subsistence. Yet this particular law, whose truth is of the first importance to Marx's whole analysis of capitalism, is in fact one of his most reckless statements. It is reckless, not because he produced no evidence in support of it (for that was not required of economists in his day), but because the second half of it contradicts some of the things said in the first half. The latter part of the law asserts that the ratio in which the money spent on wages by the whole body of capitalists stands to their total capital expenditure decreases by more than that total expenditure increases; whereas, in the earlier part of it, it is said, among other things, that variable capital (the money spent by all the capitalists on wages) does increase, though less quickly than total capital.

It is possible to make these two statements in quick succession without noticing that they cannot both be true. Yet it needs only a simple calculation to establish that, if the proportion of variable to total capital decreases by more than total capital increases, variable capital must decrease absolutely.[1] This has nothing to do with the capitalist economy but is a conclusion required by Marx's statement of his own law and the rules of arithmetic. If Marx's law is true, it follows that, in all capitalist societies, every rise in total capital must lead to an absolute fall in variable capital. Marx did not himself believe that this in fact happens when capital accumulates; he did not believe his own law, and would certainly never have proclaimed it had he been fully aware of what he was saying.[2] When I said that he spoke recklessly, I meant to be taken at my word; he just did not care what he was saying. As he dabbled in philosophy, so, too, he dabbled in arithmetic. The idea of a ratio falling more rapidly than the sum of the two quantities it relates rises pleased him, and so he used it to explain how the capitalist system inevitably produces unemployment.

Having proved mathematically much more than he wanted to prove or knew he had proved, Marx went on to elaborate his argument, until he came at last to a final conclusion, which he called the *absolute general law of capitalist accumulation*. According to this law,

the greater the wealth of society, the amount of capital in use, the extent and energy of that capital's growth, and the greater, therefore,

---

[1] It is easy to see that, if $\dfrac{A}{A + B}$ decreases proportionately as much as $A + B$ increases, then A remains always the same. Let Z be the amount by which A increases (or decreases) when $A + B$ increases by $X\%$. Then:

$$A + Z = \frac{(A + B)(100 + X)}{100} \times \frac{A \times 100}{(A + B)(100 + X)}$$

Therefore $A + Z = A$, and $Z = 0$.

If then $\dfrac{A}{A + B}$ decreases more than $A + B$ increases, A must decrease absolutely, whatever the original values of A and B and by however much $A + B$ increases.

[2] The law has several consequences that Marx knew nothing of, and in particular this one: that, *ceteris paribus*, every increase in total capital will, unless the population decreases, cause either unemployment or a fall in wages. The richer a country becomes, the fewer the people who can find employment at a given wage.

the absolute size of the proletariat and the productivity of labour, the larger the industrial reserve army. The labour power available is increased by the same causes that promote the expansion of capital. Therefore the relative size of the industrial reserve army increases with the increase of wealth. But the larger that reserve army as compared with the army of active labour, the greater the mass of the surplus population. . . . Finally, the larger the Lazarus stratum of the working class [by which Marx meant the degenerate and unemployable section of it] and the larger the industrial reserve army, the larger, too, is the army of those who are officially accounted paupers.

In other words, as unemployment increases, so do the number of the 'unemployable' and the poverty of the working class. At this stage of his argument, Marx made his meaning abundantly clear. He rebuked the economists who advised the workers to adapt their numbers to the rate at which capital was expanding, and who urged them to have fewer children. The accumulation of capital, he said, will in any case adapt their numbers to suit its own needs. 'The first word of this adaptation is the creation of . . . an industrial reserve army; the last word is the poverty of continually increasing strata of the active labour army, and the dead weight of pauperism.'

The statement and elaboration of this law, that the accumulation of capital increases unemployment, occupies two sections of Chapter 23 of the first volume of *Capital*, about twenty-two pages in all of the *Everyman* edition. The rest of the chapter, consisting of more than seventy pages, is devoted to collecting evidence. Marx, as we saw, made no attempt to prove that the ratio of variable to total capital falls as total capital increases, still less to prove that it falls more quickly. But he did draw a vivid picture of the misery caused in this country and in Ireland by the spread of industry. These seventy pages are among the most readable he ever wrote, though the information and statistics collected in them certainly do not establish the truth of what he called the *absolute general law of capitalist accumulation*. All they prove is that many workers lived in the most wretched poverty, and often in conditions worse than they had known in the past. These pages are a terrible indictment of nineteenth-century capitalism; they were much better worth writing than the general principle they were meant to establish. All honour then to their author, who felt the need to write them, and to express in this way his sympathy for the workers and disgust with their exploiters, at a time when most other economists were praising the system that produced so much misery. The fact remains, nevertheless, that Marx did enunciate a law of capital accumulation essential to his general theory about the progress and fall of capitalist society, and yet never made a serious attempt to establish it.

Marx believed that the same process of accumulation which creates unemployment and increases poverty also reduces the ranks of the capitalists. Competition is fierce, and the successful capitalists ruin and buy up those who fail. Capital increases and the number of capitalists falls. Therefore the size of the capital owned or controlled by any one capitalist or group of capitalists rapidly increases. New, larger, and more expensive machines are continually installed, and the average size of the unit of production increases. Workers are congregated together in the same place; they are all in more or less the same predicament; they are most of them tenders of machines, and their skills more easily acquired. The differences between different kinds of work grow smaller than they used to be, and labour therefore more concentrated and more monotonous. The same process that increases the pressure of exploitation reduces the number of exploiters and adds to the cohesion and the mass of the exploited. In the words so often quoted from the twenty-fourth chapter of *Capital*: 'While the number of capitalist magnates continually falls . . . there grows the mass of misery, oppression, slavery, degradation, and exploitation; but with it, too, there grows the revolt of the working class, a class always increasing in numbers, and disciplined, united, and organized by the very mechanism of capitalist production itself.'

Marx believed that the proletariat would eventually swallow up all the other classes except the capitalists, and that the number of the capitalists would continually fall. Competition always growing fiercer, and ruining the many for the benefit of the few, is enough to explain the whittling away of the bourgeoisie. But why should other classes disappear? Why should artisans, shopkeepers, and peasants all become proletarians? Because, said Marx, capitalism invades every branch of productive activity.

Its superior efficiency enables it to compete on favourable terms with all the old-fashioned small producers. The economies due to operating on a large scale are as great in the distributive as in the productive trades. As capitalism develops, the size of the market increases, and so, too, does the distance between producer and consumer. Goods are sold many months after they are made and at places far removed from the place of their manufacture. The nice adjustments of local supply to local demand are no longer possible. There are always on every market fluctuations disastrous to the small producer but affecting the big manufacturer much less. These causes will eventually destroy the class of independent artisans and small shopkeepers. As for the peasants, a class for whom Marx had no sympathy, they will give way to the much more efficient capitalist farmer. The growth of industry increases the relative size of the urban population, and the country must feed the towns. Each worker on the land must no longer feed only himself and his family, and then produce a small surplus for the local gentlefolk and the nearest market town; he must, if the great cities are to be fed, produce a much larger surplus. The peasant proprietor, already a hard worker and a small consumer, can scarcely get more out of the land than he does. If land is to become more productive, it must be differently cultivated and at much greater capital expense. The growth of industry and of the towns has already brought capitalist farming to England, and must bring it at last to Europe and the rest of the world.

This part of the Marxian analysis of how capitalism develops is largely true. The average size of the capitalist enterprise, even if we allow for the fall in the value of money, is today much greater than it was when he wrote. Though the small shopkeeper survives, he is often so dependent on the wholesaler and producer as to be almost their agent, or else so humble a member of a vast association of traders that, not he and his kind, but the representatives of the big firms take much the greater part in making the decisions that bind him. Giant capitals are locked up in the distributive trades, and the men who control them have, in their own sphere, a power as great as that of the captains of industry. The artisan, though he, too, has survived much better than Marx thought he would, has also lost his independence.

The control of industry and trade has passed into the hands of a very few people, as Marx said it would. Even the peasants are no longer economically free. They are dependent on distant markets as they never were before; they have formed co-operatives and so put themselves under discipline; they have contracted debts and mortgaged their lands; and they have taken to selling their produce to middlemen, often much wealthier than themselves, who sell it again at a greater profit. If the capitalist farmer has not replaced the peasant, if agriculture, where the peasant has survived, is still inefficient, it is none the less true that the spread of capitalism has obliged the peasant to change his methods and has deprived him of his independence.

And yet, though the shopkeeper, the artisan, and the peasant have lost their independence, though capitalism has either invaded or subjugated every branch of production and distribution, the effects on the class structure of society have not been what Marx predicted. The shopkeeper, artisan, and peasant, dependent creatures though they are, are yet not proletarians. Their habits of mind and social aspirations are quite different; they have changed, but the change has brought them no closer to the proletariat. They are still separate classes in the community. They are perhaps relatively smaller than they were but are still large enough to be politically important.

In the meantime, other non-proletarian classes have arisen or grown stronger. Production and distribution on a large scale requires many services, administrative, financial, clerical, and scientific. The ultimate control may be in few hands, but there is a great army of subordinates, whose education, salaries, and social habits put them in classes apart from the manual workers. With a large and quickly-growing civil service added to them, there are in the great industrial countries millions of people who are just as truly the creatures of industrialism as the proletarians themselves. Whether they are state officials or in private employment, it is the spread of industry which, either directly or indirectly, has created their work. They are not, like the peasant, the artisan, and the small shopkeeper, survivors from the past; their work is needed because industrial society is what it is, and because the modern state is partly its product.

Capitalism, said Marx, reduces society to two main classes, of which one grows richer as it grows smaller and the other larger as it grows poorer. It is this process that leads to revolution, because the growing and impoverished class become at last the great majority of society, disciplined, politically experienced, and determined to put an end to the system whose victims they are. This, if it were true, would be enough to account for the fall of capitalism; but it would not be an explanation in keeping with historical materialism. This polarization of society into two classes is an effect of capitalist progress, but not of a 'contradiction of capitalism,' and would presumably happen though prevailing 'relations of production' had not become 'fetters' on the forces of production. Technical progress might continue without impediment though the proletarians grew poorer and more numerous and the capitalists richer and fewer. The class war would then still be the effect of the expansion of capitalist industry; it would still have an economic cause, but that cause would not be the kind required by historical materialism. The capitalist system of property and the 'relations of production' it expresses would still be destroyed, but only because it suited the proletariat to destroy them and not because they had become 'fetters' on the forces of production. Whether such thoughts as these ever troubled Marx, no one can know. What we do know is that he was not content to leave this as the only explanation of the fall of capitalism; he also wanted to prove that the capitalist system of property becomes, as industrial production develops, a hindrance to that development. He wanted to prove that there exist, after all, real 'contradictions of capitalism,' though he had sufficiently explained the fall of bourgeois society without having recourse to them.[1]

It was the search for 'contradictions of capitalism' which turned Marx's attention to industrial crises. He and Engels made their first important statement about them in *The Communist Manifesto*: 'For many a decade past the history of industry and commerce has been the history of the revolt of modern productive forces against modern conditions of production, against the property relations on which depend the existence of the bourgeoisie and its rule. It is enough to mention the commercial crises that from

---

[1] I do not mean that his explanation is true, but merely that, if true, it is sufficient to account for the event predicted.

time to time threaten the existence of bourgeois society, each time more dangerously.' The *Manifesto* tells us no more than that these crises are caused by over-production, and that they are cured, though only for a time, by the destruction of surplus produce and also of 'a mass of productive forces.' But in the third volume of *Capital*, Marx had more to say about the 'contradictions' of capitalism and the commercial crises, which are, he thought, their symptoms. He there argued that the conditions enabling capitalists to exploit their workers do not guarantee that they can sell the products of exploited labour. Exploitation is limited by the technique of production; technical progress increases the productivity of labour, and the more productive that labour the higher the upper limit of exploitation. On the other hand, whether or not the capitalist can sell his produce depends on what Marx called the 'consuming power of society,' or, in other words, on effective demand. Effective demand depends on income. But the income of the worker, just because he is exploited, is small; and he and his kind are the great majority. Capitalism, therefore, perpetually stimulates production while it prevents or retards an increase in consumption by much the largest class in society. This, according to Marx, is a 'contradiction,' and leads to periodic crises when capitalists destroy some part of what they have produced. So obscure is Marx in the third volume of *Capital* that it is at times almost impossible to follow his meaning, but he does, I think, say at least this much in the fifteenth chapter.

Marx never really explained how it is that crises happen. It is not obvious, though he seems to have thought it so, that, because capitalism stimulates production and keeps real wages low, there must be commercial crises. Capitalism, according to this hypothesis, stimulates production and exploits the workers all the time. Both the stimulation and the exploitation are *continuous*, and it is difficult to see how, unless other causes intervene, they can lead to *periodic* crises. I doubt whether Marx, in any of his writings, gave an intelligible account of what those other causes might be. It does not follow that, because the workers produce much more than they are allowed to consume, their exploiters must find it difficult to dispose of the surplus product. The capitalists who exploit the workers presumably have their .

eye on some market or other; they produce in response to some effective demand. If the effective demand of the exploited workers is much smaller in proportion to their numbers than that of any other class, the capitalists will have a sufficient motive for producing so much the less to satisfy their needs, and so much the more to satisfy the needs of others better able to pay for what they want. Periodic crises, when capitalists find it impossible to sell all they have produced, must have some other cause than the poverty of the workers. This cause, whatever it may be, is no doubt something inherent in the uncontrolled capitalist economy, but there is no reason to believe that it is connected with what Marx called 'capitalist relations of property' or with anything 'legally expressed' by those relations.

In any case, whatever Marx's precise opinions about commercial crises and their causes, it is clear that they do no more than aggravate the struggle between the bourgeois and the proletarians. That struggle Marx accounted for by other causes, causes having nothing to do with any 'conflict' or incompatibility between 'forces' and 'relations of production,' or between the methods that capitalists use in the process of production and the system of property which gives them their social privileges. Even if there were no crises, the capitalist mode of production, if it developed as Marx said it must and had the consequences he described, would lead inevitably to a proletarian revolution. Given the truth of the Marxian account of the progress of capitalism, that revolution is inevitable whether or not capitalist relations of property act as fetters on the forces of production. In other words, it is inevitable whether or not historical materialism, as it is stated in the *Preface* to *The Critique of Political Economy*, is true. That, at least, is what we must conclude if we accept Marx's analysis in *Capital* of bourgeois production and its social consequences.

It is still the fashion among Marxists—for with them fashions change slowly—to say that the fundamental 'contradiction' of capitalism is that it 'socializes' production but not appropriation. They take for their text Marx's words in the twenty-fourth chapter of the first volume of *Capital*: 'The centralization of the means of production and the socialization of labour reach a point where they become incompatible with their capitalist shell.

This shell bursts. The knell of capitalist private property sounds.'
Engels, in *Anti-Dühring* (Part III, Ch. 2), provides the Marxists
with another text. He says:

> Hitherto [that is before the capitalist epoch] the owner of instru-
> ments of production appropriated the product because he had as a
> rule made it himself, the auxiliary labour of other persons being the
> exception; now [that is, under capitalism] the owner of the instru-
> ments of production continued to appropriate the product, although
> he had not made it and it was exclusively the product of other
> people's labour. And so the products, now produced socially, were
> not appropriated by the people who had set the means of production
> in motion and had really made the products, but by the capitalists.
> The means of production and production itself had in essence be-
> come social, but were still subjected to a form of appropriation
> which presupposed private production by individuals, with each
> individual owning his own product and bringing it to market. . . .
> In this contradiction, which gives the new mode of production its
> capitalist character, the whole conflict of to-day is already present
> in germ. The more the new mode of production prevailed . . . the
> more glaring the necessary incompatibility between social produc-
> tion and capitalist appropriation.

It is sometimes fatal to Marx when Engels comes to his assistance. What we are told in this part of *Anti-Dühring* is that a
'form of appropriation' which originated before capitalist production began survived into the capitalist epoch and so created
an incompatibility between 'social' production and capitalist
appropriation. It was apparently the rule before the birth of
capitalism for owners of means of production to take possession
of what was produced by those means, and this rule continued
to hold afterwards. But what is a 'form of appropriation'?
What does a man do when he appropriates something? He claims
it for his own, and the claim is worth nothing unless it is generally
recognized by other men. 'Forms of appropriation' and what
Marx and Engels call 'relations of property' are presumably either
different names for the same thing or for different aspects of the
same thing. If the laws of property are not what they are men
cannot appropriate as they do. Engels seems therefore to imply
that the fundamental 'contradiction of capitalism' is due to the
survival into the capitalist epoch of a law of property not suited
to the prevailing mode of production. But laws of property are

said by Marx to be the 'legal expression' of 'relations of production.' Must we conclude, then, that there would be no 'fundamental contradiction of capitalism' were it not that a pre-capitalist 'relation of production' had somehow survived into the capitalist epoch? Is this what Engels meant, or was it just another careless blow struck at historical materialism, the doctrine he thought he was elucidating and defending? For, if there are to be genuine 'contradictions of capitalism' in the Marxian sense, the forms of appropriation and laws of property (and the 'relations of production' they 'express') must be as much native to the capitalist system as the mode of production whose fetters they at last become.

The point I have made may be thought unfair to Engels. It is one thing to appropriate the product of your own labour, and another to appropriate what others have made. Capitalist appropriation is therefore different from the kind that preceded it, and the 'relations of production' it reflects are also not the same. It is one thing to own instruments that you use yourself, and quite another to own instruments used by other people. And it may have been precisely this sort of difference that Marx and Engels had in mind when they spoke of different relations of production and of property. But this is no proper defence of Engels. It was the rule, he said, in pre-capitalist society that men should keep what was made with their own instruments, and it was the survival of this rule into the capitalist epoch which made capitalist appropriation possible. The rule is the same though its social consequences differ. If the rule had been that they kept only what they had made themselves, its survival would have made capitalism impossible. What made it possible was precisely that the rule concerned the means of production. The rule was not, *Keep what you have made*, but *Keep what is made with your instruments.* If Engels had argued that the rule used to be, *Keep what you have made*, and then afterwards, as the result of changes in the mode of production, was replaced by the rule, *Keep what is made with your instruments*, he would have said what is consistent with historical materialism. He could then have pointed to a new 'form of appropriation' resulting from a new mode of production; but, in that case, he would have had to explain his 'fundamental contradiction of capitalism' quite otherwise. For this new form of appropriation must at first, if historical materialism is true, have been perfectly suited to the new mode of production, and could only have become a fetter on it at a later stage. That, however, would not have suited his formula that 'social production' and 'capitalist appropriation' are incompatible. For the capitalist mode of production is social from the moment of its birth. It is so, as Engels himself tells us, 'essentially.'

Indeed, it is absurd to speak, as he does, of social production and capitalist appropriation, as if the words 'social' and 'capitalist,' in this particular context, had opposite meanings. The social production supposed by Engels to exist under capitalism is not socially controlled; it is not *socialist* production. All that Engels means when he calls it social is that it is co-operative. Instead of one man using his own tools separately to produce goods for the market, many men work in the same factory and operate the same machines to produce a much greater quantity of goods. What they produce cannot be divided into parts of which each is the separate product of one of them; the whole quantity is the joint product of them all. Now, joint production is only one form of social production, for whatever is produced under conditions that exist only in society and according to rules prescribed by it, whether it is the separate product of one man or the joint product of many, is socially produced. Again, anything that is appropriated in society, unless the appropriation is theft, is socially appropriated. Indeed, while production is possible outside society, property is not. A man talks foolishly, then, when he repeats this empty formula about 'social' production and 'capitalist' appropriation. We cannot prove an incompatibility or, as the Marxists call it, a 'contradiction' by the simple expedient of using two adjectives as if they had opposite meanings. We could not prove it even if our two adjectives, unlike the two chosen by Engels, really had opposite meanings. We might as well say, if we are guests at a wedding: a dark man is marrying a fair woman; I predict a divorce.

What could a man mean by saying that capitalist appropriation is 'unsocial'? He could mean only that it is 'unjust.' The contrast, therefore, is between co-operative production and unjust appropriation; and it is said that the two are incompatible. Put in this way, the argument is a plain *non sequitur*. It still has to be proved that because appropriation is unjust co-operative production cannot be efficient. It was this, I suppose, that Marx tried to do in *Capital*, more especially in the third volume; and with what success we have already seen. But the Marxists—and among them I include Engels—do not rely so much on these more detailed arguments as on the simple formula that 'social production is incompatible with capitalist appropriation.' The formula is repeated as if it expressed an obvious truth. It can, they think, be elaborated, and arguments found to support it; but it carries conviction of itself. That is the belief of many honest Marxists. 'Production has become social,' they say, 'and we must now *socialize* appropriation,' or, as some of them prefer it, 'we must *socialize* distribution.' But appropriation is already co-operative; what I own is securely mine only because there are judges and policemen willing to defend my right to it. The same is true of distribution, which is always as much co-operative as production. Only consumption is still largely non-co-operative, and must be so while men's bodies remain separate. Men can share the same rooms, use the same buses, listen to the same music; but, while they have separate mouths, stomachs, and senses, they will always eat and enjoy their food separately and listen to Mozart through separate ears, though they sit at the same table or in the same hall. It is a foolish sentence that Engels wrote in *Anti-Dühring*, but as popular as it is foolish. It moves heavily from paragraph to paragraph in the Marxist text-books, as if iteration could make it true; and it somehow carries conviction. It is an article of faith.

The truth of Marx's analysis of capitalism depends in the first place on the truth of his theory of exploitation. Exploitation, he says, must grow worse because the rate of profit on capital falls. It does not much matter whether Marx's account of why that rate falls is true or not. The fact is that it has fallen, though not continuously. There have been long periods when it did not fall, though the process of capitalist accumulation still continued. Marxists have offered many explanations of why this was so. New markets were discovered and new fields of investment; the great industrial powers became imperialist, because the rich, no longer able to invest their money at a good profit at home, wanted to invest it in less developed countries where they could get a better return on it. Because they were financially interested in these countries, the capitalists wanted them to have stable governments, and therefore either spent money on maintaining native reactionaries in power or else put pressure on their own governments to annex these backward areas. Imperialist rivalries and other causes led to wars, both great and small, wars which, while they lasted, created a sudden and enormous demand for armaments, and, when they were over, for making good the damage done. Many things have interfered with the steady decline of the rate of profit, but, say the Marxists, we cannot therefore deny that the accumulation of capital causes it to fall. Marx's laws, like those of other economists, are supposed to hold good only *ceteris paribus*; they assert a tendency and not that nothing will interfere with it. The Marxists have also said that the causes which have interfered with this tendency have themselves been disruptive of capitalism, adding colonial to domestic exploitation, and forcing the nations into useless and horrible wars. These arguments have been elaborated by the disciples of Marx and Engels, but the earlier versions of some of them are to be found in *Capital* and in the later writings of Engels.

It is quite true that the rate of profit, though it fell discontinuously, had, by the second half of the last century, fallen low enough to encourage the rich to invest their money in undeveloped lands; and it is also true that the colonial rivalries of the last eighty years have been partly caused by this need for new outlets for investment and new markets. Marx lived just long enough to see the beginnings of the new imperialism, but he had already, years before it began, explained how falling profits at home drive capital abroad. All this is true. But it is not true that falling profits oblige capitalists, because they are in competition with one another, to increase the rate of exploitation. Even if they try to increase it, they will not succeed, unless the increase in the demand for labour caused by the expansion of industry does not keep pace with the growth of population. Marx, as we have seen, had no sufficient reason for supposing that it could not do so. He merely assumed, following the classical economists from whom he took so many of his ideas, that the poor are so prolific that the supply of labour will always exceed the demand for it. Instead of assuming, like Malthus, that population has a natural tendency to grow in geometric progression and the means of subsistence only in arithmetic progression, he assumed that the aggregate sum set aside by employers for the hire of labour must increase less quickly than the population. The one assumption is as gratuitous as the other; and yet both have been taken seriously by the most serious people. If Marx had not made this assumption, he would have had nothing to offer in defence of his statement that, because the rate of profit falls, capitalists do what they can to increase the rate of exploitation, and succeed only because the accumulation of capital makes labour more productive.

The Marxian account draws a curious picture of the capitalist. It is apparently not enough for the capitalist to grow richer; he is not satisfied with a larger absolute income if he gets a smaller return or profit on each unit of his capital. He will do his utmost to prevent the rate of profit falling, though his income rises in spite of that fall. He is an always desperate man growing rapidly richer. What makes him desperate is the pressure of competition. However great his prosperity, he is always in danger of ruin. While he survives he prospers, but the penalty for slackness is bankruptcy. Life offers him power and great riches, but only at the price of unremitting exertion, vigilance, and anxiety. He must move quickly forward or else be forced off the road. It is a terrible picture, and yet not altogether untrue to the facts. The capitalists of the nineteenth century were harder, more ruthless, and less comfortable than their successors; and it was no doubt competition that made them so. Marx was not unobservant. Though the laws he formulated to account for what he saw were seldom plausible, he was shrewd and imaginative. He read the reports of factory inspectors and Royal Commissions, reports that other people found dull. If he was absorbed by them, it was because he could see the living reality they described. Marx's analysis of the capitalist system, though seldom free from obscurity, sometimes illogical, and often mistaken, is nevertheless impressive. He knew what he was talking about, because he had looked at it as long and thought about it as much as anyone living in his day; but he knew it, not as he thought he did, not as a scientist knows what he studies; he had rather the feel of it than exact knowledge of how it worked. It is easy to do less than justice to Marx. He was a cruel critic of other people's nonsense, and yet sometimes talked nonsense himself. But the nonsense he talked was seldom like the nonsense he attacked. It was theoretical nonsense, the talk of a man who fancied himself a scientist and a subtle reasoner but was in fact neither. It was not the nonsense of a fool, of a man who looks and sees nothing, who has no sense of realities, who does not even begin to understand the social world he was born into; above all, it was not the pious nonsense of the man who finds excuses for cruelty. Marx discovered more than he could clearly describe or fit together into a plausible theory; and yet his account of the capitalist system, though it will not bear too close analysis, is something altogether more impressive than historical materialism. It is more impressive because it is more humane, because it is inspired, not by German metaphysics, but by pity and indignation.

Chapter Seven

THE POLITICS OF MARX AND ENGELS

I. MARX COMPARED WITH THE OTHER SOCIALISTS

Historical materialism is difficult to understand, and so, too, is the Marxian analysis of capitalism. Marx the philosopher and Marx the economist speak an obscure, involved, mysterious language, a language that seems to mean more than it says and in fact says more than it means. It is the language of a man excited by his own ideas, deeply interested in what he wants to describe, but somehow unable to find the words that exactly express his meaning. Metaphors and similes abound; the same thought is now dressed up in one way and now in another. The writer seems always to be using several different sets of phrases and never to be satisfied that he has made his meaning clear until he has expressed it in all of them. And yet his use of each set is careless, as if he thought exact statement impossible in any, and hoped that what is misleading in one would always be corrected by using the others. Persons influenced by the Idealist philosophers often write in this way, and when they do so, they can be said to express their meaning by groups of sentences rather than sentence by sentence. It is an awkward procedure, and for two reasons: because both writer and reader are apt to think that more has been said than has been, and because the many partial and careless statements of what the writer means may (and usually do) have implications he knows nothing of.

Marx the politician is more readily understood. The language he uses is more popular, and much that is vague about it belongs to ordinary speech. We can allow for it as we do for each other whenever we converse; it is not meant to be scientific, and the context usually makes the meaning clear. Marx's political opinions we can find in his pamphlets and addresses written for special occasions: in *The Communist Manifesto*, *The Address to the Communist League*, *The Class Struggles in France*, *The Eighteenth Brumaire of Louis Bonaparte*, *The Civil War in France*, and *The Critique of the Gotha Programme*, in his letters, and in the articles he wrote for the *New York Daily Tribune* and other papers. Marx the politician is Marx the journalist and revolutionary propagandist. Philosophy and economics keep on breaking in but do not greatly disturb the flow of his thoughts. Marx's political writings are quite the most readable and exciting; and, though they are popular, they are by no means superficial. Marx's shrewdness, his insight, and his persuasive powers are nowhere better displayed. Marx was a great journalist. He had deep convictions, an absorbing interest in what he wrote, a great knowledge of the contemporary world acquired by extensive reading, and a considerable experience of revolutionary movements if not of revolutions. He understood, better than most people, what was happening in France and Germany between 1848 and 1851; and again, what was happening in Paris from September 1870 until May 1871.

His political opinions he got mostly from his study of contemporary French history; for it was in France that political socialism was born, and also in France that it first became revolutionary. Indeed, properly speaking, there did not exist elsewhere in western Europe, while Marx was alive, a genuine revolutionary tradition and a revolutionary working class. In other countries there were occasional revolts, political associations which at times looked dangerous, or nationalist movements willing to resort to arms but not to make a social revolution. The nationalist movements of eastern Europe, and more particularly of the Balkans, were as much social and revolutionary as nationalist, as much directed against Turkish and Magyar landowners as against foreign domination. But Marx knew next to nothing of the Slavs; indeed, he almost despised them. Their nationalism he dismissed as reactionary. Even Ireland, though he lived next door to her, and her fight, too, was as much against landlords as foreigners, interested him only a little. He wrote a few articles and letters about her, and had a 'policy' for her that Lenin praised; but that is all. When he spoke of revolutions and class warfare, it was France he had mostly in mind, more even than his native Germany. It would, perhaps, be extravagant to say that the Marxian account of the class war is a German theory about French revolutions. Marx worked and hoped for revolution in Germany; he gave more advice to Germans than to Frenchmen; he has had, since his death, incomparably greater influence in Germany than in France. His style is German, his tricks of speech, the movement of his thought, his sarcasm, and even his wit. No man ever wrote what was more obviously not made in France. But just as he learnt his economics by studying the English industrial system, so he learnt his politics by following events in France. French history was his school of revolution. His first political experience he got in Germany, as a young journalist of the extreme left. He came from the Rhineland, the part of Germany most influenced by French ideas, and in 1844 he went to Paris, the only town in Europe where both socialist theories and the proletariat were already politically important. In *The Communist Manifesto*, written before the revolution of 1848, the proletariat are already called the only revolutionary class; but at that time they had never been engaged in serious revolutionary action except in France.

What is true of Marx is perhaps less true of Engels. His politics, from the time he met Marx until Marx's death, were much the same as his partner's. Most of his milder political pronouncements were made in the eighteen-eighties and 'nineties. They were not the effects of a latent reformism now at last given its head after the death of Marx, but of changing conditions in Europe. The German Social-Democratic Party, the largest working-class party in the world and the most Marxist, was growing so fast at the end of the century that it looked as if it might, within a generation, gain an absolute majority in the Reichstag. The workers were doing better for themselves in bourgeois parliaments than they had ever done in the streets. It was this that caused Engels to modify the revolutionary theory elaborated by Marx and himself, but he never abandoned it. The difference between Engels and Marx is that Engels lived twelve years longer into the post-revolutionary era. He was also, perhaps, rather less interested in France and rather more interested in Germany. The articles in the *New York Daily Tribune*, which appeared between October 1851 and December

1852 and were later published separately under the title *Germany, Revolution and Counter-Revolution*, are the most important Marxian discussion of political events in Germany. It used to be thought that Marx wrote them, but we now know, since the publication of the correspondence between Marx and Engels, that they were written mostly by Engels, though with the help of Marx. These letters, written by the greater German patriot of the two, make repeated mention of the political backwardness of Germany. The class war, as Marx and Engels, and in a later generation Lenin, knew, was best studied in France.

Marx was a revolutionary, and his mission to prepare the proletariat for revolution. This is the simple and important fact about him which is the clue to all his public life. The real difference between him and such socialists as Owen, Saint-Simon, and Fourier—the Utopians, as he called them, though he also spoke of them with considerable respect—was not that he was scientific and they were not. That was only the difference as he and Engels conceived it. Saint-Simon had a theory of history at least as intellectually respectable as Marx's. Long before Marx, he had taught that a new industrial society had taken the place of the 'feudal' world, that the new society was born in the womb of the old, that its coming put power into the hands of a new class, and that, in the process, all the institutions of society were transformed. He, too, had discovered, so he believed, the fundamental social process; and he had also predicted the inevitable coming of what he desired. His account, though more disconnected and less elaborate, is not less plausible than Marx's. Their philosophies of history are equally unscientific, and it may be that, if common sense had to choose between them, it would prefer the Frenchman's. Saint-Simon, though he thought economic more important than political problems, especially since the coming of industrialism, was not an economic determinist; Marx's least plausible error never attracted him. But, like Marx, he wanted to help society along the road it was in any case, so he thought, bound to travel. Marx compared Saint-Simon's theory with his own and found it unscientific; but the impartial student, looking at the two theories, finds one characteristic common to them: they both claim to be scientific. It is not true that Saint-Simon merely drew a picture of the ideal society and hoped its beauty might persuade men to recreate reality in its image. Like Marx, he put his faith in a class whose victory he believed assured by history; he, too, spoke to men of their interests, exhorting them to work for the inevitable. But he was not a revolutionary, and the industrial class he believed in included everyone who worked and not only the proletariat.

What really distinguishes Marx from the socialists falsely called Utopian is therefore not science but revolutionary zeal; and what distinguishes him from the other socialists who believed in the class war, from Blanqui, Proudhon[1] and Bakunin, is again not science but the peculiarities of the theory he invented to explain his faith in the proletariat. Proudhon had no developed philosophy of history; his theory of exploitation was different from Marx's; he wanted to abolish private capitalism without substituting for it the public ownership of the means of production and exchange; and he did not believe that the workers should try to capture political power. He was a more confused thinker than Marx, but just as determined an enemy of capitalism. Bakunin was an anarchist, an almost incoherent doctrinaire, and an irresponsible political leader, but as much a friend of the proletariat and as ardent a fighter as Marx. It is his immense learning, the greater coherence of his theories, his ability to work hard, his tenacity of purpose, his sense of responsibility and—dare I say it?—his bourgeois morality, that distinguish Marx from Bakunin.[2]

[1] Proudhon often deprecated violence and was not properly a revolutionary socialist, but he believed that there was in fact a struggle between classes, and his sympathies were all with the workers.

[2] Marx disliked and feared Bakunin more than any of the other great socialists. Marx was jealous and masterful, and could not bear to have rivals. Owen, Saint-Simon, and Fourier belonged to an older generation; and he could, with a generosity seldom difficult even to the vainest of men, praise them for having been wise in their generation, while congratulating himself on being able to see much further than they could. Blanqui was not a competitor with Marx; he was not a theorist but a fighter; he never aspired to lead the masses but only an élite chosen by himself; and he was, above all, that provincial of provincials, the Parisian who believes that nothing important can happen outside the beloved city. Marx reserved his hardest blows for the two men whose influence most endangered his own: Proudhon and Bakunin. Proudhon belonged by birth to the working class, and the influence of his doctrine over the French workers, at that time the only genuine revolutionaries in Europe, was strongest from 1848 to 1871. Bakunin had a considerable following in many countries, he had great prestige both as a man of ideas and as a revolutionary fighter, and it looked at one time as if he might win greater authority inside the first International than Marx himself. Bakunin made friends easily and soon acquired over them, merely by being himself, the sort of influence that Marx had to work hard to get and to maintain. Nearly everyone liked Bakunin, except when they found him intolerable; whereas Marx, bitter, harsh, contemptuous, and feeling

Blanqui, the most famous active revolutionary leader of the nineteenth century, was not really a theorist at all; he merely invented a social philosophy to justify his practice long after he had adopted it, and then only because it was the fashion to do so. Blanqui, like Marx, had nothing to say about the future society; it would emerge of itself and no one could know beforehand what it would be like. His business was merely to destroy bourgeois society; and to that business he devoted his whole life. Blanqui was a socialist and a revolutionary conspirator; he wanted to destroy the old society for the sake of the proletariat, but had no thought of educating the workers, of teaching them what sort of society they belonged to, and what were the interests of their class inside it. He never thought it his duty to prepare for the eventual victory of the great majority. Revolutions, he thought, are always made by minorities, and he had no interest except to make revolutions. He studied the immediate situation only, the weaknesses of governments and the courage and discipline of his own supporters; he forgot that, though it takes only a few men to make a revolution, what happens afterwards largely depends on the reactions of the others, the timorous and slothful majorities he so heartily despised. Marx admired the courage, singleness of purpose and revolutionary ardour of Blanqui, and also his contempt for bourgeois democracy; but could not admire his narrow views and lack of foresight.

Marx is the greatest of socialists because in him there is a combination of qualities not found in any of the others. He had interests as wide and a theory of society as plausible and as consistent as Saint-Simon's, but more elaborate and more formidably equipped with facts and figures; he understood the miseries and strains of the new industrialism almost as well as Fourier and Owen, and had a better cure to offer than the blue-print of a model society to be created by men of good will; he was as insistent,

an almost personal hatred for a society which treated him as an outcast, could not help offending even persons disposed to admire him. It is unfortunate for Marx's personal reputation that the two rivals he most belaboured should have been exceptionally free from his own defects. Neither Proudhon nor Bakunin was bitter, jealous, or vindictive. They were both proud of their talents and eager to display them, they enjoyed the fight against established authority, and they could give and take hard blows; but they were not sour and unforgiving. When men become enemies, comparisons are soon made between them; and with some justice, for there are few better clues to a man's character than the way he treats the people he quarrels with. From this point of view, Marx chose his enemies badly.

verbose and persuasive as Proudhon but rather more intelligible; he was as convinced a revolutionary as Bakunin and Blanqui, but more responsible and coherent than the former and more enlightened than the latter. He was not seen, as they were, on the barricades, and never went to prison, but he spent a more sedentary and safer life to much better purpose. Above all, he was the shrewdest of them, the most patient, and the best politician.

I shall not discuss all the political writings of Marx and Engels but only those that deal with matters of theoretical interest—their ideas about the proletariat and other classes, their theory of the state and its inevitable disappearance, their conception of the 'dictatorship of the proletariat,' and finally the concessions made by Engels to the reformists in the last years of his life.

II. THE PROLETARIAT AND OTHER CLASSES

(i) *The Communist Manifesto*

We are told in the *Manifesto* that, of all the classes that face the bourgeois in capitalist society, the proletariat alone are a truly revolutionary class. The other classes decay and finally disappear in the face of modern industry; the proletariat are its peculiar and essential product. 'The lower middle class, the small manufacturer, the shopkeeper, the artisan, the peasant, all these fight against the bourgeoisie to save themselves, as fragments of the middle class, from extinction. They are therefore not revolutionary but conservative. Nay, more, they are reactionary, for they try to roll back the wheel of history. If by chance they are revolutionary, they are so only because they are soon to be transferred into the proletariat; they thus defend not their present but their future interests.'[1]

---

[1] Why they should defend their future interests is not explained. Do they foresee their transference to the proletariat? It is by no means clear that Marx thought they did, for his usual assumption is that the behaviour of classes is determined by what they conceive to be their present interests. He does not credit them with long views; on the contrary, most of his explanations make sense only if it is taken for granted that political behaviour is nearly always inspired by hope of immediate advantage. How could these sections of the lower middle class know that they are destined to become proletarians? Because Marx or some other socialist has converted them to a theory which predicts this fate for them? It is, I think, most unlikely that Marx meant anything of the kind. He did not believe that any considerable section of the lower middle class could foresee their translation into another class and make their calculations accordingly. He had noticed that many people who

There are things here rather too simply put and that Marx afterwards qualified. The small business men, shopkeepers and artisans, the 'petty' bourgeois as we have learnt to miscall them in England, Marx later discovered to be not so reactionary after all. They are only destined to become so when the changes profitable to themselves have been made. According to the later version, they do not now want to put back the great wheel of history but will strive to halt it after it has reached the position that suits them. But, though Marx afterwards spoke of this class very differently, the passage I quoted gives strong expression to a belief central to his political theory: that under capitalism only the proletariat are a revolutionary class. Other classes may take part in revolutions, but only the proletariat are fully engaged. No other class have an interest in completely subverting the whole structure of capitalist society; and therefore, since social revolution is inevitable, no other class can play the predominant part reserved for the proletariat. The wheel of history, to use the Marxian metaphor, is turning, and nothing can prevent its doing so; but it is not something that carries the classes with it, something external to them whose motion they must submit to. The turning wheel is the historical process, and includes their actions. Because it turns as it does, they act as they do; and yet their actions are somehow part of its turning. The proletariat push in the direction of the wheel's turning; and if the wheel continues to turn in spite of the efforts of the reactionary classes, it does so, not because the pressure and counter-pressure are external to it and have their effects upon it, but because, somehow, the wheel, as it turns, adds strength to those who push in the direction it moves in, and makes weak those who push against it. The workers must win, and yet cannot win except by their own efforts. They are the only revolutionary class; that is to say, the inevitable social revolution can be made only by them because they alone will

were not workers were revolutionaries, and had also decided that only the proletarians were revolutionary by virtue of their class; he therefore, in order to reconcile
fact with theory, asserted that the sections of the middle class most inclined to
revolution were defending not their present interests, but the interests that would
be theirs when they had descended into the proletariat. After the revolution of
1848, Marx was no longer satisfied with so crude an explanation; he preferred to
argue that the lower middle class, in pursuing their immediate interests, might turn
to revolution, but would do so only for a time and would quickly become reactionary
as soon as their demands were satisfied. This is an explanation greatly superior to
the one offered in *The Communist Manifesto*.

acquire the strength and the will to make it. This doctrine is the pith and core of Marx's political theory, and most of his arguments tend towards it or else lead from it.

This being so, it follows that any permanent compromise between the proletariat and the other classes is impossible. The new society is not to be made by any such artificial reconciliation. There are not in society, as Marx conceived it, a number of *stable* interests to be reckoned with, and therefore no just account satisfactory to all classes can ever be made. Social and political problems are not settled by weighing rival claims against each other and striking a true balance between them. There is no generally accepted measure than can be used, no impartial judge, and no hope that what is just today will be just tomorrow. It is absurd, therefore, to treat the proletariat as one class among many whose aspirations are only part of what a just settlement must satisfy. The proletariat are the class of the future, and other classes have no rights against them. It is true, no doubt, that they also have no rights against other classes; but they have what the others have not—the task of creating the future society. Like every other class they have their interests; and, as soon as they discover what they are, their course is clear before them. What they ought and ought not to do is determined by those interests and not by abstract notions of justice common to all classes. They have no *settlement* to make with the other classes; they have, in the words of the *Manifesto*, a 'world to win.'

What the workers must do is described at the end of the second section of the *Manifesto*. They must gain political supremacy, and must use it to expropriate the bourgeois and place all means of production in the hands of the state, that is, of the workers organized as the ruling class. This doctrine, too, though he later added a great deal to it, Marx never abandoned. The workers must gain *political* power, and must not hope to transform society until they have gained it. They must not be indifferent to the political struggle; they must not waste their energies on social experiments of the kind proposed by the Utopians nor try by direct action to seize control of factories and workshops. These negative injunctions are not given in the *Manifesto*, but they are corollaries of what is said there. To be a good Marxist is never to neglect the political struggle, never to forget that political victory must come before the transformation of society. Marx could not escape the influence of an idea common to nearly all the extreme radicals of his day, the idea that political power is essentially evil, that it is of its very nature oppressive. He, too, like Saint-Simon, Godwin and Rousseau, gave vent to his hatred of the over-mighty state and spoke of it as the instrument of the idle and privileged for the exploitation of the workers. But he did not allow this hatred to blind him to the importance of the political struggle. The state, as the radicals knew and hated it, must indeed disappear and the public power lose its political character, but not until after the workers had captured it and used it to transform society.

The *Manifesto* was written on behalf of a political society calling itself the Communist League. What were these Communists to do? What should be their relation to the proletariat? 'The Communists,' says the *Manifesto*, 'do not form a separate party opposed to other working class parties. They have no interests apart from those of the proletariat . . . [They] are . . . the most resolute and advanced section of the working class parties of every country, the section that urges forward all the others . . . they have the advantage over the great mass of the proletariat of clearly understanding the line of march, the conditions, and the ultimate general results of the proletarian movement.' The Communists, then, are the people who already know the interests of the proletariat, interests which are not merely what the workers happen to want at any time but are prescribed for them by their position in capitalist society. The workers, placed as they are, have interests that can be discovered by anyone who understands that society and their situation in it. The workers have only to learn what these interests are, and they will, as a class, strive to realize them. There is no question here of the Communists imposing their will on the workers; their task is to enlighten and to guide them. Marx and Engels, like the politicians they both were, knew there could be no effective proletarian movement without vigorous leaders. If the movement is revolutionary, its success is more than ever dependent on their courage, faith and skill. 'The immediate aim of the Communists,' says the *Manifesto*, 'is the same as that of all other proletarian parties: the formation of the proletariat into a class, the overthrow of bourgeois supremacy, and the conquest of political power by the proletariat.' The proletariat, of course, are already a class; they are not made a class by men but by the spread of industrialism. When the *Manifesto* says that the Communists must 'form the proletariat into a class,' it means only that they must see to the political education of the workers, teaching them their real interests and the best means of attaining them.

Nothing could be more unjust to Marx and Engels than to read into what they say in the *Manifesto* about the Communists anything that savours of what we nowadays call party dictatorship. The Communists are not to hold aloof from the workers, to prescribe their conduct, to urge them in their own interest to do what they have no wish to do. The *Manifesto* speaks of other proletarian parties and never questions their equal right to speak for the workers.

Marx and Engels no doubt believed, even as early as 1848, that the workers would do well to present a united front to the rest of society; but this belief, though it caused them to work all their lives for working class solidarity, never tempted them to write or say a word to suggest that any organized group smaller than the proletariat could assume the exclusive right to speak in their name.

In the *Manifesto* there is nothing said about proletarian democracy, but there is also nothing to suggest that those who speak for the workers need not be responsible to them. The revolution was to be made by the proletariat; and that, in 1848, was still meant to be taken literally. It implied that whatever leaders the revolution might throw up must be responsible, in fact and not merely in name, to the class on whose behalf they acted; it implied, in other words, that the working class political movement must be internally democratic. It was not necessary for Marx and Engels to insist on something that in 1848 still seemed obvious; it was enough that they should assume it.

In the middle of the nineteenth century it was already the fashion among extreme radicals and revolutionary socialists to denounce liberalism and parliamentary government as bourgeois shams. This fashion was not created by Marx and Engels, but did affect their writings. Not a few radicals and revolutionaries had been imprisoned or otherwise ill-treated by liberal and parliamentary governments; and they therefore denounced liberalism and parliamentarism. But this denunciation never implied a belief in 'party dictatorship'; the phrase and what it denotes were in those days alike unknown. We shall see later than even 'the dictatorship of the proletariat,' a phrase not yet current in 1848, meant, when Marx and Engels used it, something vastly different.

We can take it for certain that Marx, when he called the Communists 'the advanced section' of the proletariat, had nothing in mind like the doctrine afterwards made popular by the Bolsheviks about the proper relations between the 'party of the proletariat' and the class. He was wanting, rather, to emphasize the importance of doctrine, to show that the workers could not, until they understood the society they lived in and the law of its progress, know their own real interest, which they must be taught to recognize by persons better informed than themselves.[1] The better they know it, the more they are inclined to work together as a class, to present a united front to their oppressors. The propagation of the true doctrine is therefore a means to class unity. And the victory of the doctrine is the effect of its persuasive power; it is won in open competition with other theories; it is never imposed from above. These ideas, as we shall see, were later elaborated and modified by Lenin, who—after the Bolshevik revolution, and to some extent even before it—gave them an undemocratic twist.

But in Marx's time their bias was democratic. The other socialists were, with few exceptions, less interested than Marx and Engels in the political education and solidarity of the working class. The 'Utopians' mostly believed that their schemes could be realized by a few men of good will, while many of the others either wanted the workers to neglect political action and to take direct possession of factories and workshops, or else—like Blanqui—believed that a devoted band of revolutionaries could, if they chose their moment well, destroy the bourgeois state; whereas Marx and Engels were anxious that the Communists should

---

[1] The reader may wonder, since Marx and Engels in 1848 believed that there would be proletarian revolution in the very near future, how the Communists could contrive to enlighten the workers about their true interests in time for the great event; and how, if they did not contrive it, a dictatorship irresponsible to the workers could be prevented. But the authors of the *Manifesto* did not foresee this consequence, and can therefore not be accused of desiring it.

enlighten the workers, precisely because they believed that social-ism would come only as the fruit of a political victory won by a responsible and politically intelligent working class.

(ii) *The Address to the Communist League*

The Communist Manifesto was written before the French revolu-tion of February 1848—the first in which manual workers inspired by socialist doctrines played an important part. Marx and Engels, passionately interested in contemporary affairs, were inevitably greatly influenced by that revolution and by the others that hap-pened in other parts of Europe as a consequence of it. Three of the fundamental propositions of the *Manifesto*—that the pro-letariat are the only truly revolutionary class in capitalist society, that class antagonisms are irreconcilable, and that the workers need discipline and enlightenment about their class interests—seemed to Marx and Engels to be completely borne out by the events of 1848 and the subsequent years. But they were willing to add to them important supplementary doctrines, suggested by the recent experiences of France and Germany.

Early in 1850, the members of the Communist League, for whose benefit Marx and Engels had written the *Manifesto*, expected—in spite of the victories of the 'reactionaries' the year before—a renewal of revolutionary activity in Germany. Marx, on behalf of the Central Council of the League, prepared an address which was sent by special messenger from London to the members of the League preparing for action in Germany. Marx advised them what they should do in the immediate future; and his advice incor-porates lessons he had learnt in the two years since the *Manifesto* was written.

In *The Address to the Communist League* Marx pays much greater attention than he had done in the *Manifesto* to an 'oppressed' class other than the proletariat; and in advising the League and the workers how they should treat that class, elaborates a pro-gramme for revolution incompatible with historical materialism. That programme was suggested to him by what he thought of the situation in Germany in 1850. When events belied his hopes, he forgot the programme, but Lenin in 1905 imagined another and bolder version of it. Neither Marx in 1850 nor Lenin in 1905 knew that he was making suggestions which, if they were practicable, were evidence against the truth of historical materialism. But, whereas Marx forgot his suggestions soon after he made them, Lenin used his to justify one of the greatest revolutions in history.

In the *Address* Marx distinguishes between the upper and lower middle class in Germany, and admits that their interests are so far different that, while the former have now (in 1850) become reactionaries, the latter are still willing to resort to violence to achieve reform. The Democrats, the party of the lower middle class, are powerful, and the workers must co-operate with them against the common enemy.

Both the workers and the 'petty' bourgeois are, in the Germany of 1850, oppressed classes, and their fight against reaction is supremely important. There is, nevertheless, a vast difference between them. The proletariat are a truly revolutionary class; whatever their temporary aims, their true interest, while capitalism endures, is to subvert existing society by dispossessing the present owners of the means of production. Whereas the lower middle class want no more than to make bourgeois society comfortable for themselves, to soften class antagonisms until they disappear. Once they have got what they want, they will be against revolution.

Marx does not say, as he did in the *Manifesto*, that they are a class always opposed to revolution (except when they defend their future interests); but they will, he says, be for stopping the revolution when it has given them what they want. They are therefore possible allies in a revolution, and useful too, provided the workers know what to expect from them. When Marx calls the Democrats—the party of the lower middle class—'reformist,' he does not mean that they would never under any circumstances use violence (or get others to use it) to achieve their aims; he means only that it takes relatively little to satisfy them because they do not, as a class, desire the destruction of existing society. A few reforms made in good time will quickly deprive them of all taste for violence; the first concessions made to a successful revolution will satisfy them.

During the present phase of the struggle (that is, the phase reached in 1850), the petty bourgeois are still an oppressed class, and the workers must co-operate with them. But they must take care to create and to keep a firm hold on their own separate and independent organizations, and must never allow the call for unity against the oppressor to make them forget that their true interests are not those of their temporary allies. They must be prepared for the inevitable parting, which will come as soon as the first victories are won. They must expect to be abandoned and then attacked by the Democrats: to be abandoned when the petty bourgeois have got what they want; and to be attacked when they, the workers, insist on continuing the struggle in their own interest.

When the revolution begins, the workers, and more especially the Communists, must prevent the Democrats from quenching revolutionary ardour immediately after the first victories; they must keep the people angry and excited, stimulating their hopes and their fears; they must not prevent violence but encourage it, allowing the people to take vengeance on the men they hate. They must press their own demands and exact promises from the Democrats when they take over the government; and they must not hesitate to use force and the threat of force against them, and so commit the new rulers to every sort of concession to the workers. 'From the first moment of victory,' says Marx, 'mistrust must be directed, not against the conquered reactionary party, but against the workers' former allies, against the party that wishes to exploit the common victory for itself alone.'

After the victory the workers must keep their arms, allowing no one under any pretext whatever to disarm them. They must form their own political clubs, and also unions of such clubs.[1] When the Democrats set up a national assembly, the workers must put forward their own candidates. They must have a parliamentary party of their own, separate from all the bourgeois parties. They must also demand, when the estates of the German feudal landlords are confiscated, that the state take them over. These estates must be cultivated by the village labourers, the rural proletariat; because, in this way, there are gained two advantages: the economies of large-scale agriculture, and a breach in the system of private property. The natural allies in the villages of the petty bourgeois Democrats are the peasants, the millions of

---

[1] The word 'club' used by a socialist in 1850 had a special flavour. In Paris in 1848 the extremer radicals and socialists had formed clubs, and had used them to organize demonstrations to frighten the Provisional Government and the National Assembly.

small farmers who cultivate their own land; but the allies of the urban workers are the farm labourers, who, like themselves, live on their wages.

The workers, says Marx, 'must push the proposals of the Democrats . . . to their extreme limit, transforming them into direct attacks on private property; . . . if the petty bourgeois propose the purchase of the railways and factories, the workers must demand that they be simply confiscated by the state, and the owners, being reactionaries, receive no compensation. If the Democrats propose proportional taxes, the workers must demand progressive ones; if the Democrats propose a moderately progressive tax, the workers must demand a tax with rates rising so steeply that large capital is ruined by it. . . . The demands of the workers must everywhere be adjusted to the concessions and proposals of the Democrats.' Marx nowhere in the *Address* proposes that the workers should take power; in the German revolution expected in 1850 the government is to be taken over by the Democrats, the party of the still very formidable lower middle class. The workers in the coming revolution are to be subordinate allies; they are still too few in a predominantly agricultural country to take a leading part in destroying the established order and in governing after the revolution. It is a bourgeois government's proposals that the workers are exhorted to push to so extreme a limit that they are transformed into direct attacks on private property. Marx recognizes the importance of the lower middle class and admits the power of the Democrats.

In *The Address to the Communist League* Marx was speaking about Germany, a country where industrial capitalism had by 1850 made very little progress. The Liberals, who spoke for the upper middle class, the richer merchants and professional men— the sort of people represented in France by the Orleanists—had, so Marx thought, already betrayed the revolution of 1848; they had proved incapable of destroying absolute monarchy and setting up the liberal parliamentary government that best suited the needs of capitalism. Germany had still to make, or at least to complete, her bourgeois revolution; and in default of the Liberals the initiative would have to be taken by the Democrats, the spokesmen of the lower middle class. The Democrats had, Marx thought, become the obvious leaders of the German radical movement; they represented a large and important part of the middle class, and the workers had much to gain and little to lose by making a political alliance with them against the reactionaries. The workers could not yet aspire to power, and there was little chance that the Democrats could get it without the workers' help. The workers ought therefore to join with the Democrats in their attack on the established government; they ought to help them gain power. And they ought at the same time to take care not to become the instruments of the Democrats, not to be used by them and then abandoned, as the workers in Paris had been in 1830 and 1848. This they could avoid only if they created political organizations of their own and kept them always separate from the bourgeois parties. But, with such organizations for their use, they could do more than preserve the political independence of their class; they could turn the tables on the Democrats, bully them into making concessions to the proletariat, and go a long way in exploiting the common victory for the workers' benefit.

In spite of the little respect with which Marx, in *The Address to the Communist League*, speaks of the lower middle class, he reserves for them a very considerable rôle in modern German history; and yet they are the same people—the small manufacturers, artisans and shopkeepers—of whom he said in the *Manifesto* that they are a not merely conservative but reactionary section of the middle class, because all they do (except the few of them who somehow learn to fight for their future interests) is hold fast to whatever keeps them in the middle class. They fight, according to the *Manifesto*, to preserve a precarious status, to 'save themselves from extinction' as a section of the middle class. They are described so briefly, so much in passing from one major theme to another (as if merely to show they had not been forgotten), that the reader expects nothing of them. They are almost played out, and are there only because their last hour has not yet struck. For the *Manifesto* says that all classes and parts thereof intermediate between the capitalists and the proletarians are fated to disappear, their disappearance being an inevitable consequence of the spread and development of capitalism.

Though both the *Manifesto* and the *Address* were written for the benefit of the Communist League, there is in this respect no formal contradiction between them. Marx and Engels, when they wrote the *Manifesto*, had in mind the progress of capitalism in the world, and more particularly in England and France, where that progress was most advanced; whereas, in the *Address*, Marx was thinking only of his native Germany, still at that time, when compared with France and England, an economically backward country. Capitalism was only slightly established there, and the intermediate classes, whose demise the *Manifesto* had predicted, correspondingly strong. There is therefore no formal contradiction between the *Manifesto* and the *Address* in this matter of the political importance of the lower middle class, but there is a great and important shift of emphasis. Marx in the *Address* puts forward opinions for which the Manifesto has in no way prepared us. The Democrats are in the *Address* called powerful; they are expected soon to govern Germany, and, when they do so, to make very radical proposals. They may, for instance, want the state to buy the railways and factories, and may even propose progressive taxation. Their proposals, pushed beyond a certain limit, will become direct attacks on private property. The Democrats, it is true, will not want to push them to that limit, let alone beyond it, but the workers may force them to do so. The radicalism of the lower middle class Democrats and their political predominance are predictions that certainly come oddly from one of the authors of *The Communist Manifesto*.

Much more astonishing than the rôle assigned to the Democrats is the advice given to the Communist League and to the workers. The Democrats, if they could have the help of the workers without being subject to unwelcome pressure from them, might . gain power and use it to make considerable reforms; but would do nothing to subvert the established social order, nothing likely to prevent Germany's eventually becoming a fully developed capitalist society. Marx has, in the *Address*, ascribed to the lower middle class an importance that nothing said about them in the *Manifesto* would have led one to expect, but has not suggested that they would, of their own accord, do anything subversive of capitalism, anything that might stand in the way of its future predominance in Germany. On the other hand, he has advised the Communists and the workers to oblige the Democrats, against their will, to make to their allies concessions amounting to direct attacks on private property.

What exactly is the historical significance in Marxian terms of this advice given to the German Communists and workers? How is it to be interpreted by the believer in historical materialism? The fundamental tenet of Marxism is obscure and self-contradictory, but it is in part intelligible, and that part does commit the believer to something. It commits him, among other things, to the belief that 'no social order ever disappears before all the productive forces for which there is room in it have developed'; in other words, it commits him to the belief that capitalism cannot be destroyed until all the technical improvements it allows of have been introduced. In the opinion of Marx, the bourgeois revolution had not yet in 1850 been completed in Germany, which was, he thought, economically and socially more backward than either England or France. What the German Democrats must have been trying to do, if historical materialism is true, was to destroy the last vestiges of a pre-capitalist social order—to destroy either survivals of 'feudalism' or else institutions created during the period of transition from 'feudalism' to capitalism and appropriate to neither social order. But what Marx was advising the German Communists and workers to do was to make use of a bourgeois revolution to oblige the Democrats, under the threat of proletarian violence, to take over the railways and factories without compensating their owners, and to confiscate the estates of the nobles, not for the benefit of capitalist farming, but in order to convert them into state farms; and he was also advising the levy of taxes so onerous that the great private fortunes could not survive them. Marx might not promise success to the Communist League nor to the class for whom the League claimed to speak, but would not have given the advice he did give had he not believed that success was possible.

These things, if only the Communist League and the industrial workers did what Marx told them, might come to pass in the Germany of the eighteen-fifties, a country still partly 'feudal,' where capitalist production, as England already knew it, existed only in a few places. What he said about the power of the lower middle class, and the subordinate though important rôle he ascribed to the workers after the common victory, proves how backward Marx believed Germany to be at the time he wrote *The Address to the Communist League*. And yet it was in this backward

Germany of the mid-nineteenth century that Marx expected a revolution, which, if it achieved what he advised the workers to get from the reluctant Democrats by threat of violence, would prevent for ever the full establishment of German capitalism. For a backward country, where the railways and factories, as well as the great landed estates, are taken over by the state, and where large fortunes are taxed out of existence, is already half-way towards socialism before it has become capitalist.

In *The Address to the Communist League* we have the beginnings of a doctrine that the Bolsheviks were afterwards to make much use of, the doctrine of the 'uninterrupted revolution.'[1] The workers and the Communists are invited, in a still backward country, to take advantage of middle class resistance to autocracy to steal a march on history and use an initially bourgeois revolution to achieve some at least of the 'true' interests of the proletariat. Lenin, in 1905 and still more in 1917, went much further than Marx was advising the German Communists to go in 1850; but the principle behind Lenin's policies and Marx's advice was fundamentally the same. And that principle cannot be well founded if historical materialism is true.

We also find in the *Address* a first account of how the workers should exploit their allies. Marx makes a show of moral indignation against the 'petty' bourgeois, calling them selfish and narrow; but, if we are to believe his own theory about classes, they all pursue their own interests. The workers are invited to co-operate with another class, not for the purpose of helping them, in return for agreed concessions, to get what they want, but to subvert the social order on whose continued existence the survival of that class depends. The Bolsheviks were to profit from this advice also, excepting only that they exploited the peasants instead of the lower middle class.

In 1850 Marx had not yet produced his 'classic formulation' of historical materialism. *The Critique of Political Economy* was not published till 1859; and though Marx had already adumbrated most of the ideas that make up historical materialism, he had not put them together into the form that was to serve as a guide to

[1] Not quite the first beginnings. In the last section of *The Communist Manifesto* we are told that Germany is 'on the eve of a bourgeois revolution' which will be 'but the prelude to an immediately following proletarian revolution.' But these ideas were not developed until Marx took them up again in the *Address*.

all his studies. The original version of the doctrine of 'uninterrupted revolution' was therefore given to the world some nine years before Marx had put his fundamental beliefs about society into what seemed to him good order.

Both *The Communist Manifesto* and *The Address to the Communist League* prove that Marx, in 1848 and for at least two years afterwards, hoped for proletarian revolution in western Europe in the very near future. The comparative ease with which the privileged classes, after the first shocks to their complacent power, reasserted their ascendency soon convinced him that he had been mistaken. Even the most advanced bourgeois countries—not to speak of backward Germany—were still far from ripe for proletarian revolution; and many years must pass before they reached the point of full maturity. It was certainly the disappointments of this revolutionary period that caused Marx and Engels to preach not only discipline but patience to the workers, insisting—against some other socialists—that socialism could come only in the fullness of time. In his classic formulation of historical materialism Marx felt the need to say that 'no social order ever disappears before all the productive forces for which there is room in it have developed'; and this, though he might not know it, was virtually to condemn the advice he gave to the German Communists and workers in 1850.

Though he never formally repudiated it, it was, for good Marxian reasons, advice improperly given. The Germans for whom it was meant never took it; but certain Russians, for whom it was not meant, did take it, with tremendous consequences for their country and the world.

III. THE MARXIAN THEORY OF THE STATE

(i) *The State as an Instrument of Class Oppression*

In *The Communist Manifesto* it is said that 'political power, properly so called, is merely the organized power of one class for oppressing another.' In other words, the state is essentially an instrument of class oppression, so that in a classless society there can be no state. This is the familiar, the classic Marxian description of the state.

Dislike of political power and desire to do without it are almost as old as political theory. There was no need for malcontent intellectuals to write books and pamphlets to persuade the labouring poor that public power and the laws were more favourable to the rich than to themselves. There has been for centuries a strong popular inclination towards anarchy; it has been more than balanced by an even stronger need for security, but has been nevertheless a considerable influence in many societies. Men need the protection of power, and also resent the burdens it imposes; and the poorer they are, the less they need the protection and the more they feel the burdens. It is of the essence of power that it supports rights and enforces obligations;[1] and it is inevitable that it should appear as much oppressive as protective to those who have the fewest rights.

Dislike of the state, though it was strong before the nineteenth century, was not often articulate; it was the congregation of the poor in the great towns, and also their growing confidence in their power by united action to improve their lot, that drew the attention of the educated to their grievances, and stimulated the theories whose main object was their happiness. Socialism and anarchism were plants rooted in the same soil and favoured by the same climate; their roots lay deep in feelings that had been strong for centuries, and their flowering came together.

When they called the state an instrument of class oppression, Marx and Engels were expressing opinions and feelings that many other socialists shared with them. What distinguished them from most of the others was that they could not leave this popular less-than-half-truth to work its effect merely by being often repeated, but felt the need to sustain it by argument, calling in history and sociology to their aid.

The fullest exposition of the Marxian theory of the state is a book called *The Origin of the Family, Private Property and the State*, written by Engels and first published in 1884. It purports to explain how the state arose out of irreconcilable class antagonisms, themselves caused by economic developments. It is a difficult

---

[1] It is a mistake to suppose that power is prior to right and obligation. No man has power unless his right to command is acknowledged by some at least of those who obey him; it is only because they obey him that he has power. All exercise of power is subject to rules; it is in principle regular, and cannot last long or be effective if it is often arbitrary.

book to read, for it is often almost impossible to follow the argument. At the time it was written, Engels had been a 'Marxist' for about forty years; he knew beforehand just what he wanted to prove; he was one of the two acknowledged founders of what already looked like becoming the greatest of all schools of socialism, whose senior founder had only just died. It was perhaps psychologically impossible for Engels to be fair or logical; and since he was by temperament very probably an honest man, he was forced, in his unconscious endeavours to avoid conclusions supported by facts he did not care to deny, into every kind of confusion and obscurity.[1]

The general thesis of Engels's book is that mankind passed through several stages of social organization before the emergence of the patriarchal family, slavery and private property, which in Europe were all three effects of the domestication of animals; that thereafter economic progress and an always more extensive division of labour, enriching some people much more than others and promoting trade between persons belonging to different clans and tribes, caused the breakdown of the old tribal society, substituting for it the state, whose primary function was to facilitate the exploitation of one class by another. The characteristic of the state, as opposed to the tribe and the clan, is that the task of maintaining order inside it devolves on a relatively small group of persons who, as a regularly constituted government, stand apart from the rest of society.

Before considering the arguments used by Engels to support his thesis, it is as well to notice that he did not know what had to be proved before it could be established that the state is essentially an instrument of class oppression. Even if we suppose his arguments good, he offers to prove no more than that the state was created by a privileged class to maintain their collective superiority over the rest of society, and that in all past and present states some class have used political power to exploit another. But this is by no means enough to establish that the state is essentially an

---

[1] His book is treated with the utmost reverence and studied in the greatest detail in the Soviet Union. It would be difficult to find a text better suited to become orthodox; almost anything can be read into it, so that the limits placed on the conclusions that can be drawn by authorized interpreters are few, whereas the errors of interpretation that can plausibly be imputed to their opponents are legion. It is surely no accident that men have mostly been persecuted in the name of unintelligible creeds.

instrument of class oppression. The causes of an institution's growth do not determine its functions; nor would it follow that, if all states were used by some class to oppress another, they would exist only to make this use possible. Engels admitted that an essential characteristic of the state is that the task of maintaining order devolves on a regularly constituted government, on a group of persons whose special business it is to maintain law and order. He never proved that, except where one class exploit another, there is no need for the special services of any such group; he offered to prove only that there had been no such need when mankind lived in tribes and clans. He took it for granted that, if states were first created by privileged classes, and if there had never been a state that did not enable some class to exploit another, it followed that there would be no need for a state where there was no class exploitation. It needs only a moment's thought to see that this assumption is groundless. Neither Engels nor any other Marxist has ever produced good reasons for believing that, in any except the most primitive society, there would, if there were no classes, be no need for a state—that is, for the services of a special hierarchy of persons maintaining order, if necessary by force.

But Engels never even proved what he set out to prove; he never established that the state emerged to make secure the superiority of a privileged class, which owed that superiority in the first place to economic causes. I do not mean merely that the evidence adduced to support his conclusion was sometimes false, but rather that, even if we suppose it true, it does not establish what he thought it did.

Engels believed that before society could be divided into unequal classes, the institution of private property had to emerge; and yet he never gave a satisfactory account of its emergence. He said that the domestication of animals created a new form of wealth. Hitherto, fixed (as contrasted with quickly perishable) wealth had consisted of houses, domestic implements, boats, hunting weapons and other such things, most of which were owned communally by the clan or at least by the large household consisting of several generations living under one roof. But, so Engels would have us believe, 'private property in herds must have developed at a very early stage.' This statement is the first mention in Engels's book[1] of the emergence of private property. It apparently seemed to him so obvious that this new form of wealth required a new form of property that he never troubled to explain why it should do so. Why, if houses, boats and domestic implements could be owned communally without serious inconvenience to the existing economy, could not cattle and sheep be so as well? An historical materialist ought surely to have felt the need to give a plausible answer to this, above all other questions.[2] Whereas Engels simply ignored it, admitting that the new form of wealth at first belonged to the clan, but also insisting that it soon afterwards gave rise to private property.

It is clear, too, that Engels, when he said that private property emerged 'at a very early stage' after men first domesticated animals, did not mean to be taken seriously. He often spoke of the patriarchal great family (he usually called it the gens) as if it were communistic until quite late in its development, though he treated both it and private property as equally effects of the domestication of animals. And in the ninth and last chapter of the book, the reader, by this time thoroughly bewildered by conflicting arguments, finds this confession: 'How and when the herds and flocks were converted from the common property of the tribe or gens into the property of individual heads of families we do not know to this day; but its must have occurred, in the main, at this stage.'[3] To explain the emergence of private property

[1] *Marx Engels, Selected Works,* Moscow, 1950, English edition, Vol. II, p. 195. It is also the first mention of an important economic development affecting the whole structure of society. Engels had already described four important stages in man's economic development, and also four states in the development of the family arising out of changes in the rules governing sexual intercourse; but had said nothing to suggest that these two lines of development were related to one another. Are we therefore to assume that economic determinism began to function only when man first domesticated animals?

[2] Engels—much more plausibly—attributed slavery to the domestication of animals, arguing that men had killed prisoners taken in battle until it became profitable to enslave them and use them to tend their flocks. He also argued that 'mother right' (i.e. tracing descent and inheritance through the female line) gave place to 'father right' and the patriarchal family from the same cause. When flocks and herds became important, wealth outside the house was greater than wealth inside it. But this new wealth was controlled by the men (just as inside the house it was controlled by the women); and being now greater than the old wealth, established the ascendancy of men over women. This curious argument is quite unconvincing. Engels only invented it because he had been misled by one or two contemporary sociologists into believing that the matriarchal family had everywhere preceded the patriarchal, and so felt under an obligation to attribute the substitution of the latter for the former to an economic cause.

[3] *Marx Engels, Selected Works,* Vol. II, p. 281.

from which arose the division of society into classes and thereafter the state, we are offered an argument resting on one of the
most obvious of logical fallacies: *post hoc, ergo propter hoc*. The
truth is that Engels had no idea how private property arose, and
that sometimes he came near to admitting it.

Engels, in the last chapter of his book, made a summary of the
conclusions reached in his accounts of the rise of Athens, Rome
and the western feudal states. The first great social division of
labour, he said, separated the pastoral tribes from the great mass
of the barbarians. The pastoral tribes produced not only more
than the others but a greater variety of goods. Tribe began to
trade with tribe, and eventually, as flocks and herds became private
property, trade between tribes gave place to trade between
individuals. Then came agriculture, and later the smelting of
metal ores other than iron. The division of labour grew yet more
extensive, leading to an always greater use of slaves; until society
was at last divided into two great classes, masters and slaves,
exploiters and exploited. Next came the smelting of iron ore, and
the use of iron implements, which increased the scale of agriculture. Towns arose to serve as centres and places of assembly for
tribes and confederacies of tribes. Wealth increased more quickly
than ever, but it was now the wealth of individuals.

The appearance of towns marked the 'second great social
division of labour,' separating the handicrafts from agriculture.
Slavery, hitherto sporadic, became an essential feature of the
social system. Men were now no longer content merely to barter
their surplus products against one another; they began in increasing numbers to concentrate on production for exchange, growing
or making a much smaller part of what they themselves consumed
and relying on the market for the rest. It was then that precious
metals came into general use as means of exchange.

At this stage of the economic process, the old tribal organization—until then an assembly of equals managing the common
affairs of the tribe or confederacy, either directly or through
elected chiefs—became a military democracy, an organization
for plundering and oppressing neighbouring tribes. This
strengthened the authority of the chiefs, whose office became
hereditary, though the formality of election often survived. In
this way organs that were originally mere instruments of the

popular will became independent of the people and capable of oppressing them.

Later on there arose a class of middlemen or merchants; minted money came into use, and the free sale of land was allowed. It became possible to accumulate, not only cattle, slaves, money and marketable goods, but land as well. The device of the mortgage was invented, and debtors were sometimes reduced to slavery. There emerged a new aristocracy of wealth, either inside the old tribal nobility or outside it and reducing its importance.

By this time trade ignored all tribal boundaries, bringing men, irrespective of the tribes they belonged to, into many kinds of relations with one another. Their economic interests no longer coincided with their tribal interests, and their obligations to one another arising out of trade could not be enforced by tribal authority. It was therefore inevitable that there should arise a new organization, transcending the old tribes and using new methods to maintain its authority. This new organization was the state. Engels said of it that 'it is the admission that society has become entangled in an insoluble contradiction with itself, that it is cleft into irreconcilable antagonisms which it is powerless to dispel. But in order that these antagonisms, classes with conflicting economic interests, might not consume themselves and society in sterile struggle, a power seemingly above society became necessary for the purpose of moderating the conflict, of keeping it within the bounds of 'order'; and this power, arisen out of society, but placing itself above it, and increasingly alienating itself from it, is the state.'[1]

I shall assume for the sake of argument that Engels, in the last chapter of his book, has given us a fair summary of the conclusions reached in previous chapters;[2] and shall seek to establish

[1] *Marx Engels, Selected Works*, Vol. II, p. 289.
[2] My assumption is in fact false. Engels's account of the rise of the Athenian state corresponds roughly—but only very roughly—with the summary offered to the reader in Chapter Nine. His accounts of the emergence of the Roman and western feudal states do not correspond to it, even roughly. In the case of the latter the discrepancy is easily explained and excused, for they arose as a consequence of the invasion of a civilized empire by barbarians. But the Roman state, like the Athenian, emerged directly out of a confederacy of tribes; and it ought, if Engels's summary is fair, to have emerged in much the same way. Not that the summary contains nothing taken from historians' accounts of Roman and even feudal origins, for Engels was quite capable of making a composite picture and then treating it as if it were typical.

no more than that the summary, even if it were true, would not be evidence that the state emerged primarily to maintain the supremacy of one social class over another.

The transformation of the tribal organization into the state began, according to Engels, when offices, hitherto elective, became hereditary; and they became hereditary, not because some already superior and exploiting class contrived that they should, but for military reasons. Until their offices became hereditary, the chief men of the tribe were socially on a level with the others; their social superiority was the effect and not the cause of their offices' becoming hereditary. If we suppose that this superiority made them a class distinct from, and oppressive of, the rest of society, we must then conclude that power made them a superior class and not that class superiority enabled them to get power.

Increasing division of labour and expansion of trade brought men into new kinds of relations with one another, and created obligations that tribal authorities were powerless to enforce; and there therefore arose to meet this need a new kind of authority, more professional, less popular, and more extensive than the old. The expansion of trade, the invention of money, and the free sale of land no doubt created inequalities that had not existed before; but it is surely a false inference to conclude that the new authority arose to maintain these inequalities, to perpetuate the advantage of the more over the less successful. Even if there had been no such inequalities, the new authority would have been as much needed. Moreover, division of labour does not of itself divide society into unequal classes; there is nothing about one man's producing one kind of commodity or service and another's producing another kind that puts them into different classes or makes their interests necessarily hostile. It is much more differences of income and of power that divide society into hostile classes. But these differences arise out of men's rights and obligations, which can profit them nothing if they are not enforced. From which it seems to follow that inequalities of wealth cannot arise from economic causes alone, but from them together with the system of rights and obligations actually enforced. If, then, tribal authority could not enforce the obligations appropriate to the new economy, how were they enforced? By the state? That is the answer that Engels gives us. If that answer is true, the division of society into classes must have been as much the effect as the cause of the state's emergence.[1]

Engel's account in Chapter V of the rise of the Athenian state has a good deal in common with the general summary offered in the last chapter, but there are, even in this case, serious discrepancies. It is admitted, for instance, that Solon's reforms—the greatest social and political revolution in the early history of Athens—though they strengthened the state at the expense of the clan and tribe, were made to protect debtors against creditors and to prevent their enslavement. It is also suggested that the Athenian state arose to defend the property of slave owners in their slaves. But just what slaves did Engels have in mind? Presumably not native freemen reduced to slavery through their debts, for the state was greatly strengthened at the tribe's expense precisely to prevent this kind of enslavement. Were they enslaved prisoners of war and their descendants? But this kind of slavery flourished, so Engels said, long before the state emerged. What, then, caused these slaves to be no longer amenable to such discipline as the tribe could impose? Engels said it was the great increase in their numbers, but never attempted to produce evidence to support his statement. The estimates of the Athenian slave population that he did give relate to the period after the state had emerged.

Engels's account of the origin and primary function of the state suffers from four principal defects: the facts alleged to establish his conclusions about the origins and functions of particular states are often false or doubtful; the general description of the state's origin based on those conclusions is not fairly derived from them; and would not, if it were a true description, prove that the state arose primarily to secure the superiority of one class over another; and moreover, even if it did prove it, it still would not follow that, though some class exploit another in every state, the state is

---

[1] Engels's confusion of thought about this matter is illustrated by a passage in Chapter Four (ibid., Vol. II, p. 239) reading: 'Only one thing was missing: an institution [he means the state] that would not only safeguard the newly acquired property of private individuals against the communistic traditions of the gentile order . . . but would also stamp the gradually developing new forms of acquiring property . . . with the seal of general public recognition.' But how could this new property be acquired unless the new forms of acquiring it were either generally approved or else protected against popular communistic tradition by the power of some group or other smaller than the whole society—i.e. by what Engels would call a state?

primarily an instrument of class oppression. The first of these defects must count the least against him, for much has been learnt since he wrote his book; but the others are effects of bad reasoning. Of the major classics of German Marxism, none is weaker than *The Origin of the Family, Private Property and the State.*

(ii) *The State as a Parasite on Society*

There is another Marxian theory of the state besides the one that treats it as essentially an instrument of class oppression. The best exposition of this other theory is to be found in Marx's *Eighteenth Brumaire of Louis Bonaparte*, first published in New York in 1852, but later revised by the author before the second edition appeared in Hamburg in 1869.[1] It is perhaps the best of Marx's political writings, and its purpose is to 'demonstrate how the class struggle in France created circumstances . . . that made it possible for a grotesque mediocrity to play a hero's part.'

Louis Bonaparte, elected President of France in December 1848, was put into power principally by the peasants, the least 'class-conscious' and organized of all classes, by people of whom Marx says that, in one sense, they form a class and in another do not. 'The great mass of the French nation,' he says,

> is made up by the addition of similar quantities, just as the potatoes in a sack make up a sackful of potatoes. In so far as millions of families live in economic circumstances that distinguish their way of life, interests and culture from those of other classes, they form a class. But in so far as there are only local connexions among these small peasants, and their similar interests beget no unity, no nation-wide union and no political organization, they do not form a class. They are therefore incapable of promoting their class interest on their own behalf.[2] . . . They cannot represent themselves, and must be represented. Their representative must also be their master, an authority set over them, an unlimited governmental power protecting them against all other classes. . . . The political influence of the small peasants therefore finds expression in the executive power subjecting society to itself.

---

[1] I shall be using the English translation of the Hamburg edition, which appears in Vol. I of *Karl Marx and Frederick Engels, Selected Works*, Moscow, 1950.

[2] The distinction made by Marx is between the class and the 'self-conscious' class. A class become 'self-conscious' when they come to know their interests and to organize for their defence.

Louis Napoleon, as Marx and everyone else knew, got power by first taking advantage of middle class and peasant fears of socialism and then disrupting the Conservatives, the 'Party of Order,' the loose coalition of political groups representing men of substantial property. The 'Party of Order,' though it had aristocratic supporters, was a bourgeois organization; the strongest group inside it were the Orleanists, men who represented the great financial, commercial and industrial interests of France. Louis Bonaparte, before he could get absolute power, had to disperse this party; and before he could disperse it, had to use it to shatter the parties and groups to the left of it. He made himself master of France by playing off against one another all the classes and their political organizations. The real source of his strength, if we are to believe the historians and also what Marx wrote in *The Eighteenth Brumaire*, was the active support of the army, the police, the bureaucracy and the church, and the passive support of the peasants. The men of property, landed, commercial and industrial, the petty bourgeois and the proletarians, all the politically organized classes, whose ambitions, complaints and rivalries Marx and Engels, in *The Address to the Communist League*, *The Class Struggles in France* and *Revolution and Counter-Revolution in Germany*, had passed under review as causes of the great events that had recently shaken civilized Europe—all these classes, one after the other, had seen their leaders tricked, silenced and scattered to make way for a 'mountebank,' a classless adventurer, whose only friends were peasants, soldiers, priests, policemen and civil servants. 'The executive power had subjected society to itself.' That, according to Marx, was the significance of the *coup d'état* of December 2nd, 1851, the 'eighteenth Brumaire' of Louis Bonaparte. The executive power is the army, the police and the departments of state, three of the five supports of the new dictator. Of the other two, the peasants (again according to Marx) were a class in only one sense but not in another, and the church was not a class at all. The influence of the peasants was quite negative; they did not control Louis Napoleon's government, which was in no sense their agent. The new ruler of France preserved the old system of property, the system that made possible the exploitation of the workers; he defended the class privileges of the financiers, merchants and industrialists, but he was not their agent. His government, as Marx described it, was quite certainly not a committee for the management of their common affairs.

On December 2nd, 1851 the executive power had 'subjected society to itself.' We could perhaps express the same idea by saying that the French state had conquered society. That state had therefore ceased to be an *instrument* of class oppression. Not that class oppression had for that reason ceased. While the system of property remained what it was, exploitation of one class by another, exploitation as Marx understood it, must continue. But the state, though it still maintained the conditions of this exploitation, which would be impossible without it, was no longer the *instrument* of a class. It had been such an instrument during the July Monarchy; and in *The Class Struggles in France* Marx even tells us what section of the middle class it was then the instrument of. In England, too, the state still was, and had been for centuries, the instrument of some class or other. Whereas in France the executive power had now subjected society to itself. Nor was December 2nd, 1851 the first time it had done so. The great Napoleon, so often called the child of the first revolution, was never the instrument of the bourgeois; though he, too, like his nephew, had the passive support of the peasants, he was not their agent but their master.

December 2nd, said Marx,

> was the victory of Bonaparte over parliament, of the executive over the legislative power. . . . In parliament the nation made its general will the law; that is, it made the law of the ruling class its general will. Before the executive power it [now] renounces all will of its own and surrenders itself to the orders of something alien, of authority. . . . France seems to have escaped the despotism of a class only to fall under the despotism of an individual. The struggle seems to have so ended that all classes, equally powerless and equally mute, fell on their knees before the club. . . . This executive power, with its enormous bureaucratic and military organization, . . . this dreadful parasitic growth, covering the body of French society with a net and choking all its pores, began in the time of the absolute monarchy. . . . The first French revolution, because it had to destroy all local, territorial, urban and provincial autonomies to create the bourgeois unity of the nation, was bound to develop what the absolute monarchy had begun—centralization, and with it the attri-

butes and agents of governmental authority. Napoleon perfected this machinery of the state. The Legitimist and July monarchies added nothing to it except a greater division of labour. . . . Every common interest was immediately cut away from society, set over against it as a higher and general interest, withdrawn from the control of society's members and made the object of governmental activity. . . . All revolutions perfected this machine instead of smashing it. The parties contending for power thought possession of this immense state edifice the chief spoils of the victor.

Lenin greatly admired the passage I have just quoted. It shows, he thought, a great advance on *The Communist Manifesto*, because what was there treated in an abstract manner is here discussed in much greater detail. Marx, according to Lenin, comes in these sentences to a new, precise and practical conclusion: all former revolutions have helped to perfect the state machine, and it now remains to break it.

In a paragraph omitted from the passage just quoted and which ought to be referred to now, Marx spoke of revolution as of a process that is thorough and methodical: 'By December 2nd, 1851 it [revolution] had completed one half of its preparatory work; it is now completing the other. It first perfected the parliamentary power in order to overthrow it. Having done this, it now perfects the executive power, reduces it to its present expression, isolates it, sets it up against itself as the sole target, in order to concentrate all its destructive powers against it. When this second half of the preliminary work is done, Europe will leap out of her chair and cry out in exultation: "Well grubbed, old mole".'

I dare not set myself up for an interpreter of this piece of mysticism and rhetoric. Why need the parliamentary and the executive powers be perfected before they are destroyed? The poets used to say that what is perfect cannot die; and they also said that beauty, which is a kind of perfection, must die. Both thoughts may be moving in their proper places, but neither has anything to do with political theory. What is it that students of politics need take notice of in this part of Marx's argument?

We know that Marx believed that revolutions are phases in the struggle between classes, but he now tells us that their effect is to expand and strengthen the machinery of state. It has been so in France, and the presumption is that it will be so elsewhere. Where parliaments exist, the privileged classes can, at least to some extent, control the executive; they can 'make their law the general will.' But, as society progresses, the power of the executive grows. This is true not only of France but of all countries. Marx, in the mystical passage about the methodical revolution and its works of perfection, was clearly deriving general laws from the experience of France. The executive power, as bourgeois society develops, becomes isolated. In other words, it ceases to be the instrument of society or of any class inside it. The state, continually strengthened by the class struggles, rises at last above all the struggling classes until it dominates the society which gave it birth. The aim of the revolutionary class is to destroy the state, which is a parasitic growth, feeding on its hosts, the classes that together make up the society it dominates.

Now, this is a very different theory of the state from the one put into just one sentence of *The Communist Manifesto*. It may be, as Lenin said, a great improvement on that sentence, but it is not a deduction from historical materialism. Marx was inspired to imagine it by looking at what was happening and had happened in France.[1]

Marx said that France had escaped the yoke of a class only to fall under the yoke of an individual. He explained how this had happened, what supports the despot had found in the nation. He might have gone further; he might have speculated in a general way about the possible consequences of this kind of subjection of society to the state. The government that has risen above the contending classes has power; it controls the army, the police and the civil servants. It can rely on their loyalty so long as it gives them security and sufficient pay. If it finds domestic peace threatened by the hatred of social classes for one another, why should it not work to mitigate that hatred? No doubt, it will be dangerous to make great changes too quickly; no doubt, too, the government and the great officers of state, recruited from the privileged classes, are conservative in temper. But they must have, as servants of the state, their own interests separate from those of the classes they are born into. As Marx himself noticed,

[1] If we ponder what Marx actually said of the various régimes endured by France since the monarchy became absolute in the sixteenth century, we see that he thought it possible for a country to live through a long capitalist era and yet be governed by the economically dominant classes for only a short time.

they are avid of power; they like to make it their business to look after all the common interests of society. To preserve domestic peace is their great and constant interest; and they can only preserve it by balancing the claims of the politically articulate classes against one another.

The French peasants, according to Marx, were getting into debt; their economic position was becoming precarious, and they themselves dissatisfied. Why should not the dictator who had gained so much from their loyalty do something to reward it? Why should he not think it his interest to do so? One change after another made by a powerful dictator and bureaucracy for the sake of domestic peace, a peace which is the condition of their power, can amount in not many years to a great social revolution. Once admit, as Marx has done in *The Eighteenth Brumaire*, that the state is not always an instrument of class oppression, and allow it a certain independence of all classes, and you cannot deny that it may be its interest so to act. The old French monarchy collapsed because it was too weak, too inefficient and too corrupt to do the public business of a nation rapidly growing wealthier and more civilized. It did not collapse because it attempted what Marx said was impossible, because it tried to reconcile the interests of the different classes subject to its rule; it would be nearer the truth to say that it collapsed because it made too feeble an attempt to reconcile them. It was ruined by the lawyers, its creatures; by the tax-gatherers, its servants; and by the nobles, its pensioners. It was ruined by professions and classes as much dependent on it as it was on them. Since that time the French and all other states have grown much stronger. The technical progress that transformed trade and industry, the inventions and innovations that created the capitalist system described by Marx, also multiplied the instruments of power wielded by governments. Why, then, should not these governments use those instruments to increase their hold on society? And how can they better increase it than by trying to keep the peace between the classes subject to them, or, in other words, by reconciling their interests?

In former times, when central governments were still weak, they could maintain their authority only in alliance with the privileged classes, the nobles in the country districts and the merchants in the towns, the men who were strong locally. The privileged classes were better educated, more aware of their interests and more experienced than the others. The old monarchy had to take account of them. But since then, as Marx himself has told us in *The Eighteenth Brumaire*, the state has grown immensely stronger and the less privileged classes better organized, more articulate and less docile. If this more powerful state is not, or need not be, the instrument of any one class, if the same process that strengthens it also gives unity of purpose and political experience to the proletariat and other exploited classes, is it not to be expected that governments, in their own interest, will become bolder, more enterprising and more impartial as between their subjects? When they are unjust, it will be more often for their own and their servants' sake and less often in favour of one class of their subjects against another.

Governments always pretend to be impartial, to be dispensers of an even-handed justice. Even when they are, as they often have been, dominated by the privileged, they still make this pretence. But when governments are not so dominated, when they have only to watch the reactions of the different classes and take account of them according to their strength, it is surely their interest to be as just as they dare in every dispute to which they and their servants are not parties. Why should they, when they are (and Marx said they were) growing stronger and more independent of all classes, tamely watch the proletariat grow in numbers, become better disciplined, more experienced, more resolute to put an end to their misery, even by violence—why should governments watch this process with indifference or attempt the impossible for the sake of the bourgeois? Why should they oppress a vigorous and formidable class to preserve a decadent capitalism? Why should they not, as all governments have done in the past, make concessions to the strong? Why should they, having nothing to gain by it, let it be said by men like Marx that what stands between the ever more powerful working class and the 'justice' they clamour for is an 'isolated and perfected executive power,' a power not even controlled by the bourgeois exploiters?

Not only classes but, according to Marx, all organized groups seek their own interests. Why, then, should the organized groups called governments, when once they have become independent of the social classes, prefer the interests of one of them to the others? Why should they, with great armies and police forces willing to obey them, foolishly commit suicide in a vain attempt to preserve the privileges of a class of capitalists whose numbers are steadily declining? Is it possible that they should do so without knowing what risks they are taking? Could what was so obvious to Marx— the growing power of the proletariat—remain hidden only from them? Or must we suppose them deprived of their reason by some god anxious that Marxian prophecies should come true? We cannot, as we reflect on the last pages of *The Eighteenth Brumaire of Louis Bonaparte*, help asking such questions as these.

(iii) *The Disappearance of the State*

Both the Marxian theories of the state—that it is an instrument of class oppression, and that it is sometimes a parasite superior to all classes—can be used as premises to anarchist conclusions. If the state is essentially an instrument of class oppression, it cannot· exist where there are no classes, and Marxism predicts that eventually there will be none. And if the state is a parasite on the whole of society, it is presumably society's interest to get rid of it.

These two theories of the state are not compatible with one another. If the state is an instrument of class oppression, then anything that rises superior to all classes is not a state. It may, perhaps, be objected that Marx and Engels did not say, and therefore did not mean us to understand, that the state is *essentially* an instrument of class oppression.[1] If, however, this objection is valid, it no longer follows that where there are no classes there can be no state; but this is precisely what Marx and Engels often believed did follow from their assertion about the state, which is evidence that they often thought it *essentially* an instrument of class oppression. On the other hand, if the state is a parasite superior to all classes in society, there is no reason for supposing that when society becomes classless the state will disappear. It may be desirable that it should, but does not follow that it must. Nevertheless, though the two theories are incompatible, they can both be used to support anarchist conclusions.

[1] There is, I believe, little reason to doubt that Marx and Engels, when they called the state an instrument of class oppression, were making an assertion whose predicate partly defined its subject. They spoke of the state, as such, and not of particular states, present or past.

The famous passage about the 'withering away' of the state occurs in the second chapter of the third part of *Anti-Dühring*. It reads:

> As soon as there is no longer any class of society to be held in subjection . . . there is nothing more to be repressed, which would make a special repressive force, a state, necessary. The first act whereby the state really comes forward as the representative of society as a whole—the taking possession of the means of production in the name of society—is also its last independent act as a state. The interference of the state power in social relations becomes superfluous in one sphere after another, and then ceases of itself. The government of persons is replaced by the administration of things and the direction of the processes of production. The state is not abolished, it withers away.

The belief that the state would, or at least ought, to disappear was common to many socialists and communists in the nineteenth century. Some of them believed that it would gradually pass away as men grew more civilized and learnt to do without it; and others that force alone could destroy it. Marx and Engels elaborated upon these simple themes; they believed that existing states would not pass peacefully away but had an inherent tendency to grow always stronger; and this they believed, whether they chose to regard them as instruments of class oppression or as bureaucratic parasites on the whole of society. Existing states must therefore be destroyed; and only the states coming after them—provided they were proletarian—would 'wither away.' It was thus that Marx and Engels, in spite of their strong leaning towards anarchism, set themselves and their disciples apart from the self-styled anarchists, both pacific and revolutionary. It was absurd, they thought, to expect the rulers of non-proletarian states, whether agents of the bourgeois or bureaucrats more or less independent of all classes, to prepare the way for their own disappearance; only a government responsible to a politically mature working class would undertake any such task. On the other hand, to destroy the bourgeois state and put nothing in its place, even while society was being reorganized and made classless, was to play into the hands of the reactionaries.

When the proletarian state has withered away, 'the government of persons is replaced by the administration of things.' What exactly does this curious distinction amount to? Only human beings can give and receive instructions of the kind meant by the words 'government' and 'administration' and to administer 'things' is only to give human beings instructions how to use them.

The distinction between government and administration was first made by Saint-Simon, who, when he contrasted government with administration, meant by it the giving of compulsory orders to people who need not understand why those orders are given and have only to obey them. In a society where there is government, the people obey because they must, or else from mere habit; and their governors, knowing the people's ignorance and able to use force against them, rule mostly in their own and much less in the general interest. Government, thought Saint-Simon, is good while it lasts. It is better to have an orderly society governed mainly in the interest of the few than to have disorder. But there comes a time, with the progress of science and industry, when men cease to be ignorant and need no longer be driven. They come to understand that it is useful to them to receive instructions from those who know; that, since no one can know everything, everyone must freely and in his own interest often do what he is told; and that, in every sphere, decisions must be taken for the many by the few whose knowledge and ability are the greatest. When men have progressed that far they will co-operate willingly, allowing to every man authority according to his talents, experience and good will. It will then no longer be necessary to use force to ensure obedience—or rather force will be so seldom used that those who use it will have a quite subordinate position in society.[1] They will be not rulers but policemen. They will no longer be able to use force to make themselves the masters and exploiters of mankind.

That, according to Saint-Simon, is the difference between government and administration; and therefore, as society

[1] As a matter of fact, force always has been used by subordinates. It was thought barbarous in Peter the Great that he executed some of his victims with his own hands. When discipline is maintained in an army by flogging, it is subordinates who flog subordinates. It is not the persons who use force but those who command its use who have power. Whether force is used much or little, those who use it are always subordinates. The difference between government and administration, if it is to be worth making, must lie entirely in the use of force by the one and not the other; it must not depend on the position in society of those who use force.

progresses, the former must give way to the latter. He compared the progress of society with the maintenance of discipline in French schools. In the primary school the teacher is also the dispenser of discipline; in the secondary school or lycée the professor teaches only and leaves discipline to underlings. So it must be, he thought, with society; as it grows older it must outgrow the need for government. Knowledge accumulates, industry is perfected, and mankind have at last the material and spiritual means of living together in free societies where violence and exploitation are as useless as they are immoral. There will be no armies then, no aristocracy and no police, but only a classless society of unequal men, whose inequalities are recognized and respected by them all because they rest on superiorities of talent, experience and good will—on qualities known to be useful to the whole of society but possessed more abundantly by some men than by others.

It was no doubt Saint-Simon's distinction that Engels had in mind when he wrote the passage quoted two pages back. He, too, believed that the time would soon come when men would be civilized and reasonable enough to do without government. But, though he agreed with Saint-Simon on the main point, he also differed from him in several respects. He believed, in the first place, that proletarian violence could bring to power a government willing to create conditions that would quickly make government unnecessary; whereas Saint-Simon believed that violent revolution is itself evidence that society is not yet fit to do without government, and also that no government born of violence can be trusted to prepare its own demise.

Saint-Simon cared nothing for democracy, believing that the administration of society should be the business of experts owing their authority, not to popular election, but to professional competence attested by their peers. He believed that their authority would, in a civilized and educated community, be accepted by everyone; for administration is a matter for experts, and sensible people know that, unless they are experts themselves, they cannot pass judgment on the expertise of others. Here again, Engels differed from Saint-Simon. He wanted the workers to manage their own affairs, and when they could not do so directly, to delegate their authority to persons closely responsible to themselves. It was characteristic of the state, not only that it used force to ensure obedience, but also that its authority was concentrated in the hands of a group of persons set apart from the rest of society. The state would not have 'withered away' until two conditions were fulfilled: until force was no longer used, and until the people, in fact and not merely in name, directed the common affairs of society. We do not know, because Engels never told us, how he thought this could be contrived in the enormously complex industrial societies of the modern world; but we do know at least this much: that he believed that the public business of the classless society would be more simply and better managed by all its members than by any government that has existed since the state emerged.

IV. THE DICTATORSHIP OF THE PROLETARIAT

Marxism teaches that the workers must destroy the bourgeois state and then create another to make the reforms that lead to the classless society. They must establish a *dictatorship of the proletariat*.

The bourgeois state is the instrument of a privileged class; and it is their control of it that makes that class strong. They use the army, the law courts and the police to defend their factories, their land, their commercial and financial institutions. The workers, if they attempt to take over these things without first capturing the state, are bound to fail. They may have local successes, but the wealthy and privileged will then use the armed forces and all the advantages of a highly centralized administration to defeat the workers. The ruling class, though they own and control their estates and businesses separately, are politically organized in the state. The state is the real key to their power. Until it has fallen to the workers, they cannot force their class enemies out of their privileged positions in society. The workers must therefore unite politically to gain a political victory; and only after they have gained it can they make the social and economic reforms without which society cannot become classless. The anarchists say: Dispossess the wealthy of their wealth and the state will fall to pieces. The Marxists reply: You cannot dispossess them until you have captured their state; and, while you are dispossessing them, you, too, must be a governing class, using the power of the state to destroy the last traces of the old system. When those traces have been destroyed, there will be no classes left; and the state, being merely an instrument of class oppression, will disappear. First the proletarian revolution and the capture of the state by the workers; then the dictatorship of the proletariat; and lastly, the classless society: that is the Marxian order of advance towards communism and anarchy, towards justice, equality and perfect freedom.

The *dictatorship of the proletariat* is a phrase seldom used by Marx and Engels. We cannot find it in *The Communist Manifesto*, though it is already said there that the workers must first capture the state and then use it to destroy the privileges of the old ruling class, and that only when they have destroyed them will the state disappear. But in *The Critique of the Gotha Programme*, written in 1875,[1] Marx says that ' between capitalist and communist society lies the period of the revolutionary transformation of the one into the other. There corresponds to it a period of political transition, when the state can be nothing but the *revolutionary dictatorship of the proletariat.*' He says nothing more about it; and we cannot discover from anything said in that *Critique* how the proletarian state, which is the dictatorship of the proletariat, is supposed to differ from any other state, except that it has a different ruling class intent on reforms that will make society classless and the state disappear. Of its internal organization we learn nothing. Is it, in itself, the same sort of instrument as other states? Or is it merely used by different people and for a different purpose?

If we want answers to these questions, we must look at another pamphlet, *The Civil War in France*, written by Marx in 1871. In an introduction to a later edition of this pamphlet, Engels wrote: ' Of late, the Social-Democratic philistine has once again been filled with wholesome terror at the words, Dictatorship of the Proletariat. Well and good, gentlemen, do you want to know what this dictatorship looks like? Look at the Paris Commune. That was the Dictatorship of the Proletariat.' We had better not take Engel's advice quite literally; we had better not look too closely at the Paris Commune but rather at what Marx said about it. That,

---

[1] Though Marx used the phrase 'dictatorship of the proletariat' long before this pamphlet was written, it is from it and from *The Civil War in France* (though it does not contain the phrase) that we get our best clues to what he may have meant by it.

if anything, will give us a clue to what he thought proletarian government would be like.

The Paris Commune lasted only a few weeks, it was disliked by most Frenchmen outside the capital, it achieved little and was put down more brutally by the French government than any other working class revolt in the West. It can hardly be called an heroic failure, for failure implies purpose, and of purpose the Communards had almost none. It was certainly not the proletarian revolution predicted by Marx, the revolution made by the immense majority become at last politically educated and disciplined. It was an outburst of anger, a gesture of defiance made by exasperated men, men worn out by a long siege and disgusted with the 'cowardice' and pacifism of the French provinces, men conscious of the sacrifices they had made, and determined to be insulted by no one. It was from the beginning a hopeless venture. But it was a proletarian revolt, whose leaders ruled Paris for two months.

They actually ruled, the true representatives of the proletariat, for the first time in modern history. They did not know what they wanted, except to resist the government of France; they were most of them not even socialists or at least not interested in bringing socialism to Paris. But they were the rulers of a proletarian society, and this was enough to make their government important to Marx. Every class, he thought, has its appropriate methods of government. Feudal Europe had political institutions very different from the bourgeois governments of the nineteenth century. So, too, the workers, when they seize power, must create their own instruments of government. They had seized power in Paris; and though their hold on it was precarious and temporary, they had it long enough to create something like a system of government. 'The workers,' Marx says in *The Civil War in France*, 'cannot simply lay hold of the ready-made machinery of the state and use it for their own purposes.' Why cannot they so use it? Marx gives no simple answer, but there is a conclusion to be drawn from his general argument. That machinery was created to serve the purposes of another class or else to maintain effective government during a period of transition from the predominance of one class to that of another. It was created for purposes that are not and cannot be proletarian, and is therefore an instrument not for the workers' use. 'Imperialism,' says Marx (meaning in this context the system of government of Napoleon III), 'is both the most prostitute and the ultimate form of the state power which nascent middle class society began to elaborate as a means to its own emancipation from feudalism, and which mature bourgeois society eventually transformed into a means for the enslavement of labour by capital. The direct opposite of the empire was the Commune.'

Whatever else he may have thought about proletarian government, Marx was certain of one thing: that it would be more democratic, more respectful of freedom and more humane than any of the older governments. We must not allow the hard things said by Marx of liberalism and bourgeois democracy to deceive us. He attacked them because he thought them shams; he denounced them for not being what they pretended to be; but what they would have been, had they been what they pretended, he never denounced. His ideal, and Engels' also, is expressed in the last paragraph of the second section of *The Communist Manifesto*: it is 'an association in which the free development of each is the condition of the free development of all.' This ideal was Rousseau's, Godwin's, Saint-Simon's, Owen's and Fourier's; it was even the ideal of Kant; indeed, it was the ideal of nearly all the European liberals, radicals and socialists of the last century. In the political sphere, it means either anarchy or extreme democracy. It is therefore to be expected that Marx should praise the Commune for being truly what other governments had only pretended to be—a democracy.

Let us look at his description of it:

> The Commune was made up of the municipal councillors, chosen by universal suffrage in the different wards of the town, responsible and revocable at short term. Most of its members were working men or acknowledged representatives of the working class. The Commune was to be a working, not a parliamentary, body, executive and legislative at the same time. The police, instead of continuing the agents of the central government, were at once deprived of their political attributes and made the responsible and at all times revocable agents of the Commune. So, too, were the officials in all other branches of the administration. Public service by everyone from members of the Commune downwards had to be done at workmen's wages. . . .

Having abolished the standing army and the police, the Commune was anxious to break the power of spiritual repression, the priestly power, by disestablishing and disendowing all the churches. . . . All educational institutions were made free to the people, and also free from all interference from church and state. . . . Officers of justice were to be deprived of the sham independence that masked their abject subservience to every succeeding government. . . . Like all other public servants, magistrates and judges were to be elected, responsible and revocable.

There can be no doubt about it: Marx conceived of proletarian government as being, from the very beginning, more truly democratic and liberal than anything known to bourgeois Europe; and by democracy and freedom he meant what we all mean by them, he meant government truly responsible to the governed, and as scrupulous a regard for the rights of the individual as is compatible with the existence of government. The 'dictatorship of the proletariat,' as Marx and Engels conceived it, is proletarian democracy; it is in very truth what bourgeois democracy merely pretends to be. It is class government only in the sense that, according to Marx and Engels, all government is class government; but it is less oppressive than any earlier kind of government, and can afford to be so because it is truly popular.

Marx really exerted himself to make the best of the Commune. There was, nevertheless, one thing about it he could not like, and that was its hostility to strong central government. Marx preached the eventual disappearance of proletarian government, but he wanted it, while it lasted, to be strong, He had, no doubt, in *The Eighteenth Brumaire of Louis Bonaparte*, denounced the bureaucratic and over-mighty state, which must, he said, be destroyed by the proletariat; but neither there nor elsewhere, though he had not explained how the workers should organize their state, had he wanted them to break it up into a weak national association of strong local authorities. Both he and Engels had made it clear, by their opposition to the German federalists in 1848 and afterwards, that in their opinion all modern government should, while it lasts, be adequately strong at the centre. In their articles on *Revolution and Counter-Revolution in Germany*, they had attacked the Frankfurt Assembly for not creating the strong central government so badly needed by a revolutionary power. Marx had also praised the Jacobins of the great French revolution for setting aside the first revolutionary constitution, which had given wide powers to elected local authorities, and for establishing a centralized administration more watchful, enterprising and efficient than the old monarchy. Both he and Engels had repeatedly attacked Proudhon, the inveterate enemy of the centralized state, who had encouraged the workers to mistrust all distant authority.

Now, the Communards of 1871 were much more the disciples of Proudhon than of Marx. The influence of Proudhon upon them was nowhere more evident than in their project of a Constitution for France. The Communards wanted to convert the whole country into a loose federation of communes, the ultimate power resting, not with the central government, but with the individual communes, whose mere agent that government was to be. The Communards, like Marx, wanted to destroy the bureaucratic and parasitic state machine built up by Napoleon III and his predecessors, but, unlike Marx, they did not want to put in its place, even for a short time, a strong national proletarian government.

Marx, faced with the project of a Communal Constitution for France, could do either of two things: he could denounce it or he could explain it away. He chose the second alternative. He pretended that the Communards did not intend what was in fact their plain intention; he pretended that they had no wish to destroy the unity of a great nation, which he himself thought indispensable if proletarian government were to perform its 'historic task,' if it were to prepare the way for the disappearance of all government.

We cannot know for certain why Marx decided to praise and to describe falsely what he should have condemned. He was writing to defend the Communards against their many enemies, and was defending them when they were almost universally abused. He was perhaps loth to admit anything that might seem to justify their enemies, anything that could be used by them as evidence of the political immaturity of the Paris workers and their chosen leaders. Those workers were, after all, the oldest and most experienced revolutionary proletariat in the world. If they thought their draft constitution necessary to the security of their class, Marx was reluctant to prove them wrong. Moreover, it was also Marx's opinion that every class, when it gets power, discovers for itself the governmental institutions best suited to its class rule.

He could not deny, and never for a moment thought of denying, that the Paris Commune was a proletarian government; indeed, he was enthusiastically in its favour because, for all its faults, it was, in his opinion, the first really proletarian government the world had ever seen. It was, no doubt, an imperfect specimen, but it was a specimen of something new. He wanted to justify it, to prove its unique quality, to show that the event called disastrous by all civilized Europe was not a calamity, an interval of horrid barbarism, but an imperfect image of something nobler than had yet existed among men.

'It is generally the fate,' said Marx,

> of completely new historical creations to be mistaken for counter-parts of older and even defunct forms of social life to which they may bear a certain likeness. Thus, this new Commune which breaks the modern state power has been mistaken for a reproduction of the mediaeval Communes. . . . The Communal Constitution [by which Marx meant the draft Constitution prepared for France by the Paris Commune] has been mistaken for an attempt to break up into a federation of small states. . . that unity of great nations which, though originally created by political force, has now become a powerful coefficient of social production. The hostility of the Com-mune to the state power has been mistaken for an exaggerated form of the old struggle against over-centralization. . . . The Communal Constitution would have restored to society all the forces hitherto absorbed by the state parasite feeding upon it and clogging its free movement. By this one act it would have started the regeneration of France. . . . The very existence of the Commune implied . . . local municipal liberty, but no longer as a check to the now superseded state power . . . It was essentially a working class government, the product of the struggle between the class that produces and the class that appropriates, the political form at last discovered whereby to achieve the economic emancipation of labour.

The passage just quoted deserves close scrutiny. It reveals Marx in difficulties and vainly struggling to get out of them; it brings us right up against a dilemma that Marxists somehow con-trive not to see even when they stare it in the face. Marx calls the 'unity of great nations' a 'powerful coefficient of social pro-duction,' meaning, presumably, that the massive production we are accustomed to in the modern world cannot be efficient if the largest administrative units are broken up into many small ones.

He means, in other words, that neither the capitalist nor the socialist system of production can function properly if countries the size of France are converted into loose federations of communes. Modern industrialism requires the centralized administration of large societies. That is undoubtedly part of what Marx is saying; and yet, at the same time, he, the denouncer of the parasitic bureaucratic state used by Louis Napoleon to establish his dictatorship, cannot help sympathizing with the Communards. Their argument was simple: the large state is, they said, inevitably bureaucratic, and the power of parliaments, however democratically elected, is inevitably small. Democracy in the large modern centralized state is quite impossible; the attempt to establish it leads merely to imposture and hypocrisy. Proletarian government is true democracy; and it therefore follows that, if true democracy is impossible in the large state, there cannot be proletarian government until that state is broken up into a host of sovereign communes.

That was the argument of the Communards, and Marx, the author of *The Eighteenth Brumaire of Louis Bonaparte,* could not but feel the force of it. He was willing to admit that what both he and the Proudhonists called the parasitic and bureaucratic state must be destroyed; on the other hand, he would not allow that the 'unity of a great state,' as he called it, should be broken up and a 'loose federation of communes' put in its place. What exactly did he want? Did he think it possible to have centralized administration without a large body of professional administrators? What is bureaucracy except centralized administration on a large scale? And how can there be centralized administration if units as small as the French communes have sovereign power? Marx, of course, could not answer these questions; indeed, it was his interest that his readers should not put them, and that is why, in the passage quoted, he used language to confuse both himself and them. He wanted the best of both worlds: to be still the enemy of Proudhon and the advocate of centralized administration, and yet to praise the Commune, established by the disciples of Proudhon and Blanqui, as if it were an event confirming the truth of Marxism.

In one sense, though not in a sense that ought to satisfy students of political theory, Marx did get the best of both worlds. If the Commune had a spiritual father, that father was Proudhon;

the Communards of 1871 were a good deal truer to his principles than the Bolsheviks were to Marx's in 1917 and after. Yet the fact remains that the Marxists have somehow contrived to appropriate the Commune; they have treated it as the precursor of their own revolutions and have affected to learn from it. Marx's account of the Commune has been as much admired as any of his writings. What to us looks like hedging seems to the true Marxist an almost divine tactic enabling the philosopher of genius to penetrate to the very heart of reality. Marx, when he described the Communal Constitution, hinted at many things and was explicit about none, and so gave the impression that he was getting the best of every argument, both his own and his opponents'. Hence the 'richness' of his thought, which seems to his admirers the surest proof of his genius. Precision is a kind of poverty; if we say exactly what we mean, we cannot be supposed to have said more; but if we adopt another method, there is no end to the wisdom that can be attributed to us.

Until the Russian revolutions of 1905 and 1917 Marx's account of the Commune was not very important. Engels had said that the Commune was a dictatorship of the proletariat; and it was therefore permissible to suppose that Marx's description of the Commune, whether true or false, was a clue to what he meant by that otherwise highly ambiguous phrase 'the dictatorship of the proletariat.' Marx believed at times in the imminence of a proletarian revolution, whereas Engels, after Marx's death, had perforce to set this belief a little behind him, for he lived far into one of the most peaceful and prosperous epochs of European history. Western Marxists soon ceased to believe that they would live long enough to see the proletarian revolution; and they felt that, if there were any part of Marx's doctrine they could afford to neglect, it was his difficult and obscure pronouncements about the proletarian state.

The case with the Russian Marxists, as soon as Lenin thrust his way to prominence among them, was different. Not only they, but even the Tsar's ministers, knew that there was in Russia an almost permanent danger of violent revolution. Men might differ about the nature of that revolution, but they nearly all either expected or feared it. The Russian Marxists had therefore to ask themselves whether that revolution would be purely bourgeois or whether their own intervention in it might not serve to transform it into something at least in part proletarian. If it were possible to give it a proletarian twist or even to transform it fairly quickly into a proletarian revolution properly so called, Russia might soon become, in whole or in part, a workers' state. Should that happen, what governmental institutions would suit her best? The Russian Marxists who hoped for a rapid transformation of a bourgeois into a proletarian revolution soon became interested in every sentence from Marx and Engels which could be plausibly treated as a clue to their opinions about the character of the future proletarian state. Seeing that most of these sentences are ambiguous, there was plenty of room for different interpretations; but the interpretations had to fall within the limits of what could plausibly be read into the two masters' words. Marx's account of the Commune was immensely interesting to the Bolsheviks; indeed, together with *The Address to the Communist League* and *The Critique of the Gotha Programme*, it was one of the three texts they could most often quote to justify themselves in their disputes with the other Marxists. Lenin decided that the Bolsheviks, like the Communards, must attempt to destroy the parasitic and bureaucratic state; he also decided that the Russian equivalent of the French Commune was the soviet, and that therefore the proletarian state must be based on the soviets. On the other hand, since, unlike Marx, he had to have, together with the soviets—and not merely in theory but also in practice—a strong central government, he used the Bolshevik Party to overcome the anarchy with which a loose federation of soviets inevitably threatened Russia. How he did this, and how he justified it, we shall see later.

V. ENGELS AND REFORMISM

Marx died a revolutionary socialist and Engels never ceased to be one. When Marx died, Engels kept all the opinions they had previously shared; he was a good steward, losing nothing and letting nothing decay. But he also added to the store left in his keeping, and some of his additions are important. In 1895 he wrote an introduction to a new edition of Marx's *Class Struggles in France*, an introduction published by Wilhelm Liebknecht in the German Social-Democratic paper *Vorwärts*. The Bolsheviks have since rebuked Liebknecht for omitting a number of passages where Engels spoke of future insurrections. The editor of *Vorwärts* was, they say, trying to make it look as if Engels had ceased to be a revolutionary. The rebuke is not unjust, and Engels himself made it long before the Bolsheviks. But it could, I think, be said, even more justly, that the sentences left out are unnecessary to the general argument, and that they were probably put in by Engels to avoid the impression which the article must create without them, the impression that he was no longer greatly interested in revolution because he thought the German workers were using other and more effective methods.

Marx and he had been mistaken, Engels said, in believing that a successful proletarian revolution was possible in the turbulent years after February 1848. 'History has proved us, and all who thought like us, wrong. It has made it clear that the state of economic development on the Continent at that time was not, by a long way, ripe for the removal of capitalist production; it has proved this by the economic revolution which, since 1848, has gripped the whole Continent, causing large-scale industry to take root for the first time in France, Austria, Hungary, Poland and, more recently, in Russia, and making Germany an industrial country of the first rank.'

Men believed, after the defeat of the Commune, that the militant proletariat were done for, buried in the fall of Paris, and yet the workers, especially in Germany, were now better organized than they had been and better aware of their class interests. They were winning electoral victories; they were using the liberties permitted by the Reich to multiply and consolidate their strength. But governments, too, were stronger than they had been. Their soldiers used more powerful guns and better rifles, and what Engels called the 'classic period of street fighting' was over. Even during that classic period, the victories of the insurgents had been more moral than military; they had won because the troops would not obey the orders given them, or because commanders had lost their heads, or because frightened governments had not dared do what they could easily have done. Since that time, the workers had learned to make use of the votes given them, and the class struggle had entered a new phase.

'And so it happened that the bourgeoisie and the government came to fear the legal much more than the illegal action of the workers.' Germany was setting the good example, other countries following after.

> In France, where for over a hundred years the ground was undermined by revolution after revolution, where there is not a single party that has not had a hand in conspiracies, insurrections and revolutionary activity of every kind; in France, where the government is therefore less sure of the army and conditions generally are much more favourable than in Germany for an insurrectionary *coup de main*—even in France the Socialists are learning that they can gain no lasting victory unless they first win over the great mass of the people, i.e., in their case, the peasants. There, too, it is recognized that the slow work of propaganda and parliamentary activity are the immediate tasks of the Party.

A little later in his argument Engels appealed to the 'irony of history.' What could this irony be? The unexpected happening of what Marx and Engels had never predicted? Had 'history' got loose from the great channel prepared for her course by destiny? Had she broken the bonds of historical materialism?

> The irony of world history turns everything upside down. We, the 'revolutionaries,' the 'rebels,' we are thriving far better on legal than on illegal methods of revolt. The parties of order . . . are perishing under the legal conditions created by themselves. They cry in despair with Odilon Barrot *la légalité nous tue*, legality is the death of us; while we, under this legality, get firm muscles and rosy cheeks, and look like living for ever. It we are not mad enough to let ourselves be driven into street fighting to please them, there is nothing left for them to do except to break through this legality so fatal to them.

What an extraordinary statement from the pen of a Marxist! From the pen of a man who was not a latter-day disciple, learning the doctrine in a debased form from incompetent masters, but one of the two authors of the creed! If what Engels here says is true, the 'economic basis' of capitalist society must somehow have produced a 'political superstructure' more favourable to the exploited than the exploiting class! We are told that, if Europe moves as Germany is already moving, the political victory of the proletariat is inevitable and there need be no revolution. Violence will be necessary only if the middle class parties first resort to it, only if the ruling class attempt to destroy the political order of bourgeois society, the 'legality' so fatal to themselves. What is it, then, that the 'irony of history' has turned upside down? Engels called it 'everything,' but at that moment his usual modesty must have forsaken him; for there was nothing turned upside down except a theory about history, a theory invented, with his help, by an old friend who had died twelve years earlier. Engels admired the 'irony of history,' and the sight of it gave him pleasure. That pleasure was like a man's delight at the beauty of a fire, a delight the purer because he does not know that the house which is burning down is his own. Engels was a good honest German, made happy and careless by philosophy.

Chapter Eight

THE DECAY OF GERMAN MARXISM

MARXISM is a philosophy born in the West before the democratic age. In the year that *Capital* was published—and by that time Marx and Engels had elaborated most of their characteristic doctrines—England was still an oligarchy, France was ruled by Napoleon III, and Germany dominated by Bismarck. Four years after the publication of *Capital* there happened in Paris the greatest working class revolt of the nineteenth century, the Commune of 1871. Marx called it the first proletarian revolution, and thought it the initial act in the long drama which was to be the socialist revolution of the West. From 1789 to 1794, the workers of Paris had, he thought, been the dupes and instruments of bourgeois revolutionaries; in 1830 they had become a little more independent but still subordinate to their middle-class friends; in 1848 they had been bold and tenacious enough to extort concessions from their allies; but it was not till 1871 that they had at last been strong enough to make a revolution on their own and to establish, though only for a few weeks, a real proletarian government. The Commune of 1871 seemed to Marx proof so strong that only the blind could ignore it that the workers of the West had become much more revolutionary, independent and politically experienced than they had been in 1848. When Marx died in 1883, the Commune had receded only twelve years into history, and he had therefore little reason to revise his opinion and acknowledge that the workers in the West, far from growing more revolutionary, were fast becoming reformist. The Commune had failed, and its failure had for the time being discouraged the working class, but Marx thought they would soon recover and be the stronger for their memories of the Commune.

But France became a democracy in 1871 and has remained one ever since; and with the coming of that democracy there ended the long series of French revolutions that so greatly impressed Marx. England became a democracy more slowly, but perhaps also more surely, than France; and even Germany and Italy tried to look like democracies for several decades before they became what they looked like. There is no harm done if these European democracies and the similar polities of North America and Australasia are called 'bourgeois,' for the educated classes in them are certainly much more powerful than in proportion to their numbers. They are bourgeois democracies, but they are also political systems giving the workers greater opportunities than they have ever enjoyed in any other part of the world. Even the two world wars, which Marxists call 'imperialist,' have either left the workers better off than they found them, or have impoverished them less than other classes. Bourgeois democracy in the New World, in England and France, and perhaps also in Italy, is much less bourgeois and much more proletarian in 1950 than in 1900.

Engels, who survived Marx by twelve years, lived long enough to see the German Social-Democratic Party grow in numbers and discipline until it could at last hope to win within a generation a majority in the Reichstag. He understood that new conditions had created new opportunities for the workers, but was too close to his revolutionary past and too faithful to Marx's memory to be able to abandon or revise his early doctrines. Therefore, when he died, the Marxism he bequeathed to the German Social-Democrats was still a revolutionary creed, and the German Social-Democratic leaders still thought it their duty to defend that Marxism against its reformist critics. It was, after all, a German doctrine, and was also more complete and better provided with arguments than any other brand of socialism. It was an intellectual capital amassed by Marx and Engels over a period of nearly fifty years, and therefore not to be lightly abandoned.

Marxism never was, and could not be, the creed of the German workers; it was too many-sided and too difficult to understand for that. But it had become the doctrine of their political leaders; they defended and applied it as lawyers do the law, carrying some of it in their heads, looking up in the scriptures what their memories could not hold, and putting whatever interpretations on it best suited their momentary circumstances. It had taken them a long time to commit themselves to it. The three most important German leaders, Lassalle, Bebel and Liebknecht, had learnt a great deal from Marx; but Lassalle, the most popular of them, had never been a Marxist, and the other two, though they were disciples, had at first only a small following. In 1875, eleven years after Lassalle's death, his followers joined the group of Bebel and Liebknecht to form the first considerable socialist party in Europe. It was a party greatly influenced by Marxism, but was not, until many years later, properly Marxist. Its first programme, established at Gotha, was severely criticized by Marx in one of his most famous pamphlets. Not until 1891, at a conference held in Erfurt, did the party adopt a wholly Marxist programme. From 1891 until 1914 the leaders of the German Social-Democratic Party were true Marxists; they were as much committed to Marxism and as eager to defend it as practical politicians could well be.

Generals, when they lead their armies in the early campaigns of a new war, are often guided by theories whose merits they learned to appreciate towards the end of the last war—when those theories were still useful, though destined not to remain so much longer. Practical men are often too busy to do much thinking, and are usually slow learners; they acquire great skill in the management of men and the conduct of affairs, but can use that skill effectively only while their environment remains pretty much what they have always been accustomed to. They make do with ready-made theories and opinions, and will not abandon them unless they have to. Politicians are, in this respect, very like generals; they are, of course, leaders and therefore cannot be content with the simple ignorance of lesser men; they must have theories and opinions, but, having once made their store, they do not easily change them. So it was with the leaders of the German Social-Democratic Party; they had acquired their Marxism painfully and put a great value on it. It did not occur to most of them that Europe, when Marx and Engels were young, was a very different place from what it had since become; that what the inventors of Marxism, at the age when they were most impressionable, had seen and tried to explain, either existed no longer or else was so greatly changed that their explanations had ceased to be plausible.

Politicians live closer to the intellectual world than generals do and are more easily disturbed by it. The German Social-Democratic leaders were not left in quiet possession of their theory, but had to defend it against attack. They had to protect it from people who were also socialists, who had considerable influence in the party and wanted to rid it of doctrines which, in their opinion, had been proved false since Marx's time. Bernstein, the principal heretic officially condemned by the party, wanted—so he said—not to repudiate but to revise Marxism; and so he and those who thought like him came to be known as Revisionists. Bernstein thought Marxism would do better without its Hegelian background; he believed that recent advances in economic theory made it impossible to hold any longer to the labour theory of value; he had doubts about the 'materialist conception' of history; he thought the coming of socialism desirable but perhaps not inevitable; he could see no evidence of the impoverishment of the working class which Marx had predicted; and he said that bourgeois liberal society had created many things worth preserving. This was revision so drastic that it could hardly be distinguished from repudiation. The party had only recently taken to adopting resolutions and programmes which committed it fully to Marxism, and it was not to be expected that the leaders would lightly throw away what they had not long since, and after considerable hesitation, taken full possession of. They decided to abide by their Marxism, and at two Party Conventions, in Hanover (1899) and in Dresden (1903), they condemned Revisionism. The principal defenders of Marxist orthodoxy were Bebel and Kautsky. They and a few others like them really cared about Marxism, but the great majority of the leaders, especially in the Trade Unions, were not much interested in what the quarrel was about; what mattered to them was the maintenance of discipline inside the party, and they took, in this purely theoretical matter, whatever lead was given them by the majority of the intellectuals. Being good party men, they knew that mischief makers are always a minority and must sometimes be rebuked and even punished.

It has been said that Bernstein often misunderstood Marx and that much of his criticism is therefore worthless. To say this is to divert attention from what really matters. Everyone who has read Marx has often misunderstood him, for when a man writes as he

did there are often several different and equally plausible interpretations to be put on his words. If we think we have good reason
for preferring one interpretation to the others, we must believe
that anyone who chooses one of the others has mistaken Marx's
meaning. Bernstein must have sometimes misunderstood Marx,
since God alone can know for certain what a man meant by
ambiguous statements made a long time ago. Human memory
is fallible, and the man himself whose meaning is in question,
could, were he alive to do it, give no more than an opinion slightly
more probable than other people's. How often and to what extent
Bernstein misunderstood Marx does not greatly matter; it is more
important to discover how much truth there was in what he was
saying about socialism, bourgeois society and the working class.
It ought, in any case, to have seemed more important to the
German Social-Democratic leaders, for they were practical men
and politicians who had more to gain by understanding their
contemporary world than by establishing exactly what Marx had
meant many years before.

The leaders of the German Social-Democratic Party had only
to look around them to discover that western Europe was already
much more like what Bernstein described than like what he
(rightly or wrongly) said that Marx had predicted it would become. The workers were not growing poorer but richer; they
were better housed, fed, clothed and educated than they had ever
been, and there was not the least reason to believe that their lessen-
ing poverty was distasteful either to the government or to their
capitalist employers. Germany had an efficient and devoted
civil service, and most of her governments believed that nothing
would better preserve the peace of society than a steady improvement in the lot of the working class. The greater the industrialization of Germany, the larger the size of individual concerns and the
greater the divorce between ownership and control of industry.
It was not true that increasingly fierce competition was driving
the capitalists to exploit the workers more ruthlessly; on the contrary, capitalists had never before been so mild and so understanding of the workers' needs.

The largest concerns were already so vast that they were often
managed, not by entrepreneurs who had sunk all their capital in
them, but by hierarchies of salaried officials who had at least as

much in common with the workers as with the shareholders who took the profits. Three classes of people had already become much more important than they had been when Marx and Engels were devising their fundamental theories, and they all three had interests different from those of the entrepreneur-capitalists of the mid-nineteenth century. They were the civil servants, the salaried officials in private industry, and the small shareholders. The civil servants were powerful but not wealthy, they had a strict code of loyalty to their profession and of faithful service to the state, and they had not much sympathy with the people who had recently grown rich in commerce and industry; they wanted the state to be strong and healthy, and their attitude to every class in society was governed by that wish. The salaried officials in private industry often cared more for efficiency than for distributing profits among shareholders; the concerns they managed were large, producing a considerable part of the total national output, and could not be operated efficiently except by men who had long-term policies and understood something of the workings of the capitalist economy. This new class of salaried managers were, for the most part, better educated and less ruthless than the old capitalists, and had a greater sense of responsibility both to society and to their employees. The millions of small shareholders had nothing to do with the management of industry, and all they cared about was getting a safe return on their money. They were as willing to invest in government securities as in private industry. Two of these three classes, the civil servants and the salaried managers in private industry, were among the most powerful in the state; they no doubt did not like socialism because they had been taught to mistrust and misunderstand it, but they certainly had no class interests incompatible with it.

In the political sphere, there was even more to learn unfavourable to Marxism. The German Social Democrats had taken almost no notice of *The Address to the Communist League*; it had been untimely advice when it was given, and there had been no later occasion when they could take it. They had preferred the teaching of *The Communist Manifesto*—that the proletariat would capture the state when they had become the most numerous class in society, conscious of their interests and prepared for the political struggle against their oppressors. They had been encouraged by

Engels to devote their energies to building up a vast working
class political movement, organized, disciplined, and inspired by a
single comprehensive social theory, the 'scientific socialism' invented by Marx and himself. The German Social-Democrats were
Marxists because they thought three things supremely important:
the solidarity of the entire working class in the political struggle
against the capitalist exploiters, preparation for a proletarian
revolution which could not succeed until the 'objective conditions' of its success had arisen, and loyalty to a social theory which
must guide in a general way the activities of the working class
party. They believed that loyalty to the theory would serve to
keep the class united, and that therefore every attack upon it must
tend to destroy the class solidarity essential to success. They
believed that their devotion to the Marxian theory was one of
their great political advantages; they had been encouraged in this
belief by Engels himself, who had compared them favourably
with others. The leaders of the working class in England were
notoriously indifferent to theory, and had not yet succeeded in
creating an effective proletarian political party; while in France
they were either divided into separate parties by their loyalty to
rival theories or else did not believe in political action. The
German Social-Democratic Party was, at the time of the Bernstein
controversy, much the largest of its kind in the world; its leaders
were proud of it and of themselves; they thought they knew the
causes of that greatness and were eager to preserve them. It is
one of the many advantages of Marxism that it teaches that ad-
herence to itself is for the proletariat an important condition of
political success.

These considerations—and others like them—caused the
German Social-Democratic Party to condemn Bernstein's
Revisionism.[1] And yet there was, in the political sphere, much
to be learnt from Bernstein. The workers had a party of their
own, growing steadily larger and more powerful; they were better
off and better educated than ever before; concession after conces-

---

[1] The condemnation of Revisionism did not, of course, altogether destroy its
influence. There continued to be Revisionists in the German Social-Democratic
Party, and their opinions affected many more people than were willing to call themselves Revisionists. Nevertheless, those opinions had been officially condemned;
the party, as a whole, was still supposed to be Marxist, and Marxism to be a revolutionary theory.

sion was being made to them without anyone's appearing much put out. Engels had noticed before he died that the legal order created by the bourgeois was more favourable to the workers than to themselves. The observation was true, and was also important evidence against Marxism. But Engels had not been a Revisionist; he had seldom bothered, when he acquired new opinions, to discard the old ones incompatible with them. Though he had come to believe that the legal order established by the bourgeois was more favourable to the workers than to themselves, he had saved the revolutionary character of Marxism by suggesting that the bourgeois would in the end attack that order and so precipitate a crisis. The working class would not, after all, come into their inheritance without a fight, and force would once again be the midwife of a new society. Why this should be Engels had not sufficiently explained; he had been content to make a true observation about the legal order, and then, in spite of the obvious implications of what he had observed, to maintain the revolutionary character of Marxism. Bernstein was less prudent and more consistent; he saw that the workers stood to gain a great deal even in capitalist society, he saw also that society was changing fast, and he did not pretend to know that what would emerge from these changes would be socialism.

Marx was never less a realist than when he imagined the working class, after they had become the politically organized majority in capitalist society, having to use force to take control of the state. The political organization of the great majority is no small undertaking, and in the modern state is possible only when the law allows it. Modern governments control great armies and police forces, and have so many instruments of coercion at their disposal that illegal organizations cannot grow large and formidable except with their connivance. No revolution has ever been made by an organized majority. When the minority who govern exploit the majority and fear them, they do not allow them to organize politically; and when, on the other hand, they allow them to do so, it is a sign that they do not fear them. Once the majority are politically organized they are articulate and powerful; concessions are made to them, and they soon acquire as great an interest as anyone else in social peace and stable government. The more peacefully concessions are made, the more easily they are repeated. The rich are not suddenly impoverished nor the poor suddenly enriched, but there is a smooth transition to a greater equality or else to kinds of inequality unknown before. The education and political organization of 'the masses,' required to make them, not docile servants of the ruling minority, but an independent class knowing their own interests and how to promote them, is possible only in a free society; and that society must be free for some considerable time, for it takes many years to educate and organize the masses. On the other hand, no society can long remain free unless some notice is taken of the just claims of every considerable and articulate group inside it. When classes, hitherto ignorant and exploited, acquire a little education, they soon make claims on society which can only be met at the expense of their exploiters; and, if those claims are not met, that society cannot long remain free. The conception of the politically organized majority making a revolution 'in the fullness of time'— a conception which has often been praised as a sign of Marx's superiority to the other socialist thinkers of the nineteenth century—is one of the weakest parts of his theory. It is weak, not because there is anything confused about it, but because it is not sensible. Its weakness was perhaps less easily seen when Marx was alive; but in Bernstein's day it ought to have been obvious even to the leaders of the greatest Marxist party in the world.

The German Social-Democrats were not altogether unaware that the day might never come when it would be incumbent upon them to make a proletarian revolution. They always behaved like reformists though they sometimes thought it their duty to remind other people that their party believed in revolution. In the days of opposition to the Kaiser's governments there was no need for them to practise their creed and therefore no danger in proclaiming it. They were revolutionaries engaged, in a calm and orderly fashion, in preparing the working class for a revolution not due to happen in their generation. The great fault of the early French socialists had been impatience; the lesson of their many failures had been learnt by their German successors, who thought no virtue more necessary to revolutionaries than patience. They were patient but not lazy; they worked hard to increase their party's strength in the Reichstag, and every election rewarded their efforts.

They could well afford to bide their time, for that time was pleasant; and they were, next after the Kaiser, the most applauded men in Germany.

These happy days ended when war came in 1914, and the predicament of the German Social-Democrats was quickly and unpleasantly transformed. Their leaders were, after all, no ordinary adherents of a revolutionary creed, paying lip-service to it on the special occasions when such service was required; they were its chosen guardians and most learned exponents. Marxism was a German doctrine, and their party, so proud of being the largest of its kind in all the world, was German and Marxist too. They had not long since condemned Bernstein for presuming to adapt that doctrine to circumstances unforeseen by its authors. It had been easy for them, then, to insist on the revolutionary character of their movement, for the theory supposed to inspire them did not require that they should make a revolution for many years to come. They were not to make it till capitalist society was 'ripe' for it; and of that ripeness they were to be the sole judges. Only men learned in Marxism could decide when the time had come for revolution, could discover whether or not the 'objective conditions' of its success existed.

But Marxism is as much internationalist as revolutionary; it teaches that the working classes of different nations have more interests in common than the different classes of the same nation, that war is an effect of the 'fundamental contradictions' of capitalism, and that the workers must not allow themselves to be driven like lambs to the slaughter by bourgeois governments. It might need learned Marxists to decide when the time had come to make a proletarian revolution, but nothing could be plainer than the duty of Marxian socialists in a war between capitalist states. That duty the leaders of the German Social-Democratic Party did not do.

They were not just carried away by their patriotism. When they voted in the Reichstag for the war credits, they did what the great majority of their supporters expected them to do. The German workers, like nearly everyone else in Germany, believed in August 1914 that their country was the victim of an aggression inspired by Russian imperialism and French desire for revenge. No doubt, the German Social-Democratic leaders were patriots; like other men they felt, when their country was in danger, the pull of loyalties whose strength perhaps surprised them. Nevertheless, it was not merely their own patriotism which caused them to behave as they did; had they thought of doing otherwise, had they voted against the war credits, their action would have been condemned by nine-tenths of the people in whose name they claimed to speak in the Reichstag. The German workers, like most other Germans, did not want and yet also wanted war; they would very willingly have done without it, but, believing that war had been forced on their country, they were ready to fight.

The German Social-Democratic Party did not suffer immediately as a result of the war. Even before 1914 it had had inside it two dissentient minorities; a group of Revisionists on the Right, who, believing that capitalism would survive for a long time to come, wanted the party to abandon its policy of permanent opposition to bourgeois governments and to secure for the working class, through their representatives in the Reichstag, a proper share of political power; and a group on the Left who expected a great war in the near future leading to proletarian revolution in one capitalist country after another. The majority of the Party leaders had rejected both extremes; they had refused either to collaborate with bourgeois governments or to prepare for revolution in the near future. When war broke out, they did not join the Imperial government but ceased to oppose it. They voted for the war credits and thereafter carefully avoided any action that might embarrass the government's conduct of the war; and by so doing sided, perhaps without knowing it, with the extreme Right of the Party against the extreme Left. For the time being, this move to the right, though it involved a manifest repudiation of one of the cardinal tenets of Marxism, did not disturb their consciences. The war was young and the nation ardent for war; the Social-Democratic leaders shared the people's mood and found comfort in it. Whatever they had done, they had not betrayed their country; and that was the only treachery which at that time seemed unpardonable.

As the months passed and the number of the dead grew, patriotism wore thin and was no longer the exciting and comfortable emotion it had been when the first battles were fought. By 1916 many of the workers were already beginning to tire of the war,

and there arose on the left of the Social-Democratic Party a considerable body of people who wanted to stop the war, demanding
a negotiated peace, without indemnities and without annexations.
These people, led by Dittmann and Haase, eventually broke away
from the main body of the Social-Democrats to form the Independent Social-Democratic Party. The breach was lasting, though
the original cause of it soon disappeared, as all the Social-Democrats, long before the war ended, came to want a negotiated peace.
This change of policy was not the effect of a new enthusiasm; it
was not made by confident men in an emotional hour when it
seemed both easy and heroic to sacrifice everything to a great
cause. It was made, on the contrary, by disillusioned men who
no longer felt the emotions which had made it possible for them
in August 1914 to forget that for Marxists the interests of the
working class the world over ought to come before patriotism.

They were not only disillusioned; they were also, and for obvious reasons, anxious and conscience-stricken. If the war was a
mistake and must quickly be brought to an end, why had they
done what they had done in August 1914? They could, no doubt,
make excuses; they could explain how the situation had changed
since 1914; they could argue that it would have been dangerous to
allow Germany's enemies to attack her without making a stand in
her defence. All the combatant nations had sustained great losses,
and it seemed that neither the Central Powers nor their enemies
could win the war except at the cost of perhaps even greater
sacrifices. It would surely be best to put an end to the war quickly
before Europe was completely ruined by it. These excuses and
arguments were not bad, but were not altogether convincing.
The governments at war had so whipped up the loyalties and hatreds
of their peoples that they were no longer persuadable even by the
best pacifist arguments; and, in any case, it was only too easy to
accuse the Social-Democratic leaders of faintheartedness. They
had cried out with the loudest patriots in August 1914. Why had
they since changed their minds? They must either have been
hypocrites when the war began, hiding their true feelings while
it was dangerous to show them, or else they were now behaving
like men of little courage. So long as the Imperial government
felt that there was a chance of Germany's winning the war, there
was nothing the Social-Democratic leaders could do to persuade

them to make peace immediately. On the other hand the great majority of the Social-Democratic deputies in the Reichstag and of the Trade Union officials, though they now considered themselves opponents of the government, were not willing to take the drastic action which might have made it impossible for Germany to continue the war. What they wanted was a freely negotiated peace without indemnities and without annexations; they did not want to put Germany in a position where she would have to make peace on whatever terms her enemies might choose to force upon her. Their position was uncomfortable and undignified; if the Imperial government chose not to listen to them—and it did so choose—there was nothing they could do to make their influence felt. They had proved in August 1914 that they were not good Marxists, and were now proving themselves indifferent patriots.

Their position was made yet more uncomfortable by the behaviour of Lenin. A number of Marxist groups opposed to the war had held two congresses in Switzerland, one at Zimmerwald in September 1915 and the other at Kienthal in February 1916, and it had been resolved at the latter congress that the groups taking part in it should use all possible means to bring about immediate peace. These extremist groups then broke away from the socialist parties of their respective countries, and thereafter kept in fairly close touch with one another. They did not at the time create a new international socialist organization, but it was in their ranks that the Communist International, when at last it was created, found its first recruits. Though it got its name several years later, what we nowadays call Communism was born at Kienthal, at a congress dominated by Lenin, who had been opposed to the war from the beginning but who also believed that it would so exhaust the capitalist powers and exasperate the workers that an international proletarian revolution must result from it. In 1916 it still seemed likely that that revolution would begin in the West, that the lead would be given, not by the Bolsheviks, but by western Marxists who had remained true to Marxism or had returned to it after the patriotic diversion of 1914. Lenin's task, as he then saw it, was, not so much to take the initiative in starting the world proletarian revolution in Russia, as to use whatever influence he had to induce other Marxists, perhaps better placed than he was, to take it, while he prepared the Bolsheviks for what would be their duty in Russia when the world revolution began.

Not all the Independent Social-Democrats in Germany, when their group broke away from the parent party, agreed with Lenin. Most of them wanted no more than immediate peace, and had no intention whatever of exploiting the war-weariness of the people to bring proletarian revolution to Germany. When the main body of the socialist leaders, the Majority Socialists, gave up supporting the war and in their turn demanded immediate peace, there was really nothing to separate them from most of the Independent Socialists except personal rivalries and memories of old quarrels. Only the Spartacus League, led by Rosa Luxemburg and Karl Liebknecht, really believed that the war would end in proletarian revolution and strove to ensure that it did. The Spartacists joined the Independent Social-Democratic Party but remained a separate group inside it. When the war ended in 1918, Germany had therefore, three socialist parties, of which only one—and that much the smallest—was revolutionary. At the elections in January 1919, the Majority Socialists polled eleven million votes, and the Independents two million. The Spartacists, who still belonged in name to the Independent Social-Democratic Party, did not on that occasion go separately to the polls, but at later elections which they contested as a separate group they never polled more than some two hundred thousand votes.

Nevertheless, though the partisans of proletarian revolution were always few, Lenin's behaviour had a great and unfortunate influence on the German Marxist leaders. His repeated condemnations of the 'imperialist war' reminded them of the duty they had not done in August 1914; they had, he told them, betrayed the cause of the proletariat by supporting the kind of war that all Marxists ought to oppose. Though they could rely on the votes of many millions of workers, though their party was still much larger than any other socialist party in the world, the German leaders could not, especially after November 1917, be indifferent to the insults of Lenin. They could not deny that Marx had always said that the proletarian movement must transcend national frontiers, that the workers must be taught to prefer the interest of their class to the national aspirations of their separate countries and to recognize patriotism for what it was—an emotion made use of by oppressors to keep the oppressed docile. The books, whose authority neither Lenin nor the German Social-Democrats had liked to see questioned before 1914, pronounced, on this issue, for him and against them. The fact was undeniable, and it was not the less obvious because the German Social-Democratic Party was immense and the Bolshevik faction small. Lenin's reproaches and insults were already disturbing tender Marxist consciences in Germany before the Bolshevik revolution—before the event that made the man who insulted them the most powerful Marxist in the world.

Marxism—and nobody could honestly deny it—was a brand of revolutionary socialism. The German Social-Democratic Party, only a few years before the outbreak of war, had solemnly re-affirmed the revolutionary character of their creed; and yet now, towards the end of a war which was straining capitalism to the breaking-point, the German socialist leaders, except for a few, were doing nothing to hasten the coming of revolution. On the other hand, in Russia a mere handful of Bolsheviks had taken power in the name of Marx and of the proletariat. The Bolsheviks could be accused of acting prematurely, of attempting what could not (if Marxism were true) succeed in Russia. This accusation could be and was made by the German socialists, but it was less impres-sive than the insults of Lenin. The reproaches of men who dare not to men who dare are not as disturbing as the insults hurled at the timid by the bold. Besides, the Bolsheviks were saying that they had only anticipated in their part of the world a revolution for which capitalist society, taken as a whole, was already ripe. Let the better educated, better disciplined and much more numer-ous German workers only follow the example of their Russian comrades, and the Bolshevik revolution would be justified; for it would then become what it ought to be—the prelude to more im-portant happenings elsewhere. It was impossible that the German Social-Democratic leaders should not be upset by Lenin. They could not dismiss him for a rude and fanatical leader of an alien and insignificant sect; he had always been an erudite and ardent Marxist, and had had, even before the Bolshevik revolution, a considerable influence on the extreme Left of their party; and now he and his thousands had already done what they and their millions had not even the intention of attempting. He was calling upon them to follow his example and abusing them for not doing so.

The collapse of Imperial Germany left the Social-Democratic Party stronger than any other in the country, but its leaders were no longer the confident men they had been before 1914. They did not know what use to make of their power. Though their own followers were nearly fifty times as many, they were yet afraid of the Spartacists, who, few though they might be, were already as numerous in Germany as the Bolsheviks had been in Russia in November 1917. The leaders of the Majority Socialists distrusted the councils established in the army and the factories just before and after the signing of the armistice, because they thought them too much like the Russian soviets; and this distrust kept them apart from the Independent Socialists. Ebert, Scheidemann and Noske, the leaders of the Majority Socialists, did not understand how it was that the Bolsheviks had been able to seize power in 1917, and therefore feared that what Lenin had done in Russia might be done in Germany by the Spartacus League. They were apparently not convinced that the existence of their own great party, the respect for order of an educated and disciplined people, the size and political organization of a still prosperous and confident middle class, the vigilance and efficiency of a civil service, police force and judiciary accustomed to do their duty promptly, and the conservatism of the peasants, of whom the poorest were better-to-do than most of the kulaks in Russia, put in the way of the Spartacists impediments unknown to the Bolsheviks. The Majority Socialists, had they but known it, had little to fear from Lenin or from his friends in Germany. They could safely have done much more than they did to satisfy the workers and to consolidate their own power; and, had they been bolder, they would very quickly have come to terms with the Independents. As it was, their fears and uneasy consciences made them timid and confused; they even thought it necessary to appeal to what remained of the old Imperial army for help against the revolutionaries. Their indecision, their too frequent reliance on the assistance of reactionaries, and also the humiliation by the victorious allies of the Germany they governed, soon discredited them in the eyes of their own people.

These causes, together with inflation, brought to birth and

hastened the growth of two new parties in Germany, the Communists and the National Socialists. Their constitutions and methods prove that both parties were formed on the model of the Bolsheviks; they were parties of a kind never before seen in Europe. Their avowed purpose was to make use of democratic institutions to destroy democracy, and their peculiar method, deliberately to exacerbate class and party hatreds, and to make open or secret entry into whatever organizations and professions would best serve them in the struggle for power. Though the two parties were rivals and used the same methods, the victory of the Nazis over the German Communists was easily won, partly because the Nazis were not controlled from abroad and partly because they could afford to be more unscrupulous than it was yet possible for Marxists to be in a country where Marx's theories were still well-known and freely discussed. Of the men who have profited from Lenin's example none has had a more spectacular career than Adolf Hitler.

An encumbrance that the German Social-Democratic leaders did not recognize, and therefore could not get rid of, was their too great respect for Marxism. If they had not made so much of it before 1914, if they had not been so active in its defence, if they had not so officiously proclaimed its truth even when that truth seemed most doubtful, they would not have been so much embarrassed when circumstances obliged them to behave like the prudent, gentle and patriotic men they really were. Engels had said that their love of theory was one of the great advantages of the German Social-Democrats, but it proved in the end more harmful than profitable to them. They would have done well to follow the lead of Bernstein, for, had they done so, they might have become resolute Revisionists and not remained irresolute Marxists. They would, no doubt, have been bitterly attacked by the extremists in their own party, and by Lenin too, but would at least have known their own minds. They would not have found themselves in the precarious position of men whose loyalties and instincts do not accord with their explicit beliefs, and who are both too intelligent not to notice the discord and too honest not to be made uneasy by it. They were not fanatics; they could not do just what they wanted with their consciences, nor could they get free of the prejudice in favour of consistency which is so remarkable in western Europeans. They could never have used Marxism as the Bolsheviks used it; they had neither the ruthlessness nor the lack of intellectual scruples needed for the successful defence of an apparently rigid orthodoxy in a changing world.

Rosa Luxemburg, one of the Spartacist leaders, said that, after 1914, the German Social-Democratic Party became a 'stinking corpse.' It became a corpse, apparently, because it ceased to be a revolutionary organization, and it stank because its leaders had betrayed their Marxist faith. This insult gave great pleasure to Lenin who often repeated it; and yet it ought not to have been difficult for him to understand how foolish and misplaced it really was. He knew that the German Social-Democratic Party was in 1914 the largest in the world, he knew that the workers belonging to it were as well educated as any members of their class anywhere, and he knew also that Marxism had nowhere been preached so long and so ably as in Germany. There, if anywhere, was a politically organized, massive and educated proletariat, which had been exposed for a quarter of a century (and parts of it for much longer) to Marxist indoctrination. It ought therefore, if Marxism were true, to have become by 1918, after a disastrous war, the proletariat not only best able, but also most willing, to make a revolution. It is, according to Marx, Engels and Lenin, the true interest of the working class to adopt some such theory as Marxism; and as soon as a class know their interest, they follow it. The ideology best suited to the interest of a class may not be invented by members of the class, but as soon as that ideology, whatever its origin, is brought to the class, it quickly, unless its progress is impeded by reactionary governments, makes its way among them; and it does so precisely because it 'corresponds' to what the Marxists call their 'objective interests.' Now, if Marxism is true, the 'objective interests' of the German proletariat must have been determined by the progress of capitalist society as Marx described it; and, since Marxism was preached to the German workers almost without let or hindrance for twenty-five years before 1918, they should by that time have become ardent revolutionary socialists. The First World War had, according to Lenin, strained the German capitalist economy to breaking-point, and military defeat had quite discredited the old ruling class. How, then, could the leaders of German Social-Democracy have contrived to betray Marxism?

How could they even have dared attempt such treachery? Would they not merely, had they attempted it, have played into the hands of the extremists by flouting the will of the great majority of German workers? And why, in any case, should they have wanted to flout it? They were powerful and important only because they were the acknowledged leaders of the proletariat. Would they have risked losing that position, and with it the chance of ruling Germany, merely to become the 'lackeys of the bourgeoisie'—and lackeys without power or honour or even great material rewards?

We are often more blinded by theory when we pass judgment on other people's actions than on our own. As we shall see later, Lenin did not mind taking the greatest liberties with Marxism whenever it suited him to do so, but he expected the German Social-Democrats to be much more literal and pedantic in their application of the theory in Germany. His Marxism, though it did not prevent his making what most Marxists would have called a 'premature' revolution in Russia, did prevent his understanding the German situation. Four years of war had not really strained the German capitalist economy to 'the breaking-point,' but had only modified it and left it as efficient as before; the German workers, though they were glad to see the war ended, were almost as peaceful and orderly as they had been before 1914; and the only friends of violence, apart from the Spartacists (most of whom were more given to praising revolution than to making it), were retired army officers who resented their own diminished importance in a defeated and plebeian Germany. The German Social-Democratic leaders made no revolution after the war because the workers on whose support they depended had no intention they should—as they very plainly showed at the elections held in November 1918. Moreover, to have attempted revolution would, even had the workers wanted it, have been mere folly, for the Allies would certainly have intervened to stop it. It mattered much more to them what happened in the centre of Europe, in a country easily accessible to their armies and which had recently proved itself strong enough to wage war for years on two fronts against several of the greatest Powers, than what happened in far-away, impoverished and barbarian Russia.

Lenin did not know it, but the Marxian theory of revolution

had proved very exactly false. It was precisely because the German workers were numerous, well educated and politically organized, that they had no intention of making a revolution; they had gained too much without it and they stood to gain much more. Though they were the most 'indoctrinated' of all the world's workers, Marxism had made only a slight impression on them; they had, in spite of it, sense enough to see that revolution could only ruin their country and themselves with it. It was precisely because the conditions that Marx thought necessary for a successful proletarian revolution did exist in Germany that there was no desire to make it; and it was also because they did not exist in Russia that Lenin was able to seize power in the name of Marx and the proletariat.

PART TWO

RUSSIAN COMMUNISM

Chapter Nine

RUSSIA AND THE BOLSHEVIK REVOLUTION

I T is wasted labour to describe the inconsistencies of the ambitious and to show what little respect fanatics have for the creeds they make use of to impose their wills on quieter men. The Bolsheviks have done what they pleased with Marxism, and what they have pleased to do has not improved its quality as a social theory. Passing from German to Russian Marxism, we leave the horses and come to the mules. The Russian doctrines, though they have moved men to action in many countries, have been—from the intellectual point of view—sterile and unprofitable; they have done nothing to help us understand social and political matters better than we could before. It would be as foolish to attempt making a coherent theory out of them as to build a house of sand. They are in sober truth beyond criticism, and interesting only as historical and psychological events.

But, as such, they are interesting and ought to be explained. How was it possible that able men should come to believe what we now call Communism? Part of the answer to that question lies in Russian history. For the Bolsheviks, though illogical, were not arbitrary in their operations upon Marxism; they distorted it to meet their needs, which were only to some extent effects of their ambition. They had to make their way as revolutionary socialists in Russia, a country unlike most others and with a peculiar history of its own. Bolshevik additions to and distortions of Marxian doctrine were made to justify policies adopted to take advantage of Russian conditions. Unless we know something of what kind of country Russia was when Marxism was introduced into it, and also of the circumstances that enabled the Bolsheviks to make their successful bid for power, we cannot understand how Russian Communism came to differ from German Marxism.

More particularly, we must know something of the peasants and their attitude to the landowners and other classes; of the Russian state and the causes that prevented its dealing effectively with the problems created by the introduction of foreign techniques and ideologies into a still primitive country; of the social theories that flourished before the coming of Marxism; of the circumstances that caused the quarrel between Bolsheviks and Mensheviks; of the effects of war and the opportunities it gave to the Tsar's enemies; and of Lenin's tactics during the summer and early autumn of 1917. Unless we know how the Bolsheviks got power, we cannot understand what difficulties faced them afterwards, forcing them upon courses that made Russia something quite different from what even they had expected. The Bolsheviks were one-eyed men leading the blind, but Argus himself could not have been more confident that nothing escaped his vision.

I. PEASANTS AND LANDLORDS

Serfdom came to Russia much later than to western Europe and was not abolished until 1861. In the fifteenth century, which is the last that belongs to what the West calls the Middle Ages, most Russian peasants were still free; there were some slaves among them and rather more serfs, but the majority of the peasants were not tied to the soil. They had taxes to pay, and for the assessment and payment of them every group of so many villages and hamlets were collectively responsible; but the peasant, his obligations fulfilled, was free to move from one part of the country to another. The transformation of the various kinds of peasants, of whom only a few had been slaves and serfs, into the two broad categories of bonded serfs and state peasants began in the sixteenth century. It was then, too, that Muscovy became a strong military Power, eager to strengthen her hold over her subjects, because by so doing she would be better provided with money and soldiers, and therefore more formidable to her neighbours. Thus in Russia autocracy and serfdom increased together at a time when in western Europe, as the centralizing royal power grew stronger, serfdom either disappeared or became milder.

By the eighteenth century, nearly all the peasants in Russia were either bonded serfs or state peasants. The former lived on the private estates of noblemen,[1] to whose jurisdiction they were subject in most things, and to whom they owed at least three days' labour in the week; the latter had a rather greater though limited power of self-government in their village communities, but paid rent for their holdings and also heavy taxes. All the peasants, the private serfs and those attached to state lands, were liable to military service; they did not all do it, but those who did might well be away with the colours for half their adult lives.

The growth of the state power and of serfdom had not only increased the peasants' dependence on the nobles and the government; it had also bound them more closely to their comrades in the village communes. These peasant communities, controlled by the landowners on the private estates and by officials on the state lands, had to see to it that their members carried out their many obligations. They also, in many parts of Russia though not in all, from time to time redistributed the land among the peasant households. This practice was apparently unknown before the sixteenth century, but from that time onwards spread over the greater part of European Russia until, just before the emancipation of 1861, it affected about three-quarters of the peasants. The power of the peasant communes and the widespread practice of redistribution caused many nineteenth-century socialists to believe that a kind of primitive communism had survived among the Russian peasants. The belief was mistaken, for there is no record of the redistribution of land before the rise of the Muscovite autocracy and the loss of peasant liberties in the sixteenth century.

The Muscovite rulers had imposed heavy burdens on both landowners and peasants; their state was autocratic and military; they expected all their subjects to spend a great part of their lives in its service. But in the eighteenth century the privileges and exemptions of the nobles were increased while the burdens put on the peasants were made heavier. Peter the Great subjected the peasants, but not the landlords or priests, to a poll-tax; Peter III published in 1762 an edict exempting the nobles from compulsory

---

[1] By 'noblemen' I mean all landowners. It is true that in the nineteenth century persons who were not accounted noble bought landed estates, but until then nearly all landowners were noble.

service in the army and the administration;[1] and in 1767 the bonded serfs were deprived of their last rights of appeal against the tyranny of their masters. As the Russian historians put it, the nobles were emancipated a hundred years before their serfs. It was in the eighteenth century, too, that the peasants on the state lands were first obliged to pay rent for their holdings; that many of them were pressed into service in the mines and factories established by Peter the Great; that the peasants on noble estates in the Ukraine had their two days' servile labour increased to three; that Catherine and Paul made to their favourites presents of land so extensive that over a million state peasants were reduced to serfdom; and that the masters were given the right to decide which of their serfs should go to the army for twenty-five years' service with the colours. The eighteenth century, which brought European manners and refinements to the nobles, saw the peasants reduced to conditions worse than any they had known before; and their two most brutal oppressors were Peter and Catherine, the most famous among Russian Princes, who between them made their country one of the three or four Great Powers of the world.

The Russians have never been a docile people, and the great majority of them, the peasants, bitterly resented the servitude imposed upon them. Some fled into the wild steppe country recently liberated from the Tartars, where they were out of reach of the nobles and the ordinary state administration. They formed free communities of peasants there, admitting some sort of allegiance to the Tsar but not directly controlled by his officers. The first refugees, the older Cossacks, settled in areas so remote that they were quite cut off from the peasants left behind in the more thickly populated and regularly administered parts of Russia; but the ones who fled later, and had perforce to settle in areas nearer the frontiers of officialdom and serfdom, had close and con- tinuous contact with the peasants. They were the beggar Cossacks who took a leading part in stirring the peasants up against their masters. In the seventeenth and eighteenth centuries, there were five great peasant revolts in what is now called European Russia, four in provinces already subject to the Tsar, and the other in 1648 in the Ukraine while it was still Polish. The last and the most

---

[1] They mostly continued to go into the army or the state service, but were no longer obliged to do so.

famous of these revolts happened in Catherine's time; it broke out in 1773 and was not put down completely until 1775. Its leader, Pugachov, was a Cossack, and among his followers were not only Cossacks and bonded serfs but also state peasants doing forced labour in the mines and factories established by Peter the Great and his successors. These revolts were great indeed, and the areas affected by them larger than most European countries. In the nineteenth century the Tsars at last made terms with all the Cossacks, who became their allies in the southern border regions, and the serfs lost their one support in the free world. There were no more great servile revolts, but there was perpetual restlessness and frequent defiance of authority. The Russian peasants believed that all the land had once been theirs, and that they had since been wrongfully deprived of it together with their freedom and happiness.

The emancipation of 1861 did little to improve relations between the peasants and their former masters. The nobles were heavily in debt and many believed that they could make their estates pay only if they farmed them in the western manner, hiring free labour. Serfdom had been good enough when the nobles had rather simpler tastes and expected to produce most of what they needed on their own estates; but as they grew more civilized they acquired more needs that could only be satisfied by purchases made in the towns. They could increase their money incomes only by selling the produce of their estates on the market, and they soon learned how inefficient their agricultural methods were. The serfs were emancipated, not only from liberal motives, but also because their servility was no longer thought profitable by their masters; there were better ways of using them than exacting day-labour from them.

The edict of emancipation allotted to the peasant households whatever land they held at the time it was passed, and left to the masters their personal domains. The landowners were supposed to be compensated by their former serfs only for the land they lost and not for the labour, but redemption prices were often so fixed that it looked as if the landowners were also being compensated for the labour. The peasants did not purchase their land outright, not having the means to do so; the government paid the landowners for it, and arranged to be repaid by the communes over a period of forty-nine years. The state peasants did better out of emancipation than the private serfs; the agreements made by them were less unfavourable to them and they also got larger holdings. The peasants on the Imperial Estates—and there were as many as eight hundred thousand registered males among them—made the best bargain of all.

Emancipation did not weaken, but perhaps even strengthened, the authority of the commune. The land ceded to the peasants was vested in the commune, the practice of redistribution continued wherever it had existed, and it was still the duty of the commune to see that the peasants carried out all their obligations, to itself and to the government. The peasant had ceased to be a serf but was not yet a free man; he was tied to the commune and could not leave it until he had met all his obligations, which now included finding his part of the money needed to repay the government for the sum advanced to the landowner on behalf of the commune. Nor did the peasant, after the emancipation, become an ordinary citizen; he still belonged to a separate social 'estate' with institutions and laws peculiar to itself.

The communal control and periodical redistribution of the land prevented any improvement in agricultural methods. The peasant holdings were not compact but made up of scattered strips; and in about three-quarters of the villages did not pass regularly from father to son. The land therefore continued to produce about as much as before emancipation, but the peasant mouths to be fed by that produce multiplied rapidly. Between 1861 and 1905, the peasant population of Russia increased by about three-fifths (from fifty to nearly eighty millions), but the total acreage of peasant holdings by not more than one tenth. The peasants, as might be expected, soon fell into arrears over the payment of redemption dues; in 1886 the poll-tax was abolished and in the eighteen-nineties the payment of debts deferred and in part cancelled. And yet the peasants grew poorer and more hungry.

Meanwhile, their former masters had also fallen on bad days; they had not been able to convert the estates left to them (though many of them were very large) into efficiently run farms. They had been obliged to sell some land to the peasants and even more to the new rich from the towns; and when, in 1885, a Nobles' Land Bank was established to help them, many of them quickly mortgaged their estates. Both nobles and peasants were growing poorer, and no one prospered except in the towns. The most numerous class in the country, the peasants, were disaffected, and had been for generations; the landowning class, on whose service and loyalty the autocracy had long depended, were losing their wealth and their old confidence in the society where they held the first places; while the only people growing rich were without political experience, and also too few and timid to take over the duties of government.

II. THE RUSSIAN STATE

Imperial Russia fell because the nobles, on whom she most depended, lost confidence in her, and there was no other class strong enough to take their place. The nobles might, conceivably, with the help of able men from other classes, have reformed the state, making it flexible and strong enough to meet the strains and shocks that a primitive country is liable to when it is exposed to foreign influences. Japanese experience proves that it is possible for a privileged class to adapt their country, quickly and without violence, to a world transformed by forces outside their control and whose influence they cannot escape. But the Russian nobles and their associates failed to reform the state in time to prevent its ruin and the destruction of their class. They failed for many reasons—partly for lack of political experience outside the state service; partly from having no liberal Emperor strong enough, not only to take the initiative, but to persist on a set course for several decades; partly because they were not trusted by other classes, whose complaints, perpetual restlessness and occasional violence frightened the Tsars and their advisers; and partly, also, because, being themselves (more perhaps than any other class) influenced by foreign ideals and prejudices, they too often acquired consciences so tender that they lost courage and despaired of themselves and their country.

Unlike the nobility and gentry of England they had no experience either of strong local government or of national institutions of a truly representative character. They had been, from Catherine's time until the emancipation of 1861, masters on their own estates and almost absolute rulers over the villages belonging to them. But they had never had the *public and collective* responsibility of English Justices of the Peace for the maintenance of order and the relief of distress. Their power had been private and irresponsible, and outside the circle of its use they had been entirely subservient to government. Not until the eighteen-sixties were the nobility and gentry given their first real opportunity of being independently useful, outside the limits of their own estates and the Imperial administration, to the society that gave them so many privileges; but even that opportunity was quickly restricted.

There was perhaps nowhere in Europe more intelligence, more sweetness of character, a more fervent and modest desire to earn, by service to the community, the privileges they were born to, than among the nobles of Russia in the late nineteenth century. The possessors of these qualities were no doubt a minority of their class—for the best things are everywhere given only to the few—but they were as richly endowed with them as the ruling classes of the well governed and much more prosperous countries of the West. The Tsars and their advisers allowed the nobles, by their education, to acquire the best that Europe had to give, but did not know how to contrive that they should use that best in the service of their country.

The Tsars, from Peter's time onwards, tried to make Russia a strong and efficient power on the European model, and they had therefore, whether they liked it or not, to expose her to many kinds of western influence. In the eighteenth century, when the Austrian and Prussian military monarchies seemed strong, western influences did not weaken, but rather strengthened, the Tsar's authority. The object of Peter's reforms had been to make Russia militarily powerful, and he had known that she could not become so unless she were given an efficient administration. He therefore not only laid the foundations of a modern army and navy, but also attempted something much more difficult—the reform of governmental institutions. Though his reforms were only partly successful, his object was always to increase his own effective control over all classes of his subjects. The next great reforming Tsar, Alexander I, still further strengthened the bureaucracy, making it more efficient and conditions of service inside it more attractive. But it was not till Alexander II's reign, a century and a half after

Peter had begun the Europeanization of Russia, that the first serious attempts were made to liberalize her institutions, to make her more the sort of country that the educated classes exposed, since the French revolution, to liberal influences had been taught to consider civilized. Alexander's reforms were well-intentioned and long overdue; they were also, unfortunately, timid or ill-conceived or spoilt by his successors.

Russia had in the beginning of the twentieth century a peasant class several times more numerous than any other, barbarous still and ill-disposed to the better-to-do and more civilized parts of the nation; and from this class were recruited the workers in the industries quickly growing in the towns. Neither the peasants who stayed in the villages nor the men who went to town needed to be taught to dislike either the old masters or the new; they were already convinced, without the help of German socialism, that they were the perpetual victims of injustice, men kept poor that others might be rich. The nobles were no longer the confident master class they had once been; their western education had not made them love their country less but had made them almost too sharply aware of its miseries and their own defects. They knew only too well what was wrong and too little how to set it right. They could serve the state, but must accept the terms on which the autocrat chose to make that service possible; and this too often meant that they could serve only at the sacrifice of their principles. The Russian bureaucracy was dilatory, mediocre, arbitrary and yet easily discouraged; it bored the intelligent and made men of good will unhappy. Russia seemed too vast and illiterate to be governed properly, like a huge prehistoric animal unfit to survive because its brain is too small for its body. The nobility and gentry of Russia, a class made known to the world by one of the world's most excellent literatures, were true patriots; their country seemed to them unique and wonderful, to be loved and wept for, but how, just how, to be saved? The new middle class, in their pursuit of wealth and happiness, were no doubt rougher and more impatient, but there were not many of them, and in political matters they were too much at cross purposes and too little experienced to do anything useful for their country. Though many of them thought themselves liberal, they were still engaged in the most illiberal of human occupations: they were busy getting rich, and sometimes affected to despise the men intent upon the so much more difficult and important business of government.

III. IDEOLOGIES BEFORE MARXISM

It was the Germans who first taught the Russians to philosophize about their country. In the eighteenth century, the Russians, in their literature and their theories, had copied the French, who had not—in those days—speculated about the destinies of nations but rather about the passions and rights of men. It was the German Idealist philosophers, first among them Hegel and Schelling, who set the Russians thinking about the peculiarities of their national character and the probable fate of their country. Two schools of thought, both deeply influenced by German Idealism, soon arose among them; of which one, the Westerners, believed that Russia would develop much as the other European nations had done; while the other, the Slavophiles, believed that Russia's destiny must be peculiar to herself because her 'spirit' is essentially different from that of the West.

The Westerners,[1] with Bielinsky and Herzen at their head, thought Russia backward; what she needed most was freedom, to be given her head a little to enable her to use her vast energies to catch up quickly with the West. She was fresh, resourceful and unspoilt, and would know how to make the best of her opportunities. The Westerners did not want Russia merely to imitate the West, for they had faith in her native genius and were among the most fervent admirers of her young literature; but they also believed that she belonged entirely to Europe and could not attain her full stature, could not become completely and maturely herself, unless she opened her doors wide to western influences. The Russians, they thought, were too vigorous and too gifted a people to be in danger of being swamped by foreign influences; they were Europeans, and being in need of education, must go to school in Europe. They must become full members of the European community, and there was no danger that they would thereby cease to be Russians.

The Slavophiles wanted to preserve the Russian character of

---

[1] S. I. Potugin, in Turgenev's *Smoke*, is a good example of a Westerner. See his conversation with Litvinov given in the fifth chapter of that novel.

their people, whom they believed to be quite different from the Europeans of the West. The Russians, they thought, did not belong to the same family of nations as the French, Italians, Germans, and English, differing from them only in the sort of ways that they differed from each other; the difference between the Russians and these western peoples was altogether more profound. The Russians were not individualists and rationalists, and put only a small value on political constitutions and the rule of law; they were believers in Orthodoxy, and had much greater faith in conscience and right instinct than in reason; and in the peasant commune they had an institution peculiar to themselves and unknown to the West. The Russians must not try to make themselves what they could not of their nature become; the attempt would fail and must spoil their native genius.[1]

Socialist ideas began to influence Russian intellectuals in the eighteen-fifties, before the industrialization of their country had seriously begun. The first Russian socialists were therefore more interested in the peasants than in any other class in society; and they soon persuaded themselves that the Russian peasant was a born socialist. Like the Slavophiles, they thought the commune an institution peculiar to Russia; and they cared nothing for constitutionalism, believing that their country would develop quite differently from the West. Again like the Slavophiles, they used western ideas to preach a philosophy asserting the unique character of their country. These early Russian socialists—or Populists (Narodniki) as they were called—took their ideas from many western sources, from Feuerbach, Vogt and Buchner, from Spencer and Darwin, from Fourier and Proudhon. They were not Idealists but materialists; they were interested in the application of Darwinism to the development of human societies, and they were socialists who believed in direct rather than political action. Their general philosophy (that is, their materialism) they

---

[1] The Slavophiles either did not know or did not care to remember that the western Europeans had been rationalists, individualists, and believers in constitutional government for only a comparatively short time; and that, before they were civilized, they had possessed most of the virtues that the Slavs suspicious of the West now took pride in. The historians had not yet explained that the peasant commune would probably not have survived into the nineteenth century, were it not that it had proved convenient for administrative purposes to governments organized on the German model—governments too little interested in the welfare of the peasants, the least westernized class in Russia.

mostly borrowed from Germany, their ideas on social evolution from England, and their socialism from France. They had more than a little in common with the other important schools of thought in Russia: they shared the Slavophiles' belief in the peculiar destiny of their country and they also idealized the peasants. They were not obscurantists and Slav soul-worshippers, but, like the Westerners, rationalists willing to learn from people better instructed than themselves; and like the Marxists who came after them, they were materialists and socialists who wanted to subvert society for the benefit of the exploited poor.

The Populists were in their prime during the sixties and seventies. In 1874 they decided 'to go to the people,' putting their knowledge, energy and good will at the disposal of the humble and oppressed, and awakening in them a proper sense of their rights and opportunities. But their missionary zeal was not rewarded by the peasants, who received them with curiosity and suspicion.

Their failure to win the confidence of the peasants taught the Populists a lesson; they learnt that political action matters after all, and that nothing much can be done for the people by a party having no influence on government. Some of them resorted to violence, while others sought by peaceful means to achieve civil rights and parliamentary government—things once despised as bourgeois trash, but which now seemed good to them. The campaign of terror organized by the minority culminated in 1881 in the assassination of Alexander II; it, too, was unsuccessful, and its effect merely to strengthen the autocracy and excuse its repressive character.

For many years after 1881 the Populists were quiescent, until in 1900 they formed the Socialist-Revolutionary Party. They had by that time considerably changed their principles, having ceased to believe that socialism could come to Russia directly through the efforts of her peasants; they were no longer opposed to political action, admitted the fact of industrialization and even welcomed it, and strove to create a socialist movement supported by industrial workers and intellectuals as well as by peasants. Their ideas about their country had been affected by Marxism, but they had not become Marxists. They were still much more occupied with the peasants than with any other class, and they never won any considerable support except in the villages.

IV. MARXISM

Marxism appeared in Russia in the early eighteen-eighties. Its first exponents, Plekhanov, Axelrod and Vera Zasulich, had all been Populists. In *Socialism and the Political Struggle* (1883) and in *Our Differences of Opinion* (1884), two works published in Geneva, Plekhanov explained why he had become a Marxist. Russia, he said, was already becoming a capitalist country and there were no longer good grounds for believing, with the Populists, that capitalism might pass her by, that she might, owing to the communalism of her peasants, move directly from her present condition to socialism. The Populists had misunderstood the peasant commune; they had believed it to be an institution already half socialist in character, whereas it was only maintained by the government for fiscal purposes. In Russia as elsewhere the socialists must rely for support on the urban workers and not on the peasants; they must expect new industries to grow quickly, the peasant commune to disappear and the bourgeois to predominate for a time.

Plekhanov was also the first Russian Marxist to warn his people against the dangers of a premature attempt to establish socialism. In *Socialism and the Political Struggle*, he argued that a revolutionary socialist party seizing power immediately in a backward country like Russia would be faced with this dilemma: either to try to organize production in the way approved of by modern socialism —an attempt that must fail because of the workers' ignorance and their not yet having acquired the habits and moral attitudes that make loyal and intelligent collaboration possible; or else to fall into a patriarchal and authoritarian communism of the kind that existed in Peru before the Spanish Conquest, with this difference, that production would be controlled by a privileged class of socialists instead of by the Incas and their officials. Plekhanov believed that, though the Russians were not yet, by far, civilized enough for anyone to be able to establish real socialism in their country, they were already too advanced to put up with what he called 'Peruvian tutelage.' He thought himself a prudent man, a cool head among hot ones, but, like so many of his kind, he underestimated both the patience of the multitude under oppression and the ruthlessness of oppressors.

Plekhanov, Axelrod and Vera Zasulich created in the 'eighties the first Russian Marxist organization, 'The Emancipation of Labour,' which in 1898 made way for the Russian Social-Democratic Party. They were the 'first generation' of leaders, and they led the party from abroad, where they were more free than they would have been in Russia to keep the party's headquarters in continuous being and to direct its work. They were joined in 1900 by the younger leaders, Lenin, Martov and Potressov; and the six of them for a time jointly edited a journal called *Iskra* (The Spark). These six and their collaborators—known as the *Iskra* group—convoked the first Congress of the Russian Social-Democratic Party, which met in Brussels, and then, to escape the too close attentions of the police, moved to London.

It was at this Congress that the party, only five years old, split into two groups, the Bolsheviks and the Mensheviks. They quarrelled about an apparently unimportant matter—the conditions of membership of their party. The Bolsheviks wanted no one admitted to it who did not 'take part in person in the activities of one or other of its organizations,' while the Mensheviks were content to let anyone in who gave it 'continuous personal support under the direction of one of its organizations.' Behind these harmless-looking phrases were hidden two very different conceptions of how the party should be organized and what it should do; the Bolsheviks wanted it confined to militant socialists, with whom service to the party took first call on their time, while the Mensheviks were willing that mere sympathizers should also join it and have a say in deciding its policies. The Bolsheviks got their majority—and thus also their name—because Plekhanov voted with Lenin in favour of a narrow party organization, and carried many of the delegates with him.

Soon after the London Congress, Plekhanov quarrelled with Lenin, so that the Bolsheviks—despite their name—were a majority for only a very short time. Plekhanov's defection left Lenin easily the most powerful leader among them, and they soon became little more than the faction of Lenin. For fourteen years they remained a minority, often a small one, among the Russian Social-Democrats, their only advantage over the majority being the clear ascendency among them of only one man. They were not always loyal to him, and were often quarrelsome; but they did at least share his conception of an exclusive and highly disciplined party of militants acting as 'the vanguard of the proletariat.' They formed no separate organization of their own until 1912, for Lenin was more anxious to convert the whole party to his views than to use a rump against the main body.

The Mensheviks were never dominated by any one leader, and often quarrelled as bitterly with one another as with Lenin. They were, on the whole—except for Trotsky—much less willing than the Bolsheviks to take liberties with Marxist doctrine, but this more scrupulous orthodoxy did not keep them at peace with one another. They did not believe in severe party discipline, and were as often several factions as one. Not until Lenin returned to Russia in April 1917 did common hostility to him unite them more than their different opinions separated them. They had long known him for an aggressive doctrinaire and dangerous opponent, but they did not, until too late, think the danger so pressing as to sink their differences in union against it.

V. THE FALL OF TSARDOM

The Russia of the Tsars was a military state and was ruined by unsuccessful war. The victories of the Japanese in Manchuria—the first great victories won by Asians over Europeans since the Ottoman triumphs of the seventeenth century—provoked widespread disorders in Russia. Marxists and other revolutionaries tried to make the most of them, and there was spasmodic fighting for many weeks before order was completely restored. It was then that the workers formed their first councils or soviets, institutions that seemed to Lenin specifically proletarian because (to him) they looked so much like the Paris Commune. The abortive revolution of 1905 made a deep impression on the two boldest and ablest Marxists in Russia, Lenin and Trotsky, suggesting to them both that conditions peculiar to their country might enable the proletariat and their party to get power much earlier than orthodox Marxism allowed for.

The Tsar and his advisers were also deeply impressed by so much evidence of their own unpopularity, and they decided to make large concessions. The Manifesto of October 30th, 1905, prepared for the Emperor by Count Witte, gave Russia her first legislative assembly. The franchise was wide but election was not, except in the towns, direct; in the country districts deputies were to be chosen by electoral colleges, and election to these colleges was so contrived that the landowner's vote counted for much more than the peasant's. Despite these precautions the first Russian parliament, or Duma, was very little to the Tsar's taste. The elections to it were boycotted by the two parties most bitterly hostile to the established order, the Socialist-Revolutionaries and the Social-Democrats, but the Duma was, nevertheless, much more radical than the Tsar had expected. The Constitutional-Democrats (the K.D.s or Cadets), the party of the middle class and the more liberal landowners, won a hundred and ninety-six seats, nearly twice as many as the next largest group, the Labour Party (Trudoviki). Russia's first parliament, in spite of the electoral devices used to favour the privileged, had a small Right Wing, a large Centre and a considerable Left, which was moderate only because the revolutionaries had boycotted the elections.

The first Duma lasted only two and a half months, and was dissolved in July 1906. Its successor, the second Duma, elected on the same franchise, was even more hostile to the Tsar; there were only fifty-two conservatives in it, including both moderates and diehards, ninety-two Cadets, one hundred Trudoviki, and as many as a hundred and thirteen Socialist-Revolutionaries and Social-Democrats. Though the franchise was neither universal nor equal, there were twice as many revolutionaries as conservatives. Nowhere else in the world, not even in Germany or France, was the Extreme Left so well represented, and the peculiarity of Russian revolutionaries was that they did not merely preach eventual violence but were willing to use it even now. The second Duma was almost as short-lived as the first; it lasted just over three months and was dissolved in June 1907. These two Dumas accomplished nothing, but their composition did at least prove how completely the régime had lost the confidence of the Russian people.

The third Duma, which lasted five years, was the only Russian parliament that did for the country anything worth doing. It was elected on a much more biased franchise than the first two, and was very predominantly conservative, though more moderate than die-hard. The largest party in it, the Octobrists, were constitutional monarchists, more cautious than the Cadets and less enamoured of liberty, though not less opposed to autocratic rule; they were led by an able parliamentarian, Guchkov, who knew how to co-operate with the Tsar's chief minister without diminishing the authority and dignity of parliament. That minister, Stolypin, was himself a man of great courage and ability, who saw that Russia could never have social peace until the peasants were made as free of their communes as they had been of their masters. He made it possible for the peasant householder to withdraw from his commune, and to become, with or without its consent, the full and independent owner of his holding, able to dispose of it as he liked; he abolished the practice of repartitioning the land; and he made it easier than it had been for the peasant to consolidate the separate pieces he held into one small farm.

Stolypin wanted to help the more enterprising peasants to become prosperous farmers; he foresaw that they would, in course of time, buy up the holdings of the unsuccessful, who would either have to move into the towns or else become wage-labourers on the land. The peasants who grew rich would soon become (as they had already done in the West) firm supporters of the social order which gave them their opportunities, while the others, the unsuccessful many, would at least be no worse off than before, and probably a good deal better. The land would be better farmed, and it would no longer seem to the peasants that there was not enough of it to feed them. This was Stolypin's famous 'wager on the strong,' and it was a risk well worth taking.

The peasants, no doubt, except for a minority among them, would at first resent the new inequalities resulting from the gradual dissolution of the communes, but they would, in the end, grow used to them and accept them as they had in the past accepted the old order. Stolypin's reforms, well-conceived though they were, could bring about only a slow improvement, and might for a time be resented by many more peasants than welcomed them. The evil was deep rooted, and the cure could be neither easy nor quick. Time and peace were needed for Stolypin's reforms to do the good intended of them; but Russia went to war in 1914, and in 1917, when she was so exhausted that she could fight no longer, much the greater number of her peasant holdings were not yet consolidated into small farms.

When Stolypin was assassinated in 1912 the Tsar lost his ablest minister. He might perhaps have found others strong and wise enough to save his dynasty, but he chose to be governed by his wife and, through her, by an illiterate, drunken and debauched monk, who soon became so dangerous to Russia that he had to be killed like a mad dog. Nicholas II was not nearly as respectable a prince as Charles I of England or Louis XVI of France; he was not a man ordinarily weak and irresolute who was ruined because he had not courage and intelligence enough to deal with a situation quite out of the ordinary; he was disgracefully weak and ended his reign a dishonoured man, who had brought monarchy so low that, when he abdicated, even the most conservative courtiers breathed a sigh of relief.

If the Tsar had made a better choice of ministers, or if, though he had remained as foolish as nature and his wife made him, there had been no war, the old Russia might have survived and have become in time a stable constitutional monarchy. The war quite ruined her. She fought, not as she had done against Napoleon, on the defensive and in the far interior, but on her own frontiers and even in the enemy's territory. She had of all the belligerents to maintain the longest lines of communication, although, being economically the most backward of the Great Powers, she was the least able to bear that burden; and she also, on several occasions and for her allies' benefit, mounted great offensives which exhausted her more than they hurt the enemy. As she had been against Napoleon and was to be in the Second World War, so also from 1914 to 1917 was she more prodigal of her resources than any of the other Powers. But the economic consequences of the First World War—waged on so much vaster a scale than the defensive campaign against Napoleon, and by a country which (though backward still) had a more intricate and vulnerable economy—were much more disruptive of Russian society; and there was not, as there was to be from 1941 to 1945, at the head of the state a government long used to controlling every part of the nation's life and willing to take the most severe action whenever they thought it necessary, either in their own or the national interest.

The war brought inflation and famine, which must in the end ruin any government incapable of mitigating their effects. Already before the war, many of the peasants had not been able to produce food enough to feed themselves and their families adequately, and now the government were taking millions of them off the land and sending them to the army, where regulations prescribed for them a better diet than most of them were used to at home. Agricultural prices rose, and the peasants who stayed behind in the villages had at first a sufficient motive for growing and marketing as much food as they could. There was no doubt a considerable increase of efficiency. But the peasants soon had more money than they could spend; the factories in the towns, where production was also increasing,[1] were so much absorbed in making munitions and the equipment needed by the armed forces of a great country engaged in total war, that they could produce little to satisfy the villagers' needs. The government did not even contrive that industry should produce agricultural implements more abundantly, though the peasants would have been only too pleased to invest their growing profits in them. As it was, they found no way of spending their money usefully to themselves, and so in the end decided to grow less food for the market. The manufacturers, too, were making big profits. There was inflation everywhere, both in the villages and the towns; and in the latter there was the threat of famine as well. Russian agriculture and Russian industry had never been more efficient, and yet the country was threatened with economic ruin.

Meanwhile at the front the chances of war were always against the poorly equipped Russian armies, who lost several lives for every death inflicted on the enemy. The burden of war was altogether too great for a still primitive country ruled by incompetent ministers chosen by a Tsar whose most trusted adviser had for several years been a debauchee monk, and who, when that monk was killed, seemed quite lost.

VI. THE TRIUMPH OF THE BOLSHEVIKS

The March revolution of 1917 was not made by the Bolsheviks. It was an effect of famine and unsuccessful war; it began in a small way, was not quickly put down, and so, since Tsarism was rotten,

---

[1] Production increased by about 10% between 1914 and 1916 in spite of the loss to Germany of the most important industrial areas of Russian Poland.

soon destroyed it. Like every revolution, it was weak in its infancy, and grew strong only because it was allowed to do so. Tsardom collapsed because scarcely anyone thought it worth while making an effort to defend it. There was no Mirabeau to make a last attempt to reform and save it, for Nicholas II had brought it into such contempt that every change from it seemed for the better.

As soon as Tsardom fell, Russia acquired two governments, one official and the other unofficial, both weak and each suspicious of the other. The first, the Provisional Government, came into existence on March 14th; it consisted of the leaders of the more liberal groups in the fourth Duma, with only one Social-Democrat, Alexander Kerensky, among them. The second, the unofficial one, was the Soviet of Workmen's and Soldiers' Deputies, elected by the factory workers and soldiers in Petrograd at the instigation of the Marxists. Very soon afterwards there arose other soviets in the important towns and the country districts of Russia, but the Petrograd Soviet was, until after the Bolshevik revolution, easily the most powerful among them. The March and November revolutions both happened in Petrograd, where Tsardom fell and Bolshevism triumphed.

The soviets did not at first contest the authority of the Provisional Government; they were dominated in the towns by the Mensheviks and in the villages by the Right Wing Socialist-Revolutionaries, who had no desire to govern Russia but only to be the formidable critics of her government. The Mensheviks believed that the time had not yet come for the party of the proletariat to govern; for Russia had only just had her bourgeois revolution, and many years must pass before she could be ripe for socialism. It was therefore the obvious duty of a Marxist party, socialist and revolutionary though it might be in principle, to leave the actual business of government to the bourgeois. The time of bourgeois predominance had come and must be lived through to the end, like years of adolescence before the full maturity that brought socialism. Though the Mensheviks did not want to govern, they did want to make their power felt, and were too caught up in their own theories to understand that that policy, unless they collaborated closely with the government, must lead to disaster. They thought it their Marxist duty always to be suspicious of a bourgeois government, to harass and oppose it, and above all to add strength to the oppressed classes.

The Mensheviks were in 1917 merely following the example set by the German Social-Democratic Party, and by so doing, also the advice given to that party by Engels before he died. They were neither cowardly nor irresponsible; they did their best to follow what they thought was the distinct line of their duty. It has been said—no doubt rightly—that they were ruined by their pedantic Marxism. They were pedants, not because they believed that a proletarian revolution was impossible in the Russia of 1917 —for history has, in this matter, proved them right and the Bolsheviks wrong—but because they did not understand, until too late, that, by refusing to co-operate with a bourgeois government, they were only making it easier for revolutionaries more ambitious than themselves to seize power in order to attempt the impossible. The Mensheviks, believing (as they did) that a Russian revolution made in 1917 in the name of the proletariat could not be properly proletarian nor lead to socialism but only to what Plekhanov had called a 'Peruvian tutelage,' ought to have made every effort to ensure the stability of the bourgeois government. That government, after all, was new; its members had no experience of power, and the parties they led were loose and undisciplined; the industrialists, merchants, small tradesmen and professional men, on whose support a bourgeois government must—according to Marxism— principally depend, were not a numerous class and were unused to power; the armies at the front were barely able to defend their positions against the enemy and were too disaffected for the government to be able to use troops to maintain its authority; Russia had ceased for a while to be a police state and her new rulers believed in democracy and mild government; the civil departments were discredited and in any case no longer knew what was expected of them. The Provisional Government, bourgeois though it was in a Russia supposed to be entering 'the capitalist epoch' of her history, was so weak that it needed every assistance to keep alive. But all it got from the Mensheviks, until the abortive Bolshevik coup of July 1917 thoroughly frightened

---

[1] A Menshevik and a Socialist-Revolutionary joined the government on May 19th but it was not till July that the Mensheviks understood that it was their interest to strengthen governmental authority.

them, was suspicion and censure; and by that time the Mensheviks themselves had begun to lose favour with the workers.

Not that the Mensheviks were ever really powerful. When it is said that they dominated the urban soviets, no more is meant than that they took a leading part in their deliberations and were more often listened to than any other group. They were not, however, a disciplined party; and, even if they had been one, could never, having no force at their disposal, have imposed their will on the soviets. Their hold on them was precarious, just as was the later hold of the Bolsheviks, until Lenin's revolution and the need to defend it against the Whites enabled the government to create new and formidable instruments of coercion. The Mensheviks were never the 'party of the proletariat'; the workers never understood their theories and were only to some extent amenable to their advice. Nevertheless, they did for a time listen to the Mensheviks more than to anyone else, and the Mensheviks could have used what influence they had in the urban soviets to strengthen the authority of the Provisional Government. It would, no doubt, in many cases, have been beyond their power to prevent the workers taking over the factories, but they could, perhaps, when the workers began to discover their own incapacity to run them, have persuaded them to accept a considerable measure of government control. If the government had learnt to trust the Mensheviks—which, being aware of its own weakness, it might well have done had it received a little support from them— they could have given it advice badly needed. They could have warned it against taking the offensive militarily and advised a withdrawal to lines more easily defended; they could have used their influence to persuade it to make quickly the concessions that could not be long withheld without danger of a new revolution; and in particular could have urged it to satisfy the land hunger of the peasants without further delay. Prompt action, that only the government could take, to legalize what everyone knew was inevitable would have enabled the Right Wing Socialist-Revolutionaries, who were well disposed to both the Provisional Government and the Mensheviks, to retain their authority among the peasants, instead of losing it to the Left Wing of their own party, who were friends of the Bolsheviks. Such tactics as these, had the

Mensheviks adopted them, might not have succeeded, but were at least worth trying.

The position of the Bolsheviks, after Lenin's return to Russia in April 1917, was much less difficult. They had for a time, until their leader joined them, not known what to do, and he had scolded them for their dullness and inadequacy; but as soon as he was back among them, the world had seemed once again a simple place. Lenin was not given to anxiety about the remoter consequences of his actions, and, though he often changed his opinions, was always very sure of their truth while they occupied his mind.

He had, as he followed the course of the First World War from his refuge in Switzerland, persuaded himself that so terrible a conflict could end only with the collapse of capitalism. After the massacres on the battlefields would come proletarian revolution. His Marxism would not let him believe that the war might transform society without the need for domestic violence, that the wealthy and powerful might grow used to the discipline imposed on all classes for the sake of victory, and that therefore, when the war was over, it might prove easier than before 1914 to tax the rich heavily for the benefit of the poor. Lenin had for several years looked forward to the early ruin of western capitalism; and after his return home he quickly discovered that he and his Bolsheviks might, if they made good use of other people's mistakes, soon get a chance of taking power in the name of the Russian proletariat. If they took that chance, they would not, he thought, be making a 'premature' revolution; they would merely be putting it in the power of Russia, in spite of her backwardness, to profit from the collapse of world capitalism to be expected in the almost immediate future.[1]

His mind once made up that it was his duty to do what he most wanted to do, Lenin set about preparing the Bolshevik seizure of power. As early as May 1917, at the first conference of the Bolshevik Party held freely on Russian soil, Lenin proclaimed the

---

[1] Lenin also saw signs in Russia—for nothing favourable to his ambitions escaped his notice—of monopoly capitalism, which is (according to the Marxists) capitalism's last stage, reached when society is about to pass into socialism. But he put much greater faith in world revolution. It was as if he were saying to the Mensheviks: 'Russia is not as backward as you think, and there are signs enough for those who can read them that she is quickly growing ripe for socialism; but, in any case, our cause is international, the world proletarian revolution is at hand, and our obvious duty is to prepare for it and to do our best to associate Russia with it.'

three policies that were to make his party within six months the rulers of Russia. At the time of the conference the Bolsheviks were still greatly outnumbered by the Mensheviks, and were not more than a few thousand in the whole of Russia; but courage and resolution had lately been restored to them, like life to thirsty plants when at last they get water. They were now obedient to Lenin and therefore formidable.

His three policies, and the slogans that expressed them, were well chosen. The first was immediate peace, the second to give all the land to the peasants, and the third to vest governmental power in the soviets. The Provisional Government wanted to continue the war, and the Mensheviks though they liked the war much less, would do nothing to stop it, believing that Russian soil must be defended against the Germans. But the soldiers, unlike the politicians, had no more stomach for war. They knew that only the Bolsheviks promised immediate peace; and peace, now that they despaired of victory, and were quite tired out, and knew that they could hurt the enemy only a little at the cost of hurting themselves much more, was what they wanted above all. Soldiers were deserting from the army and making their way back to their villages, bringing disorder with them. As summer passed into autumn it was clear that Russia could resist the enemy no longer; there was no more hope of taking up new defensive positions, and there was nothing to do but make peace. The Bolsheviks, who had clamoured for peace ever since May, found themselves growing quickly popular.

The slogan, 'All land to the peasants,' was not less effective. The peasants wanted the landlords' estates and were no longer willing to give the government time to arrange for the legal transfer of the land to themselves. Almost nothing had been done for the peasants;[1] they had been exhorted time and again to be patient and obey the laws, as if they had not for generations believed that all the land belonged properly to them and had been taken from them by trickery and the wicked laws made by their masters. The Bolsheviks and their allies in the villages, the Left Wing Socialist-Revolutionaries, instead of preaching patience to the peasants and obedience to the masters' laws, encouraged them to

[1] Kerensky, just before the Bolshevik revolution, took more vigorous measures to satisfy the peasants—but too late.

take what was theirs without waiting for the permission of a remote and weak government.

The cry, 'All power to the Soviets,' was not so immediately useful to the Bolsheviks. By calling for immediate peace they were asking for what millions of soldiers wanted, and by demanding that all land be given at once to the peasants they were setting them against a government that expected patience of them; but the soviets were, until October, dominated by the Mensheviks in the towns and by the more conservative Socialist-Revolutionaries in the villages. It would seem, then, in May 1917, when the Bolsheviks first raised this cry on behalf of the soviets, and also for several months afterwards, that they had nothing to gain by it. After the manner of politicians, the Bolsheviks hated those groups most that stood closest to themselves, and therefore hated the Mensheviks above all others. Why, then, should they seek to give all power to soviets dominated by the Mensheviks and their allies?

The calculations of Lenin were quite simple. The Mensheviks did not want to govern, and did not even think it proper, at that stage in Russian history, that they should govern. The cry 'All power to the Soviets' could only embarrass them; though they could not take it up, they must, if they resisted it, appear timid and weak. The workers and peasants, on the other hand, knowing nothing about the difficulties of wielding power, were not averse to getting it. It flattered them that the Bolsheviks should think the soviets, consisting mostly of workers and peasants, fit to govern Russia. This slogan, therefore, was one more reason, added to the other two, why the Bolsheviks quickly grew popular.

The workers and peasants were, despite Bolshevik flattery, quite unfit to govern. Should power ever pass to the soviets, it could do so only after the Bolsheviks and their friends had gained control of them. Lenin's third slogan therefore meant in practice 'All power to the Bolsheviks.' Lenin knew how unequally power is distributed in the modern bureaucratic state. Revolutionaries, if only they can establish their authority in the capital and in a few of the larger provincial towns, can quite easily become masters of the state. It would have been impossible for the Bolsheviks at any time in 1917 to win a general election or even to force their way into the Provisional Government; their only hope was to get power through the soviets; and it was not even necessary that they should, in order to get it, control many soviets. Political victory in Petrograd and in a few provincial capitals would be enough.

Meanwhile, the Bolsheviks also enjoyed the support of the more extreme wing of the Socialist-Revolutionaries, whose influence in the villages was growing fast; but these rural allies, precisely because they were rural, would, whether they liked it or not, be subordinate.

Everything happened as Lenin had hoped, and on November 7th, 1917, only a month after gaining control of the Petrograd Soviet, the Bolsheviks made their bid for power. It was quickly and completely successful and for several months afterwards there was almost no organized resistance to them. But, though the Bolsheviks got power, that power was not great, for Russia was without an army or police force or competent civil service. Every organized body, political, administrative and military, was weak, and the Bolsheviks were merely the least weak among them. They owed their victory to their promises and their courage. But neither the workers nor the peasants knew what the Bolsheviks wanted to do in Russia; they knew nothing at all of Marxism, and, had they known it, would certainly not have liked it. The Russian Bolsheviks, at the moment of their triumph in November 1917, had far less than the German Social-Democrats the right to call themselves 'the party of the proletariat.' Only their Menshevik enemies knew them for what they were; the workers and peasants knew nothing about them except the promises they had made as a means to getting power.

Chapter Ten

BOLSHEVISM BEFORE THE REVOLUTION

Marxism, by the time that Russians began to be seriously interested in it, had already become the most influential of all schools of socialism. Though still a revolutionary doctrine, it owed its great influence in the West to conditions that made revolution less likely than it had been in any earlier part of the century. Marxism was spreading fast and growing milder; it was the doctrine of revolutionaries who had learnt to be patient. Many decades had passed since Marx and Engels had expected an early revolution, and much ink had flowed from their pens. Their doctrines were perhaps not less confused than they had been forty years earlier, but their manifest tendency was to encourage revolutionaries to make a long preparation for ultimate success. *The Communist Manifesto* and *The Address to the Communist League*— the pamphlets most encouraging to the impatient—were written, as Marx and Engels had themselves admitted, at a time of illusion and ill-founded hopes. Bitter experience had taught them since then that capitalism was still full of vigour and the workers far short of the discipline required to destroy it. Marx had written, in the passage accepted by all Marxists as the classic exposition of his fundamental doctrine, that 'no social order ever disappears before all the productive forces for which there is room in it have developed, and new, higher relations of production never appear before the conditions of their existence have matured in the womb of the old society.'

It was the patient Marxism of Marx's middle and later years that Plekhanov imported into Russia; and he used it to shatter the 'illusions' of the Populists, which he had himself once shared. Russia, he said, could not, while still a primitive peasant country,

217

become socialist; she was already on the threshold of capitalism and must pass through the whole of that phase of her development; she must become a mature industrial and bourgeois society before she could hope to establish socialism. Not the peasants, but the urban workers—the proletariat—would make the socialist revolution, and could not do so until they had become the most numerous class in society. This was the orthodox Marxism that Plekhanov explained to the Russians. Not all that Marx and Engels had said was consistent with it, but it was the doctrine of their later and presumably wiser years.

Marx and Engels had noticed that the bourgeois capitalists were changing the whole face of the earth, but had never had time to consider how these changes were affecting the economically more backward peoples. They had said, in the *Manifesto*, that 'all, even the most barbarian, nations' were being drawn 'into civilization' and compelled, 'on pain of extinction, to adopt the bourgeois mode of production.' But were they thereby being made exactly like the bourgeois nations? They were, after all, being subjected to influences that the western nations had never known. The 'bourgeois mode of production' and the 'civilization' so powerfully affecting them were not native products; they had not appeared among them because social conditions had brought them to birth but had been imported from outside. What happens to a 'barbarian' society, still by many centuries too primitive to bring forth capitalism out of its own womb, when what it could not give birth to is brought to it from a society more 'civilized' than itself? Its condition must surely be quite unlike any known in the past to the more civilized society? And—since from different causes spring different effects—must not its future also be different?

Marx and Engels assumed that there is a normal course of social evolution—the course followed by the western society which alone was familiar to them. They knew that not all societies are alike, that some are profoundly affected by others; but this knowledge did not cause them to qualify their assumption or even to question it. Though it is possible to find in their writings several passages virtually admitting that societies do not all develop in ways that are broadly similar, there is perhaps not one that betrays an inkling of what these admissions might imply for their fundamental theory. If societies are not insulated against one another, if they can and do profoundly influence each other, how can there be a normal course of social evolution? Or—if they have been so insulated in the past but are so no longer—how can the course of the backward societies (presumably the most susceptible to external influences) continue to be normal?

The Russian Marxists did not attend to the questions neglected by their German masters. They, too, assumed that there is a normal course of social evolution which Russia would follow as the West had done; and Plekhanov even used that assumption to confound the Populists. As a premise to arguments directed against the older, non-Marxian socialists at a time when Russia was fast acquiring new industries, the assumption might be effective; but it could not save the Russian Marxists from the need to make decisions of a kind that their western partners in the faith never had to make. They lived in a country which, on the threshold of industrialism though it might be, was in most ways more primitive than the West had been in the early stages of the industrial revolution. They were adherents, in a still predominantly pre-bourgeois society, of an ideology whose social function was to unite the proletariat in their struggle against the bourgeois. The next revolution in Russia must, given the truth of historical materialism, be made by the bourgeois and lead to a period of bourgeois ascendancy. What, then, in this situation not foreseen by Marx, should the Russian Marxists, the Social-Democrats, do? This question they could not avoid, however much they might ignore the wider theoretical issues raised for the historical materialist whenever an 'advanced' society exerts a deep influence on a 'backward' one.

Many of them decided that there was not, for the time being, much they could do. The Russian proletariat—the class they aspired to serve and to guide—were a very small part of the nation, and generations must pass before they would be numerous and literate enough to be knit together into a massive and enlightened political movement capable of making a proletarian revolution. It was the task of the bourgeois to destroy the Tsarist autocracy, and until that was done, the workers and Marxists must be content to play a not very important rôle. No doubt, Russia, following in the footsteps of more advanced countries and subject to their influence, would be more quickly industrialized than they had been; the capitalist stage of her development would therefore be shorter, and her workers and Marxists would need less time to prepare the destruction of bourgeois society and the establishment of socialism. But, in the meantime, they must learn to be patient, putting first things first, according to the order inexorably laid down by the law of social progress. In a still largely pre-bourgeois society, it was not for them to take the lead in political opposition to the Tsar's government; they must leave that business to the class whose historic function it was. The immediately important task for the workers was to form effective trade unions, protecting their day-to-day interests against their employers; and the Social-Democrats ought chiefly to concentrate on encouraging them to do so. It was, of course, the workers' interest that the bourgeois should bring Tsarist autocracy to an end; and it was possible to disagree widely about just how far social democrats and pro-letarians should go in helping the bourgeois against the common enemy, without contesting their right to take the leading part.

Some of the Social-Democrats—Lenin chief among them—were less willing to be patient. They saw opportunities that escaped the notice of others; and whenever the danger of premature action was pointed out to them, persisted in finding excuses. They did not deny, as a matter of principle, that Russia would develop as the West had done; but from time to time advocated policies that must be absurd unless she were already developing differently. They did not hesitate, on appropriate occasions, to point to these differences, for they could hardly justify their policies without doing so; but they never made a serious and scrupulous attempt to adjust Marxian theory to them. On the contrary, they believed themselves to be the most orthodox among orthodox Marxians, and often—no doubt sincerely—loudly proclaimed the principles which, in their policies, they were tacitly repudiating. They were people who, without knowing it, were determined to have their cake and eat it. As their tacit repudiations of Marxian doctrine were unsystematic and unconscious, they could seldom afford to be clear and logical about matters of theory. They made up for the obscurity of their doctrines by the vigour and clarity of the practical conclusions those doctrines were meant to justify.

Broadly speaking,[1] the patient Marxists were the Mensheviks, and the impatient, the Bolsheviks, companions and disciples of Lenin. Bolshevism—both the political theory and the movement inspired by it—is the creation of Lenin, the projection of his personality stamped with his image. Perhaps no man, since Mahomet, has changed the world so greatly in so short a time.

Lenin was not a philosopher or social theorist of even secondary importance. To think otherwise is quite to mistake the nature of his genius. His more theoretical works, had anyone else written them, would now be read by no one; he never understood the intelligible parts of dialectical and historical materialism, and so— despite his good intentions—was never able to defend them except by quoting their authors and abusing their critics.

Lenin was a Marxist of a peculiar kind, who thought himself a resolute defender of the pure faith and yet added to it, in order to excuse immediate policies, riders whose further consequences he never foresaw—consequences that have turned Marxism inside out. He wanted to justify proletarian revolution in a country where it and the socialism it was meant to lead to were alike impossible, and was convinced that he could do so without distorting Marxism. He saw, more clearly than any other Marxist, that a band of revolutionaries might, in a backward country already deeply affected by industrialism and western ideas, exploit the ambitions, hatreds and fears of all classes and political groups to so good effect as to be able to take power in the name of the proletariat; and he found it possible to persuade himself and others that this seizure of power would be a proletarian revolution.

Lenin made two capital additions to Marxism before the Bolshevik revolution;[2] he elaborated a theory about the proper

[1] Trotsky was neither a patient Marxist nor a Leninist; Plekhanov, in the matter of party organization, was at first with Lenin against the first Mensheviks, and yet must be reckoned with the patient Marxists. This distinction between patient and impatient Marxists tallies only roughly with that between Mensheviks and Bolsheviks. We cannot, however we choose to classify them, put the same men into the same classes at all times.

[2] Lenin's account of imperialism, which he called 'the highest stage of capitalism,' has also been accounted important, though it is superficial and derivative. J. A. Hobson's *Imperialism*, to which Lenin acknowledged his debt, is no doubt a good book; but it takes a fervent Communist to believe that Lenin improved on it. Lenin was never at his best except when he was discussing his native Russia or the organization and policies of his own and other parties.

organization of the Russian Social-Democratic Party and its relations to the class it claimed to serve; and he explained how the Party
might take control of a 'bourgeois revolution' and exploit it in the
interest of the proletariat.

II. THE PARTY OF THE PROLETARIAT

Lenin was concerned to show that the Russian Marxists, even
though their country was not yet properly capitalist, must be
politically active, bringing the true doctrine to the workers and
preparing them, even now, for the political war against the
bourgeois.

In *What Is To Be Done?* (1902), his first important pamphlet,
Lenin argued that a revolutionary proletarian movement does not
arise spontaneously out of the workers' struggle against their
employers. The workers create trade unions to protect themselves
against exploitation, to get better wages, and to improve the
conditions of their employment. This is the class struggle at the
'economic level'; and the workers engage in it of their own accord
as soon as capitalism emerges and gathers them together in large
numbers in factory towns. Their sufferings are the same, and the
same immediate remedies occur to them; the employers are the
enemies and exploiters of them all, and the workers therefore
unite against them. But this union does not of itself enable the
workers to understand the society they live in; they still do not
know that they are the victims of much more than their employers,
that their predicament is the result of their position in society, and
that they can find a real and permanent remedy only by destroying
that society. Trade unionism does not of itself give birth to a
political and revolutionary proletarian movement.

Before the proletariat can become a revolutionary class, politically conscious and disciplined, they must come to understand the
general structure of society and the law of its development. They
must be taught their place in history and the tasks that lie ahead
of them. They must be supplied with a theory, for 'without a
revolutionary theory there can be no revolutionary movement';
there can be neither discipline nor unity of purpose.

The workers are uneducated, and so cannot be expected to produce the theory that is to unite them into a solid revolutionary

class. It must be brought to them from outside their ranks by intellectuals whose knowledge and understanding enable them to create and explain it. 'By their social class, the founders of modern scientific socialism, Marx and Engels, belonged to the bourgeois intelligentsia. So, too, in Russia, the theory of social democracy arose quite independently of the spontaneous growth of the labour movement. It arose as a natural and inevitable outcome of the development of ideas among the revolutionary socialist intelligentsia.'

Lenin did not mean either to deny the political capacity of the workers or to flatter the Marxist intellectuals; he meant only to show that they were necessary to each other. Nor did he mean that political doctrines are mere products of discussions among intellectuals. Marxism could not have been invented in any society earlier than the capitalist; for how men think about society is determined, in the first place, by the nature of the society they live in, and in the second, by whatever doctrines become popular because it is men's interest that they should. Marxism is a theory produced by middle class intellectuals, but could only have seen the light of day at a certain stage in history, and would not have become important unless it had suited the proletariat.

Lenin had, in fact, but little faith in intellectuals. He admitted that they perform the indispensable social function of producing ideologies, but he found them undisciplined, disputatious and unreliable, always eager, in defence of their vanity and caprice, to allege their right to criticize freely. He found the workers more patient of discipline, less vain and more devoted to whatever cause they made their own. Lenin's ambition was to endow Russia with a strong and disciplined Marxist party including both intellectuals and workers, a party strong enough to restrain the caprice of the intellectuals and give them a sense of responsibility by binding them to the workers in common loyalty to a cause. He believed that, without devotion to a comprehensive social theory, there could be no party discipline; and also that, without party discipline, there could be no sustained devotion to theory. Faith must support discipline, and discipline faith; for the workers needed both if ever they were to become a formidable revolutionary class.

Lenin's concern in *What Is To Be Done?* was to denounce the 'intellectual vices' of the Russian Marxists.[1] Many of them were saying that, during the period before the bourgeois revolution (which all the Russian Marxists, none excepted, were then agreed must be the next to happen in Russia), trade unionism could be the only really important proletarian activity. Lenin argued against them that it was the duty of Russian Marxists, even now, to form a revolutionary socialist party, recruiting into it the ablest, most active and bravest workers. It was their duty to teach the workers, even before the bourgeois revolution, that the political struggle is of capital importance, and that its object must be, not merely to remedy grievances, but to destroy the old society and put a new one in its place. The proletariat, even at that stage of Russia's development, must be taught to fight, not for their class alone, but for all the oppressed; in other words, they must be encouraged to take a prominent part in the fight against Tsarist autocracy.

Lenin wanted the Russian Social-Democratic Party kept as narrow as the need to maintain doctrinal integrity and strict discipline required. It would be wasted effort to extend the party to include as many workers and sympathizers as possible, if it were thereby weakened and made ineffective.

If we begin with a solid foundation of a strong organization of revolutionaries, we can guarantee the stability of the movement as a whole and carry out the aims both of social democracy and trade unionism. If, however, we begin with a wide workers' organization supposed to be accessible to the masses, when as a matter of fact it will be accessible to the gendarmes and make the revolutionaries accessible to the police, we shall achieve the aims neither of social democracy nor of trade unionism . . . I assert: 1. that no movement can endure without a stable organization of leaders to maintain continuity; 2. that the wider the masses drawn into the struggle . . . the more urgent the need for such an organization . . . 3. that the organization must mostly consist of persons professionally engaged in revolutionary activities; 4. that, in an autocratic state, the more we confine the membership of the organization to professional revolu-

[1] Lenin was also concerned, by arguing the need for party discipline and doctrinal orthodoxy, to condemn the German Revisionists. But that part of his polemic is less interesting; he did not understand, either then or later, what was happening to Marxism in Germany. He objected to the disruptive influence on the German Social-Democratic Party of intellectuals who, in the name of free criticism, called in question the fundamental tenets of Marxism.

tionaries trained in the art of combating the police, the more difficult it will be to destroy the organization; and 5. the greater will be the number of workers and members of other classes who will be able to join the movement and do active work in it.

Lenin, when he used these arguments, was thinking of Tsarist Russia, which was not yet, in the opinion of Russian Marxists, a properly bourgeois state. The revolutionary and conspiratorial organization he had in mind was to work in a country ruled by an autocrat, an illiberal bureaucracy and a secret police. Lenin admitted that conditions were different in bourgeois Germany, where the Social-Democratic Party could work freely and in public. All its members could easily discover what it was doing, and so, too, could anyone else who took the trouble to follow its much publicized activities. Lenin called the German party 'democratic,'[1] saying that 'no one would call an organization hidden under a veil of secrecy from everyone except its own members' democratic. He wanted for Russia, while Tsarist autocracy continued, a revolutionary socialist party working in secret and therefore so organized that its officers could not be responsible to the generality of its members, seeing that the very nature of their work required that each 'should conceal his identity from nine out of ten of them.'

It is easy for us, who know what happened to Lenin after 1902, to read more into these early statements than he put into them. There is nothing specifically undemocratic about the opinions so vigorously expressed in *What Is To Be Done?* Lenin nowhere suggested that the leaders of a Social-Democratic party, no matter where that party is active, need not be responsible to their followers; he said no more than that they could not be so in Russia while the party, to be effective, had to work secretly. Where, as in Germany, there was no police state, publicity and the free election of officers—the two conditions of internal party democracy— ought always to prevail. Lenin still believed, in 1902, that Russia would cease to be an autocracy long before she became a socialist state, and that there would therefore be ample time to build up a broad and democratically organized workers' party before the proletarian revolution. He never, when he wrote *What Is To Be Done?* intended that the 'party of the proletariat' should drive and

[1] Meaning, of course, that its leaders were responsible to the rank and file.

bully the workers, or even that it should make their revolution for them, and then govern Russia in their name but without taking the trouble to consult them. The party was merely to educate and guide them, to raise them, as Lenin said in a later pamphlet, up to 'its own level of consciousness.'[1] Unless this were done there could be no proletarian revolution to establish socialism in Russia.

Lenin was, no doubt, always an unaccommodating and opinionated man, intolerant, unjust and abusive. He was by temperament an autocrat, but that did not prevent his being, at least in theory, a democrat of the Marxian kind until he became ruler of Russia. Being a Marxist, he thought it impossible that free discussion and the counting of heads should reconcile the interests of different classes; he believed that parliaments and general elections are bourgeois shams invented to disguise the oppression of the poor by the rich; but he also believed that those who speak and act for the workers should be in fact, and not merely in name, responsible to them.

Had there been no Bolshevik revolution in 1917, had Russia become a constitutional and fairly liberal bourgeois state long before anyone took power to try to make her 'proletarian,' had Lenin remained always in opposition to government, the doctrines expounded in *What Is To Be Done?* would never have acquired their present significance. We should not venture to call them undemocratic, but merely say of them that they were advice perhaps well enough adapted to the needs of a revolutionary party active in Russia in the first decade of the twentieth century.

But the Bolshevik revolution did happen, and was made by a small and irresponsible party, and was never preceded by a period of stable and fairly liberal 'bourgeois' government. The 'party of the proletariat' never had time to become a massive and internally democratic class organization. Indeed, it never even became

---

[1] In *One Step Forward, Two Steps Back* (1904), he again discussed the relations of the party to the proletariat, saying that 'it would be Manilovism [i.e. complacent stupidity] . . . to think that at any time under capitalism the whole class, or almost the whole of it, could rise to the level of consciousness and activity of its vanguard, its Social-Democratic Party.' The reference here is no longer to the Russian party while the Tsarist autocracy lasts, but to any proletarian party 'at any time under capitalism'; and the passage, by insisting so much on the difference between an organized body speaking for a class and the class it speaks for, rings somehow false to democracy. But even here we must be careful how we interpret Lenin.

what Lenin thought it should be during the period of Tsarist autocracy, for Russia was still in 1917 without a united and doctrinally pure Marxist party, and almost none of the 'masses' had been 'raised' to the level of 'consciousness' of their still chaotic and quarrelsome 'vanguard.'

The union, discipline and doctrinal purity of the party were achieved *after* the revolution made by Lenin on behalf of the proletariat; and it was then, too, that the 'raising of the masses' seriously began. What ought to have been done before the 'proletarian' revolution was not seriously attempted until after it, when the party already controlled the state and could achieve by more forceful methods what, in opposition to established government, it could only have done by persuasion.

Pamphlets written for the benefit of a small band of Marxists harassed by a powerful and intolerant bureaucracy have now become the sacred texts of rulers who wield greater power than Lenin ever had to oppose. Their principles inspire the conduct of men whose influence depends, not on the quality of their arguments and their honest devotion to the working class, but on the massive political apparatus they control. No wonder then that those principles have come to mean something quite different from what Lenin intended when he first put them into words!

III. THE UNINTERRUPTED REVOLUTION

The defeat of the Russians by the Japanese in Manchuria weakened the authority of the Tsar, causing widespread disorder, mutiny in the navy and fighting in the streets of several towns. The Russian Marxists believed that their country was on the brink of revolution and their theory taught them that that revolution must be bourgeois. Plekhanov, Russia's proto-Marxist, had 'exposed' the Populist fallacy that a peasant country could pass directly to socialism without first becoming capitalist. No country could be made socialist until it had become industrial, and the historic rôle of the bourgeois was to provide the industries. Marxism had been brought to Russia by a man who proclaimed, against the Populists, that there would be no short cut for Russia, no passing capitalism by. And Lenin, who had got his Marxism from that man, believed that the revolution just beginning in

Russia was bourgeois, and also that the socialist revolution, when it happened, would be made by the proletariat. While keeping a firm hold of these two 'truths,' he boldly denied what to most of the other Marxists seemed to follow from them. He was determined that his party should exploit to the full the calamity about to descend on the country. To justify this policy, he wrote the pamphlet, *Two Tactics of Social Democracy in the Democratic Revolution*,[1] which perhaps more than any other has given to Russian Communism its special character.

Not that there was no Marxian precedent for Lenin's policy. There was *The Address to the Communist League*, the strange advice which the Germans could not take in 1850, and had ignored ever since. Marx had in that pamphlet urged the German workers, whom he thought of as the weaker partners in an alliance with the lower middle class, to exploit an expected bourgeois revolution in such a way as to force Germany half way to socialism before she had become properly capitalist. It was advice that an historical materialist ought never to have given, but it did prove the revolutionary zeal of the giver. It was so much in keeping with Lenin's temperament that in 1905 he more than took it; he improved on it. The coming revolution in Germany should, so said Marx in 1850, be made by the bourgeois with the help of the workers, and should give power to the former. His advice to the German Communist League and to the workers had been to remain independent and suspicious, to keep the revolution moving fast, to jolt and harry their allies, to prevent or retard the reactionary purposes that would inevitably be theirs as soon as the revolution had given them what they wanted. These hustling tactics, effectively used, might force the bourgeois to move towards socialism before they had time to get properly used to the ways of capitalism, just as the terrors of the jungle sometimes make animals run almost before they can walk.

What was enough for Marx in 1850 did not satisfy Lenin in 1905. What he expected was also a bourgeois revolution, but what he expected of it was much more than Marx had dared to hope in 1850. Russian appetites and digestions are stronger than German. What Lenin wanted was no less than that the workers

---

[1] Published at Geneva, in August 1905. *The Essentials of Lenin*, Vol. I, pp. 343–434.

should make the bourgeois revolution and rule the bourgeois state.

If Marxism were really what Marxists think it is, this suggestion would be so fantastic that we could not believe a Marxist had made it. If Marxism were a coherent theory and Marxists were persons who believed in it and acted in consequence, Lenin, a real Marxist if ever there was one, could never have written this absurd and important pamphlet. But men sometimes do the most natural things, which seem incredible to us only because we take those men at their own valuations. Marxism is a collection of doctrines having a strong family likeness between them, but its powers of assimilation are considerable. Indeed, since the Russians took over Marxism, these powers have increased. The further east we move in Europe, the less consistency and coherence matter. That is why the Slavs, though they have not enjoyed much freedom and do not greatly respect it, have such accommodating minds. They kill each other in defence of orthodoxy, but there is almost no opinion of which we can say beforehand for certain that it will shock or even disturb them. It all depends on the way the opinion is put to them, on the occasion, on prevailing moods and sympathies. Under the veil of a Slavonic orthodoxy almost anything is possible.

To prove the innocence and sincerity of Lenin, let me quote a few passages from this remarkable pamphlet. The next Russian revolution, Lenin knows, cannot be socialist; and he gives his orthodox reasons:

> The degree of economic development of Russia (an objective condition) and the degree of class consciousness and organization of the broad masses of the proletariat (a subjective condition inseparably connected with the objective) make the immediate complete emancipation of the working class impossible. Only the most ignorant people can ignore the bourgeois nature of the democratic revolution which is now taking place; only the most naïve optimist can forget how little as yet the masses of the workers are informed of the aims of socialism and of the methods of achieving it. . . . A socialist revolution is out of the question unless the masses become class conscious, organized, trained and educated in open class struggle against the entire bourgeoisie. . . . Whoever wants to arrive at socialism by a different road, other than that of political democracy, will inevitably arrive at absurd and reactionary conclusions, both in the economic and the political sense.

A few pages later Lenin says:

> Marxists are absolutely convinced of the bourgeois character of the Russian revolution. What does this mean? It means that the democratic changes in the political system, and the social and economic changes that have become indispensable for Russia, do not in themselves imply the undermining of capitalism, the undermining of bourgeois domination; on the contrary, they will, for the first time, really clear the ground for a widespread and rapid . . . development of capitalism; they will, for the first time, make it possible for the bourgeoisie to rule as a class.

These premises, so clearly and vigorously stated, do not prepare us for Lenin's conclusion:

> Only the proletariat can be a consistent fighter for democracy. It may become a victorious fighter for democracy only if the peasant masses join its revolutionary struggle. If the proletariat is not strong enough for this, the bourgeois will be at the head of the democratic revolution and will impart to it an inconsistent and self-seeking nature. Nothing short of a revolutionary democratic dictatorship of the proletariat and the peasantry can prevent this.

And then, a little later:

> The revolutionary-democratic dictatorship of the proletariat and peasantry is unquestionably only a transient, provisional aim of the Socialists, but to ignore this aim in the period of a democratic revolution would be plainly reactionary.

And then, again:

> the proletariat fights in the front ranks for a republic and contemptuously rejects the silly and unworthy advice to take care not to frighten away the bourgeois. The peasantry includes a great number of semi-proletarian as well as petty bourgeois elements. This causes it also to be unstable and compels the proletariat to unite in a strictly class party. But the instability of the peasants differs radically from the instability of the bourgeois, for at the present time the peasantry is interested, not so much in the absolute preservation of private property, as in the confiscation of the landed estates, one of the principal forms of private property. Though this does not cause the peasantry to become socialist or cease to be petty bourgeois, the peasantry is yet capable of becoming a wholehearted and most radical adherent of the democratic revolution. The peasantry will inevitably become so if only the progress of revolutionary events,

which is enlightening it, is not interrupted too soon by the treachery of the bourgeois and the defeat of the proletariat. Subject to this condition, the peasantry will inevitably become a bulwark of the revolution and the republic, for only a completely victorious revolution can give the peasantry everything in the sphere of agrarian reforms—everything that the peasants desire, dream about, and stand truly in need of.

Do these quotations prove the folly or the wisdom of Lenin? Let me avoid the question and say: they prove that this devoted Marxist could take what liberties he chose with the object of his devotion, and also that he was a shrewd politician. The coming revolution must, he says, be democratic and bourgeois; neither the economic condition of Russia nor the political education of her workers and peasants (and these things go together) allow her to become socialist in the immediate future. Capitalism will come and with it the rule of the bourgeois. What, then, must the workers do? They must, together with the peasants, take control of the revolution and establish their joint dictatorship. But how can the bourgeois rule if the workers and peasants make themselves masters of the bourgeois state? And if the bourgeois do not rule, how can the state, after the democratic revolution, become bourgeois? It is useless to put these simple questions. Had they occurred to Lenin, he would have written a different pamphlet and the Communists would lack one of their most important texts. It is easy to discover the folly of Lenin, to point to the grossest contradictions even in the polemical writings whose subtlety is most praised by his admirers. It is the nature of fanatics to strain at gnats and swallow camels. Using the martial vocabulary of their creed, they dress up their arguments like soldiers in battle formation, whose general thinks them invincible because their fine appearance excites him.

The shrewdness of Lenin's political judgments is less obvious. He spoke, in this pamphlet, of the 'instability' of the bourgeois and of the peasants. What had he in mind? And why did he think them 'unstable' in different ways? The Russian bourgeois and the peasants were 'unstable' from the point of view of the proletariat. The bourgeois were 'unstable' because, though they wanted to destroy the autocracy, they were also afraid that the classes and parties to the left of them would use the revolution to get more than the bourgeois were willing to concede. The French bourgeois in the great revolution had been more afraid of reaction than of the excesses of the Jacobins; they had been, in their time, a revolutionary class. But socialism had since come into the world, and fear of it had inevitably affected the policies of the bourgeois even in the most backward countries. There were now enemies to both sides of them and they had to make their calculations accordingly. They might even find it politic in Russia to make a compromise with the Tsarist autocracy. The Russian bourgeois were therefore an 'unstable' class in this sense—that they wanted to put an end to the autocracy and yet feared the consequences of its fall. The workers could not count on their unrelenting hostility to the régime; they might, for a little while and with considerable reluctance, make use of the workers, but would quickly betray them and unite with the autocracy for their punishment if they asked for too much or seemed too powerful. The Russian bourgeois liberals were therefore unreliable friends and potential enemies of the workers and peasants. They were so already, though Russia had not yet become a bourgeois and capitalist society.

The 'instability' of the Russian peasants had a different cause. They were not more conservative but more revolutionary than the peasants in the West. Very few of them were prosperous and independent farmers, substantial yeomen who found it their interest to stand, in the last resort, with all other owners of property. They were mostly poor and growing poorer, they were used to the discipline of the village commune, they felt strongly that all peasants were their friends and all landlords their enemies. They were no longer serfs but their minds were still servile; they were the 'people' and the others, the landlords, were the 'masters,' to be placated because of their power but whose domination was unjust. They were an exploited and resentful class, more intent on dispossessing the masters than concerned to defend their own property. They knew nothing of a socialist threat to all property; they knew only that they could scarcely get a living from their primitive farms, and that the best land still belonged to the masters. In the West the peasants were the natural and docile allies of the bourgeois, but in Russia they were still friendless outside their own class. If there were timely reforms, the Russian peasants might yet become allies of the bourgeois, but there was still time for the Social-Democrats to win them over. By the 'instability' of the peasants, Lenin meant that they had not committed themselves to an alliance with any of the politically more active classes and might therefore be won over by the proletariat and their party.

The Tsarist autocracy was rotten, the bourgeois were weak and timid, and the urban workers were in close touch with the peasants—the great and undocile majority of the Russian people. Why, then, now that the inevitable 'bourgeois' revolution was on the way, should not the workers and peasants, led by the Social-Democrats, unite to take control of it, and then use their united power to prevent reaction and drive Russia towards socialism as quickly as she could go? · The other leading Russian Marxists (with the exception of Trotsky, who then, as always, had opinions of his own) were saying that, because this revolution was of necessity bourgeois, the workers must leave it to the bourgeois to take the leading part in it. Lenin's reply was that conditions peculiar to their country gave the Russian Marxists and workers an opportunity it would be folly to neglect. If that opportunity were not taken, the eventual coming of socialism would be greatly delayed; and it could not be taken, unless the Social-Democrats contrived a revolutionary alliance between workers and peasants.

Lenin was not the only Marxist who in 1905 conceived that it might be possible for the proletariat and their party to take control of a 'bourgeois' revolution and use it to hasten the coming of socialism. The same idea occurred at about the same time to Trotsky, who was far from being Lenin's disciple and even mistrusted him for his too great love of discipline and arrogant contempt for what he liked to call 'intellectual caprice'; but it was Lenin who was the first to understand the uses to which the Social-Democrats might put peasant discontents. Stalin has praised Lenin for his discernment; that praise is just but needs to be qualified. Lenin did not care for the peasants as peasants, and meant to do good to them by changing their condition. He had never the least intention, despite the phrase he coined, that there should be 'a revolutionary dictatorship of the proletariat and peasantry.' He may perhaps have imagined that the 'dictatorship of the proletariat' could be exercised for the workers by the

Social-Democrats without the rights of the class being usurped by the party; but he made it abundantly clear that the peasants were not to be allowed to get, or if they got it to keep, what he knew they wanted. He meant to do good by them, but in the manner of Mr. Murdstone to David Copperfield.

In an article published in September 1905, on *The Attitude of Social-Democracy Toward the Peasant Movement*, we find the words: 'We support the peasant movement, in so far as it is a revolutionary democratic movement. We are making ready . . . to fight against it in so far as it becomes reactionary and anti-proletarian.' Lenin said not a word about 'reconciling' the interests of the two classes whose revolutionary alliance he wanted to contrive; though the peasants were many times more numerous than the workers, he always intended that their interests should be sacrificed to those of their allies. He foretold a future conflict between the richer and poorer peasants, explaining that the Social-Democrats must take advantage of it. He promised that 'from the democratic revolution we shall at once, and just in accordance with our strength, the strength of the class-conscious and organized proletariat, begin to pass to the socialist revolution. We stand for uninterrupted revolution. We shall not stop half way.' And if 'we' do not promise all kinds of socialization immediately, it is only because we do 'not gloss over but reveal the new struggle that is maturing within the ranks of the peasantry.'

It is clear that Lenin believed, even in 1905, that the alliance between workers and peasants must be only temporary, that after the bourgeois revolution the poor peasants must be set against the rich ones, and must in any case always be controlled by the party of the proletariat. He reckoned with the peasants more than any Marxist before him had done, but he never thought it possible to establish socialism in Russia except against the wishes of the more independent among them, who had achieved the ambition common to all their class—a decent living earned by their own work on their own land. The peasants on whose collaboration he counted after the bourgeois revolution he called 'semi-proletarians,' thereby implying that their position in the class they were usually assigned to was precarious. They were peasants, no doubt, but peasants with a difference, having interests uncharacteristic of the petty bourgeois class they belonged to; they were disinherited, not in virtue of their class, but because—numerous though they might be—they were abnormal specimens of it.

The Communists defend Lenin against the charge of heresy by saying that the doctrine of 'uninterrupted revolution' has good Marxian authority behind it. Lenin may have wanted to go further in 1905 than Marx in 1850, but the principle behind their policies was the same; each proposed that, in a still predominantly agricultural country, a small and scarcely organized urban proletariat should make, and then exploit for socialist purposes, a temporary alliance with another and larger class, which, being semi-proletarian, was inclined to revolution. If Lenin chose a different ally for the Russian proletariat from the one chosen by Marx for the German workers, he did so only because the condition of Russia in 1905, socially and politically, was different from Germany's in 1850.

Though the Communists are not unreasonable in their defence of Lenin, they overlook the stronger part of the accusation against him. By the time Lenin wrote the *Two Tactics*, the authors of Marxism were both dead and their works long familiar to their disciples. Historical materialism had received its classic formulation, and there were ample commentaries upon it. Not all its knots had been unravelled, but there were already common opinions about it enough to make some conclusions improbable. History, as Marx and Engels had described it in their later, quieter and more voluminous works, moves so slowly on its predestined course that neither they nor their Russian disciples could reasonably hope to make the proletarian revolution—the event they lived for and continually foretold. They could proclaim the promised land and set the chosen class on the road to it, but could not reasonably hope to get even as near it as Moses had done. The justification of their lives must come some considerable time after their deaths. Marx and Engels had been impatient in their youth, but had afterwards made amends for that impatience.

The proletarian revolution, more by far than the classless society that comes after it, excites the imagination of the ambitious Marxist; it is for him the last great fall of the waters of history on their course to the open sea of communism, the last battle and the last occasion for heroism. To live through it and help make it is the greatest of adventures, the crowning glory of a revolutionary's life. Though Lenin could not reasonably hope to witness that great event, he so longed for it that, when he saw what appeared to be signs of its coming sooner than historical materialism allowed for, it was more than he could do to take that appearance for illusion. It was faith in historical materialism that made him hope for proletarian revolution, and yet, when that revolution seemed nearer than his faith gave him the right to expect, it was faith he put to one side. This is the origin—simple, human and far removed from intellectual causes—of the strange doctrine of the 'uninterrupted revolution,' which begins by being 'bourgeois' and ends by being 'proletarian,' the doctrine of which Marx was the less and Lenin the more reckless exponent. It is a doctrine that every historical materialist ought to reject, but that no one not an historical materialist has ever accepted. Marx invented the milder form of it for a special occasion, and when that occasion was past said no more about it. Lenin revived it to serve a greater ambition.

The doctrine of the 'uninterrupted revolution' is no more true than the historical materialism it denies by implication. There has never been, since the world began, a bourgeois revolution that turned into anything partly or wholly proletarian; and Russia, in particular, has never known either a bourgeois or a proletarian revolution. Only a small minority of either class took part in the revolutions of 1905 and of March and November 1917; of which the first is called 'abortive' because it failed to put an end to Tsarist autocracy, and the second and third 'successful' because they caused the fall of the governments they were directed against. But the March revolution was not properly bourgeois nor the Bolshevik revolution proletarian; the former would not have happened had the workers not revolted, and the latter gave power to the Bosheviks and not the proletariat. The Bolsheviks could not have seized power in November 1917 except with the support of the workers, but that no more makes the Bolshevik revolution proletarian than the support of the Paris mob makes the dictatorship of Robespierre a working-class government. If a revolution is proletarian only when the men and parties that make it are truly representative of the workers and use their power to establish working-class government (and that is what Marx and Engels meant by it), then the revolution of November 1917 was not proletarian.

Though Lenin used words improperly when he spoke of the three Russian revolutions of the twentieth century, he did not misunderstand the situations that made them possible. Marx, when he wrote his *Address to the Communist League* in 1850, expected a revolution which never happened; the advice he gave could not be taken because the political situation in Germany was not in fact what he thought it. Lenin, however, understood the realities of Russian politics rather better than Marx had understood the Germany of 1850; it was true that the bourgeois in Russia were weak and timid, that the workers could be easily persuaded to attempt the violent overthrow of the régime, and that the peasants could, at least for a time, be won over to the revolutionary cause. It was true that Russia, a backward agricultural society suddenly exposed to the impact of western industrialism and western socialist thought, was in a condition peculiar to countries of her own kind and unknown to the wealthier and more civilized parts of Europe and North America; and it was above all true that that condition could be exploited by a band of determined revolutionaries to seize power in the name of the workers and peasants. The simple mistake that Lenin made—and he had to make it or else abandon all hope of the triumph, while he lived, of the class to whose service he had dedicated his life— was to suppose that whatever was done in the name of the workers by the party calling itself proletarian[1] was done by the workers.

[1] Not by *any* party calling itself proletarian but by that one among them to which Lenin belonged. The fanatic devotes himself to a cause, the egoist to himself; but the fanatic puts himself at the centre of the cause he makes his own, taking spiritual possession of it. He treats whoever abandons the cause as a traitor, and arrogates to himself the right to decide what treachery is. When he parts from another man, it is always the other who has betrayed the cause. The fanatic is 'selfless,' but only in the sense that he has put his self into something that to him appears external to himself, though to others it is merely himself writ large. He has sacrificed himself to this external and superior thing, and thinks that he has thereby acquired the right to sacrifice others. The egoist and the fanatic are both unjust, but in the fanatic there are also seeds of madness. There is a great difference between fanaticism and faith. The act of faith is a submission to what is felt to be superior, and the man who has submitted knows that, being human and weak, he may be unfaithful. Whereas the fanatic believes that, while others can betray, he can never be a traitor. The distinction I make has nothing to do with the truth or falsity of men's beliefs; it is merely psychological. The man of faith may sometimes be as harmful as the fanatic, and both faith and fanaticism can be religious or political or different from both; but whatever their objects and though their results are on occasion similar, the difference between them is absolute. Faith is no more like fanaticism than it is like doubt. It may be that these two words, 'faith' and 'fanaticism,' have not often been used to make just this distinction; but there is here, nevertheless, a real and important difference between two emotional attitudes, and these two words are perhaps

This mistake, as necessary to Lenin's ambition as it was obvious to his critics, has had the gravest consequences. If the 'party of the proletariat' can make a 'proletarian' revolution without greatly caring what the workers think, if it can know what is good for them better than they know it themselves, if it can both speak for them and reduce them to silence whenever it chooses to find it to their interest to do so, why should it not act on their behalf even before there are enough of them to constitute an important class in society? Just as Lenin improved on Marx, so the later Communists have improved on Lenin. They have formed parties of the proletariat where no proletariat exists; they have done it in China and Yugoslavia. The members of those parties are nearly all intellectuals or peasants, but their avowed purpose is to establish a proletarian state. They first make a revolution and then set about creating the industries without which, according to Marx, no proletarian state can exist. They first capture the 'superstructure' and then use it to transform the 'foundation'— so that 'proletarian revolution,' from being an effect of mature industrialism, becomes the prelude to it.

The doctrine of 'uninterrupted revolution' was severely criticized by the Mensheviks who denounced it as a travesty of Marxism. In a country to which Plekanhov had introduced Marxism by proving that the Populist hope of passing capitalism by and moving quickly to socialism was groundless, it was not possible for Lenin to ignore this criticism, which was supported by texts more numerous and plausible than his own, and was also in keeping with what the German Social-Democratic Party accepted as orthodox Marxism. He therefore made use of an argument intended to meet the Menshevik accusation that he was advocating premature revolution.

This supplementary argument, though it was invented as early as the main doctrine,[1] was not prominently used till the First

the best suited to express it. Fanaticism is not just faith miscalled; for we seek faith to bring peace to our own minds, while fanaticism urges us to make war on others. The fanatic may have faith, but his fanaticism consists in this, that he makes his faith an excuse for seeking power over others. Moreover, fanaticism is destructive of faith, because it makes the fanatic distort his faith to serve his ambition. Faith is often the refuge of the humble, while fanaticism is the effect of a secret and abominable pride.

[1] In an article on *The Provisional Government* (1905)—which Stalin quotes from in *The Foundations of Leninism*—Lenin argues that the fall of Tsarism in Russia will start off a proletarian revolution in the West, whose repercussions will enable

World War. Lenin believed that the major industrial Powers engaged in war were exhausting one another and putting an intolerable strain on the capitalist economy. The war could, he thought, end only in proletarian revolution, affecting several— if not all—of the major belligerents. Since the great industrial countries dominated the world, they could carry their weaker neighbours along with them in whatever direction they moved. If they were ripe for proletarian revolution, then the world was also ripe for it. Marxists everywhere, whatever their nationality, owed their first duty, not to a nation, but to a class; and must serve the interest of that class according to the world situation. Whatever the conditions peculiar to their own country, they must exploit them for the benefit of the world proletariat; and that benefit, now that capitalism was strained to the breaking-point in the most powerful industrial states, was to be found only in proletarian revolution.

Lenin, when he arrived in Petrograd from Switzerland in April 1917, was convinced that the Russian Social-Democrats, by seizing power in their own country in the name of the workers, could precipitate proletarian revolutions in the West. If one or two of the great industrial states turned proletarian, the others would soon follow their example and the world would get the revolution and the socialism for which, taken as a whole, it was already ripe. The wealthy and powerful countries, by giving help to their backward neighbours, would prevent the evil consequences of what might otherwise have been premature attempts to establish socialism where 'objective conditions' did not allow it.[1]

The leaders of Social Democracy in the West had betrayed the working class, and were no longer fit to take advantage of the predicament created for moribund capitalism by the most terrible of wars; but the chain of imperialism, forged by the strong to

Russia to achieve socialism much more quickly than she otherwise could. He said that the 'revolutionary wave in Europe will sweep back into Russia and convert a few revolutionary years into an epoch of several revolutionary decades.' But he made little use of this argument in 1905, and never put it in the *Two Tactics*. He revived it later, making much more of it.

[1] Lenin also used arguments tending to show that 'objective conditions' in Russia were already much more favourable to socialism than the Mensheviks supposed; but these were lesser arguments. The most effective and plausible was the one we have been discussing.

bind the world to dependence on them, might be broken at its weakest link, which happened to be Russia, by the ruthless energy of the Bolsheviks. The Russian David could not slay the Goliath of Imperialism, but could strike the first and bravest of the many blows needed to bring him down. To what other group of men was given an opportunity of so glorious service to the world? Who would hesitate with the timid and pedantic Mensheviks rather than risk all in so noble a venture?[1]

IV. THE PROLETARIAN 'HALF-STATE'

The doctrines of Lenin so far considered have remained to this day essential parts of Communist theory; they have been reinterpreted but not neglected or given wholly new meanings; they still help us to understand the ambitions and behaviour of Lenin's successors.

There is, however, another side of Lenin's teaching which, though it adds nothing important to Marxism and no longer inspires the behaviour of the Communist Party, is yet well worth studying for the insight it gives us into the character of the greatest revolutionary of our age. Lenin has been called a realist, and indeed was one, and yet was also a Utopian simpler and more credulous than most. If we look at *The State and the Revolution*, perhaps the most often read of all his pamphlets, we can see how narrow the understanding and how little the foresight of the man who, more than any other, has changed our modern world.

The State and the Revolution consists of quotations from Marx and Engels so put together and explained as to justify the revolutionary Marxism of the Bolsheviks and confound all their critics. The too ample commentary on the quotations is a rude[2] defence of the 'pure doctrine' against the Majority Socialists in Germany and the Mensheviks in Russia. Lenin's pamphlet seeks to prove, against the German Social-Democrats, that Marx and Engels

---

[1] The reader may find this attitude too romantic for hard-headed Marxists. But, then, most revolutionaries are romantics. Their's is the romanticism of the embittered and would-be tough—the most common variety in the modern world.

[2] Marx was a most rude and scornful controversialist, and his disciples have mostly imitated his manners, whose freedom from 'bourgeois hypocrisy' they have greatly admired. It seems not to have occurred to them that discourtesy, by causing men from motives of vanity to defend the indefensible and to waste time on irrelevancies, is a serious obstacle in the search for truth. Or if it has occurred to them, they have disregarded it in practice.

never ceased to be revolutionary socialists, but does not offer us a coherent theory of the state. On the contrary, it draws attention to what might otherwise have escaped notice—to the absence of any such theory in the writings of Marx and Engels; it also draws attention to other faults invisible to Lenin, to the reckless assertions and bad logic of the two men who seemed to him the most profound of thinkers.

We can find in Lenin's pamphlet arguments—as if by anticipation—against much that happened in Russia after 1920 and that Trotsky later condemned. The pamphlet is, of course, still printed in Russia and approved by the authorities, who do not think it dangerous to themselves. It is an authorized text subject to official interpretation, and therefore not to be taken literally. It has proved easy enough to teach the youth of Russia to admire it without drawing from it any inconvenient practical consequences. They are made familiar with it, and the familiarity breeds a kind of careless reverence not far removed from contempt.[1] But the fact remains that the pamphlet can be taken literally, and that those who so take it, if they happen to be Marxists, will soon find themselves looking at the Russia of Stalin through the eyes of Trotsky.

Marx produced two doctrines of the state, and would neither explain how they are connected nor abandon one of them. He said that the state is an instrument of class oppression, and also that it is often a parasitic growth on society, making class oppression possible even when the government is not the agent of any class. Lenin accepted both these doctrines without noticing that they are incompatible or attempting to adjust them to one another. He also accepted the theory of Engels that the state emerges as soon as there arise in society classes with irreconcilable interests, its function being to keep the peace between them. Lenin, like Engels, never thought it necessary to explain how it is that the peace cannot be kept except by sacrificing the interests of all classes but one to that one class. Nor did he explain how the

---

[1] We, too, are brought up in the same way. When we are young we are taught to admire the saying: 'Sell all that thou hast and give to the poor.' When we first hear it, it can do us no harm, for we are children with nothing to sell and nothing to give. And when we grow up, we quickly discover that the advice is impracticable. This process of inoculation against the impossible virtues, which we ought to admire but not to practise, is a usual part of nearly all education. Whether it is necessary, the psychologist must decide.

keeping of peace within society differs from the conciliation of interests; he merely said, repeating Engels, that the function of the state is to keep the peace between 'irreconcilable' classes, and to keep it in the interest of only one class among them. Lenin had fewer doubts than either of his masters and was never tempted to question their assumptions; he therefore never pondered their curious doctrine that, though the social classes have *irreconcilable* (and not merely different) interests, it is somehow possible to keep the peace between them. He quietly accepted in the way of doctrine whatever they offered him, including this far from self-evident assumption that to maintain social peace and order is not to conciliate interests. For the difference between these two functions he had never a thought to spare.[1]

In *The State and the Revolution*, Lenin repeats, again following Engels, that the existence of armies and police forces is proof enough that class interests cannot be reconciled. Special instruments must, he thinks, be created to maintain the supremacy of the ruling class. The alternative hypothesis, which is perhaps more plausible, that these instruments were first created in the

---

[1] Interests are not solid things of determinate shapes, which, like the parts of a jig-saw puzzle, either can or cannot be fitted into each other. How is one man's interest reconciled with another's? There are two words of uncertain meaning in this question—'interest' and 'reconciled.' A man's interests can surely be no more than the objects of his more persistent desires, the things for whose sake he works and makes sacrifices; and the interests of a class merely the objects of the most persistent desires common to persons having more or less the same status in society. The interests, whether of individuals or classes, very frequently conflict; if one man gets all he wants another must often get less, and so it must also be with classes. How are interests 'reconciled'? They are 'reconciled,' presumably, whenever the men or classes that pursue them observe the rules whose general observance is social peace. How then, if the rules are observed, can interests be irreconcilable? We can perhaps say, as many philosophers have done, that the more rules are observed because they are felt to be just, the greater the harmony between men's interests; and that, conversely, the more they are observed from fear of punishment, the less that harmony. This, at least, is a distinction which makes sense; but, in that case, what becomes of the 'irreconcilable' interests of different classes in a society where, say, bourgeois morality prevails? Let us suppose for a moment that some travellers' tales are true, and that American workers really do not mind their employers being ten or a hundred or even a thousand times richer than themselves, that they would rather keep their one chance in ten thousand of becoming rich than have governments, however democratically elected, take over the factories they work in; let us also suppose that they require no more of governments than that they should tax the rich to give everyone modest provision against ill-health, unemployment, and old age. Are their interests and those of their employers 'irreconcilable' still? What could be meant by calling them so? When classes are at peace and little force is required to keep that peace, surely the man who calls their interests 'irreconcilable' merely betrays his desire that there should be disputes where there are none, or that what disputes there are should be more bitter.

common interest and then enabled those who controlled them to become a ruling class, never occurs to him, though he also repeats the argument of Engels that the state arises out of the need to hold class antagonisms in check, a need presumably felt by all the classes and whose satisfaction is therefore a common interest.

On the basis of this theory of the state—or, rather, of this collection of ideas about the state—Lenin seeks to establish as orthodox Marxism two propositions neglected or denied by the German Majority Socialists: 1. that the bourgeois state and all its instruments must be destroyed by the proletariat, and 2. that it is the 'dictatorship of the proletariat' (that is, the proletarian and not the bourgeois state) which is destined to 'wither away.' There are interesting corollaries of these propositions, but they are the two major theses of the pamphlet.

The Majority Socialists did not want to remember that Marxism is a revolutionary doctrine. They, too, hoped eventually to capture the German state, to use it to establish socialism, and then to see it (though they did not know quite how or when) disappear. Their theory of the state was a considerably modified version of the doctrine baldly asserted in *The Communist Manifesto*. The workers must first capture the state, and then use it to establish the kind of society inside which the state (i.e. the organized use of force) can gradually subside to nothing. The German Social-Democrats no longer saw the capture of the state as the result of a violent assault upon it by the workers; they hoped that an electoral victory might suffice to give them power, and that, if they had to use violence, it would be to suppress an illegal *putsch* made by the defeated reactionaries.

To establish his first proposition, that the proletariat must destroy the bourgeois state, Lenin chose for his texts quotations from the last chapter of *The Eighteenth Brumaire of Louis Bonaparte* and from *The Civil War in France*. In the former, Marx had said that 'all the revolutions had perfected this (state) machine, instead of smashing it'; and in *The Civil War in France*, that 'the working class cannot simply lay hold of the ready made state machinery and use it for its own purposes.' To prove that these two ideas were not unconnected in the mind of Marx, Lenin also quoted some sentences from a letter written by Marx to Kugelmann during the time of the Commune: 'If you look at the last chapter of my

Eighteenth Brumaire, you will find that I say that the next attempt of the French revolution will no longer be to transfer the bureaucratic and military machine from one hand to another but to smash it; and that is a preliminary condition for every real people's revolution on the Continent. And this is what our heroic Party comrades are attempting.' This doctrine, that the workers, when they make their revolution, must destroy the bourgeois state and substitute for it the 'dictatorship of the proletariat,' which is the last state, the state destined to wither away, is, so Lenin tells us, the fundamental thesis of Marxian political theory.

The bourgeois state must be destroyed because it cannot be used for proletarian purposes. Lenin's assumption is that every ruling class dominates society in its own peculiar way, and therefore require its own political institutions, its peculiar instruments of government. The bourgeois state has a natural tendency to grow stronger and more elaborate, to become an always fatter parasite feeding on the body of society. It maintains an army, a police force and a bureaucratic machine, whose interests cannot be those of society as a whole. The bourgeois find it easy to tolerate this parasite, because, while it exists, it maintains the conditions of their economic and social supremacy.

The dictatorship of the proletariat, the workers' state or 'half-state' (as Lenin sometimes called it), is not a growing parasite whose function is to maintain the social conditions of class exploitation; it is the instrument of the workers and peasants, of the great majority, who use it to destroy the last traces of class exploitation.

It is therefore the dictatorship of the proletariat and not the bourgeois state that will wither away. The workers' state is strongest at the moment of its birth, and must from that moment weaken until it dies. Lenin called it a 'half-state' because its function is not to perpetuate the conditions of its own life but to destroy them. It is repressive and therefore a state; but it is also the instrument of the great majority. In the words of Lenin: 'Since the majority of the people themselves suppress their oppressors, a "special force" for suppression is no longer necessary! In this sense the state begins to wither away.' In the bourgeois state, the minority exploit the majority, and the condition of this exploitation is the growing strength of certain instruments of government, of organizations that perpetuate themselves because their members have corporate interests of their own. In the proletarian state the majority suppress the minority, and, being the majority, have no need to use for instruments organizations that are self-perpetuating and parasitic. On the contrary, the organizations they use are democratically controlled, and they gradually disappear as the work of suppression is completed.

Lenin, when he wrote *The State and the Revolution*, had never had even a day's administrative experience. He had been for years a member of the Russian Social-Democratic Party, an undisciplined and quarrelsome body, and had later created his own Bolshevik organization; but he had never taken even a subordinate part in governement. That is why he could write,[1] only a few months before the Bolshevik revolution, that 'the great majority of the functions of the old state power have been so simplified and can be reduced to such simple operations of registration, filing and checking, that they can be easily performed by every literate person.' Lenin believed that capitalism makes the tasks of government easier. Why, then, has the bourgeois state become so massive? Lenin's answer is that successive revolutions have made it so; that the parasite has fed on its host and is swollen with its blood. This was the simple answer that satisfied Lenin in 1917, when he still refused to believe that the spread of industry makes society so complex that only a large, varied and highly trained administration can control it. 'We ourselves,' he said, 'the workers, shall organize large-scale production on the basis of what capitalism has already created . . . we shall reduce the rôle of state officials to a simple carrying out of our instructions as responsible, revocable, and modestly paid "managers". . . . Overthrow the capitalists . . . smash the bureaucratic machine of the modern state —and you will have a mechanism of the highest technical equipment, free from the parasite, capable of being operated by the workers themselves, who will hire their own technicians, managers and bookkeepers, and pay them all—as, indeed, all state officials in general—ordinary workmen's wages.' Only a Bolshevik could have been so innocent in the summer of 1917.

[1] The explanation falls short of the truth. In matters so simple common sense can enlighten us even when we have no experience. Such blindness as Lenin's is the effect not of inexperience but of devotion to false doctrines.

The German Social-Democrats, of course, knew better. They had outgrown Marxism, though not the vanity that made them cling to their reputations as leading Marxists. They had hitherto not needed to reject the more irresponsible utterances of Marx and Engels; it had been enough to take little notice of them. But with the Bolsheviks in the ascendant, and their own extremists restive, they had learnt to dislike what they had previously ignored. Above all, they had come to dislike the phrase 'the dictatorship of the proletariat,' and now wanted to minimize its importance. Experience had taught them that the bourgeois state is not merely an instrument of class oppression, that it is not a mere parasite feeding on the social body, that the departments of state established by the old society would be necessary to the new one; they knew, in short, what we all know when we have no special motive for refusing to admit the obvious; they knew that the government of modern industrial society is altogether too difficult to be entrusted to persons not specially trained for it. They knew that direct rule by the workers is impossible, and that the most to be hoped for is as much responsibility to them as the devices of democracy will allow. The administrative machine must not be smashed; it must be preserved and adapted to new uses. For without it socialism is impossible—socialism which requires so great an intervention of public authority in the daily business of our lives.

Kautsky, who, after the reunion of the Independents with the Majority Socialists, could speak for the whole of the German Social-Democratic Party, knew the truth and was embarrassed by it, while Lenin exulted in his own and Marx's nonsense. What made Kautsky unhappy and Lenin happy was the one thing common to them: their devotion to Marxism. Whatever Kautsky might say, the texts meant what Lenin said they meant. Marx had indeed written the last chapter of *The Eighteenth Brumaire of Louis Bonaparte*, and had also written *The Civil War in France*. What was written there could not be unwritten; and though the expressions used by the master were not precise, there was a limit to their possible meanings. The scriptures weighed heavily on Lenin's side, and Kautsky, who knew them better than any Russian, could not really believe otherwise. The Paris Commune was—Marx had said it—a proletarian government. That government Marx had attempted to describe, and whether or not he described it accurately does not matter. The fact remains that what he there described could not be established unless the modern bourgeois state were destroyed or completely transformed.

It is odd that Marx's description of the Commune, his disingenuous account of a government inspired by the doctrines of his great rival Proudhon, should have been the stone that broke in two the great international socialist movement most of whose leaders called themselves Marxists. What is less odd—for nothing is more usual than that men's actions should give the lie to their doctrines—is that, within a year or two of writing *The State and the Revolution*, Lenin should have proved that Kautsky was right after all. Lenin soon found himself obliged to establish a highly centralized administrative machine in Russia, finding that he could not govern without it. The constitution of the new Bolshevik state was federal, but that federalism was a mere pretence; all real power belonged to the closely disciplined Communist Party. Most of the old departments of state were brought to life again, albeit under new names; and the political police were soon more active than they had been under the Tsars.

We cannot ignore *The State and the Revolution*, though its logic is bad and its facts mistaken. It is, with Marx's *Civil War in France* and his *Critique of the Gotha Programme*, one of the three doctrinal disasters of Communism. It is nonsense, and yet not sufficiently nonsense; it can be partly understood, it can excite and mislead, and can therefore influence men's actions. It is not mere abuse, and noise, and abstract argument; it gives advice that men can take at their peril, and more particularly at the peril of their neighbours. The advice it gives is to destroy what the adviser thinks harmful but what is in fact indispensable.

One of Lenin's slogans during the October Revolution was: 'All power to the Soviets.' He mistook the soviets for organs of proletarian democracy, and may perhaps have at first intended that they should control everyone exercising authority in Russia. The Bolshevik Party would, he hoped, give a lead to the people inside the soviets without destroying their democratic character. He believed that soviet democracy was the political instrument especially fitted for making a socialist revolution.

Lenin was the victim of Marx's evasive arguments in *The Civil*

War in France, where he praised the democracy of the Paris Commune, its project of a federal constitution for France, its hatred of bureaucracy, and yet also pretended that there would remain a national authority strong enough to transform French society more radically than it had ever been transformed before. Marx knew that the Communards intended that the provincial authorities and the national government should be responsible to the communes, and should consist of mere delegates revocable at will. Much less knowledge of human affairs than Marx possessed could have taught him (had he been willing to learn) that a national government so constituted has almost no power; and that, if it acquires power, it does so only because it has ceased (whatever the appearances) to be what the constitution made it—power having in fact shifted from the communes to the centre, so that the national government has somehow acquired effective instruments, which it alone controls. Marx knew that only a strong central government can transform a capitalist society into a socialist one. Indeed, this belief, as much as any other, distinguishes his theory from anarchism; and yet he also contrived to praise the Paris Commune and its projected constitution for France. Where Marx was evasive, Lenin, in theoretical matters always more blind and therefore bolder than his master, was positive and explicit. And so the world acquired *The State and the Revolution*, the most simple-minded and improbable of all famous political pamphlets.

Lenin was a shrewd and masterful politician, but as a political theorist much less admirable. When he wanted to establish the truth of his opinions, he seldom discussed the relevant facts: he did not study society and government but only what Marxists, orthodox and heretical, had to say about them. He took the opinions opposed to his own and then collected a number of texts from Marx and Engels to refute them with; he took these objectionable opinions one by one and dealt with each in turn until it seemed to him to fall to pieces, battered by his sarcasms and withered by his scorn.

He became in time a master at this game, and mistook it for argument. He was amazed at the variety of the texts he was able to collect; the richness of Marxism and its adequacy for all occasions astonished him; and where he was grateful, his praise was loud. He struck blow after blow, and when he had taken what exercise he needed, was sure that his adversaries were all knocked down. Or else he merely paraded his opinions with a triumphant air, as if he thought the sight of them enough to silence his enemies. This tough and primitive controversialist thought himself a philosopher; and he also believed himself invincible in argument, so strong was his desire to win and his confidence in Marx and Engels. He felt that if they were proved wrong, truth itself would be betrayed. He imagined himself the servant of an infallible doctrine which he alone could interpret, and so could afford to be always modest and yet always right. 'It is not I but Marx' or 'it is not I but Engels who says': these are the unseen beginnings of all his arguments; and their perpetual conclusion: 'and therefore I am right.' When a hint of inconsistency troubled him, he took refuge in a phrase.

Chapter Eleven

BOLSHEVISM AFTER THE REVOLUTION

I HAVE discussed the theories of Lenin before the Bolshevik revolution, theories that still go by the name of Leninism. The books, pamphlets and articles setting them out have given to Bolshevism its special character—a character which, like so much that is human and individual, is as difficult to define as it is easy to recognize. Lenin was neither a philosopher nor a social theorist; he was a man of action excited by ideas. When he turned his mind to philosophy and to social theory, he was not trying to find solutions to difficult problems, he was not making hypotheses and weighing the evidence for and against them; he was merely defending his heritage of ideas, polishing his intellectual armour and sharpening his weapons for the war of words. What genuine thinking he did was about political warfare; it was only then that his mind was engaged with realities. He delighted in the Marxian philosophy, he repeated its phrases and hurled them at his enemies; they passed so often through his mind and came so readily to his pen that it never occurred to him that he did not understand them. They were familiar to him; and, being a simple man, he made the mistake of thinking that what is familiar is understood. It is the sign of the born philosopher that he does not easily make this kind of mistake.

Lenin and the Bolsheviks seized power; and they were the first doctrinaire revolutionaries[1] in modern times to keep it for more than a few months. Indeed, some of them only lost it by dying a a natural death, and not because Stalin killed them. Even Stalin was a Bolshevik; he had as good a right to call himself one as anyone, except Lenin, ever had. The Bolsheviks are still in power;

[1] They were much more doctrinaire than the French Jacobins, who were influenced by several philosophers and many ideas but by no one more or less coherent theory of society and the state. Though Robespierre carried *Du Contrat Social* in his pocket, he was less Rousseau's disciple than Lenin was Marx's.

250

they are not quite the same kind of Bolsheviks as the old ones, but they are still Bolsheviks. It would be pointless to deny it. How, then, has power affected the doctrine of the Bolsheviks? How have they adjusted Marxism and the Leninism of before 1917 to suit their later convenience? These are not unimportant questions, provided they are put, as the French say, 'en connaissance de cause,' provided we know what we are about when we put them.

There has never been any such thing as a coherent Marxian doctrine that a man could hold to consistently. But that does not mean that Marxism is a mere collection of doctrines to which new doctrines can be continually added without regard to what they are. Marxism has its own vocabulary, and its dominant themes. The vocabulary is easily recognized; and I hope that, by this time, we can also recognize some of the dominant themes. They are such doctrines as these: the inevitability of the class war, the special revolutionary rôle under capitalism of the urban working class, the need to capture and to destroy the parasitic bourgeois state, working class democracy after the revolution, the abolition of all private property in the means of production, the eventual coming of the classless society. These doctrines were often asserted and never denied by either Marx or Engels, and they were fully, explicitly and repeatedly accepted by Lenin before the Bolshevik revolution. Nothing that he taught before October 1917 about the rôle of the party as the vanguard of the proletariat, or about the dictatorship of the proletariat, or about the opportunities of the Russian Social-Democrats in the bourgeois revolution, or about the need for an alliance with the peasants—and these were his favourite themes, the themes he devoted much more attention to than Marx and Engels had done—abated anything from any one of these doctrines. No doubt, Lenin, like all Marxists and more boldly than most, attended only to those parts of the Marxian teaching that suited him best, but he never, even by implication, denied any of these doctrines before 1918. And even afterwards, he never denied them; he merely acted in ways that made it impossible to apply them. What is true of him is also true of Stalin. Let anyone go to Russia and repeat, as boldly as he likes, any one of these dominant themes, and no one will molest him. He will please some people and perhaps bore others, but no one will think him seditious. That is, of course, provided he does not go into too much detail, and uses the Marxian vocabulary.[1]

I. THE FIGHT FOR POWER AFTER THE REVOLUTION

The revolution that Lenin made quickly developed in ways unforeseen by him. He had honestly believed in 1917 that he and his Bolsheviks were 'the party of the proletariat.' They had not been strong in April 1917, but they had, during the summer and autumn of that year, won the confidence of the industrial workers. In October 1917 and for several months afterwards they deserved, more than at any earlier or later period of their career, to be called 'the party of the proletariat.' The Bolshevik leaders mostly came from the middle class, but they were already, in October 1917, the leaders most listened to and applauded in the urban soviets, the councils formed by the workers to defend their interests. The soviets were not created by the Bolsheviks but by the workers themselves; and until the late summer of 1917, they had, as we have seen, been dominated by the Mensheviks. Lenin could therefore claim that his party had won them over from their rivals, and that the allegiance given to the Bolsheviks by the urban and factory soviets was freely given. The Bolsheviks did not dominate the rural soviets; the political leaders most listened to there were Left-Wing Socialist-Revolutionaries. These men were not Marxists but they were revolutionaries and, unlike the Mensheviks (who were Marxists), believed in immediate revolution. Lenin saw in the Left-Wing Socialist-Revolutionaries the 'natural'

---

[1] To say what Marx said in words of your own choosing may be fatal. The Communists are very familiar with Marx's writings but can no longer afford to understand him. Their authority requires that they should both defend the letter of Marx and punish whoever would be true to his spirit. Since the Communists are human, they mostly wish to be honest; and they could not be honest, if, while calling themselves Marxists, they understood the Marxian doctrine and punished people for conforming to it. It is therefore their interest to misunderstand Marx. This is easily done in Communist countries, where everyone repeats the same things; but in the West the predicament of the intelligent and honest Communist is much more difficult. We ought, therefore, to draw this maxim: Never discuss Marxism with a Communist. If he thinks you know nothing about it, he will engage with you readily and pelt you with quotations. If he suspects that you know his scriptures as well as or even better than he does, he will try to avoid the discussion; or, if he cannot avoid it, he will try to spoil it, to confuse both himself and you, so that, neither of you understanding the other, you both hold to the positions you started from. Tennyson said of Sir Lancelot that 'faith unfaithful kept him falsely true.' The Communists want to be both faithful and honest, and the strain on them, in countries where they are exposed to criticism, must often be great. They must wriggle like eels to retain the appearance of honesty.

allies, at that stage of the revolution, of the 'party of the proletariat.' He had for years believed that an alliance[1] between
workers and peasants would enable the Social-Democrats to get
power in Russia long before the country had become properly
capitalist. In November 1917 he had seen his opportunity and
had taken it—all the more willingly because he believed that the
Bolshevik example would lead to proletarian revolution in the
West, first in Germany and then in other great industrial countries.
In the late autumn of 1917 everything had seemed to play into the
hands of Lenin; and it was, for a time, easy for him to believe that
the government of Russia was in very fact a dictatorship of the
proletariat and peasantry, exercised on their behalf by the trusted
Bolsheviks. No professional revolutionary had invented the
soviets; they had emerged and challenged the authority of the
Provisional Government long before the Bolsheviks got control
of them. The urban workers had on their own initiative begun
to take over the factories, and the peasants to carve up the great
estates; they had of their own accord made the attacks on
bourgeois property which proved them genuine revolutionaries.
If the Bolsheviks had become powerful, it was only because they
had correctly interpreted the people's wishes. They had been but
fifty thousand strong in April 1917, and their number had afterwards grown rapidly only because their party was fast becoming
popular. When they seized power, they were not a well-organized
and disciplined body; they had been bewildered and without a
policy until Lenin's return to Russia in April, and had afterwards
multiplied too quickly to have time to put much order into their
ranks. They could never have seized power directly against the
people's will; they were too weak for that. They owed their
triumph to their popularity,[2] which, though far short of universal,
was yet wide enough to give them power.

[1] Seeing that the peasants, still the great majority of the people, were to be subordinate to the workers, with ultimate control lying always with the Bolsheviks,
and seeing also that Lenin foretold a future struggle against a large part of the
peasantry, it is clear that the association between the two classes, as he imagined it,
scarcely deserves to be called an alliance. He meant to 'dish' the peasants just as
thoroughly as any other non-proletarian class. Indeed, there was only one class—
the proletariat—that he came to oppress without having foreseen that he would
need to do so.

[2] It was just before this triumph, and borne up by this popularity, that Lenin
wrote *The State and the Revolution*. It is the work of a man whose great ambition is
about to come true, a man who has lost his head a little because reality looks for a
moment so like a cherished dream.

The real struggle, as so often in politics, came after the victory. The Bolsheviks were popular, but they were also weak; and it was not likely that they would long remain popular. They got power because they made promises which the other parties, more timid or more conscientious, were not willing to make; they did not get it because the people understood and approved their ultimate purposes. The workers and peasants, when they decided that Lenin was the man to follow, had not thereby changed their characters; they were still as illiterate, as undisciplined, as much inclined to anarchy as ever. The workers, much more than the peasants, put their trust in the Bolsheviks; and yet even the workers were not really of one mind with them. The Bolsheviks might lead them easily enough while they promised them what they wanted; but the workers were not 'indoctrinated,' they cared only for immediate benefits and would respond only to immediate dangers. They were not aware that the Bolsheviks were in any peculiar sense 'their' party; they looked upon them merely as persons who, for the time being, were talking the kind of sense that simple men could understand.

The Bolsheviks owed their triumph to a popularity which, though it was shallow, was yet wide. They owed it even more to the weakness and scruples of the other parties. The middle-class Provisional Governments had wanted to continue the war; they had been pestered by the soviets and had not known how to assert their authority against them; they had proved themselves equally incapable of maintaining order, of waging effective war and of making peace. The Mensheviks, though they had used the soviets to harass and annoy the Provisional Governments, had not wanted to use them to get power. The Socialist-Revolutionaries were supported only by the peasants, and that support was not enough to enable them to rule Russia. The Bolsheviks alone saw the opportunity and were willing to take it. Their number had grown five or six times between April and November 1917, and yet they were only a quarter of a million strong when they took over the government of Russia. The older Bolsheviks had not even had time to indoctrinate the new recruits, so that, when he took power, perhaps not more than one member in four of his own party understood how Lenin's theory differed from the other brands of Russian Marxism.

It is easy to exaggerate the popularity of the Bolsheviks. The urban workers actively supported them, and the peasants, led by the Left-Wing Socialist-Revolutionaries, were willing to tolerate them. They had made attractive promises to both the workers and the peasants; the poor and the illiterate mostly spoke well of them. They had, for a time, no effective rivals. But that does not mean that they were universally popular, nor even that, where they were popular, they were trusted. This is proved by the elections to the Constituent Assembly, where the Bolsheviks got only a minority of the seats. The Bolshevik faction inside the Assembly, seeing that most of the members were hostile to the new government, moved for a dissolution on the ground that the Assembly represented 'a stage already passed by the Revolution.' As the Assembly was elected after the Bolsheviks took power, the argument was not convincing and the motion was lost. The Bolsheviks then left the Assembly, which was dispersed that same evening, never to meet again.

We cannot, of course, say that because the majority of the Constituent Assembly mistrusted the Bolsheviks, the people who elected them did so too. The electorate, especially in an illiterate country, know very little of the purposes and rivalries of the politicians they vote for. Though we cannot infer from the hostility to them of the Constituent Assembly (chosen by universal suffrage at the freest elections ever held in Russia) that the Bolsheviks were unpopular, we can say that the great majority of the people, on the one occasion when they were free to choose, preferred other parties to them. Mr E. H. Carr, in his book *The Bolshevik Revolution*, has said of the election to the Constituent Assembly that, 'as a verdict on the government set up by the October revolution, it was a crushing vote of non-confidence.'[1] This is, I think, to interpret the event too much as if it had happened in England; in the villages the peasants, when voting for the Socialist-Revolutionaries, were not voting against the Bolsheviks, while in the towns the Bolsheviks won an overwhelming victory over the Mensheviks and the middle-class Cadets. It would be better to say that the only free election in Russia was not a vote of confidence in the Bolsheviks rather than it was a vote of non-confidence in them.

[1] Vol. I, p. 110.

The Bolsheviks justified their seizure or power by predicting that one of its consequences would be proletarian revolution in Germany. This did not mean that, should their prediction prove false, they would abdicate. They were bold and ambitious; what they wanted was an excuse for taking power, and they had no time to consider beforehand what they must do should their excuse turn out a bad one. Having made themselves the rulers of Russia, they had perforce to rule; and, as soon as their power was challenged, they defended it as best they could. Whenever they found themselves obliged to do what they had condemned in their predecessors, they called it a temporary expedient. They believed that their ultimate purposes were good, and therefore thought they had a better right than anyone who had ruled Russia before them to use every means necessary to consolidate their power. The more ruthlessly they defended that power, the more enemies they made; and the more enemies they made, the greater the dangers they were exposed to if ever they lost power. The Bolsheviks were as honest as most men, but they also put as high a value on their lives; it was not to be expected of them that they should abdicate for no better reason than that circumstances drove them into courses which every Marxist in the world would have condemned without qualification before November 1917.

It is doubtful whether the Bolsheviks would ever have consolidated their power had they not had to fight a civil war. They had no effective rivals at the end of 1917. The Socialist-Revolutionaries were supported by the peasants, and were much the largest party in the Constituent Assembly; but the centres of political power were in the towns, and in the towns the Bolsheviks were supreme. The ease and completeness of the Bolshevik victory were astonishing; even when they dispersed the Constituent Assembly there were very few protests except from the leaders of the other parties. The Russian people had not learned to care for their first sovereign parliament merely because they had elected it; it never occurred to them that a blow aimed at it was also aimed at them. They were no more offended than were the French peasants in 1848 by the government's contempt for an assembly they had so recently elected; they had not yet learnt to identify themselves with parties and politicians. When they were asked to vote they did so with a good grace, and they voted for the candidates who best pleased them; but what happened to those candidates afterwards was no particular concern of theirs. The Bolsheviks, by dispersing the Constituent Assembly, destroyed what might soon have become a centre of opposition to themselves; but they in no way offended the Russian people. They destroyed an unvalued and alien thing, whose uses were not known to the great majority of the peasants. Yet the completeness of their victory had not made the Bolsheviks powerful; they still had no effective instruments of government in their hands. They had no army, no police force, no loyal civil service, and even no disciplined party. While they swam with the tide there was no danger of their drowning, but it was not their purpose to swim with the tide for long.

It was the good fortune of the Bolsheviks that their power was challenged before they had time to begin using it to make Russia socialist. Had they tried to impose discipline in the factories to ensure the smoother working of a state-controlled economy, or to oblige the peasants to sell the produce of their farms in quantities and at prices fixed by authority, they might have raised an opposition they were powerless to resist. They claimed to speak for the workers and the peasants, but they were, as yet, without the means of controlling them. The Mensheviks in the towns and the Socialist-Revolutionaries in the villages would certainly have rushed to the defence of the people against their 'new oppressors.' The new recruits, attracted to the Bolshevik party by its popularity and by its apparent concern to give immediately to the workers and peasants what they wanted, would perhaps have deserted it. The Bolshevik leaders, had their only motive been the need to coerce the classes in whose name they had taken power, might have found it impossible to agree among themselves to create anew the 'bourgeois' instruments of government they had so recently condemned. Would it have been easy even for Lenin, that devout and unscrupulous man who found so many things possible, to persuade himself that the workers and peasants were traitors to the revolution for no better reason than that they resisted the authority of his party?

The Civil War saved the Bolsheviks because it enabled them to pose as defenders of the revolution against the class enemies of the workers and peasants. The Bolsheviks had promised peace and had made peace. In March 1918 they had signed the Treaty of Brest-Litovsk, ceding a large part of Russia to the Germans. This episode was more than many officers of the old Tsarist army could stomach; they made their way to South Russia where they got into touch with the Cossacks, who had never taken kindly to the new régime. A few weeks later, some Czech and Slovak regiments, trying to make their way to the western front the long way round through Siberia, quarrelled with the local Soviet authorities and quickly put them down. A few foreign soldiers stranded in Siberia had won an easy victory over the Bolsheviks along a great stretch of the Trans-Siberian railway. Their example was catching. If foreigners far away from their native land could do so much so easily, why not the Tsarist officers and dispossessed landowners? Would it not be possible for them, used to war and good discipline as they were, to form a small but efficient army strong enough to destroy an incompetent régime fast losing the little popularity it had ever enjoyed? The officers and landowners soon created forces—the so-called White Guards—capable of quickly liberating vast territories. Their early successes impressed the Allies, who had not found it easy to forgive the Bolsheviks for taking Russia out of the war. A little intervention would, they hoped, go a very long way towards helping the Whites to 'liberate' Russia.

As soon as they saw their old officers and landlords in arms against the Bolsheviks, the peasants, who were already beginning to grow tired of their new rulers, found themselves in a quandary. If they joined neither side, they would become victims of both; if they joined the Whites, they would bring the landlords back to the villages; if they joined the Reds they would at least be defending their most recent acquisitions. The poorer peasants, and they were the majority, decided to throw in their lot with the Bolsheviks. The decision was the easier because the Bolsheviks made it their policy to favour the poor against the rich peasants. On the other hand, the Whites did little or nothing to gain the confidence of the peasants neglected by the Bolsheviks. The inevitable consequence was that the Bolsheviks enjoyed the loyal support of the poorer peasants, while the Whites had no friends in the villages on whom they could equally rely. It was in the richer provinces away from the two capitals—in the Ukraine, in Siberia, in the Don and Kuban territories—that the peasants were most hostile to the Bolsheviks; in Great Russia itself, where the land was poor and there were not many well-to-do peasants, the Bolsheviks were much stronger than their enemies, even in the villages.

There was no need of the Civil War to reconcile the factory workers with the Bolsheviks; and yet it was, even with them, a source of strength to the new government. It made the workers amenable to discipline; they had to supply the Red Guards with the arms and ammunition they needed, they had to produce what the government, waging a war against the enemies of the Revolution, told them to produce. They knew that without discipline the war could not be won, and they also knew that the discipline would have to be imposed from above. They submitted to the yoke willingly enough, knowing that the Bolsheviks, alone of all parties, were determined to win the war at any cost.

The same causes that brought discipline into the factories brought it into the Bolshevik party. There were cases of disillusioned or corrupted Bolsheviks going over to the enemy. If the party were not severe with itself, how could it be severe with others? The direction of the war fell naturally to Lenin, Trotsky and the other Bolshevik leaders; loyalty to the Revolution was loyalty to them. If the party were to survive, it must learn to act as one body; and it could learn that most quickly by acquiring the habit of immediate obedience to its leaders. The institution of the 'purge' was invented to rid the party of undesirables, and this institution (so easily justified at the time) was itself enough to prevent the party's ever becoming what Lenin had once wanted it to be—internally democratic.

The Bolshevik leaders, when they began hurriedly to create an army, had to use the services of many professional soldiers; they also soon discovered that they could not govern a vast country without the assistance of the old civil servants. They had, perforce, to employ servants on whose loyalty they could not absolutely rely; they had also to maintain their authority over the factory workers through the trade unions, and over the peasants through committees of village poor; they had, above all else, to keep the party absolutely loyal to themselves. How could they better achieve these aims than by creating a new political police?[1] Its existence, they said, was indispensable to victory over the enemies of the Revolution. They were no doubt right. It was, from their point of view, the supreme instrument of government; for, until they had it, they could not rely on any of the others. The Bolsheviks were the best soldiers of the Revolution, the most reliable, the most willing to take risks and the most ruthless; to ensure the loyal and energetic co-operation of all other organizations it was necessary that Bolsheviks should occupy the first places inside them. Thus it was that the Red Army, the trade unions, the committees of village poor, the urban and rural soviets, and the departments of state all became subordinate to the Bolshevik party; and to keep that party united and strong, there was the institution of the purge and also the political police owing an almost personal allegiance to the leaders.

There is no need to follow this process through in detail.[2] The Civil War exhausted Russia but left the Bolsheviks immeasurably stronger than they had been in the summer of 1918, just before it broke out. They were, no doubt, much more hated than they had ever been, and by many more people; but that, now that all their enemies were defeated and all rival parties eliminated, made little difference to their strength. The revolt of the Kronstadt sailors was a severe blow to them, not because it shook their power, but because it proved that they had lost the confidence of their oldest allies, the men who had helped them gain control of Petrograd in November 1917. The Kronstadt revolt, though an impotent gesture, was galling to the pride of Marxists who thought themselves the spokesmen of the men who took arms against them. The Bolsheviks had won the civil war, but had used such brutal methods that even their friends, now the enemy was defeated, were turning against them. The Kronstadt sailors had not revolted in vain; they had taught the new masters of Russia that their subjects had reached the limits of endurance. The Bolsheviks, though they liked to make free use of their spurs, meant to ride, not a worn-out jade, but a strong, though docile, mare. On Lenin's

---

[1] The Cheka was actually created in December 1917, half a year before the outbreak of civil war; but it was not until after the war had started that it became really powerful.

[2] It has been done, fairly and fully, by Mr. E. H. Carr in *The Bolshevik Revolution*, Vol. I.

advice, they pressed on with the milder régime known to history as the 'New Economic Policy.'

II. LENINISM AFTER THE REVOLUTION

When the civil war ended, there was no longer hope of proletarian revolution in the West, and Russia's system of government was already as different as it could be from the simple, loose and gentle policy described by Lenin in *The State and the Revolution*. Bolshevik theory had therefore to be adapted to two situations not foreseen before October 1917: the existence of only one 'proletarian' state in a predominantly capitalist world; and the presence within that state of institutions hitherto denounced by all Marxists, in Russia and abroad, as incompatible with proletarian democracy. The process of adaptation was neither easy nor short. Men ordinarily shut their eyes to difficulties for some considerable time before they begin trying to explain them away; and when they are as busy as the Bolshevik leaders have been since the summer of 1917, they have not much leisure to take stock of their situation.

The Bolsheviks were strangely little embarrassed by the failure of the world to behave as they had expected. If there had been no proletarian revolution in the West, the fault, they thought, lay with proletarian leaders corrupted by too long and close an acquaintance with bourgeois politicians in bourgeois parliaments. The German Social-Democratic Party, if it had done its duty, would have made the revolution which Lenin predicted to justify his own seizure of power in November 1917. It was no fault of his that the German leaders had proved unequal to a great occasion; nor was he to blame that the Spartacists, who did believe in revolution, had proved unable to make one against the opposition of the moderates. While he had still hoped for a German revolution, Lenin had both abused and exhorted the German socialists; when that hope faded he merely abused them. The one idea that never found lodgment in his head was that his own diagnosis of Germany's situation might have been entirely wrong, that there had perhaps been no proletarian revolution in Germany because the German workers, being literate and having no Bolsheviks to guide them, had never wanted to make one. It may be that more courage was needed than even Lenin possessed to entertain such an idea, for—if it were true—the only plausible Marxist excuse for the October revolution fell to the ground. Lenin, like others before him, was blind when it was not his interest to see. He continued (when not too busy with other things) to preach world revolution and to abuse the western Social-Democratic 'lackeys of the bourgeoisie' who somehow contrived to prevent it, but did not care to remember that he had once used the immediate prospect of it to refute the Mensheviks who were saying that a revolution made in the workers' name in a country as backward as Russia could bring neither proletarian government nor socialism.

Early in 1919, at the first meeting of the newly-created Communist International, Gregory Zinoviev had said: 'Within a year we shall already be beginning to forget that there was a struggle for Communism in Europe, because within a year all Europe will be Communist.' It was no longer possible, after the civil war, to make such wild prophecies; it remained only to continue working for world revolution and meanwhile to look to the security of the Soviet Union in an unfriendly world. The long struggle had brought many disappointments but had also ended in victory; it had left the Bolsheviks with such immense and immediate tasks on their hands that they had no time to spare even for fundamental problems of Marxist theory.

Lenin was a prolific writer and copious speaker all the years of his political life. The published record of what he wrote and said after the revolution is long indeed, and some of it is important even to the student of Bolshevik theory. But it is not important in quite the same way as what he wrote before October 1917. It is not merely that, as an opponent of the established régime, he had had time to elaborate his doctrines, and that when he came to rule Russia he no longer had the leisure to explain just how he differed from or agreed with other Marxists about matters of theory. It is also that he had found it much easier to defend his own brand of Marxism while there had as yet been no need to put any of it into practice. But with power at last in his hands, he found 'proletarian' Russia quickly becoming what he had never expected her to be; he found her growing progressively more unlike his own description of the 'dictatorship of the proletariat.' The less the world looks like what his creed teaches him to expect, the greater a man's reluctance to ponder that creed and follow out its implications. It is perhaps the condition of his retaining his faith in it that he should speak of it as often as possible and think about it as seldom as he can.

After the revolution, Lenin wrote only two long pamphlets dealing primarily with matters of theory: *The Proletarian Revolution and the Renegade Kautsky* (1918) and *Left Wing Communism, An Infantile Disorder*, written in April 1920. The first is a long, tedious and abusive reply to Kautsky, who had attacked the Bolsheviks, their revolution, and their methods of government. We can learn nothing from this pamphlet about how the possession of power had affected Lenin's theories; and it is important only because it is often quoted.

Left Wing Communism, An Infantile Disorder is greatly superior to it, and is an even richer source of quotations. It is a criticism of the western Communists who, professing disgust at what they called the 'betrayal' of the proletariat by the Social-Democrats, refused to co-operate with them against the bourgeois parties. The importance of the pamphlet is obvious: it treats of a matter still important to us—the behaviour of Communists towards other socialists in the West;[1] a matter that Lenin was better fitted to discuss than the nature of the proletarian state. The getting of power, the making and unmaking of political alliances, the uses to which trade unions can be put by a revolutionary party: when he is discussing such topics as these, we can rely on Lenin's really addressing his mind to them. He did not know the West, and many of his judgments reveal this ignorance; but he did understand politics—not parliamentary politics, but the politics of the working-class movement in the factories, newspapers and streets. When he was wrong he was so because he did not know the facts, and not because he was juggling with words and ideas beyond his power to control.

He advised the Communists not to cut themselves off from the Social-Democrats nor to leave the trade unions whose leaders

[1] The capital letter used for the Communists and not for the socialists is not a mark of respect reserved for the former. It is merely that 'socialist' is nowadays mostly used to refer to a person holding certain opinions or belonging to any party subscribing to those opinions, whereas 'Communist' is used to refer to a member of a specific international organization subscribing to a doctrine defined by authority. I write 'socialist' as I would 'deist,' and 'Communist' as I would 'Roman Catholic' or 'Social-Democrat' (i.e. partisan of the Second International).

had 'betrayed' the working class. The Communists must, he said, keep in touch with the workers wherever they are to be found; they must not abandon any working-class organization they might later control on the ground that its present leaders have been corrupted by the bourgeois; they must not refuse to work with the Social-Democrats merely because they have become the 'lackeys' of the bourgeois. So long as they keep their own party separate and intact, so long as they retain their revolutionary zeal and grasp of doctrine, the Communists have a plain duty to make whatever use they can in the proletarian cause of all other working class organizations.

Lenin, in this pamphlet, puts a question to the Communists, who, to keep themselves pure, would refuse to have anything to do with the Social-Democrats and their corrupted Trade Unions: 'To carry on a war for the overthrow of the international bourgeoisie, a war which is a hundred times more difficult, protracted and complicated than the most stubborn of ordinary wars between states, and to refuse beforehand to manoeuvre, to make use of conflicts of interest (even though they should be temporary) among one's enemies, to refuse to temporize and compromise with possible (even though temporary, unstable, vacillating and conditional) allies—is not this ridiculous in the extreme?' He rebuked Will Gallacher and Sylvia Pankhurst for saying that the British Communists ought to have nothing to do with Parliament. On the contrary, he said, they should do their utmost to help the Labour Party win a parliamentary majority, so that the workers, having direct experience of Labour in power, should turn away from them in disgust and seek out the Communists.

Infiltration into all working-class organizations, collaboration for limited objects, careful manoeuvre and temporary compromise: these are the proper methods of the Communists in their constant endeavour to gain control of the working-class movement in the sham democracies of the West. The Communist 'vanguard' must keep a firm hold of the truths of pure Communism; if they do this, they will not be corrupted, they will not be tempted to betray, as the Social-Democrats and Trade Union leaders have done, the cause of the proletariat. But the mere propagation of these truths by an uncorrupt élite is not a sufficient preparation for revolution; it is also necessary that class organizations hostile to the Communists should have weakened themselves by quarrelling with one another, that the unstable and hesitant groups (and among them Lenin includes the Social-Democrats) should have proved themselves ineffective and disgraced themselves, and that the workers should at last have come to support the boldest revolutionary action against the bourgeois. It is when these conditions hold, when the exploited and oppressed no longer find the old system tolerable, and when their exploiters are so perplexed and divided that they can no longer rule effectively in the accustomed ways, that the hour of revolution has come. The duty of Communists is to create these conditions by whatever methods seem best to them.

This doctrine of Lenin's is perfectly clear, and it is the fruit of his experience during the three years after the Bolshevik revolution. The pure truth of Communism, he now tells us, is the possession of an élite, and within their circle must be kept pure. But when men work for revolution, they must 'count not in millions but in tens of millions,' and it is therefore far from enough that the vanguard should preserve and publish the pure doctrine. Lenin's argument has implications not the less obvious for being left unexpressed: the doctrine is primarily for the vanguard, and the vanguard are a small minority. When it comes to preparing a great country for revolution, the propagation of the doctrine is of relatively minor importance. We are expressly told that 'when it is a question of the practical action of the masses . . . of the alignment of all the class forces of the given society for the final and decisive battle, then propaganda habits alone, the mere repetition of the truths of pure Communism, are of no avail.' What *then* matters is that bourgeois parties should be at loggerheads, the Social-Democrats and other 'unstable elements' disgraced, and the workers so disillusioned and exasperated as to be willing to follow the lead of the boldest revolutionaries.

This is not the same doctrine as the one expounded in the pamphlets written long before the October revolution, in *What Is To Be Done?* and *One Step Forward, Two Steps Back.* This is not advice given to revolutionaries working in secret against the Tsarist police state; it is advice given to Communists working in countries whose governments still tolerated them at a time when Lenin had already suppressed in Russia every party except his own. Not even in the most advanced industrial countries was 'proletarian revolution' to be made by a united, disciplined and politically conscious working class; it was to be made by a Communist élite profiting from the mistakes of others, out-manœuvering them, and using them for purposes not their own. The Bolshevik recipe, used successfully in backward and illiterate Russia in 1917, was to be applied—though with appropriate differences—to the whole world. The leaders of the proletariat, as Marx and Engels had imagined them, were guides and teachers primarily, and also organizers of massive and internally democratic proletarian political movements; but by 1920 they appeared to Lenin in the guise of conspirators.

III. STALINISM

Left Wing Communism, An Infantile Disorder contains only a small, though important, part of what Lenin added to Bolshevik doctrine after the revolution. The other parts lie scattered through a vast collection of articles, speeches and addresses, whose purpose, when they were made, was not to discuss theory but to explain and justify policy. It is not possible to discover the meaning of generalizations made on particular occasions by a man discussing practical matters unless we know something about those matters. It would not be proper to make a collection of Lenin's theoretical statements made after 1917 and simply call them 'post-revolutionary Leninism'; and yet it would be infinitely tedious to trace each of them back to its source and discuss the occasion when it was made.

It is, fortunately, less our purpose to discover exactly what Lenin meant by these statements than how they were officially interpreted. For, in a sense, until they were so interpreted, they were casual, loose and indeterminate, not yet included in the corpus of orthodox doctrine, not yet solid enough to be used for the confounding and putting to death of heretics. But, soon after Lenin's death, his statements about theory were collected and interpreted, and by no less a person than Stalin. I shall therefore call the collection and the comments upon it made by the collector by another and safer name; I shall call it 'Stalinism.' Not that I wish to accuse so devoted a disciple as Stalin of originality; it merely happens to be easier to discover how he understood Lenin than what Lenin really meant. And it also matters more, for Lenin ruled Russia for less than six years, and Stalin for about twenty-eight.[1] It is mostly Stalin's version of Lenin's post-revolutionary theoretical announcements that have governed Soviet policy. I shall not, however, hesitate to follow Stalin's example, and shall quote freely from Lenin whenever I find it useful to do so. Stalin may have sometimes distorted Lenin's meaning, but much less often than those people say who, while they now abuse Stalin, still praise Lenin.

In April 1924 Stalin gave some lectures in Moscow, which were later published under the title *The Foundations of Leninism*; and in January 1926 there appeared his second important book, *Problems of Leninism*. These are his two principal works discussing matters of theory, and both were written within a short time of Lenin's death. Stalin had been one of the leading Bolsheviks still in Russia when the first revolution broke out in March 1917; he had, like his colleagues, been taken quite unawares and left for the time without confidence and initiative; he had then witnessed the sudden transformation of the spirit and fortunes of his party after the arrival of Lenin at the Finland station in Petrograd. Though not an intimate friend of the great leader, he had been close enough to him to know that, without him, there would have been no October revolution and no Bolshevik state. In 1924 and 1926 Stalin was still deeply impressed by his memories of the greatest man he had known. He never ceased to be a disciple of Lenin, to quote and to praise him, and never accused him of error unless Lenin had first accused himself. Only one man, he thought, ever had the right to rebuke or correct Lenin—and that man was Lenin. Stalin had no ambition to be right where Lenin had been wrong; it was enough for him that he should be Lenin's only infallible interpreter. Stalin's devotion never ceased, but its quality changed. He was in 1926 still at considerable pains to discover Lenin's meaning; and if he sometimes failed to do so, it was either because Lenin had been careless or he had himself lacked

[1] Lenin died in January 1924 but for many months before his death had been too ill to be in effective control of the state. Stalin's supremacy was already established by April 1925, when a Party Congress accepted his thesis that it was possible for socialism to be established in only one country. His power was then smaller and less secure than it afterwards became, but was already much greater than anyone else's. He was already more—much more—than *primus inter pares*.

skill. But as Stalin's power grew, so, too, did his confidence in himself; until he came in the end to think that it was enough that he should have spoken for Lenin's meaning to be beyond dispute. The considerable part of *The Foundations of Leninism* devoted to a defence of Lenin's version of the doctrine of uninterrupted revolution adds nothing worth noticing to Marxist theory; it is dull and unperceptive, and quite misses the point made by Lenin's critics—which is that, given the truth of historical materialism, it can never be possible to make a proletarian revolution and establish proletarian government in a country as backward as Russia was in 1917. Stalin explained how the Bolsheviks had taken power in the name of the working class, and was simple enough to believe that this amounted to a proof that they had made a proletarian revolution. The details of a paralogism so inept need not detain us.

Otherwise, Stalin's main concern in *The Foundations of Leninism* was to explain what the 'strategy' and 'tactics' of the Bolsheviks should be now that they controlled one of the world's largest states. They must use that state as a base for the overthrow of 'imperialism,' and must therefore consolidate the dictatorship of the proletariat in it. Their principal ally in the struggle against imperialism must be the industrial workers in capitalist countries, but the Bolsheviks must also win the support of the peasants in Europe and of militant nationalists in the colonial dependencies of the Great Powers. They must persuade the workers and peasants in the more advanced countries to abandon the bourgeois democrats and the parties of the Second International—the weak and treacherous exponents of a policy of compromise with imperialism.

This part of Stalin's argument is merely the translation of the class war into the region of international politics. The rulers of the Soviet Union, being the leaders of a proletarian party bound by common loyalties to all other such parties in the world, must use their governmental power to prepare the victory of the 'world proletariat.' Their policies as rulers of a great state must follow logically from their policies as revolutionary opponents of Tsarism. For them, diplomacy and war must be only the continuation of the class struggle by other means.

Stalin distinguished three principal stages in the political activities of the Russian proletariat and their Bolshevik vanguard. From 1903 until February 1917 they had been fighting to destroy Tsarism; their chief allies had then been the peasants, and the aim of the Bolsheviks had been to prevent the bourgeois parties, the liberal opponents of Tsarism, from winning the confidence and support of the peasants. The second stage had lasted from the February to the October revolution of 1917. The main object of the workers and their vanguard had been to destroy 'imperialism' in Russia and to put an end to the war, their chief allies then being the poor peasants; and the aim of the Bolsheviks had been to prevent the petty bourgeois democrats (Mensheviks and Socialist-Revolutionaries) from gaining the support of either the workers or the peasants.[1]

The third stage, because it began after the Bolsheviks had become the rulers of a great state, inevitably widened the responsibilities of the Russian workers and their vanguard; they now had not only to fight their class enemies in Russia but also to use their governmental power on behalf of the world proletariat. They had to 'consolidate the dictatorship of the proletariat'—that is, to strengthen the machinery of the Soviet state and the party's control over it—in order to use the Soviet Union as a base for the overthrow of imperialism. This meant in fact—though the fact was not insisted upon indiscreetly—that the dictatorship of the proletariat, instead of being a 'half-state' preparing its own demise, had to be a political colossus strong enough to destroy imperialism and (should the need arise) to take the shock of the capitalist world in arms against it. The chief ally of the Bolshevik and proletarian state must be, not any other state—for all other states were still capitalist and therefore enemies of the Soviet Union, with whom only temporary accommodations could be made—but the industrial workers in the advanced countries. Their subsidiary allies must be the poor and dissatisfied among the peasants of Europe and other politically independent regions; and in the colonies and protected states of Asia and Africa, they must be the native patriots and enemies of European ascendancy. The last twenty-five years have shown that the industrial

[1] This account is, of course, largely fanciful. The workers and peasants have never been political allies; their grievances and ambitions remained almost unchanged during the first two of Stalin's three stages, and the Bolsheviks were never the 'vanguard' of any class.

workers of the West, whom Stalin hoped would be the staunchest allies of the Soviet Union, have not been much attracted by it. The better they have known it the less they have liked it.[1] The Bolsheviks have profited much more from peasant discontent in Eastern Europe and from Asian dislike of landlordism and European ascendancy. Nevertheless, though some of his hoped-for allies proved cold towards him, Stalin did, in *The Foundations of Leninism*, give us a clearer and more systematic account than any to be found in the speeches and writings of Lenin of how, as a result of the Bolshevik triumph of 1917, the class struggle should affect international politics.

In both *The Foundations* and in *Problems of Leninism*, Stalin's account of the rôle of the party in the new proletarian state is derived entirely from Lenin. There is, however, a matter-of-factness about it and a blindness to difficulties that a more perceptive mind would have taken care to evade; and this makes it interesting. Stalin, as a political theorist,[2] was often a clumsy speaker who revealed the truth to others though he did not see it himself. Marx could often cover up his tracks so completely, could mix up his arguments so thoroughly, that no one—perhaps not even himself—could tell how he had arrived at his conclusions. He dived boldly into a Sargasso sea of German polysyllables, was lost for a time to view, and then suddenly emerged in an unexpected place holding some intelligible fragment of the Doctrine in his hand. Lenin, less nimble and less mysterious, splashed about so vigorously that the manner of his progress often could not be seen. But Stalin's slow and deliberate movements in shallow waters are easily detected, and that is why he is sometimes more instructive than his masters.

In the fifth section of *Problems of Leninism* it is denied that the dictatorship of the proletariat means in practice the dictatorship of the Communist Party. Stalin quotes freely from Lenin to prove that only one party must lead the proletariat; and he has already argued, in an earlier section, that, though the peasants are allied

---

[1] Bolshevism has appealed more strongly to intellectuals than to workers in the West. Perhaps they like the energy with which it drives the 'inarticulate' and 'stupid' masses to work hard for the ultimate good of society.

[2] As a political theorist only. As a politician he was patient, calm, deliberate, ingenious, and without pity. He was crafty and shrewd where others were brilliant. Never a good speaker, his words acquired weight and authority only after his power was undisputed and his opinions uncontradicted.

to the proletariat, they never take the initiative but are always guided by their allies, the actual work of guidance being done by the vanguard of the proletariat, a party that never shares power with any other. But this, thinks Stalin, does not make the dictatorship of the proletariat equivalent to a party dictatorship, because there also exist other organizations beside the party—the trade unions, the soviets, and the League of Communist Youth—through which the party maintains contact with the people. Stalin, following the example of Lenin, calls these bodies 'transmission belts' because they are indispensable to the dictatorship of the proletariat. He does not forget to add that the party must not force or bully the people but must guide and persuade them; it must correctly interpret the interests of the proletariat. Stalin quotes with approval the dictum of Lenin: 'First we must convince and then coerce. We must at all costs first convince and then coerce.'[1]

These are the arguments of a child to impress children. Even the most brutal tyrant must have officers through whom he transmits his orders to the people; he too must have his 'transmission belts,' and does not cease to be a tyrant because he cannot do without them. No phrase could have been invented that marks more clearly than this one the absolute subordination of all other bodies to the Communist Party.

Stalin was, in this matter, the true interpreter of Lenin, who had boasted in the spring of 1920 that 'not a single important political or organizational question is decided by any state institution in our republic without the guiding hand of the Central Committee of the Party.' The Party at that time was only just over 600,000 strong, and yet Lenin thought it too big. 'We have,' said Lenin on the same occasion, 'a formally non-communist, flexible and relatively wide and very powerful proletarian apparatus by means of which the Party is closely linked up with the class and with the masses, and by means of which, under the leadership of the Party, the dictatorship of the class is exercised.' It was absurd, thought Lenin, to try to distinguish between the dictatorship of the leaders and the dictatorship of the masses; it was, to use his

---

[1] Stalin was impressed with the mildness of this dictum. In the eyes of a Georgian peasant, a tyrant drives men as a cow-herd drives cattle; but the man who offers reasons, and does not punish unless his reasons are not accepted, is no tyrant; he is rather the father of his people who gives them what they need.

own simile, like discussing whether a man's left leg or right arm
is more useful to him. Lenin believed that the Russian system
was incomparably more democratic than the parliamentary
governments of the West, because the soviets mostly consisted of
working men while the bourgeois parliaments drew nearly all their
members from the educated class. And yet he did not deny, either
that the soviets were in fact subordinate to the Communist Party,
or that the party was not responsible to the proletariat.

This theory—that the party is the 'vanguard of the proletariat'
—put forward in a country dominated by that party means something very different from what it meant when Lenin first elaborated
it in 1902. At that time, the Russian Marxists were a small group
of persecuted revolutionaries; they could not prevent other parties
seeking the support of the workers, and could not themselves control the workers unless they first won their confidence. Under
the circumstances then existing, the Russian Marxists could never
hope to do more than persuade and guide the proletariat. Had
they then succeeded in winning the confidence of the workers to
such an extent that no other party could stand comparison with
them, they would in very truth have become *the* party of the proletariat. That, of course, is what Lenin wanted them to become;
that was his ambition for his party in the days of opposition.
While those days lasted, his ambition was never realized; it was
not even nearly realized. The Bolshevik Party did not become the
only party claiming to speak for the proletariat until after the
October revolution, after the suppression by force of all other
parties, including even the Mensheviks, who were also Marxists.
Lenin did not get the party he wanted until he had created such
conditions in Russia that it was impossible to discover whether
or not the workers really trusted that party, until it was impossible
to know where guidance ended and coercion began. Lenin had
perhaps not intended, when he seized power in 1917, to eliminate
all the other parties; he still had allies at that time, and there is not
sufficient evidence that his real purpose, even then, was to use his
allies until he could destroy them. Later on, he had come to differ
from them and to believe that the counter-revolutionaries must
win unless the Bolsheviks, by whatever means, always got their
own way; his allies had resented his methods, and he had destroyed them. He was, he said, fighting for the revolution and

would allow no scruples to deter him. The Bolsheviks, having acquired a monopoly of power in Russia, still held to their theory, invented some eighteen years earlier and under quite different circumstances, about the proper relation of their party to the proletariat. It was only natural that they should use that theory to justify the absolute predominance that their victory in the civil war gave them.

It was natural, but it also obliged them to close their minds to reality. Neither Lenin nor Stalin could afford to think honestly about the conditions of proletarian democracy. The whole Marxian political theory rests on the assumption that not only every class but every organized group pursues its own interest when they know it. The church, the army, the civil service, though they are not classes, have separate group interests of their own; and they have often in capitalist countries, as both Marx and Lenin admitted, pursued those interests even at the expense of the bourgeois, the class most of their leaders came from. If these groups can win a considerable independence of a wealthy and educated class like the bourgeois, though they were at first their mere instruments, why should not the 'party of the proletariat' in a country as poor and illiterate as Russia win an even greater independence of the class in whose name it acts? Is it not inevitable, on Marxist premises, that it should do so?

In the world as Marx described it, the proletariat, like every other class, have their 'objective' interests determined by their position in society, and the rôle of the party is to teach them what those interests are and guide them in their endeavours to satisfy them. Those interests are not arbitrarily chosen by the party; their existence is not their being perceived by those who urge the workers to clamour for their satisfaction; the interests are there all the time, though no one should correctly describe them. They are recognized for what they are by the class only when the party has interpreted the essential needs and permanent, though often unconscious, aspirations of the workers. If the party is incapable of guiding the class as they ought to be guided, if it is mistaken about their real interests or else betrays them, it loses the con- fidence of the class, and therefore ceases to be 'the party of the class,' 'the vanguard of the proletariat.' There is a proper road for the class to take, and the business of the party is to discover that road and to guide the class along it. But the class, apparently, are not blind; for though they do not in the first place discover the road, they do, when they have strayed off it, come in time to know that they are out of their way. The party must guide the class, but the class will know sooner or later whether or not they are being properly guided. If the party proves a bad guide, the class will eventually lose faith in the party and abandon it. The party no more creates the interests of the class than a water diviner calls into existence the water he discovers. That is the orthodox theory of the relations between party and class as the Marxists—and more especially Lenin and Stalin—have always interpreted it.

Now, these relations cannot exist unless the class are free to repudiate the party, unless they are free to place their confidence in other leaders. The class cannot promote their own interests, cannot even know them properly, until they have become politically active; they therefore cannot do without a party, and that party must take the initiative. All this is good Marxian doctrine, and—provided we do not quarrel with the assumption that classes have 'objective' interests[1]—it is also quite good sense. But the party must be truly responsible to the class, for otherwise (since, on the Marxian theory, every irresponsible group sacrifices the good of others to its own) it will use power to further its own and not the class interests. No doubt, if the party first got power by

[1] When a class are badly led by their party, they suffer and their sufferings enlighten them. New leaders arise and are listened to, and the authority of the old ones is undermined. The Marxists, like Abraham Lincoln, believe it impossible to fool all the people all the time. The workers, no less than other classes, need enlightenment and leadership, but they are not so foolish that they cannot see, after a time, what leaders are unprofitable to them. They have 'objective interests'; they may not be able to describe them nor discover how best to promote them, but they cannot, apparently, be led astray for long without their suspicions being aroused. Wherever there is a political movement, there are leaders and led, and the former, devoting their lives to politics, are of necessity in many ways much better informed than the latter; but this does not mean that leaders cannot be truly responsible to their followers and justly found wanting by them. This much, at least, is implied by the Marxian conceptions of 'class interest' and 'class consciousness,' just as it is by the modern conception of representative democracy. The peculiarity of the post-revolutionary Bolsheviks is their belief that the responsibility of the party to the class can be made effective without the devices which we in the West consider the necessary (though not always sufficient) conditions of all genuine political responsibility. The people must, we say, be free to criticize their rulers; they must also, at general elections regularly held, be free to choose between candidates who do not all belong to one party or to a group of parties that have ceased to compete against each other for popular support; and they must have the right, should they wish it, to form new parties as well as organizations of other kinds, professional, religious, or cultural, to promote whatever purposes they choose to consider important.

gaining the support of the class, its own and the class interests were once largely coincident; but the longer it retains power and is not responsible to the class, the smaller that coincidence. It cannot be responsible to the class unless the class have the power to repudiate it. No amount of self-criticism by members of the party, no purges, no denunciations of heresy, can create responsible government where it does not exist. The conditions of its existence are well known; it is sometimes difficult to discover whether those conditions obtain in a particular country, but there is no mystery about what they are. Neither Lenin nor Stalin has ever said that they do obtain in the Soviet Union; they have merely denied that they are conditions of responsible government. In other words, they have denied the obvious; they have denied what Marx knew just as much as we know it, and what Lenin himself affirmed until it became his interest to speak otherwise.

In *The Foundations* and in *Problems of Leninism*, Stalin claims to be the pupil and expositor of Lenin. The claim is, on the whole, a just one. If I have called the doctrines there expounded 'Stalinism' rather than 'Leninism,' it has been for three reasons: because Stalin collected them into two books, thereby making it easier to get at the gist of them and also often betraying their true nature; because they have inspired his policies for a much longer time than they ever could Lenin's; and because for Lenin, though not for Stalin, they are additions made on many separate occasions to an older and more systematic pre-revolutionary doctrine, additions whose total significance he was perhaps never aware of. In the life of Lenin they are explanations made to justify actions and policies whose necessity he had not foreseen before the revolution; in the life of Stalin they are an entire philosophy of Bolshevik statesmanship.

Stalin did, however, produce one doctrine that is his own and not Lenin's; and it is his own though he tried to foist it on Lenin. In the preface to *On the Road to October*, dated December 17th, 1924, Stalin attacked Trotsky's doctrine that the establishment of socialism in only one country, and that country as backward as Russia, is impossible. The attack is made in the approved Bolshevik fashion; there is no attempt to argue the matter, and Stalin does no more than collect quotations from Lenin in his own favour. This time the quotations are not conclusive, they are not sufficient evidence that Lenin ever agreed with Stalin in this matter. All that the quotations prove is that Lenin wanted to build socialism in the Soviet Union as quickly as possible and that he had good hope of success.

Lenin had, indeed, said that the Russia of the New Economic Policy could be made socialist; he had described her condition at that time—her large industries owned by the state, the state controlled by the workers, and the peasants in subordinate alliance with them. That condition was not yet socialism, but it was the basis on which socialism could be built. But Lenin, when he said this, did not also say that this could happen even though the rest of the world remained capitalist. He had no occasion to consider the matter later at issue between Stalin and Trotsky, to decide whether Russia could be made socialist though no proletarian revolutions happened in the West. Stalin's many quotations[1] are not real evidence that Lenin would have sided with him in his great dispute with Trotsky.

Trotsky contended that, though special circumstances had enabled the proletarian revolution to happen in Russia before it happened elsewhere, socialism could not be brought to so backward a country while it remained isolated in a capitalist world. Before there could be real socialism in Russia, there would have to be proletarian revolution in at least some of the more advanced countries; and it was therefore the paramount duty of the Bolsheviks to bring that revolution about. In answer to Trotsky, Stalin argued that, though the new Russia could never be secure in a predominantly capitalist world, she could in time become socialist, even though the bourgeois remained supreme in every other major country.

[1] Lenin rebuked the fainthearted, pointing out to them whatever in the Russian economy and social order would, in his opinion, make easier the establishment of socialism. He did not, on these occasions, say that Russia could not be made socialist until after there had been proletarian revolution in the West. But neither did he say the opposite. If it is borne in mind that Lenin had frequently argued against the Mensheviks that the Bolshevik revolution was not premature because it was the opening move in a world proletarian revolution, for which the world, being capitalist-dominated, was, as a whole, ripe, it is easy to see that Stalin failed to make his point. In the light of Lenin's argument against the Mensheviks, the only sufficient evidence that he believed it possible to make Russia socialist, no matter what happened abroad, would be his having said in so many words that it was possible. Stalin's quotations prove only that Lenin found several things in Russia favourable to socialism; they do not prove that he thought these things enough to make the transition to socialism possible.

Stalin and Trotsky were not arguing about the need to promote world proletarian revolution; they both admitted that it is always the duty of Communists to do so. Nor were they arguing about the need to make Russia a great industrial power and to eliminate her last traces of private capitalism. Indeed, Trotsky was the more urgent of the two even in this matter; he wanted to force the pace of industrialization in Russia and at the same time to press for proletarian revolution abroad. The argument between them turned entirely on the conditions for creating socialism in Russia. Revolutions abroad are inevitable, said Stalin, and the Soviet Union cannot be secure until they happen; but it can create socialism within its own borders even before they happen. Trotsky agreed that revolutions abroad were inevitable and that the Soviet state could not be secure while it remained a Bolshevik island in a sea of capitalism, but he added that it could not even be made socialist except with the help of more advanced countries—help they would not give until they, too, had become proletarian.[1]

We cannot know for certain that Lenin, had he lived longer, would have sided with Trotsky against Stalin. We cannot even know whether, when he began to despair of early proletarian

---

[1] Stalin attacked Trotsky for advocating 'permanent revolution.' According to Trotsky, it was the duty of the Comintern to work continually for world proletarian revolution. There must be no interval of quiescence between the Bolshevik revolution and similar revolutions in other countries; there must be no letting up of energy, no putting other things first on the pretence that they were more urgent. Stalin, though he believed in the eventual (and even early) coming of world proletarian revolution, thought it inopportune in the middle twenties to incite the workers to make it. The incitement would exasperate bourgeois governments and unite them in common action against Bolshevik Russia. The Communists must bide their time, knowing that the not-too-distant future would bring new opportunities. But they must recognize that, for the moment, the times were unpropitious. Russia was still weak, and the capitalist world had recovered much of the strength lost during the war.

We must distinguish the doctrine of 'permanent revolution' attacked by Stalin in 1926 from the other doctrine of 'permanent' or 'uninterrupted revolution' expounded by both Lenin and Trotsky in 1905. The earlier doctrine asserted that circumstances peculiar to Russia (or to countries like her) made it possible for the Russian proletariat and their vanguard to take a decisive part in the 'bourgeois' revolution against the Tsarist autocracy, and then to use their power to change the character of that revolution until it became 'proletarian' and 'socialist.' This doctrine, expounded with considerable vigour by both men (though rather more clearly by Trotsky than by Lenin), was inspired by one revolution and was revived on the eve of the next. Whereas the doctrine of 'permanent revolution' attacked by Stalin in the middle 'twenties advocated the devoting of Communist energies, everywhere and continuously, to making the revolution that would destroy world capitalism. The two doctrines are not unrelated—for Trotsky believed that there could be no uninterrupted progress towards socialism in Russia unless there was world proletarian revolution.

revolution in the West, he ever came to believe that it might, after all, be possible to establish socialism in a Russia surrounded by capitalist states. We know only that he was by temperament an optimist, and that, as one hope faded, another grew quickly to take its place. It may be that, had he lived longer, he would have taken the step that Stalin took. But this is mere conjecture; the fact remains that it was Stalin who took it.

It is perhaps worth noticing that Stalin was himself of Trotsky's opinion until only a few months before he decided to differ from him. We find him, in *The Foundations of Leninism*, putting this question: 'Can the final victory of socialism be achieved in one country, without the joint efforts of the proletariats in several advanced countries?' and answering that it cannot. Eight months later, in December 1924, we find him attacking Trotsky for giving precisely the same answer. It was not until 1926, in *Problems of Leninism*, that he explained how he had come to be mistaken. He had, he said, failed to distinguish between establishing socialism in one country and making that country secure against aggression in a capitalist world; it was only the second, and not the first, of these objects that could not be achieved. Stalin had learnt his mistake, and now understood that Lenin had always taught that socialism could be established even in an isolated Russia. But if that was what Lenin had always taught, how was it that Stalin and the other Bolsheviks were so long mistaken? For it was not until April 1925 that the Communist Party officially decided that it was possible to establish socialism in only one country.

This decision, inspired by Stalin, was momentous. Whether we treat it as repudiating Marxism or as transforming it is perhaps a matter of taste, but it cannot be plausibly denied that it did either the one or the other. The old Marxism, the doctrine of Marx and Engels, obscure in some respects, was crystal clear in others; it did not teach that men of good intentions and noble ideals, provided they have power, can make a backward country socialist, but rather that there can be no socialism where the 'objective' conditions of it, economic and social, do not exist. If the Bolsheviks now decided that they could, by their own unaided efforts, create those conditions, were they not implying that men who have political power can, if they so wish, establish socialism? Lenin had said, time and again, that Russia had natural resources enough to enable her to become a great industrial Power, and had taken it for granted that that Power would be socialist. But he had never put the one question that was really awkward: could the Bolsheviks, using the political instruments forged during the civil war (instruments of a kind long denounced by all Marxists as incompatible with proletarian government) make the Soviet Union socialist despite her primitive economy and the illiteracy of her people? It was perhaps too difficult even for the boldest of the older and more intellectual Bolsheviks to forget past opinions and controversies so completely as to take this question literally and give an unequivocal answer. It was perhaps best left to a rough Georgian, brought up in the intellectual innocence of an orthodox seminary, to put the question without embarrassment and find a confident answer. He said, quite simply, Yes; and on that affirmative Communism, as we today know it, rests.

The Stalinist differs from the old-fashioned Marxist in two important respects. He does not ask himself whether his country is ripe for socialism but only whether his party can get power. He studies 'objective conditions' (the state of the economy and relations between classes), not to discover whether they are a proper foundation on which to erect a socialist superstructure, but to find out what political opportunities they afford to the party which, inconsiderable and unpopular though it may be, he chooses to call 'the party of the proletariat.' He takes it for granted that if that party, by whatever means, can get power the 'objective conditions' of socialism are thereby proved to exist. No successful revolution can ever be premature even if it is made in the most primitive country—provided the Communists make it. The Stalinist, though he still calls himself, in honour of a doctrine he no longer understands, an economic determinist, is in fact a political determinist.

He also differs from the old-fashioned Marxist in identifying the interests of the proletariat with the interests of a single Great Power. He refuses to admit that the rulers of that Power, because they allow no one to compete with them for popular favour, are not properly the spokesmen of any class. On the contrary, it seems to him that they are, even in the countries they do not rule, somehow more truly the spokesmen of the working classes than the parties those classes actually vote for. How this can be he cannot intelligibly explain, but he believes it nevertheless.

Though twenty-seven years have elapsed since Stalin published the second of his two famous books, nothing really important has since been added to the body of Communist doctrine. For by 1926 Russian Communism, though still wrapped up in Marxian phrases, had lost its Marxian backbone; it had abandoned, in fact if not in words, economic determinism; it had become the incalculably pliable doctrine of inflexible masters. It has since that time remained virtually the same though Russia has changed more quickly than any other country. The doctrine has been put to new uses but has not been renewed. No doubt, it looks different to the Bolsheviks of 1953 from what it looked to their predecessors twenty-seven years ago; they see it with different eyes, and to that extent it is different. But they have not thought it out afresh nor consciously modified it to suit new circumstances. The words, phrases and arguments that embody it have not changed—which is evidence enough that in the Soviet Union people have ceased to think seriously about social and political theory. For though set phrases ring differently in the ears of succeeding generations, men who think for themselves like to choose their own words.

Chapter Twelve

TROTSKYISM

WHILE the Bolshevik revolution was happening, and for many years afterwards, the two most famous Bolsheviks in the world were Lenin and Trotsky. Lenin was the great leader and Trotsky his principal lieutenant, a lieutenant so able and independent as to be almost an equal. That was how the two men appeared to the outside world between the autumn of 1917 and the year of Lenin's death. To those who knew nothing of the new Russia, it might in 1924 have seemed almost inevitable that Trotsky should succeed Lenin. And yet in the contest for the succession Trotsky was easily defeated. Some say that he withdrew from the contest too soon and that more patience and energy would have given him the victory; others—and they are the better informed— say that he withdrew quickly because he knew he could not win. A man may have a great reputation among foreigners and yet not be popular at home; and he may even be popular at home and yet have too little influence among the powerful to be able to rest his supremacy upon it.

What sort of man was Trotsky? The Bolsheviks now say that he was always at heart a Menshevik, and that he was never a reliable member of their party. It is true that Trotsky did not join the Bolsheviks until 1917, that he had often before that been at odds with Lenin, and that, even after he joined the party, he was more impatient than conciliatory with many of its leading men. Trotsky was certainly not 'reliable' in the way that Molotov or Malenkov or Beria have been; indeed the word 'reliable' has come to be more strictly interpreted since Trotsky left Russia. Trotsky was never a good party man; he was, perhaps, like so many brilliant and ambitious men, temperamentally incapable of loyalty to a political party not dominated by himself. He could be loyal to a creed or to a friend but not to an organization of professional politicians.

Yet to call Trotsky a Menshevik is quite misleading. The Mensheviks never were what the Bolsheviks at last became, a body of men owing allegiance to a single leader or group of leaders. There were always several different groups among them, and those groups were not even stable. There never was a Menshevik party before 1917. The members of the Russian Social-Democratic Party who voted with the minority at the London Congress in 1903 were called Mensheviks, and those who voted against them were called Bolsheviks. Because Lenin was already by that time a leading Russian Marxist and because he voted with the majority in 1903, it soon became customary to call the Social-Democrats who supported him Bolsheviks. Those who thought with Lenin were not always a majority, but, because they had been so in 1903, the name stuck. The Mensheviks, on the other hand, were merely those Russian Social-Democrats who were not followers of Lenin; and they were, between 1903 and 1917, nearly always the majority. Lenin did not form an organized group of his own until 1912, and it was never a loyal and disciplined body until the eve of the October Revolution. When Lenin returned to Russia in April 1917, he found the Bolsheviks bewildered and hesitant; they did not know what to make of the new situation until he was there to explain it to them.

We must therefore be careful how we use the words 'Bolshevik' and 'Menshevik' when we apply them to the Russian Social-Democrats before 1917; we ought to mean by 'Bolshevik' merely 'supporter of Lenin' and by 'Menshevik' 'not a supporter of Lenin.' We must not imply that there was less disagreement among the Mensheviks than between them and the Bolsheviks. Lenin was, no doubt, even before 1917, the strongest personality among the Russian Marxists, but that does not mean that support of, and opposition to, his policies constituted the major difference between them. They were all Marxists who often disagreed, either about what Marx and Engels had taught, or about how their doctrines should be applied in Russia. If the division between those who supported Lenin and those who did not is now treated by the Communists as more important than the others, that is merely because Lenin lived to be the founder of their party; it is not evidence that, in matters of theory and policy, what divided Lenin from his opponents in the years before the revolution was felt by them to be more important than what divided those opponents from each other.

It is less significant that Trotsky was a Menshevik before 1917 than that he became a Bolshevik that year and remained one until he quarrelled with Stalin; for the Bolsheviks were in 1917 and for many years afterwards a band of men who had committed themselves irrevocably. They had dared seize control of and refashion the largest country in the world, and had done so in the name of a small, unorganized and almost illiterate proletariat. They might quarrel among themselves, some applauding what the others regretted, but for them all the same die was cast. They had crossed the Rubicon with Lenin; indeed, they had crossed it with Lenin and Trotsky, for both men were leaders and there were no others like them, none so bold, resourceful and commanding. They were orators who knew how to make what the timid thought impossible look as if brave men might accomplish it. The Bolshevik revolution is the revolution of Lenin and Trotsky. No other men, not even Robespierre and Saint-Just, have used men's hopes, fears and hatreds to so great effect in so short a time.

The idea that had to be firmly lodged in a considerable number of heads before the Bolshevik revolution could be made—the idea of the 'uninterrupted revolution'—was as much Trotsky's as Lenin's. It occurred to both men at about the same time, in the autumn of 1905. The revolution occasioned by the Russian defeats in Manchuria had already begun, and Trotsky took a very active part in it. It was his behaviour during that revolution which made his reputation among Russian Social-Democrats. Contemplating the situation of Russia in 1905, Trotsky, like Lenin, noticed the timidity and anxiety of the middle class parties and the 'revolutionary zeal' of the urban workers. The bourgeois were too few and already too frightened of the Marxists and other revolutionaries ever to strike hard blows at the Tsarist bureaucracy. They were not, and were not likely to become in the conditions peculiar to Russia in the early twentieth century—conditions in important respects unlike those prevailing in France before 1789—a truly revolutionary class. This was, thought Trotsky, the great lesson of 1905. The defeats in Manchuria had destroyed what remained of the prestige of Tsardom; the régime had never been weaker, and yet the middle class parties, though they disliked and were even ashamed of that régime, though they wanted parliamentary government and a constitutional monarchy, were afraid of revolution. It had been the workers who had taken up arms and who had, for a few weeks, threatened to destroy Tsardom. Because the bourgeois liberals were timid and the Imperial bureaucracy rotten, the proletariat could, in spite of their small numbers, attempt a revolution with good hopes of victory. They were much weaker than their class in western Europe, but so too—and more so— were their corrupt, frightened and ill-assorted enemies.

Now the workers, if they made the revolution and afterwards took control of Russia, would not use their power for the benefit of the bourgeois; they would use it to make their country as quickly as possible socialist. Trotsky imagined that, after the success of the revolution, there would be an uninterrupted advance towards socialism. That advance might take many years, or even 'an entire historical epoch,' but it would be smooth and continuous; there would not be in Russia what there had been and would be in Western Europe: first bourgeois revolution, then a period of bourgeois ascendancy and then at last, in the fullness of time, proletarian revolution. Trotsky, nearly always more lucid than Lenin, did not wrap up his doctrine in confusion and paradox. He did not, as Lenin had done in *Two Tactics*, first set out to prove that the revolution of 1905 must be bourgeois and lead to capitalism and the political ascendancy of the middle class, and then go on to show how the workers could nevertheless use it to establish a 'revolutionary dictatorship of the proletariat and peasantry.' Trotsky was content to argue that Russia's peculiar situation would ensure that, if the revolution of 1905 were not put down, real power would belong to the workers and not to the bourgeois. The revolution, if successful, would not bring socialism to Russia, but it would give power to the workers and enable them to make the transition to socialism smooth and rapid. Trotsky believed with Marx that socialism cannot exist except in an advanced industrial economy; he therefore believed that the Russia of 1905 would need to be greatly changed before she could be made socialist. What he imagined in 1905 has since become one of the essential tenets of Communism; he imagined that the workers, led by the party of their class, might first make a revolution and then use political power to create the advanced industrial economy which is alone (according to Marx) compatible with socialism. Like Lenin in the *Two Tactics*, he placed *after* the revolution what, in the opinion of Marx and Engels, should come *before* it. This simple inversion, which makes nonsense of historical materialism, is the essence of Bolshevism.

Confronted with the revolution of 1905, Lenin and Trotsky reacted to it in much the same way; they both read into it signs that the proletariat could seize power immediately and use it to deprive the bourgeois of their inheritance. There was, however, one important difference between them. Lenin counted on a revolutionary alliance between workers and peasants, an alliance which meant little to Trotsky in 1905. This difference was important, but not as much so as the enemies of Trotsky later pretended. It was no doubt one of Lenin's great merits that he understood how the peasants could be won over to support the urban workers and Social-Democrats rather than the middle-class parties; he understood that, without their support, the urban workers and their political leaders would not, in spite of the weakness of the bourgeois and the decay of the régime, be strong enough to take power and hold it. The revolution would need a broader base than the diminutive Russian proletariat could provide, if it were to be used as both Lenin and Trotsky intended that it should. This Lenin saw clearly and Trotsky did not. As in 1905 so in 1917, it was Lenin who knew what ought to be done about the peasants; and in 1917 he was there to do it. It was he who invented the few simple slogans—among them the one calling for all land to be given to the peasants—which brought power to the Bolsheviks.

But, though Lenin understood better than Trotsky the uses to which in a backward country determined revolutionaries can put peasant discontent, he, too, reserved the principal rôle for the proletariat. The peasants must, he said, be made allies of the workers, but must always remain subordinate. Not only would the workers, acting through their party, carry the great burden of the revolution; they would also control the transformation of Russia into a socialist and industrial society—a kind of society that the peasants, left to themselves, would never find attractive. Lenin, no more than Trotsky, believed that the peasants had, as a class, the same interests as the workers. They might be won over to a revolutionary alliance against Tsarist autocracy, but, the revolution once made, it was to be expected that the peasants should offer considerable resistance to the conversion of Russia into a socialist society. Lenin's later writings show that he thought the alliance of workers and peasants merely temporary, and that he conceived of the 'dictatorship of the proletariat and peasantry' as something almost entirely proletarian and intellectual.

Trotsky did not forget the peasants; he did not say that no use could be made of their grievances to advance the cause of the revolution; he merely thought them unreliable friends and potential enemies of the workers. He was less disposed than Lenin to believe that they could be won over to whole-hearted support of a revolution made by the workers and the Social-Democrats; and he was also more afraid than Lenin of the obstacles the peasants might put in the way of a post-revolutionary government intent on making Russia socialist. He put a smaller value on their alliance, and was more prone to fear that the price to be paid for it might be excessive. Trotsky, for a time and under the influence of Lenin, changed his mind about the peasants; he approved of the Bolshevik policies towards them in 1917 and during the civil war. After that war and during the period of the New Economic Policy, the old mistrust revived; and it was Trotsky who first warned the Bolsheviks that they could not bring socialism to Russia until they had solved the peasant problem, until they had 'socialized' agriculture. This mistrust of the peasants was not peculiar to Trotsky;[1] all the Bolsheviks felt it, but with him it was stronger than with most of the others. He thought that the fewer the compromises with the peasants the better in the long run for the proletarian cause, whereas Lenin was willing, for a time at least, to go a long way to meet the peasants, believing that it would not otherwise be possible to establish a dictatorship of the proletariat in his own lifetime.

Trotsky, from 1905 (when he first became prominent) until

---

[1] It was not an effect of the usual dislike felt by the urban Jew for the class of Christians most remote from him. Trotsky spent a great part of his childhood among peasants, and had none of Marx's contempt for them. He merely believed that their customs and traditions were such that Russia could be made socialist only against their will. It was inevitable that they should, sooner or later, resist the Bolsheviks; and that resistance must be overborne.

1917, belonged to none of the Marxist factions; he disagreed for one reason or another with most of the leaders of the Russian Social-Democratic Party; he was a Marxist *sui generis*. He could not agree with the Mensheviks because they repudiated proletarian revolution and dictatorship in their own time, believing that no such dictatorship could be established in Russia for many years to come—or that, if it could, it would not make Russia socialist. Trotsky wanted the revolution made while he was alive to enjoy it; he was not the kind of man who can be content with the small beginnings of a vast enterprise not to be completed for generations after his death.

On the other hand, Trotsky could not, before 1917 and during the years of opposition to Tsardom when there was as yet no prospect of immediate revolution, feel at home among the Bolsheviks. They were too much dominated by Lenin, too narrow and mistrustful; he did not like their conception of a severely disciplined and exclusive party. Trotsky was a clever man who valued his independence. He was also vain and moody, neither a good subordinate nor a leader who could inspire lasting confidence in his followers. He was more admired than trusted, more envied than feared. He cared for doctrinal purity about as little as for party discipline; if he was ruthless, it was not in the defence of orthodoxy but for victory's sake and in the quest for power. Lenin before 1917 was too masterful and exacting, too fond of preaching discipline, too careless of freedom, too verbose and confused, too much addicted to quoting from the scriptures as if he were in sole possession of their truth, too much surrounded by men duller and weaker than himself, to be attractive to Trotsky.

The year 1917 changed everything. It revealed to Trotsky a Lenin greater than he had yet suspected him to be. Trotsky had courage and imagination; he no sooner understood that Lenin intended to get power and had better ideas than other men about how power was to be got and used, than he joined him. He became a Bolshevik, and was thereafter loyal to Lenin until Lenin died. There were differences of opinion between them and heated arguments, but the two men understood one another. For all his belief in discipline, Lenin was often a patient and generous leader. Besides, the Bolshevik party had not been tightly organized before the revolution—for Lenin had never been able to put his theory into practice; and after the revolution the party grew at such a pace that it was several years before there could emerge inside it the efficient machinery that would make it quickly responsive to a single will. This rapid growth was indeed in the end to make it easier to establish the present autocracy within the party, but during the early years after the revolution, the men at the top could still discuss policy with considerable freedom. In those days the man in Russia with the greatest influence after Lenin was Trotsky, and that influence he owed to his services in the cause of the revolution and to the respect that Lenin felt for him. Lenin knew his faults but had a great opinion of his talents.

Trotsky, on his side, knew—and never sought to deny—that it was Lenin who, more than any other man, made the Bolshevik revolution, the event so longed for by himself, the convulsion that enabled him to make a great figure in the world. Lenin gave Trotsky his chance in history, gave him work which absorbed his energies and satisfied his ambition. For several years—the most wonderful years of his life—Trotsky was a devoted Bolshevik, and, though never exactly a disciple of Lenin, had for him a respect he felt for no other man. Trotsky's great years were the years of his friendship and collaboration with Lenin; and it was he and Lenin who in 1905, alone among the Russian Marxists, conceived of a revolution that might bring immediate power to the proletariat and to the party acting in their name. Different though they were, there was more than a little in common between the two men whose friendship has made a greater difference in the world than any other between two Russians.

Nevertheless, when Lenin withdrew from public life and later died, when the struggle to succeed him began, there was not much hope for Trotsky. He was the next most famous Bolshevik after Lenin, but he was not a Bolshevik in quite the same sense; he had never inspired the same loyalty, and had not known how to acquire control of the party machine. In spite of his fame he was easily defeated.

His easy defeat did not cause Trotsky to respect his enemies; he ascribed their victory for the most part to a course of events which neither they nor he could control (but which he, unlike them, could understand), and partly also to their having qualities which he thanked God he did not possess.

Trotsky's explanation of Stalin's victory is the greater part of the theory nowadays called Trotskyism. That theory is not much attended to, either in Russia or in the West. In Russia, of course, no one is allowed to know anything of it; but the indifference of the West is not so easily explained. For the theory is, in its way, a very good one; it is convincing to anyone who accepts the Marxist assumptions of its author. And even if he does not, there is no reason why he should not accept many of Trotsky's conclusions, though he will have to account for them in a rather different way.

Trotsky's best account of Stalinism is *The Revolution Betrayed*, a book written in 1936, and translated into English by Max Eastman. It is a good book, and a more effective condemnation of Stalinism than any other. It is written by a man who, unlike the Communists who have stayed in Russia, has never lost the habit of discussing public affairs with intelligent men of independent judgment; it is a book written in the hope of convincing just such men, men whom the author, if he does not happen to persuade them, cannot coerce. It is a work incomparably better and easier to read than any written by Stalin or Lenin, especially since they adopted for the government of both Russia and the Communist Party the nursery rule: First try to convince and then coerce. Nothing makes a man a more careless reasoner than the knowledge that he can, should the need arise, use another and a shorter method of persuasion.

Trotsky would not be a Marxist if he did not preach from a text. The text of *The Revolution Betrayed* is a sentence taken from *The Critique of the Gotha Programme*: 'Law can never be higher than the economic structure of society and the cultural development conditioned by that structure.' In other words, no society can enjoy a system of laws and rights that does not correspond to its economy and to the culture appropriate to that economy. If an attempt is made to impose any such system, it will surely fail; the new rights and laws will exist only on paper, and will either be ignored or so distorted as not to be what they seem. This judgment is a proper deduction from historical materialism, and Marx felt no need to qualify it in *The Critique of the Gotha Programme*.

But Trotsky, being one of the two original exponents of the doctrine of 'uninterrupted revolution,' had perforce to qualify it. He did so by repeating the arguments used by the Bolsheviks in

1917 to prove that their revolution was not premature. These arguments have already been sufficiently considered, and it is enough to remind the reader that their intention was to show that, since the Russian revolution would be only an episode in the fall of world imperialism, the Bolshevik attempt to make Russia socialist in spite of her economic and cultural backwardness need not fail.

Trotsky wanted both to condemn Stalin's doctrine of 'socialism in one country' and to justify the Bolshevik revolution. Stalin's doctrine, he said, was—though Stalin might not know it—a repudiation of a cardinal tenet of Marxism; it implied that men could seize power and then use it to transform, not merely an obsolescent political and legal superstructure, but the economic basis of society as well. Trotsky believed that the Bolsheviks were right when they took advantage of circumstances peculiar to Russia to make the October Revolution; they were right because international capitalism was rotten to the core, and their action could only hasten its collapse. The risk they took was worth taking, for they took it in reasonable expectation of proletarian revolution in Germany. That revolution had not yet happened, but it did not follow that the Bolshevik diagnosis had been wrong. The exact date of a revolution cannot be foretold, though its causes are easily seen and its coming inevitable. The West was ripe for revolution, and the duty of the Bolsheviks was to hasten its coming. Their excuse in 1917 for seizing power in the name of the proletariat in so backward a country as Russia had been that they would thereby precipitate a world revolution; they had not seized it under the illusion that, whatever happened in the West, they could make a socialist society in their own primitive and illiterate country. The first duty of the Bolsheviks was, and always must be, to use all the means in their power to foment and sustain proletarian revolution all over the world. To neglect that duty was to endanger the Bolshevik régime—a régime that nothing except revolution in the capitalist West could save from decay.

Neither Marx nor Lenin, said Trotsky, ever foresaw the possible consequences of a proletarian revolution in a backward country; Marx because he never thought such a revolution possible, and Lenin because he always looked upon the Bolshevik seizure of power as an incident in a world revolution. Lenin never expected, and therefore never made a theory about, the prolonged isolation of the Soviet State. No doubt he already saw emerging, and strongly condemned, some of the evil consequences of that isolation, but he always hoped it would soon end; and so he never troubled to analyse its peculiar problems. That task was reserved for Trotsky; and his best attempt at it is his book *The Revolution Betrayed*.

The urban workers, the only ardent supporters of the Bolsheviks in 1917 and during the civil war, were, Trotsky admitted, a very small minority of the Russian people; and they were also more primitive and illiterate than the corresponding class in the West. The peasants might support the Bolsheviks against the landlords and the Whites, but their interests, while they remained peasants, could not be compatible with those of the workers. Trotsky believed that, since Russia was poor, backward and illiterate, she could not be transformed into a modern industrial society with the consent and willing co-operation of the great majority of the people. Her rapid industrialization had increased the value of the services of her few competent technicians and administrators, who had to be suitably rewarded for what they alone could do, and could do efficiently only while they were much better off than the ordinary workers. There had therefore arisen since the Bolshevik revolution privileges that no one could have prevented—very considerable inequalities of income unacceptable to the common people who could not understand the need for them. For the defence of these misunderstood and resented privileges, the workers' state had found itself obliged to create anew the special instrument, the police force, long used by the bourgeois for a similar purpose.

If Russia had been an advanced industrial society, her proletarians would have been the majority, or at least a large minority, of the people. They would have been literate and would also have lived much more comfortably than they in fact did; and so, too, would her peasants. Technicians and administrators would then have been less scarce, and their privileges much smaller. A numerous and educated proletariat would have given the workers' state a broader and a more solid base. With less inequality and a better understanding by both workers and peasants of their country's needs and their government's benevolent purposes, the newly founded state would have been from the first truly democratic. Whereas, poverty and ignorance being general in Russia, and the most useful workers (the technicians and administrators) scarce and unable to work efficiently unless they lived very much better than the manual labourers, there was of necessity great inequality and widespread coercion. The situation of the new Russia, as Trotsky imagined it, was that of a queue of people awaiting the distribution of scarce and indispensable commodities: while everyone in the queue gets an equal or nearly equal share, even though not a sufficient one, a natural sense of justice keeps the people quiet and orderly; but as soon as some get much more than the others, who get less than they need and for reasons which, good though they may be, are unintelligible to them, the unsatisfied grow angry with the lucky ones, and there is need of policemen to keep the queue in order.

Where force must be used, those who use it cannot be responsible to the people they use it against; and, being irresponsible, they soon learn to use it to create and defend what suits them best rather than whatever, under the conditions prevailing, is the most just—that is to say, the most likely to transform, as quickly and easily as possible, the existing imperfect society into a society of equals. Privileges, created in the first place because they are necessary and thereafter maintained against the wishes of an ignorant people who cannot understand the need for them, soon grow into something much greater than can be justified. Privilege breeds arrogance, and arrogance breeds indifference and contempt for the unprivileged. This is the simple process whereby the powerful, whatever their intentions when they seize power, acquire interests different from those of the rest of the people. With the passage of time, these interests become always more incompatible with the popular interest, and the business of defending them more elaborate. That is what must happen, according to Trotsky, when an attempt is made to build socialism in an illiterate and poverty stricken society. Lenin knew this; he admitted the special dangers to which Russia was liable, and struck hard at the evil growths wherever he saw them. The difference between him and Stalin—this, of course, is the verdict of Trotsky and not of the impartial historian—is that Lenin always strove to avert and mitigate these inevitable tendencies, and always hoped and worked for the world revolution which would save the

Bolshevik régime from them and from internal decay; whereas Stalin thrived on the decay and counted so little on world revolution that he might as well never have given a thought to it. He gladly accepted the bureaucratic privileges and social inequalities that Lenin strove to avert, taking no other precaution than to call them by new names to hide their true character.

The Left Opposition—the opposition inspired by Trotsky—was defeated by Stalin, not because Stalin's arguments were better but because they pleased the powerful bureaucracy then emerging in Soviet Russia. The revolution had exhausted the people, morally even more than physically; they were apathetic and cynical, doubting whether any action of theirs could prevent the triumph of the evils they saw around them. Revolution squanders a large capital of hope; and when that capital is spent, the people are docile and a new generation of privileged rulers get their chance to install themselves in power. Trotsky called Stalin and his companions in the government of Russia 'men of Thermidor'; they were Bolsheviks who had outlived the heroic period of the revolution, men who, while still calling themselves revolutionaries, had allowed circumstances and their own love of power and wealth to turn them into reactionaries. Like the Jacobins who overthrew Robespierre on the 9th Thermidor (July 27th, 1794), Stalin and his companions rode to power on a counter-revolutionary wave; they were the minor actors of the great period, persons brought to the fore after its close by their own persistence and the general weariness and desire for quieter and less exacting times. They were the kind of men wanted by the new bureaucrats, and what they wanted they were already powerful enough to get. In Trotsky's own words: 'The bureaucracy conquered something more than the Left Opposition. It conquered the Bolshevik Party. It defeated the programme of Lenin. . . . It defeated all these enemies, the Opposition, the Party, and Lenin, not with ideas and arguments, but with its own social weight. The leaden rump of the bureaucracy outweighed the head of the revolution. That is the secret of the Soviet's Thermidor.' After Lenin's death, Stalin opened wide the gates of the party, that the revolutionary vanguard might be lost in what Trotsky called 'raw human material, without experience, without independence, and yet with the old habit of submitting to the authorities.'

Trotsky said that there was democracy inside the Bolshevik party from 1917 to 1921, though there was civil war in Russia for most of that time and the capitalist powers were sending troops to fight the revolution. The party was then, on good Leninist principles, exclusive: it took great care who should enter it, but to those who entered it allowed full freedom of debate and criticism; every Bolshevik had then an opportunity to take part in defining the policy of his party.[1] Trotsky admitted that the Tenth Congress of the Party, held in 1921, condemned 'fractionalism' (i.e., the formation of separate groups inside the party for the purpose of influencing its policies); but that, he said, was an exceptional measure meant to be abandoned as soon as possible. Stalin's doctrine that such groups cannot be tolerated in the party is, according to Trotsky, 'a myth of the epoch of decline.'

As soon as the new bureaucrats had, by the victory of Stalin, established their predominance in the state, they set about consolidating their position. It did not suit them—the few hundred thousand persons holding positions of real authority in the administration of the state, of industry and of agriculture—that they should be isolated from the rest of the people, that there should be a long gap in the social ladder, with many rungs missing and no hope left to the humble of climbing the ladder without them. They were afraid of too solitary an eminence, and thought their own position would be the stronger for having other privileged but more modest groups around them. The greater the inequality among their subordinates the more secure their own pre-eminence. They therefore encouraged the emergence of lesser aristocracies, that they might themselves be the tallest of the tall, and not giants among pygmies. When they set up collective farms, some of these farms were much richer than others, and the government did nothing to make them more equal. They also allowed as great inequalities inside the farms as had formerly existed between the peasants. The new inequality was different in kind; it was based, not on unequal property in land, but on the division of labour inside the collectives, the desk workers getting much larger real incomes than the men who worked in the fields.

[1] This is not true, but Trotsky said it. *The Revolution Betrayed* is not a fair book, it is a clever one. Trotsky dilates on the dangers that attend a 'proletarian revolution' in a primitive country, but was not by any means so sharply aware of those dangers before he quarrelled with Stalin.

Because the workers in industry were paid not time wages but piece rates, the more efficient were everywhere drawn away from the others and converted into privileged groups distributed widely over the whole economy. No doubt, it was necessary to increase efficiency, but inequalities in industry and in agriculture soon became much greater than could be excused by this need. Stakhanovism was unpopular with most of the workers but was encouraged by the government because it created an aristocracy of labour. That was not the government's only motive, but it was, said Trotsky, an important one.

It used to be a doctrine held by almost every kind of socialist in Europe that large professional armies are instruments of bourgeois exploitation. They find their officers among the educated class, and attract into the ranks by a promise of security a considerable section of the working class, who are then put into uniform, kept apart from the rest of the community, and trained in habits of unquestioning obedience to their superiors. They are thus cut off from their class, both physically and mentally, and so can be relied upon to defend the system that exploits that class. The proletarian state must therefore destroy the professional army and put in its place a citizen militia, an armed force not divorced from the people but always close to them and responsive to their moods.

It was in France that the theory about the socially oppressive function of the professional army was invented, and it was from the French socialists that Marx took it over. The Bolsheviks had accepted it, and had at first acted upon it. The old army of the Tsars was completely disbanded. The Red Army was a new creation; it was intended to be a people's army and was organized as a territorial militia. But unfortunately, owing to the general ignorance of the people and their lack of technical training, it could not long remain a pure militia; and Trotsky himself, then in charge of the military defence of the state, had established a part of it as a professional force on the European model. He had soon come to believe that a territorial militia cannot be highly efficient except in a technically advanced and civilized country. The introduction of regular units into the Red Army had been merely one example among many of the falling away from theory forced on the reluctant Bolsheviks by the backwardness of their country. But the regulars had, according to Trotsky, been a mere stiffening of a very predominantly militia force, and the military commanders had not been allowed to become a corps of officers on the western model, a military caste separate from the troops and in no way responsible to them. As late as the beginning of 1935 the Red Army was still predominantly a citizen militia, three-quarters of it consisting of territorial units and only one-quarter of regulars. In 1935 and 1936, the army was greatly expanded, and the proportion of territorials to regulars in it almost exactly reversed; and in September 1935 the corps of officers was restored and with it all the military titles abolished by the revolution. The reason given for these drastic measures was the rise to power of Hitler in Germany. Trotsky did not deny the duty of the Soviet Government to make provision for the military defence of the state; he was neither a pacifist nor a believer in disarmament. But he did take this rapid conversion of a citizen militia into a professional army for another symptom of Bolshevik degeneracy. He thought the restoration of the corps of officers especially significant. The Red Army would soon become as divorced from the people as the older professional armies of the West, and therefore as well suited to be the instrument of an exploiting minority.

Trotsky considered the Stalin Constitution of 1936 another betrayal of Bolshevism. It had been a favourite belief of the Marxists that proletarian democracy differs in kind from bourgeois democracy, and uses quite different organs of government. The central parliament elected by a people divided into artificial territorial constituencies, though it looks democratic, in fact ensures that government cannot be responsible to the people. The territorial constituency is not a social unit, it has no common interests and therefore no common 'will'; the man who 'represents' it does not speak for a true community, but is merely the person least unacceptable to the different classes and groups in that constituency. He must stand for what is common to them, and that is mere pious sentiment; he must speak to please them all, to excite them without making them dangerous, to give them hope without their quite knowing what it is they are hoping for. He is a compromise candidate endeavouring to attract as many votes as possible among people having nothing more in common than that they live within so many miles of one another, and he is able to attract them only because he and the party supporting him make harmless promises which mean nothing and can therefore neither be kept nor broken. Parliamentary democracy is an elaborate make-believe; the politicians are all in the same profitable game together; they are mere seeming enemies, like actors playing Montagues and Capulets on the stage, earning their living by making a show of passion. The real business of bourgeois politicians is to get power and sell the use of it to the highest bidder. Nothing important can be decided at general elections, which serve only to confuse the people and to keep their minds away from realities; the decisions that really matter are taken by the politicians and civil servants in the capital, where they are exposed to all the pressures that powerful financial, industrial and professional corporations can bring to bear on them, pressures not the less effective because it would so often be harsh to call them bribery or intimidation. In a parliamentary democracy the common people are the occasional audiences of the politicians; they listen to their speeches, but the real business of government is never discussed with them or in their presence. This is inevitably so, being the effect of institutions whose function is to make possible government in the interest of the few with the apparent consent of the many. It is the political machinery of exploitation appropriate to the last stage of capitalist society.

This theory does not require that bourgeois politicians should be hypocrites. The system is profitable to them, but they did not deliberately make it for the sake of those profits. Trotsky, being a Marxist, did not believe that institutions are contrived for the benefit of the ruling class; they are, he knew, the effects of many men's actions over long periods of time, and none of the men, the consequences of whose actions they are, need ever have foreseen or understood them. Men seek to promote their interests, and there slowly emerge, as a result of their endeavours, institutions profitable to the most powerful among them; and there also arise, together with these institutions, the myths and codes of behaviour appropriate to them. The democratic theories of the capitalist world do not describe how institutions work there; they merely cause them to work more smoothly than they otherwise would. Institutions are ways in which men behave as a matter of convention; they would not behave in these ways unless they had acquired certain habits of mind, certain kinds of response to their social environment.

Men are not only conventional, they are also inquisitive and rational, and therefore devise theories to justify their conventions. The more civilized they are, the more important the theories. Again, the more important any institutions to the predominance of the ruling class, the more sacred the theories about them. There was a time when theology mattered greatly, but that time is now past; and in the modern world it is the political opinions of their subjects which interest governments most. When Trotsky and the Marxists call parliamentary democracy a 'sham,' they mean to accuse no one of hypocrisy or cynicism. Indeed, the fewer the hypocrites and cynics in high places, the more impressive the sham. When their wealth and power depend upon it, men will put their very souls into the parts they play on the world's stage; they will believe themselves to be what they pretend.

Serious matters cannot, according to this theory, be discussed at general elections, nor yet by central parliaments consisting of men elected by constituencies which are not true communities. And yet something must be discussed at them or by them; the actors must be kept busy and must look important. There therefore arise false issues and insignificant problems to occupy men's minds and divert their passions. The very system they operate forces confusion on them and makes them each other's dupes. On the other hand, professional, industrial and financial corporations require real services from bourgeois governments; they are suitably organized to advance their interests, they know what difficulties face them and what opportunities come their way; they therefore make precise demands. They find it easy to negotiate with the politicians and permanent heads of departments, and ways are soon found to accommodate what they ask for with the current vague notions of the public good. The negotiators are satisfied, appearances preserved, and consciences untroubled. Parliamentary democracy of its very nature creates two orders of political phenomena: the processes whereby the ruling class deceive their victims (and themselves) that a majority 'will' is being elicited and given effect to, and the amicable but hard-headed negotiations that result in the making of laws and executive decisions in the interest of the capitalist class. Not that parliamentary democracy

brings no benefits to the workers; where there is so much talk of
the people's will and their needs, something must be done for
them or else no one will be deceived. There is an element of compromise about it, and the poor do get their pickings; for the
system would never have arisen could exploitation have remained
as naked as before. Its appearance in the world is a concession
made by the rich to the poor; it is the interest—though not the
conscious purpose—of the rich that the concession should be
illusory, but it cannot bring them social peace unless it is also to
some slight extent real.

Now, under the system which emerged in Russia in 1917 and
afterwards, the soviets did not represent large territorial constituencies; they were formed in the factories, in the armed forces
and in the villages; and were therefore thought by the Bolsheviks
to be proper organs of working class government. The people
who belonged to them or who elected their members did form—
so Trotsky believed—true communities having important interests
in common; the soviets were instruments of government allowing
realistic discussion of those interests and making easier their pro-
motion. They were true organs of popular democracy, and did not
confuse the people but brought their minds to bear upon the issues
that most deeply affected them. Many thousands of soviets made
their appearance in Russia, some of them before but most of them
after the Bolsheviks seized power, and each of them was the
organ of a true community, of a group of people who felt the need
to act together in defence of a common interest, because they
belonged to the same factory or village, or were in some other way
drawn to one another to form a political unit of their own, and
were not a mere collection of people who happened to live within
an area whose boundaries were drawn by some external authority.
These communities and groups could formulate precise demands
giving expression to common needs and aspirations.

Trotsky did not deny that the Bolsheviks had already, while
Lenin was still alive, refused the vote to many classes of people,
to employers of labour, to priests and to other 'unreliable
elements'; he did not deny that the pyramid of soviets was from
the first so constructed that every urban worker's vote counted
for several times as much as a peasant's. These, he thought, were
precautions necessary to preserve the 'dictatorship of the pro-

letariat' in as backward a country as Russia. Soviet democracy had always been far from perfectly democratic, but that did not prevent the soviets from being, at least in principle, much better organs of democracy than the parliaments of the West. Trotsky also admitted that the soviets had in fact lost all real initiative long before Stalin invented his new constitution. The illiteracy and political inexperience of the working people, in the towns and the villages, had made their democracy fall an easy prey to the Stalinist reaction. Soviet democracy had long been a sham before Stalin decided to put another sham in its place. But the soviets, paralyzed though they were, had once been alive; and they were, at least potentially, true organs of proletarian democracy. The workers had once used them, clumsily and foolishly perhaps, but they had used them—and might be tempted to use them again. Stalin felt strong enough in 1936 to get rid of them, and to replace them by something much more easily controlled from the centre, by a system perfected by the bourgeois for the very purpose of exploiting the people while seeming to consult them.

The arguments used by Stalin to recommend his new constitution seemed to Trotsky childish and cynical; they amounted to a scarcely veiled rejection of what the Bolsheviks had always understood by proletarian democracy. Trotsky spoke with particular contempt of Stalin's defence of the one party system. The Bolsheviks had during the civil war been obliged by circumstances to suppress the other parties because their activities had endangered the survival of the Soviet state; but they had never pretended that by so doing they were acting democractically, still less that the workers and peasants must have one party and one party alone. During the civil war there had been freedom inside the party, though the fate of the revolution had still been uncertain and the dangers much greater than at any time since. No one had then dared make such a mockery of Marxism as to say that socialism existed in Russia. But Stalin did say in 1936 that 'socialism had conquered finally and irrevocably,' and yet had found it necessary to abolish the soviets, to maintain the political monopoly of one party, and to allow no freedom inside it. It is, according to Trotsky, a pitiful argument that, where there is only one class, there need be only one party, as if a social class were homogeneous, as if there could be no important divisions of interest inside it, as if no part of it could ever feel the need to form a political organization of its own. Stalin had to preserve the one party system because it was the ultimate defence of the new bureaucracy against the people, the workers and the peasants, whom they now feared even more than they feared their foreign enemies. It was a fear made stronger by their betrayal of the revolution. In a country where there has just been a great revolution in the name of equality, new privileges 'burn their possessors as a gold watch burns the pocket of an amateur thief.' The Stalin Constitution was the consummation of evils begun long before; it was an attempt made by the murderers of proletarian democracy to bury the corpse. A system of government is not like a man; when the spirit has left it the body does not immediately decay, and there is for long afterwards the danger that it may come suddenly to life again. When it is killed it must be buried, or the killers may find that they have soiled their hands in vain.

This in brief is Trotsky's account of what happened in Russia after Lenin's death and his own exile. It is an account very generally accepted by Marxist critics of the Soviet Union. Russia, they say, has never yet been and is now no longer in the way of becoming a socialist society. Lenin in all sincerity wished to make her one, though he knew how difficult it would be, seeing how ignorant and poor she was. Whereas Stalin merely rode to power on the reactionary current that Lenin had always resisted. Far from striving to avert the dangers that a backward country was inevitably liable to, Stalin made the best use he could of them to fasten his hold on Russia.

Trotsky believed that one of two things must happen in Stalin's empire: there must be either a political revolution to destroy the new bureaucracy and restore a true 'dictatorship of the proletariat,' or else a social revolution made by the bureaucrats to give a more solid basis to their ascendancy. This social revolution would destroy the system of property established by Lenin and the old Bolsheviks; it would, if it happened, restore in some form or other the right of inheritance and of private property in the means of production. Trotsky did not pretend to know which of these two things would happen, but, being (in his own way) a Marxist, he thought it must be either the one or the other, that either the political system would be forcibly adjusted to the new system of property, or else the latter so altered as to become a solid basis for the predominance of a new ruling class.

He did not think it likely that the bureaucrats would leave the system of property alone, that they could long continue to enjoy their privileges (and even pass them on to their children) while the state remained the sole owner of the means of production, distribution and exchange. He did not think it likely, because he was a Marxist and therefore had rather too simple ideas about the connexion between property and power. In the quarter of a century since Trotsky left Russia, the Stalinists have done almost nothing to increase the economic *independence* of the new rich. The bureaucrat or technician lives off his income, which, large though it may be, he must still earn; and he must also be satisfied with what opportunities are given him to put his children in the way of earning similar incomes when their time comes. This can be done without destroying any of the state's many monopolies; and it is, indeed, the interest of the rulers of the Soviet Union that it should be done that way and not another. The superiority of the new rich in the Soviet Union is a collective superiority; it is maintained by the state and the party, and it cannot, in present circumstances, be maintained any other way. There is great inequality within the ranks of the privileged, but every privileged individual is equally subject to the discipline that maintains the hierarchy he belongs to. The independence of the state power enjoyed by the feudal lord, by the squire, and, later, by the western merchant, manufacturer and professional man, is impossible in Bolshevik Russia; there the privileged must exploit and oppress collectively or else not at all. Independence of the state is impossible in the modern industrial world, in the West as well as in Russia, but in Russia much more than in the West. When a premature revolution is made in the name of Marx and of the working class, that class, if they are to be exploited, must be so by means of a system which at least looks like socialism. Provided they are clever enough, men can often in this world be grossly and successfully unjust, but only if they preserve whatever 'decencies' may happen to prevail where they live. The Bolsheviks may or may not be exploiters; but the society they rule calls itself socialist, and they could not exploit it unless they contrived to look like socialists.

As an indictment of Stalinism, Trotsky's account of Soviet Russia is formidable. So much so, indeed, that some version or other of it has been adopted by nearly all Stalin's more plausible critics. But the account is not only an attack on Stalinism; it is also an apology for Trotsky and Lenin. For it was their revolution that Stalin betrayed, misunderstood and corrupted.

As an apology for the Bolshevik revolution, Trotsky's account is not impressive. It makes the assumptions that Lenin made about the condition of western capitalism and the prospect of immediate world revolution. Trotsky, no more than Lenin, understood how it was that the German Social-Democrats, nourished on Marxism and enjoying in their own country incomparably greater working-class support than the Bolsheviks had ever done in Russia, could not make a proletarian revolution. He, too, spoke of treachery and corruption in a bourgeois environment. It never occurred to him that the German workers, knowing the 'sham democracy' of the bourgeois better than he did, might have learnt to like it and to prize the benefits it brought them. Every sign of disorder in Germany seemed to him to announce the coming proletarian revolution in the West—the revolution so much needed by the Bolsheviks to justify their desperate hazard of 1917 but which the German workers felt they could do without. Blinded by Marxism, Trotsky even mistook the great and rapid increase in the number of civil servants in western countries for evidence that bourgeois repression was increasing as bourgeois predominance grew less secure. Though he survived Lenin by many years, he would not—perhaps because he dared not—recognize the emergence of the democratic welfare state. That state has, no doubt, inefficiencies and injustices peculiar to itself, but they are not faults that lead to proletarian revolution. The welfare state is no more bourgeois than the Communist state is proletarian. These old-fashioned categories no longer apply, but the Communist still believes that they do, and therefore systematically misdescribes the world he lives in.[1]

[1] Not only the Communist but the westerner also. We still commonly speak of England and France as capitalist countries, though they are no longer capitalist in the sense understood by Marx and his contemporaries. The political and social theorist cannot avoid using words with several or changing meanings, but he can take care not to treat an argument which is valid when a word is used in one sense as if it were valid when it is used in another. Communists, whether followers of Trotsky or Stalin, usually neglect this simple precaution.

The Bolshevik revolution was never betrayed, for both Lenin and Trotsky miscalculated when they made it. They quite misread the situation in the West; for there never was reasonable hope of proletarian revolution in Germany or in any other major industrial country during or after the First World War. The Bolshevik revolution was premature and the coming of Stalinism, whose causes Trotsky described so well, was therefore (on Marxian premises) inevitable. If Marxism is true, not all the valiant efforts of Lenin and Trotsky could have prevented the emergence of some such system as Stalin later stood for. The 'objective conditions' of his success were created by the Bolshevik revolution—which was itself a betrayal of Marxism but which no Marxist could betray.

Nor were these efforts as valiant as Trotsky, after his quarrel with Stalin, tried to make them out. In *Two Tactics*, the long and elaborate pamphlet in which Lenin first put forward the doctrine of 'uninterrupted revolution,' there is nothing said about the Russian workers and Social-Democrats slightly anticipating in their country a movement soon to sweep the whole capitalist world. That argument was lightly touched upon in 1905, but was not made much of until many years later, when it seemed to Lenin that war was exhausting all the Great Powers and that Tsardom had not long to live. The doctrine of 'uninterrupted revolution' was revived, and this argument used to defend it against the Mensheviks. Trotsky himself, who was a more lucid and consistent advocate of 'uninterrupted revolution' than Lenin, long thought it inevitable in Russia whatever happened elsewhere.

Moreover, most of the evil consequences of premature revolution were already apparent before Lenin died. They were, indeed, consequences of courses that the Bolsheviks had felt themselves driven to in their 'valiant efforts' to retain power. They had had to fight hard to defeat numerous enemies, and most of the institutions that Trotsky afterwards considered preclusive of socialism had been created to give victory to the Bolsheviks. After the civil war they had somewhat relaxed their hold on an almost stifled economy but had kept all their instruments of coercion; and Trotsky for one had never suggested that they could do without them. His strong dislike for these instruments was not evident until there was no longer a hope of his using them.

There can be no doubt that Stalin was right and Trotsky wrong in the dispute between them about the imminence of proletarian revolution outside Russia. There was not, after 1920, even the glimmer of a hope of it in any great industrial country. Had the Bolsheviks exerted themselves to stimulate it, they would have failed miserably and have united all the Powers against them. Western governments were willing enough to let the Bolsheviks play the masters in exhausted Russia, provided they kept their hands off the rest of Europe. It did not greatly concern them who killed whom, or how many millions starved, in so remote, impoverished and barbarous a country. They were too much occupied with their own quarrels and too little recovered from the effects of war to embark on new adventures in Russia. They had, for a time, while they thought the Whites might beat the Reds, thrust their little fingers just a short way into the Russian mess, but had got nothing for themselves or their friends by doing so. Russia, they now thought, was best left alone. She was the victim of a dreadful and catching disease, and should be kept away from other nations and allowed to cure herself as best she might. The western governments wanted to have as little to do with her as possible, and she was therefore safe from them. Only the reckless policy advocated by Trotsky could have caused them to change their minds, and drive the Bolsheviks out of Russia before they had time to make her and themselves formidable.

Chapter Thirteen

MARXISM AND COMMUNISM

I. THE MARXIAN LEGACY OF IDEAS

Marxism has been often attacked, and at almost every point; and yet still remains, even in the West, the most important of all systematic social and political theories. There have certainly been greater political theorists than Marx; Plato stands head and shoulders above him, as he does above all the others, and Aristotle, Aquinas, Hobbes, Montesquieu and Rousseau are every one of them, though each for different reasons, superior to him. Aristotle was not more the disciple of Plato than Marx of Hegel, Ricardo and the early French socialists, and he was a better reasoner, more lucid, orderly, exact and economical, than the inventor of historical materialism. Aquinas expressed more elaborately and clearly than anyone before him the political ideals of the Middle Ages, ideals to which western civilization is as much indebted as to the Greeks. This deeply religious man was by temperament exceptionally tolerant and intellectually honest, and it is easy to detect, under the dry formalism of his scholastic philosophy, the wide sympathies and good will that dispose a man to put a high value on justice and freedom. Like Immanuel Kant, he had moral excellence and intellectual power, and was therefore admirably sane.

Hobbes was the innovator who broke with the traditional political philosophy whose greatest exponent had been Aquinas; he made political theory amoral, treating it as if its function were merely to devise the organization of power most likely to give security to individuals. Such was the force of his arguments and his style that, though he was never popular, his influence was immense. No political thinker ever put so much into one book as Montesquieu into *De l'Esprit des Lois*, and anyone who wished to make a list of its merits (or of its defects) would find it hard to

306

know where to begin. Perhaps the book's greatest merit is that it directs the reader's attention, not to the origins of political society or to problems of political obligation, but to customs, laws and institutions, their relations with one another and with the moral attitudes and ideals that accompany them. If originality is the main ingredient of intellectual greatness, it would be difficult to find any political thinker since Plato greater than Montesquieu.

Rousseau,[1] scarcely less original than Montesquieu, was perhaps his most perceptive admirer and the first to understand that his true greatness lay, not so much in his apology for the English political system or his liberalism, as in the elaborate and subtle account he gave of how institutions, laws, customs and social ideals affect one another and thereby mould the characters of men. Rousseau's other master was Plato, the spirit of whose political philosophy he (though not a classical scholar) understood better than did any of the moderns before him.

But Rousseau, unlike Plato and Montesquieu, was a believer in equality, the greatest and most eloquent of modern radicals, the idol of the first revolutionaries, the denouncer of class exploitation who believed that men could be moral and free only in a society of equals. The beliefs to which life and fire were first given by Rousseau later became assumptions common to all schools of socialism. It was he who argued that, whenever a part of the community are much wealthier than the others, they impose on them conditions that make them their mere instruments. It was he, too, who argued that, though equality is right and natural (i.e., necessary to the happiness of creatures constituted as men are), the bias of nearly all institutions is against it, leading in the political sphere to oligarchy, and in the social, to a division of the community into a number of hostile classes. Equality must therefore be deliberately contrived and maintained by the authority of the entire community. The margin is indeed narrow that separates Rousseau's brand of radicalism from nineteenth century socialism. Kant, who more than most of his admirers has done justice to him, took from him two major principles: that freedom is obedience to the law we prescribe for ourselves, and that it is morally

---

[1] Though Madame de Staël, whose enthusiasm for new ideas was like a philatelist's passion for stamps, never noticed the fine specimens he had to offer, and could presume to say of him that he 'discovered nothing and inflamed everything.'

wrong for any man to treat another merely as a means to his own ends.

Even if we compare Marx with the other socialists, it is by no means obvious that he was the most original. We can already find in the writings of Saint-Simon many of the favourite themes of nineteenth-century socialism: the belief that economic and political phenomena are intimately related; the condemnation of militarism and organized religion as survivals from the past whose social funtion is to protect the privileges of the rich and powerful; the belief that industry cannot be fully efficient, nor its products justly distributed, unless it is socially controlled; the explanation of political struggles as effects of class antagonisms; the condemnation of political liberalism and the language of the rights of man; the belief that all that has gone before has prepared the coming, now at last imminent, of the just society; the division of history into a number of epochs, of which each coincides with the predominance of a different class; the distinction between 'administration' and 'government,' of which the latter is fated to disappear as mankind become more enlightened and the use of force unnecessary; the treatment of all earlier social philosophies as metaphysical fantasies whose only use was to justify the claims made on behalf of some social class or group. All these things are in Saint-Simon— not lightly touched upon but often repeated and with great emphasis by a man convinced of their importance. But Saint-Simon was not even as systematic a thinker as Marx; and was also, take him all in all, much less formidable and impressive, without the passion, the scorn, the learning and the shrewdness which have added so much to the power of Marx's writings over his readers' minds. Marx was not a great writer, but there was something about him, revealed even in his clumsy style, to compel attention and respect. Whereas Saint-Simon was intolerably diffuse, repetitious and disorderly. *L'Organisateur*, the most lucid, cogent and well constructed of the essays that go under his name, was put together for him by his sometime friend and disciple Auguste Comte. Despite his originality, many of his best ideas did not make their full impact on the European mind until Marx had placed his imprint upon them. Even in the intellectual world, the stronger personality sometimes puts the weaker in the shade, and the larger reputation in the end sucks the life out of the smaller one. While he lived, Marx was one socialist among many, though already, towards the end of his life, considered one of the two or three most important; but since that time his superiority over the others has seemed to grow always more evident. This is partly an illusion due to our increasing distance from him. Just as the largest star in a cluster seems to absorb the light of the lesser ones, so all that is memorable in a past epoch is attributed to the greatest names surviving from it.

Yet Marxism is, in its own right and apart from its having inspired great political movements, a social theory of the utmost importance. Even if politicians, agitators and revolutionaries had taken no interest in it, it would still be worth studying; and might, indeed, in that case, be easier to study, for it would not have been so often and so variously misinterpreted. Almost everyone who is at all concerned with it is so much more familiar with common opinions about it than with the theory itself, that it has become, as it were, surrounded by a cloud of multicoloured dust through which its real shape is dimly seen. There are, I think, three great services done by Marxism to social theory.

In the first place, it has taught us a lesson that Montesquieu, Saint-Simon and Hegel failed to bring quite home to their contemporaries; it has taught us that the proper study of politics is not man but institutions. Montesquieu, no doubt, studied institutions; he did not, like Hobbes or Locke, begin with man in an imaginary state of nature and then explain all social institutions as human contrivances for human ends. But Montesquieu, though himself an innovator, was not fully aware of the sterility of the older method; and, in particular, did not understand that theories like those of Hobbes and Locke cannot explain the facts but serve only to justify certain practical conclusions. Moreover, Montesquieu still retained some of the old conceptions—for instance, that of *jus naturale*—and even treated them as if they were somehow prior to institutions.

Rousseau, in *The Origins of Inequality Among Men*, tried to imagine how political societies came gradually into existence, and described a process which, while it was entirely an effect of men's actions upon and reactions to one another, was yet uncontrolled by human purposes—a process which, while it elaborated institutions, quite changed man's primitive character, making him rational, moral and subject to ambitions and emotions he could never have known outside society. Rousseau's account of the probable origins of the state has also this great merit, that it does not treat men's social interests (as distinct from the primitive appetites they are born with or acquire as a mere consequence of physical maturity) as in any way prior to their morals. He understood that the things a man most wants, his more permanent ambitions and preferences, determined though they are in large part by his social status, are nevertheless profoundly affected by prevailing notions of right behaviour and of the kind of life best worth living; that interests no more determine morals than they are determined by them; and that this must be so even though men should be selfish and corrupt beyond redemption. Yet, though Rousseau knew all this and often said it, he never abandoned the old methods; he was always the disciple of Hobbes and Locke as well as of Montesquieu.

Saint-Simon and Hegel did, no doubt, quite give up the old methods; they discussed institutions, how they develop, how they affect and are affected by men's morals and ideals, and they never attempted to explain them as human contrivances; but Saint-Simon made only a small impression on his own and succeeding generations, while Hegel wrapped up his sense so tightly in nonsense that it could scarcely be got loose from it. It was not until Marxism pervaded the social studies that the old method of starting from man's essential nature and explaining social institutions as means to that nature's satisfaction was almost universally abandoned—by the opponents of Marx not less than by his supporters. It may be that the combined influence of Montesquieu, Saint-Simon and Comte sufficed to teach this lesson to French students of society, but outside France it was not properly learnt until Marxism became a widely discussed theory. Marxism has also this merit, that, while it rejects the old method and treats only of social phenomena, there is no trace in it of state worship. Marx put no value except on individuals, and assumed[1] that that society is best which enables every member of it to lead a full and free life.

It is to Marx, too, that we largely owe our appreciation of the

---

[1] This assumption is not part of historical materialism; it expresses only a belief that Marx in fact held.

historical importance of classes, their activities and enmities. Saint-Simon appreciated it before Marx, but it was Marx and not Saint-Simon who convinced the intellectual world. Of course, in a sense, men have always known that social classes are important, that the way in which a community is divided into classes is one of the most important facts about it. Not only did Thucydides, Plato and Aristotle understand it, but almost every able politician and historian from their day to Saint-Simon's and Marx's. Montesquieu, Burke and Hegel thought the existence of unequal classes inevitable and even good for society, while Rousseau and his radical posterity (including the French socialists) strongly condemned it; but they all ascribed great importance to it. What is new in Saint-Simon and Marx is the attempt to establish a connexion between the evolution of social institutions and the emergence and decay of classes. Though they took rather too simple a view of the matter and made several mistakes, their hypotheses have proved among the most fruitful advanced by the social theorist. They have not perhaps been verified, but they have inspired the most profitable researches.

Marx carried the analysis of social classes and their activities much further than Saint-Simon had done. Saint-Simon, indeed, did not even distinguish between capitalists and workers, but treated them both as one industrial class having interests opposed to those of the old nobility; whereas Marx made many distinctions. They were not all peculiar to him but occurred to several of the more intelligent observers of social and political developments in France and England during the first half of the nineteenth century. Yet not one of these observers was as shrewd as Marx, and certainly none of the other socialists had anything like his understanding of contemporary political and social antagonisms. Marx said so much that was later proved false that it is nowadays easy to reckon a long list of errors against him. He wanted to do too much. He wanted to advise the workers how they might take advantage of every shift in the balance of social power to prepare the overthrow of an oppressive régime, and had perforce to be always interpreting events and making predictions. He had decided he was a scientific socialist, and therefore an adequate, subtle and always ready counsellor of the proletariat; and with these pretensions, it was inevitable he should be often mistaken.

He was eager to help make great changes in the world, and convinced that he could best do so by explaining events and showing where they would lead. Though the catalogue of his errors is not short, he has taught us much, much more than any other man about social classes and their political behaviour.

Marx provided himself, while still a young man, with a comprehensive social philosophy, and yet found it possible to learn a great deal from experience. In 1852 he understood contemporary politics much better than he had done four years earlier; and we can discover, by comparing *The Eighteenth Brumaire of Louis Bonaparte* with *The Communist Manifesto*, how much he had learnt from only four years of French history, with nothing to help him except newspaper reports and the prejudiced accounts of revolutionaries who had failed. Marx predicted that all except two classes would disappear as capitalism grew older, and the prediction has proved false; but that did not prevent him from appreciating the very great complexity of the social structure of capitalist society. The longer he lived the better he appreciated it. Marx was less inhibited by Marxism than a good many of his disciples have proved themselves to be. Since his time, the social structure of western Europe has greatly changed, and mostly in ways that Marx did not foresee. The attempt often made by Marxists to discuss our twentieth century Europe as if it were more or less the same as Marx's Europe, or as if it had substantially become what he said it would be, is a very fertile source of error. And it is even more absurd to speak of Slavonic Europe as if the Marxian analysis of social classes, the enmities between them, and their respective rôles in times of revolution, applied there. Slavonic Europe has been deeply influenced by the West, and that is one reason among the most important why the whole course of its development has been profoundly different. There are no two words in the Marxian vocabulary more often used than 'bourgeois' and 'proletarian'; and yet Russia, a country now ruled by Marxists, has never yet had either a bourgeois or a proletarian revolution. These epithets can be (more or less) properly applied to the series of revolutions which happened in France between 1789 and 1871; but they are more misleading than informative when used to describe social disturbances in twentieth-century Russia. It is, among other things, because, long before Russia was industrialized, Marxism was introduced there and had important political consequences, that there never has been, and now probably never will be, either a bourgeois or a proletarian revolution in that country. Nevertheless, though their pedantry leads the Marxists, whenever they discuss contemporary politics, to misdescribe the world they live in, it still remains one of their master's great merits that he taught us to appreciate the importance of social classes and of the conflicts of interest between them. Marx, in his own generation, tried to think for himself, and did so very often to good purpose; it is not his fault that so many of his disciples have not followed his example but have merely repeated his words. To blame him for their pedantries would be as unjust as to blame Aristotle for imposing his categories on European philosophy for over two thousand years.

Another of our major debts to Marx is that he taught us to recognize the importance of ideologies, that is, of theories whose social function—whatever the intentions and illusions of their authors and propagators—is to protect the privileges or justify the pretensions of some class or group in society. Saint-Simon, in this as in so much else, anticipated Marx; he explained, for instance, that the principles of the great revolution, the doctrines of the rights of man and of popular sovereignty, were metaphysical and, properly speaking, neither true nor false. Taken literally, they were absurd; but, interpreted as claims made against the old privileged classes on behalf of the new classes challenging their predominance, they were historically significant. They were put forward as if they were general conclusions derived from man's essential nature, and therefore universally valid; whereas they were at bottom mere demands made by some classes on others at a particular stage in European history. Saint-Simon, the enemy of all unearned privileges, thought nothing more absurd, when taken literally, than the revolutionary dogma of 'equality.' Whatever the respects in which we choose to compare men, some will always be superior to the others; and the dogma of equality, therefore—to the extent to which it is not metaphysical nonsense —is merely a denial that certain privileges are just. But Saint-Simon, though he anticipated Marx, did not by any means provide him with a ready-made doctrine about class ideology. He explained the principles of 1789 in this way, but did not construct a more general theory about the social functions of ideologies; nor did he, as Marx did, distinguish between classes before and after they had become 'politically conscious,' that is, aware of themselves as separate from other classes and having different interests. We can find in Saint-Simon only a few rudimentary ideas about the social functions of class and group ideologies; the mature theory comes to us from Marx.

Like most important theories, it is mixed up with more than a little that is false. Marx and Engels often spoke as if all moralities were (or at least had hitherto been) class moralities, as if the primary social function of every one of them was to justify the claim made on society by some class or other. This is, I think, a mistake, and for two reasons: because it assumes that interests are prior to morals, that what men thus and thus situated in society commonly strive for determines the general character of their moral judgments more than it is determined by it; and also that, to the extent that interests do affect morals, those common to the whole community have a smaller effect than the ones peculiar to this or that class. Neither of these assumptions is plausible. Not only are men's interests profoundly affected by the moral codes prevailing in their communities, but the division of society into classes is itself not possible except where certain rules (e.g. those governing property) are generally respected. Before some men can become socially superior to others, there must be rules governing the acquisition and transference of whatever it is their superiority rests on. Even power presupposes morals. As Rousseau argued in *The Origins of Inequality Among Men*, what a man can oblige others to do by virtue merely of superior strength, courage or intelligence is little indeed. Without institutions there can be neither power nor wealth; and without morals there can be no institutions, and therefore no classes or class interests or class ideologies. This is not to say that morals are prior to institutions, for to treat either as a mere effect of the other is clearly absurd; it is only to say that unless men were moral—that is, creatures having rights and obligations—there could arise neither classes nor governments among them. But, classes and governments having once arisen, they in their turn affect morals: and it is therefore quite proper to speak of class moralities and ideologies, so long as it is not assumed, either that all morality is class morality, or that the moral rules peculiar to a class are more affected by their class interests than they affect them.[1]

Marx was an individualist; he put a value only on the well-being of individuals and was not in the least inclined to sacrifice it to 'the good of the community.' If he preached working-class solidarity, it was because he believed that only the united efforts of the oppressed could save them from their oppressors. And yet, like many another social theorist reacting against the natural rights and Utilitarian philosophies of previous generations, he did exaggerate the importance of group behaviour and group attitudes. From the correct assumption that it is in society that men become rational and moral and acquire interests, he drew the doubtful conclusion that the activities of groups and classes are more important than the idiosyncratic behaviour of individuals as explanations of the course of human history. He knew that men have different natural qualities, and no doubt thought that these natural differences, being presumably much the same from generation to generation, cannot explain how the institutions, morals, cultural standards and ideologies of one society differ from those of another, nor yet how they change in any one society. He was probably right in so thinking, but it does not follow, even then, that the idiosyncrasies of individuals are not a causal factor as important as the activities and attitudes of classes and groups.

For society, though it moulds men's characters and imposes conventional uniformities of behaviour upon them, also (and by the same process) accentuates the differences between them. Were a woman in Rousseau's imagined state of nature to give birth to identical twins, they would, though each lived apart from the other in the forest, be very much alike after fifty years; whereas, if they lived in society, the differences between them would be much greater. It is social environment, much more than natural, which affects character; and every man's social environment is unique. Every man in society is a member of many groups, and every one of these groups affects him in a different way. The smaller the

---

[1] People who treat interests as prior to morals often believe they are being 'objective,' hard-headed, and unsentimental. Bentham and Marx, who did so treat them, rather fancied themselves as realistic and unsentimental persons. But neither Montesquieu nor Rousseau, who avoided this particular mistake, had a high opinion of mankind. They both understood that it is because men are moral creatures that they are capable of being selfish, oppressive, and nasty.

group, the fewer the people who have shared the experience of belonging to it; and the number of small groups is legion. It is only when we forget this simple fact that we can suppose that 'society,' because it moulds our characters, tends to make us alike, and that, if it does not quite succeed, this is only because we are born different. We are, indeed, born different, but society makes this difference greater by far than it would have been otherwise. Society is not like the air around us, exerting an equal pressure on us all. It treats everyone of us differently from the rest; it makes us rational and moral, but also provides us with an experience, and therefore with prejudices and emotional responses, peculiar to ourselves. Because we are rational and moral, we are inevitably —dull and timid though we may be—not only each other's critics but critics also of every group we belong to. Every man stands to some extent apart from all the social groups he belongs to; he is, indeed, conscious of himself as a unique individual only because society has made him self-conscious.[1]

Moreover, the smaller and more intimate a social group, the greater its influence on its members, and yet the more one member's position inside it is unlike another's. It is a very different thing to be a husband than a wife, or a father than a son, or a son than a daughter; and the better we know any two families, the more we are aware of the differences between them. There are innumerable group moralities, uniformities of behaviour and emotional responses that men acquire, almost without knowing it, by the mere process of living together; and over against them there are the normal peculiarities of every person who, born different from the others, has also had his character 'moulded' by

---

[1] Some careless people have argued that, because there are no natural rights and no moral codes or habits of approval and disapproval not socially determined, the individual has no rights 'against society.' The conclusion is either trivial or suggests what is false. Since rights are held only against persons, and no social group— except in a fictitious sense—is a person, there are, strictly speaking, no rights against society. When we say we have rights against 'society,' we mean only—if we mean anything—that we have rights against certain persons in virtue of their special position in society. In that elliptical sense, we very certainly do have rights against society. We cannot, by showing that rights are socially determined, prove that no one can have them against persons holding authority in society. As a matter of fact, we have more rights against such persons than against the others, for the simple reason that they have greater obligations to us. One sometimes important right, that of tyrannicide, can only be held against a person having authority. That it has been abused is no more a reason for denying it than the occasional condemnation of innocent persons is a reason for denying the authority of judges.

a unique social experience. Class morality is only one among many kinds of group morality; and the more complex, sophisticated and free a society, the less important any one of these.

II. BOLSHEVISM

Had the influence of Marxism been confined to the West, it would probably have done much good and little harm. Its authors thought it a revolutionary creed, but its effect among the advanced peoples has been, on the whole, to make revolution unnecessary. Marx and Engels condemned premature violence; they prescribed many years of preparation before the ultimate revolution, and wanted it made in the fullness of time by an immense and politically organized working class. Their influence served therefore in their own day more to prevent violence than to encourage it; and their programme for the working class, had it been fulfilled, would have made violence unnecessary in the future. The political organization of the proletariat in the industrial countries of the West has proved so vast an enterprise that it could only be achieved in free societies; and in them, every large organized group, just because it is organized and large, possesses great political influence. The political organization of the working class has quite transformed the free societies which have made it possible; it has led to so many drastic reforms in the interest of the working class that the capitalist economy known to Marx no longer exists. This great and peaceful social revolution was not foreseen by Marx, but the influence of his doctrine has been one, and not the least important, among its causes.

Marxism has in western Europe been the socialism of the post-revolutionary epoch. In France it had little influence until after 1871, when the long series of French revolutions was over and the workers could elect deputies to free parliaments. In Germany the socialist movement which survived Bismarck's mild persecutions very quickly became the largest party of its kind in the world. That party condemned Bernstein's attempt to revise Marxism, but the future was nonetheless with Bernstein. Indeed, not more the future than the present, for though the leaders who condemned Bernstein were true to the letter of Marx's teachings, they were no longer, except in name, revolutionary socialists. Marxism has in the West been a parliamentary socialism, and has flourished only in countries where the régime denounced by Marxists as a 'bourgeois sham' has been more or less firmly established. Indeed, the western Marxist parties, before they began to be affected by Bolshevism, were among the most responsible, intelligent and enterprising of socialist movements. They had their faults, but they were not ruthless, or avid for power, or indifferent to freedom. They were competitors for power, but also convinced democrats who competed strictly according to the rules, because they knew—whatever they might sometimes affect to believe—that those rules were as profitable to themselves as to their rivals. Their Marxism was wearing thin, and they would probably soon have let it slip quietly from them. They had in the past profited by it, but it was likely, if they kept fast hold of it, to prove in the future more embarrassing than useful. Bernstein's theories were twice officially condemned, but their influence was quickly growing. Marxism as an active force in politics was dying a slow and natural death, and a death that was honourable. For what more can a fallible mortal ask than that his doctrines should have a great and beneficial effect on mankind for some fifty years?

But Marxism went to Russia and was there transformed. It became the doctrine, not of a working class party in a highly industrialized and literate society, but of a group of intellectual malcontents in a country which, though still primitive, was profoundly affected by the spread of western industrialism and western social and political ideas. Bolshevism is the distorted Marxism of a backward society exposed to the impact of the West. This is not a condemnation of it; it is a mere statement of fact. Since Marxism, as it left the hands of Marx and Engels, was as much compounded of error as of truth, a distortion of it may well be no more, or even less, open to criticism than it is itself. In any case, Bolshevism is only one kind of distorted Marxism among several; for no social and political theory can be used by practical men in the shape given it by its authors; it must always be greatly simplified and often considerably changed.

The process of distortion has been a long one, and the additions and alterations made have therefore been numerous. From 1902 until 1926 German Marxism—the doctrine of Marx and Engels—was gradually transformed into what is nowadays called

Communism. This comparatively new doctrine, though it has adherents all over the world, is specifically Russian; its other (and perhaps less misleading) name is Bolshevism. For Bolshevism, though some of its roots are in Marxism, is not really the kind of doctrine that can properly be called either communist or socialist in any of the older nineteenth-century meanings of those words. Western communism[1] and socialism, before they began to be affected by the Russian 'experiment,' used always to advocate either extreme democracy or anarchy, whereas Bolshevism is the creed of ruthless and irresponsible minorities who use the state power to transform society in the ways that seem to them best. It is still in some parts of the world a revolutionary creed but has to all intents and purposes ceased to be democratic.

As soon as a Marxist group arises in a primitive and undemocratic country, it is at once faced with two problems: it must decide what its mission is, and also how to order its ranks to be able to execute that self-imposed mission with as little interference as possible from the government. The German Marxist doctrine was put together by its authors for the use of the working class in countries that were already capitalist and accustomed to constitutional and fairly mild, if not exactly democratic, government. The Russian Marxists had to decide what a Marxist group must do in a country not yet capitalist, and also how to set about doing it in defiance of the Tsarist autocracy and secret police. Whatever the first decision—unless it were to do nothing—the second must be to engage in clandestine activities. Any Marxist party in Russia, no matter how mild its programme, would have had to be, at least until 1905, a secret political organization; and it was impossible for an organization of that kind to be democratic. Nor would it have been easy for it, even after 1905, to become democratic, for the constitutional régime established by the October Manifesto was precarious, and the secret police active and oppressive without interruption until March 1917. The socialist movement in Russia had perforce, whatever the theoretical preferences of its leaders, to be undemocratic. Had it been a purely intellectual activity, had it consisted only of conversations in academic and

---

[1] I refer to communist doctrines since the birth of modern radicalism in the second half of the eighteenth century, and not to such older theories as those of Plato and More.

polite circles, it need never have been organized; but as soon as the Russian socialists decided to influence the classes in whose welfare they were interested, they had to organize themselves into a political party, and that party could not be democratic. This was as true of the Socialist-Revolutionaries as of the Marxists.

The peculiarity of the Bolsheviks was not that they recognized that an effective socialist party could not be democratic in the Tsarist police state; it was that they wanted a more strictly disciplined and exclusive party than the Mensheviks were willing to tolerate. It is one thing to admit that in a police state a socialist party, if it is to be active on any considerable scale, cannot resort to many of the practices needed to keep the party internally democratic; but it is quite another to want to make it an exclusive élite devoted to an agreed body of doctrine. Though the Russian Social-Democratic Party could not, because it was always watched and harrassed by the police, be properly democratic, most of the Mensheviks in it were by temperament inclined to democracy, whereas the Bolsheviks were not. Not that the Bolsheviks were in principle opposed to the democratic organization of the party; they willingly admitted that, had Tsarist Russia enjoyed even as much freedom as Imperial Germany, the party ought to have been democratically organized. But they accepted the situation as they found it without regretting the expedients that it seemed to impose on them; though they were democrats in principle, it was without reluctance that they acted undemocratically. They wanted the party to be a united, disciplined, active and irresponsible élite, indoctrinating the workers and teaching them how to fight their oppressors. The party was not to be the only organized group, but the first among many and in control of the others. It was to be the select vanguard of a growing army. The Bolsheviks believed that the condition of Russia made it their duty to create such a party, and they welcomed the opportunity its existence would give them. They thought doctrine important, but were impatient of doctrinal disputes and tender consciences. Lenin knew that the party could not do without intellectuals, but wanted it so organized that they could always be called to order.

The Bolsheviks also decided—or, rather, Lenin decided for them—to take a leading part in what they chose to call the Russian bourgeois revolution. When that decision was taken by Lenin in

1905, he explained that the Russian working class, weak though they were, had two peculiar advantages: they had to reckon with a middle class who, while they wanted to put an end to Tsarist autocracy, were yet too few and too easily frightened of the socialists to the left of them to dare stake the future on a revolution; and the workers could, if they acted in time, make a political alliance with the peasants, who were not in Russia (what they were in the West) humble and inarticulate supporters of the established order, but a restless, resentful and land-hungry class willing, should the need arise, to use force to get what they conceived to be justice. Lenin did not suppose that Russia was in 1905 ripe for a proletarian revolution; she had still, he thought, to have her bourgeois revolution, and was indeed only just beginning to have it. But why, he asked, should not the proletariat, allied with the peasantry, take control of the bourgeois revolution, and then govern Russia while she passed through the bourgeois phase of her development? Was it not evident that the Russian middle class lacked the courage to do in their country what the French bourgeois had done in France during the great revolution, and that the brunt of the attack on Tsardom was already borne—and not only in the streets—by the workers and their political vanguard? Why should not the workers and peasants destroy the Tsarist autocracy, not to give power to the bourgeois, but to set up their own dictatorship? These questions, had historical materialism been true, would have been foolish; for only the bourgeois can make a bourgeois revolution[1] and govern a bourgeois society. And yet, in the conditions prevailing in Russia, they were not foolish. Marxism was an ideology that first saw the light of day in capitalist society, and could hardly have done so elsewhere; but

[1] Though, of course, the actual fighting, as both Marx and Lenin knew, is always done by a 'rabble.' The great French revolution deserved, if any did, to be called bourgeois, but the rôle of the mob was indispensable. That mob consisted of workers and was controlled by the bourgeois radicals of the Jacobin Club. The Russian liberals dared not rouse the mob against Tsarism, fearing they would quickly lose control of the revolution once it had started. Lenin, knowing their fears, and knowing too how prone to violence the workers and peasants were, thought it incumbent upon the Social-Democrats and their political friends to use that violence to destroy the common enemy of the bourgeois, the workers, and the peasants. The Social-Democrats would play, in the Russian 'bourgeois' revolution, the part played by the Jacobins in the French revolution. But it would be absurd of them, the Russian bourgeois revolution once made, to abdicate power; they should therefore use it to establish what he called a 'revolutionary dictatorship of the proletariat and peasantry.'

its influence could not be confined to the region of its birth. Neither Marxism, nor capitalism its matrix, could have emerged from inside the Russia of the late nineteenth century; but both could be brought in from outside. They were so brought, and there therefore arose in Russia a situation not accounted for by the Marxism of Marx. Russia acquired a proletariat while she was yet, in most ways, socially and economically more primitive than the West had been when capitalism first arose there. Russia had by 1905 both a proletariat and a Marxist party, and the leaders of that party had to decide what to do in a situation not predicted by the philosophy of history they had put their faith in. Lenin, being a bold, ambitious and shrewd man, caring more for power than consistency, did not mind putting these questions, and could even find in Marx's *Address to the Communist League* texts to support the answers he gave.

It was not Lenin's habit to push an explanation further than was needed to justify the course of action he proposed. He believed in 1905 that Russia's next revolution must be 'bourgeois,' and he was also certain that the Social-Democrats, if he could knock some of his own sense and courage into them, could use it to establish a 'dictatorship of the proletariat and peasantry,' with the latter as subordinate allies of the former. He said no more about this dictatorship than that it would serve to get Russia through her bourgeois phase as quickly as possible, and bring her to the point where she could be made socialist. Just how she could be bourgeois and at the same time have a dictatorship of the proletariat and peasantry, he did not properly explain. Would the workers and peasants, while they ruled Russia, allow her to develop a capitalist economy on the western model? If they could govern, why should they not also control the national economy? And if they could control it, why have a bourgeois phase at all? Lenin spoke of 'uninterrupted revolution,' of a continuous and rapid transition to socialism, but never put or answered these questions clearly and fairly. He took many liberties with Marxism, but tried always to take no more than were needed to justify whatever decisions seemed to him important at the time. All the rest he left vague and undecided. He never looked far ahead, and possessed to an astonishing degree the faculty of shutting his eyes to what it did not suit him to see. Though not a peasant, he had a large share of that almost wilful stupidity which is an essential part of peasant cunning.

Lenin did not even inquire what kind of government a 'dictatorship of the proletariat and peasantry' might be in the Russia of 1905. He welcomed the soviets as organs of popular democracy, but did not explain how, in a country where the peasants greatly outnumbered the urban workers and both classes were mostly illiterate, it would be contrived that the latter class and not the former should be the senior and controlling partner in the alliance between them. Since both workers and peasants were ignorant, it was not possible for them, however many the soviets at their disposal, to govern Russia. Their 'dictatorship' would therefore have to be exercised in their name by whatever parties could plausibly claim to speak for them. Would the Socialist-Revolutionaries, who has as good a right to speak for the peasants as the Social-Democrats to speak for the workers, accept a subordinate rôle? And if they were somehow obliged to accept it, could they still presume to speak for the peasants?

When Lenin, in 1902, had argued that the Russian Social-Democratic Party could not, while the Tsarist police state lasted, be democratic, he had implied that it must become so when that state was destroyed. He had spoken with approval of the German Socialist Party, and had explained why it could be democratic. He had then looked forward to a time when Russia would be what Germany already was—a bourgeois society allowing at least as much freedom as would enable a socialist party to be truly responsible to the working class. But in 1905 he was proposing a 'dictatorship of the proletariat and peasantry' at a time when his own party, which he called 'the party of the proletariat,' was still by his own admission far from being responsible to the proletariat. It was not even a united and disciplined party, for Lenin had not succeeded in imposing his will upon it. If the 'bourgeois' revolution of 1905 were to lead to a 'dictatorship of the proletariat and peasantry,' what could that dictatorship be? The workers and peasants were manifestly incapable of governing Russia or even of contriving that the parties claiming to do so in their name should be responsible to them; and the Socialist-Revolutionaries would not willingly accept a subordinate part in a political alliance with the Social-Democrats. What, then, in the Russia of 1905, could the dictatorship that Lenin clamoured for amount to except the irresponsible power of the Social-Democratic Party? Lenin, of course, admitted no such thing. He was less interested in the probable consequences of the policy he advocated than fearful lest the Russian Marxists should not rise to a great occasion; and other people's fears, discordant with his own, merely annoyed him. His instinct was to urge bold courses on the timid, and to let the future take care of itself.

Though Lenin did not know it, the course he chose for his country in 1905 was impossible. There could be no 'dictatorship of the proletariat and peasantry' among an illiterate people unaccustomed to all the processes of organized power. Neither the workers nor the peasants could rule, in alliance or separately. The ignorance which put it out of their power to rule their country also made it impossible for any political party to act for them. In a large country, no class can rule except through deputies; and there cannot be deputies unless institutions exist to ensure that persons supposed to be responsible to others really are so; and these institutions cannot function properly except where there is freedom. There can be no freedom unless the people—and more particularly that part of them active in public affairs—have acquired the habits and prejudices of democrats. Lenin spoke of his party and of the class to whose service that party was bound as if they were so intimately related that the rule of the party was, to all intents and purposes, the rule of the class. It did not suit him to understand that so intimate a relationship could not bind political leaders to their followers in a country like Russia, precisely because there existed neither the institutions nor the habits that make up democracy. No party can justly claim to speak for a class except in a democracy; and no modern democracy has known for more than a few years what could properly be called 'the party of a class.' Indeed, it is a thing dangerous to democracy, though democracy alone makes it possible.

Russia has never had a 'party of the proletariat.' Were this name given to the British Labour Party, it would describe it falsely; and yet not so falsely as it describes the party of Lenin. The Russian Social-Democrats were disunited and quarrelsome from 1902 until after the Bolshevik revolution, and the relations that bound them to the workers were always uncertain and precarious. Nor were their quarrels the effects of dissensions within the class whose 'vanguard' they called themselves; they related mostly to matters of doctrine beyond the understanding of the Russian workers. The Russian Social-Democracts no more had the right to call themselves 'the party of the proletariat' than a man has the right to call himself a woman's husband merely because, though she does not know it, he intends to marry her. If the man believes a magician who foretells his marriage to this woman, it is perhaps difficult for him not to think of her as already his wife, and not to anticipate his rights. It is the common error of hopeful men to behave as if the future were already in some way present; but it is an error nonetheless, and no woman is a man's wife merely because he has his reasons, unknown to her, for believing that his offer must be accepted in the end. The Russian workers were for the most part not even aware of the kind of relations that the Social-Democrats hoped would eventually unite them to their class. They knew only that the Social-Democrats were well disposed to them, and that it was sometimes worth their while accepting their support and their advice; and the Bolsheviks, when they at last in 1912 formed a party of their own, were certainly no closer than the Mensheviks to the workers. Not until the eve of the October revolution did they enjoy the confidence of anything like the majority of the industrial workers; and even that confidence was limited, for it was given merely because Lenin's promises were attractive, and not because the workers understood and cared for the doctrines and ambitions of the Bolsheviks. The party of Lenin had some shrewd and bold ideas about what to do with the workers in their own supposed interest, but was never, except in this meagre sense, 'the party of the proletariat.'

The decision to seize power once made, the Bolsheviks were driven to all the courses which, in the eyes of their critics, have made nonsense of their professed Marxism. But—and this too ought always to be remembered about them—they would never, had they not been Marxists, have been driven to these courses. The revolution they attempted was 'premature,' and yet their excuse for it was Marxian, for they said that they were only anticipating in backward Russia what would soon happen in other countries, where it would be, not premature, but a timely and long step forward, bringing great benefits both to the advanced peoples and to the others who were necessarily dependent on them. Having taken power in the name of the Russian proletariat, the Bolsheviks quickly discovered that the class whose vanguard they claimed to be would not always follow them; and, seeing that the class were ignorant of what seemed obvious to themselves, did not scruple to drive where they could not lead. They had spoken of a 'revolutionary dictatorship of the proletariat and peasantry,' and had therefore made allies of the Left Wing Socialist-Revolutionaries, who stood to the peasants as they did to the workers; but, when they found that their allies would not accept the minor rôle allotted to them by Lenin, they set about suppressing them.

The Bolsheviks, applying their principles to the contemporary world, made a number of calculations about what was possible in Russia and probable elsewhere, and then decided that it was their duty, as good Marxists, to become the rulers of their own country. Their calculations were partly right and mostly wrong; they were about right enough to enable the Bolsheviks to get power, but not to precipitate the world revolution they hoped for, nor yet to use power in Russia to establish what Marx or Engels (or even Lenin before 1917) would have called a 'dictatorship of the proletariat.' They watched the course of events in the world, saw only a small part of what was happening, interpreted that part in the light of their faith and to serve their ambition, and then decided to intervene in the world's affairs at the moment most propitious to themselves. It was only afterwards that they discovered they had foreseen almost none of the obstacles standing in the way of their using power to reach the ends for whose sake they had taken it. The world has been greatly changed by them, though not in the ways they intended; and it has also greatly changed them. They are no longer today the Bolsheviks of 1917. If we are to count them successful, it must be, not as Marxian socialists, but as ambitious men and lovers of power. They have played a great part in the world, but what that part was to be they did not know when they took control of one of the world's two largest states. They looked only a short way into the future, and made several bad guesses.

As Marx saw it, the progress of mankind towards communism

is by successive stages, each presided over by a different class, and every passage from stage to stage marked by a revolution made by the only class capable, at that point of the progress, of making it. The stuff of history is a succession of class conflicts, the victor in each (except the last) being the vanquished in the next; and the succession itself is the effect of a long process of economic development, a process for the most part ignored or misunderstood by the warring classes. The proletariat, and therefore *a fortiori* the party of that class, can make only the last revolution.

The Bolsheviks have changed all that. They believe that, wherever Marxism finds lodgment in the minds of men banded together in the service of their faith, those men—provided only they are orthodox—are, whatever the society they live in, the 'party of the proletariat.' Not for them to wait until society has progressed so far that it is ripe for proletarian revolution. On the contrary, it is their duty, using every means in their power, to force progress upon it, whatever the stage of its development. No society can be so primitive that, if there are Communists inside it, there is nothing for them to do; for every society having Communists must have been affected, in one way or another, by world capitalism and the social conflicts it engenders. No society can live any longer to itself alone, but is always considerably dependent on the rest of the world; and that dependence must continually increase. The great conflict now in the world is between 'proletarian' and 'bourgeois' states, and every class in every society is already, or must soon become, a party to that conflict. Therefore, the duty of Communists everywhere is either to push their country into the community of proletarian states or else, should this not prove possible, so to divide and weaken it that its alliance is of little value to the enemies of the Soviet Union. Whenever, in a primitive society, Communists have the chance to get power, they must take it, and then use it to create the economic and social conditions that Marx and Engels had thought must exist before they could get it; they must establish a 'dictatorship of the proletariat' in order to make their country what, according to Marx and Engels, it must already have become before there could be any such dictatorship.

The Communists, the self-styled 'party of the proletariat,' believing themselves possessed of a doctrine that explains how society must normally develop, suppose themselves competent to control the destinies of every society. Marx, they believe, discovered how any society, unaffected by societies more advanced than itself, must develop; and they, since Marx's time, have discovered how contact with advanced societies affects the development of backward ones. That development is 'abnormal,' but is also in principle calculable by anyone possessing the Marxian philosophy and knowing the relevant facts. Seeing that capitalism now affects—and always more strongly—every part of the world not dominated by the Communists, the development of all backward societies is, from the Marxian point of view, abnormal. It therefore appears to the Communists their duty, wherever they find themselves, to seize power if they can get it, because they alone possess the science enabling them to control the abnormal (but also, if properly controlled, much swifter) progress of backward societies towards the goal common to all societies—which is communism. The Communists believe that, whatever the appearances against them, they have a better right than other people to call themselves 'the party of the proletariat,' even in countries where there is no proletariat, or one so small as to be insignificant, or one that mistrusts them and turns elsewhere for guidance; for the business of the Communists is always and everywhere to prepare the coming of the classless society—the task assigned by Marx and Engels to the proletariat.

To us it may seem obvious that the Communists are doing the opposite, but they, like other fanatics before them, cherish nothing more obstinately than their illusions. The more successfully they control the development of a backward society and the more quickly they endow it with industries and 'collectivize' its peasants, the more proletarian they think they make it. They therefore do for the workers what they, had they been literate, organized and numerous enough, would have done for themselves; and the better they do it, the more their government comes to look like a 'dictatorship of the proletariat.' In this double sense, though neither is quite literal, they are (so they imagine) the party of the proletariat. They look upon themselves as the only competent midwives of every society, because they alone understand the inner workings of every social process. They believe that they are come, not to deny Marx, but to fulfil him;

and have taken it upon themselves to accomplish in a few decades what he thought might occupy many generations.

Nevertheless, though they choose to think otherwise, they have denied him. They have not merely declared possible what must be impossible, if his theory is true; they have also created new kinds of inequality and oppression as extensive and self-perpetuating as the old. They have used force, not to assist what the old Marxists would have called a timely and natural birth, but to refashion society from the foundation upward; they have been, not midwives, but surgeons, and have not been able to foretell the results of their operations. The world they have so greatly transformed is as much a surprise to them as to their enemies. They never imagined it, and still do not understand how their actions have helped make it. It would be presumptuous to call them blinder than their neighbours; their sight is perhaps as good but no better; and yet they claim to see much further. It is mostly this that makes them so great a nuisance in the world. Life in a house where everyone's sight is weak becomes burdensome to all when one of the inmates insists on behaving as if he had the eyes of a lynx. The Communists are altogether too enterprising in a world whose processes are but slightly known to any of us. Their greatest fault is their immense and inextinguishable conceit.[1]

III. BOLSHEVISM AND THE WORLD

Marxism, transformed in Russia into something very different from, though in some respects closely related to, its original self, has become a creed attractive to the peoples called backward because they are poor. The Communist stronghold is still in Europe, but the nations looking hopefully towards it are mostly outside.

Communism's swift advance into Europe after the Second World War was not an effect of popularity but of Soviet military power. The Russians moved into Germany across the territories of weak and sometimes divided peoples, and so found it easy to establish among them by force and intrigue governments on whose obedience they thought they could rely. Though little resistance

---

[1] They are not the less satisfied with themselves as a group because they live in mortal fear of one another as individuals. Indeed, this fear probably increases their conceit, which must compensate them for being deprived of so much.

was offered to the Russians, they were not welcome. In many regions they were as much objects of hatred and fear as the departing Germans. They were resisted almost not at all because resistance was deemed hopeless. The small Slav nations, exhausted, disillusioned and impoverished, lay prone before the Russians, and passed quickly and quietly into their power. They had lost confidence in the western Powers, who had encouraged and praised them while they were the resentful and defiant victims of Hitler, but could do nothing for them now that they were threatened by Stalin. The moral defeat and humiliation of the British and French at Munich in 1938 had taught the small nations a bitter but important lesson: that even the best and most civilized of the Great Powers will do nothing for their weaker allies until they feel themselves threatened by the aggressor. This lesson had been well learned before 1914, but after 1919 it was hoped that times had changed and that small peoples might look for better treatment from great ones. Munich destroyed the last illusions created by the Treaty of Versailles. In 1939, and more especially after 1941, it was worth while offering resistance to the Germans, who had enemies as powerful as themselves; but in 1945 all the Great Powers were—or were anxious to appear—friends, and it would therefore have been disastrous for the smaller Slav states had they offered to resist the Russians. They had no alternative but to submit, and they submitted.

In every European country bordering on the Soviet Union, however poor it may be and however much oppressed some sections of its people, Bolshevism has been almost universally unpopular ever since its establishment in Russia. This is not surprising, for the Bolsheviks, though their achievements are great, have brought more suffering to the workers and peasants than to any other class. One of their ultimate purposes may be to make Russia a rich country, but in their efforts to fasten their grip on her they at first nearly ruined her and afterwards always proved willing to sacrifice the present welfare of her people to their future aggrandizement. This was well known to Russia's immediate neighbours and counted heavily against her. In these small countries Fascism has been more attractive to the rich than Communism to the poor.

The nations of Europe do not consider Russia a civilized

country, and are not accustomed to take lessons from her. Had Germany and not Russia turned Communist after the First World War, the prestige of Communism would have been much greater. The smaller Slav nations, though they have sometimes sought Russian protection against the Turks or the Germans, and though they have (except the Poles) felt a warmer affection for the Russians than for most other peoples, have not greatly respected nor sought to imitate them. They have considered the Russians even more backward than themselves. Sharing with the other European nations a belief in 'progress,' they have looked to the French, the English, and even the Germans, for models of what civilized European communities should be like. These small nations, compared with the great ones to the west of them, are poor and unlettered; but they are also richer, in proportion to their size, than most Asian and African peoples, and have made their own much more of western culture and ideas. Until 1945 they had a considerable and growing middle class, a free peasantry, and departments of state most of whose highest posts belonged to persons educated in the West. Though the arrogance of western peoples was often resented, they were felt to be, not alien and remote conquerors, but merely more fortunate and successful members of the European community of nations. There was felt towards them something of the mixed envy and annoyance that the French provinces feel towards Paris; and yet their countries were recognized as the cultural centres of the European world that all white men inevitably belong to.

In only one East European country did the Communists come to power partly because they enjoyed considerable popular support. In Yugoslavia they could justly claim to be more popular than any other party in several of the more remote, illiterate and sparsely populated provinces. In Bosnia and Herzegovina, when the Germanophile and bloodthirsty Ustashi had laid down their arms, they had no serious rivals, and they were also popular in parts of Montenegro and Macedonia. But in Croatia, Slovenia, Serbia and Voivodina, in all the more thickly inhabited, prosperous and civilized parts of Yugoslavia, they had very few supporters until the end of the war, when the Russian armies had reached the frontiers and had even crossed them, and the allies had made it clear that they would help none of Tito's opponents. Nevertheless, the Communist-dominated Yugoslav Partisan Army was popular in a considerable part of the country, it was native to the soil, and had fought with courage and tenacity against the enemy. Some of the leaders were trained in Russia, but the great mass of the army were patriots convinced that only a social revolution could make their country healthy and strong. Though the Partisans and their supporters were only a minority of the people, there was, even among their political opponents, a reluctant admiration for the resistance offered by them to the Germans. Everyone in the country knew that, in order to induce the allies to give them more help and to abandon their rivals, they had grossly exaggerated their achievements; but, though they had in the true Gascon and Yugoslav manner boasted of impossible things, they had yet done much. They were offensive, intolerant and often brutal, but it was still possible to be a little proud of them.

Yugoslavia's position in Eastern Europe was exceptional. She alone had in 1945 a Communist-controlled movement enjoying a considerable though limited measure of popular support; and she alone has since been able to throw off the Soviet yoke. These two facts are not unconnected. The Yugoslav Communists have risen to power largely by their own efforts; they have taken great risks to get it and are determined not to share it. Ideological ties once bound them to the Russians, but they value their independence and will not be treated in their own country as the servants of foreigners. They bore with the Russians for three years, and then at last resolved to defy them. They did so with reluctance, hoping that the Russians would understand their motives and respect their pride. There was no dispute about theory behind the quarrel between Moscow and Belgrade; it was due only to the refusal of men who felt themselves equals to be treated as subordinates. The Yugoslav Communists behaved in their own country as their Russian colleagues were behaving in Russia, and it was not until many months after they had quarrelled with Moscow that they discovered that Stalin and his companions had betrayed the doctrines of Marx and Engels, doctrines whose only true exponents they now think themselves. It was concern for their own mastery that led the Communist rulers of Yugoslavia to defy Stalin; but, having defied him, they feel the need to condemn him and justify themselves on other than personal grounds. They now want their kind of Communism to be visibly different from his, and they also seek the approval—because they need the help—of the western Powers.

They may find it expedient to adopt milder courses and slowly transform their system of government, if not into democracy, at least into something that maintains the rule of law and protects the personal freedom of citizens. Should they have or acquire any such purpose, they will find it difficult to achieve; for they have spilt much blood and have made many enemies among a people whose last virtue is forgiveness, and must therefore keep a close hold on the country if they are not to be destroyed. They waged a most terrible civil war to get power, they have mortally offended the Russians, they have scarcely the means of bringing prosperity to their country, they dare not become liberal, and it is unlikely that the western Powers will make large sacrifices for their sake. Neither their position nor that of the peoples subject to them is enviable. And yet, all things considered, they are perhaps the best of European Communists, the least servile, the most manly and the least corrupt. If they are a fair sample of their own peoples, they are probably better provided with courage than political skill; but which of these two virtues is the more useful to persons placed as they are, I do not know.

Except in Yugoslavia (the Slav country furthest removed from the Soviet Union) the Communists can count many supporters in only two parts of independent Europe, France and Italy. The French and Italians know nothing of Russia, which is to them the most remote and mysterious region of Europe. About it they are free to cherish whatever illusions best please them. They carry on their domestic conflicts with great bitterness, and use the Soviet Union as a symbol of their hatreds and their hopes. The wealthier classes, the conservatives and the Catholics look upon it as something dreadful and satanic, while the poor often admire it, sometimes for no better reason than because their class enemies fear it. In France and Italy class enmities go deeper than in England and North America, and the Communists, who never forget to take the class war seriously and are ready at all times to advocate extreme courses, therefore have a considerable following. Yet there is little understanding of Soviet Russia in either France or Italy, and the sympathy felt for her is not strong. The French and Italians who vote for the Communist Party do so from many and different motives, of which most have nothing to do with enthusiasm for Russia or desire for proletarian revolution. There are millions of Frenchmen voting for the Communists whose respect for property is beyond question; they use their vote to express their resentment, or because they fear war, or because the Communists have promised them some not-very-drastic reforms they despair of getting from anyone else.

This is not to say that the French Communist Party is not dangerous to the western democracies; it can use its great influence to make trouble for them, for its leaders are servants of Moscow. A Communist Party can be obstructive and even dangerous though most of its supporters care nothing for Communism and have no strong desire for a social revolution. There could easily arise situations when the Communists of France or Italy could destroy French or Italian democracy, but that does not mean that revolutionary Communism is a truly popular force in either country. The general proposition still holds, that what the Russians have made of Communism is either misunderstood or else is repulsive to nearly all Europeans, whatever the region of their birth and the social class they belong to.

There is no longer a revolutionary socialist movement in any part of Europe. The Social-Democrats, though their debt to Marx is still great, are everywhere believers in parliamentary democracy, and their object is to make gradual reforms peacefully. Before 1914 they were still, on the Continent, predominantly Marxist, but since the First World War that Marxism has worn thin. The continental Social-Democrats, though they use a rather different and more Marxian vocabulary, now have much the same ambitions as the British Labour Party. The Communists are either agents of Moscow or else persons who, knowing nothing of the Soviet Union, vote for the Communist Party from many different motives, of which few, if any, derive from hope of proletarian revolution. In the countries bordering on Soviet Russia, and also in Germany, where more is known about Russia than in any other western country, the more common motives making Communists of men are ambition, fear, despair and cynicism. Genuine enthusiasm for the Communist ideal is rare; it has been almost killed

by the terrible events of the last thirty years, events that have
stopped up men's more generous emotions and made them prudent and cynical calculators. The Communists are more pitiless
and exacting than other men, they are powerful and expect obedience, and they allow no services done in the past to weigh with
them when they measure out punishment for present offences.
They are greatly to be feared because they dare not allow themselves to be moved by compassion; they live in terror of one
another, they are watchful and suspicious, and are therefore des-
potic and cruel. From the Russian border to the line that cuts one
half of Germany off from the other, they have behind them the
tremendous power of the Soviet Union; everyone outside their
ranks has cause to fear them, while they need fear no one except
their protectress and each other's malice and treachery. They are
at once slaves and tyrants, and their power, while it lasts, is as
absolute as their personal security is small.[1] What worse masters
can a nation have than persons who are mortally afraid of one another but not of the people?

Only the most ignorant people still believe that the Communist
Party anywhere in Europe is a revolutionary organization of the
working class. No such organization has yet existed in the world,
and Europe has seldom been less likely to produce one than today.
In the part of Europe not subject to the Bolsheviks, Communist
parties are merely competitors for power whose methods are
unscrupulous and peculiar to themselves; while in Russia and the
satellite states they are privileged corporations. Indeed, the class
struggle is nowadays much less a reality than the struggle between
parties for power; and the recent history of Europe has taught us
that whenever a political party—whether or not it calls itself a
class party—wins a monopoly of power, it is always a party that
rules and never a class.

These things are not unknown to the rulers of the Soviet Union.
They know what kind of support they receive in the satellite
countries, and probably have few illusions about the Communist
Parties of France and Italy. It is doubtful whether they are much
put out by their lack of popularity in Europe. What they want is

---

[1] The Nazis, with some exceptions, dealt more gently with one another, and many
of them contrived to be happy in their brutalities. Whereas the Communists have
laid a great load of anxiety upon themselves; they are tormented as well as tor-
mentors.

power, and they are more interested in getting it than in being liked or understood. They do not, to do them justice, want power for no other reason than to enjoy the use of it; their purpose is to get power and then use it to transform the societies they control. But it does not much matter to them how they get it. They remember their own predicament in Russia in 1917, when they were a small and misunderstood minority, who owed their success to their ruthlessness and skill in exploiting the dissensions, timidities and misunderstandings of other people. They were not the spokesmen of a proletariat become the vast majority in a powerful industrial nation; their country was exhausted and primitive, their convinced supporters were few, and they were surrounded by enemies, domestic and foreign. And yet they triumphed, and in only one generation made their country formidable to the whole world. Lenin taught them to rely for success on the divisions between their enemies more than on the numbers, intelligence and enthusiasm of their friends. The party must keep the doctrine pure and discipline severe, but need not be large; while the quality of the support given it outside its own ranks does not much matter. Popularity, understanding, and perhaps even gratitude, will come later, as society is transformed and the masses begin to receive the benefits prepared for them by the wise and devoted Communists. The Bolsheviks have discovered that men who have power can, though they are harsh and impose great sacrifices, make themselves loved; they can advertise themselves and their virtues so persistently that none can escape their image and testimony; they can use the schools to turn themselves into gods in the minds of little children. Political power has grown a monster with so many tentacles that those who have it can use it even to make their victims grateful to them.

There are great obstacles in the way of Communism in western Europe. There were more Communists in Germany when Hitler became Chancellor, and there are more today in France and Italy, than there were in any Slav country when it became a Russian satellite. Small minorities were able in some countries to do what much larger ones found impossible in others. This circumstance is easily explained—partly by the presence of the Red Army, and partly by the absence of well-organized democratic parties, trade unions and professional bodies in the more backward of the lesser

Slav states. Where the Communists alone are united, disciplined and purposeful, they can, though a small minority, get power easily; but where they are only one political body among many, and are more generally disliked and suspect than the others, they can sometimes be excluded from power even where millions vote for them. In France, for instance, the democrats have been able to quarrel with one another endlessly, though the Communist Party is large and likely long to remain so; they can afford this luxury because they are willing to act together to keep the Communists out of power—and because no war has yet brought the Red Army across the Rhine. The French have long been accustomed to freedom and are among the most ingenious and resolute of European peoples. The large Communist Party in their midst has proved less dangerous to them than the much smaller ones active in the two Slav countries (Russia and Yugoslavia) where the Communists got power mostly by their own efforts.

The western Europeans, including even the Germans and Italians, have—by Russian standards—enjoyed considerable freedom during the last hundred years. Their poorer classes, in spite of two world wars, are much better fed, housed and educated than they were when Marx and Engels wrote their *Manifesto*. Liberalism and democracy have brought great benefits to them, so that they now have much more to lose than their chains. They have also learnt a great deal about the Russian Communists since 1939. For many years, only the Poles, Rumanians and Baltic peoples knew much about them, but they have recently penetrated deep into Europe and have made themselves unpopular everywhere. Even the French, the most insular of civilized peoples, are beginning to know them.

It is much more because the Red Army is strong than because their creed is attractive that the Communists are formidable in Europe. In Asia matters stand differently. There are fewer political traditions there strong enough to withstand the influence of Communism, fewer organized parties with leaders accustomed to the intricacies and subtle conventions of democracy, fewer professional and trade organizations; while the mass of the people are ignorant and desperately poor. It is much more of them than of the Europeans that we can say: they have nothing to lose but their chains.

How can this profit the Communists? What have they to offer but chains? These are questions prompted by what Communism looks like to us, but to the Asian it may look different. The Red Army has gained victories only in Europe, and none but Europeans are acquainted with the blessings of the Soviet peace. The Soviet Union, though it stretches across Europe and Asia, has its centres of power and culture much nearer to us than to the thickly populated and civilized parts of Asia. The tens of thousands of refugees who have fled from Communism have come to our countries and not to Asia to describe how men live where the Communists rule. The highest mountains in the world separate the Soviet Union from India, and vast deserts separate it from China. To the Asians, except in Mongolia and Manchuria, the Russians, since they became the bearers of Communism, have been almost unknown. In Asia, interference from outside is still, very predominantly, interference by the West; so that the cry 'Asia for the Asians,' whenever it is raised—and it was never more popular than today—is raised much more against us than against the Russians. In the eyes of most non-European peoples, it is still the British, the French, and now the Americans, who are the arch-imperialists,[1] the hated white men, the arrogant conquerors and hypocrites who think it their duty to come uninvited to manage the affairs of people whose society they disdain. The Russians have made themselves virtual masters of Manchuria, and the theft has not passed unnoticed by the Chinese; but Red China has meanwhile been engaged in another and for the moment more urgent quarrel, and the people's anger is turned against the West.

The Communists have one great virtue in Asia: they are not afraid of simple and drastic action on a gigantic scale. To the complex and delicate economies of Western Europe such action might do irremediable harm, but in Asia it can bring immediate benefits to millions of people. The Chinese peasants paid rent to landlords who did nothing for them in return, and the

---

[1] I do not like to speak of 'imperialism'; it is a word covering many activities, some good and some bad; and to use it indiscriminately is falsely to suggest that they all amount to much the same thing. It is just another of the words used to make us feel guilty without our knowing what it is we are feeling guilty about. But the fact remains that the word is used indiscriminately and still possesses the emotional overtones given to it by the Marxists; and it is also true that what 'imperialism' there is in Asia (not to speak of Africa) is mostly British or French.

Communists, wherever they went, deprived the landlords of their land. They also imposed taxes on the peasants, collecting them even more efficiently than the landlords their rent; but they did relieve the peasants of the burden that seemed the most unjust. The taxes they levy are mostly used, not to provide themselves with luxuries, but to arm China against the hated foreigner; they can be justified for the present and promises made to reduce them later. Communism is popular in China; though oppressive, it is not felt to be alien. No doubt many, perhaps most, Chinese do not like it. But it is popular in the sense that it is a Chinese movement, depending for its success on the energies, loyalties and ideals of Chinese people. In this sense, the Roundheads were once popular in England and the Jacobins in France, though the historians cannot tell us what most Englishmen and Frenchmen really thought about them. Their ascendancy, however, was not due to the support of foreigners but to the strength they could draw from their own countrymen.

Russian Communism or—to give it its better name—Bolshevism, is a creed in some ways remarkably adapted to the needs of illiterate and poverty stricken peoples brought into contact with western civilization. It does not tell them that they must, being backward, remain eternally subject to the Europeans, or that they cannot hope for real independence until they have become industrially strong, or that the process of acquiring strength is slow and must be controlled by foreigners. Bolshevism offers 'backward' peoples a short cut to equality with the wealthy and arrogant white men; they have only to follow the example of the Russians. According to the Bolsheviks, Imperial Russia, despite her potential wealth, vast size, large army and formal independence, was fast becoming a dependency of the western capitalists, when Lenin and his party, only a few hundred thousand strong, took control of her destiny, shaking her free of the tightening stranglehold of alien capitalism. In a single generation, exhausted though she was by foreign and civil war, she became a country so powerful that all the capitalist states in league against her were yet afraid of her. If this was done by an illiterate and almost prostrate Russia while she was the only proletarian state, might it not be done rather more easily by other nations now that one of the two greatest Powers is proletarian? To follow the road trodden by the Russians might still be painful, but is there another that leads so quickly to independence and prosperity?

Many Asian governments that are not Communist are either corrupt or timid; they will not or dare not take the drastic measures which alone can cure the evils that arise whenever an economically backward people are brought into close contact with western civilization. The vast majority of Asians are so poor that they can scarcely be made poorer, and they have almost no freedom to be taken from them. They have always been oppressed, either by their own rulers and landlords or by the Europeans. Violence and injustice have always been done to them. They have surely nothing to lose, and perhaps, in the long run, much to gain, if they are driven painfully forward by the Communists rather than trodden underfoot by native landlords and European administrators and capitalists?

These arguments are perhaps too simple, but to many Asians they are convincing enough. They know that Communist rule is painful, that it excludes liberty and drives the people harder than anyone drove them before. But they have also heard of its immense achievements in Russia. If the mass of the people are to be lifted out of the squalor they now live in, if independence is to be won or preserved, if Asians are ever to be treated as equals by Europeans, what the West did in several centuries must be done in Asia in two or three generations. For how otherwise can Asia ever draw level with Europe? The slow and patient efforts of the past are no longer enough. If 'backward' and dependent peoples are quickly to be become the equals of prosperous ones, they must make such efforts as the Europeans and North Americans never made. But how can ignorant and poverty-stricken masses be persuaded to make these efforts? Does not the experience of Russia prove that they cannot be persuaded and must be driven? The quick transformation of old and backward societies is a stupendous undertaking. Only men who have the kind of faith that moves mountains will attempt it; and in the modern world that kind of faith is to be found among the Communists alone. Considerations such as these sometimes make even intelligent and gentle Asians educated in the West conclude that only the Communists have courage and self-confidence enough to attempt the tasks that Asia cannot long defer.

Though the Bolsheviks have behaved like tyrants in Europe and have made themselves hated in all the satellite states, it is probably a mistake to suppose that they either wish or will be able to behave in the same way in Asia. They thought it necessary to their security to advance far into Europe, and they had to make sure of the obedience of the small countries that passed into their orbit. Most of these countries were wealthier[1] and more westernized than Russia, and had inside them considerable and influential minorities of democrats, or Catholics, or persons who, if they despaired of democracy, preferred Fascism to Communism. Not one of these countries could be trusted to prefer the Russian alliance to the friendship of the western Powers. The invasion of their country during the Second World War convinced the Russians that they could not be secure unless a large territory to the west of their frontiers were held by governments on whose loyalty they could absolutely rely. They were therefore willing to go to any length, short of provoking a third world war, to ensure that those governments should be loyal, and they could not be known for certain to be loyal unless they were made subservient and Communist. But it is not thought necessary to the security of the Soviet Union that the government of the Chinese republic should be docile to Moscow, and it is, in any case, beyond Russia's power to make it so. The Bolsheviks will get a sufficient reward for the help they give the Chinese and other Communists in Asia in the quarrels which those Communists, of their own accord and unprompted by Moscow, are sure to pick with the 'imperialists' and European 'aggressors.'

True though it may be that what the Russians have made of Communism is more attractive to backward peoples than to the prosperous Europeans and Americans, it does not follow that the victory of Communism in Asia is inevitable. It has so far triumphed only in China, and may never do so in Japan or India. The Japanese turned their country into a great industrial Power long before the Russian kind of Communism became important in the world, and have, except for one short interval, enjoyed independence and stable government for the last hundred years.

---

[1] I have in mind, not industrial production, but the real incomes of peasants and workers. Before 1941 people lived better, on the whole, in the western half of Poland, in much the greater part of Czechoslovakia, in most of Hungary and Rumania, and in the northern provinces of Yugoslavia, than in the Soviet Union.

India and Pakistan have been independent for only a few years, but they, too, have known stable government for several generations. Their present rulers have stepped into the shoes of the British, and are deeply imbued with British notions of government. They are new to the business and therefore not always efficient, but their political assumptions come mostly from Europe. Whether the mass of the people, who are much less affected by European ideas, will trust them for long or ever come to understand them, no one can say; but there is always the chance that they may do so; and if they do, then those rulers may, provided they get generous assistance from the West, be able to bring what the world now calls 'progress' to them by other methods than the Communists use. There were no doubt reasons making the Communist victory especially easy in China. Nevertheless, Asia has less to lose and apparently more to gain than Europe from the Russian brand of Communism.

We often do less than justice to the Communists, not so much when we condemn their methods of government as when we estimate the motives of their international policies. They are not more aggressive than they think it necessary to be in a world where the greater power is still in the hands of their potential enemies. We may say that there was a time, after the common victory over Germany, when we wanted to be friendly with them, but we ought not to be astonished that they find it difficult to believe us. We should remember that their Leninist Marxism teaches them that conflict is inevitable between the middle and working classes, and therefore between bourgeois and proletarian states. That conflict, just as it need not occasion much bloodshed between the classes engaged in domestic strife, so it need not cause war between states dominated by different classes. But the conflict, whatever the form it takes, is inevitable; and it is quite out of the power of the parties to it to bring it to an end. This is still an article of faith with the Communists; it is what they think they know before they even begin to look at the facts. No doubt, they have not been truer to their faith than other people, and have contrived to do and to get many things in spite of it. It is not impossible that this article, too, like some of the others, will eventually be set quietly aside—though not, of course, abandoned. But this has not yet happened.

There are several reasons why it has not done so. The Bolsheviks have been (or at least have felt) obliged to impose heavy sacrifices on the people, which they have had to justify. It was not enough to say that Russia must be industrialized quickly in order to be made socialist, or that the achievements of the revolution would be lost if the kulaks were allowed to retain their wealth and consolidate their position, or that only the boldest and most ruthless policies could prevent the forces of reaction from growing too strong to be repressed and making Russia capitalist. These arguments might seem good to the Bolsheviks, but there was nothing to recommend them to the people generally. What was needed was to persuade the people that, unless Russia grew strong quickly, she must fall an easy victim to the foreigner, so that only the most drastic measures could save her. She must devote all her strength and courage to building up her industries and reforming her agriculture at a speed never before attempted, and she could succeed only if her energies were directed by the state. The Bolsheviks had to persuade the people that Russia was in great danger, with only a few years' grace to gain security by becoming as formidable to her enemies as they were to her. They had to enlist the patriotic sentiments of the people in the cause of socialism. They were not, however, hypocrites, using arguments they did not themselves believe to persuade others. On the contrary, no one believed them more fervently than they did, and they thought they had good reason for doing so. The western governments had intervened against them during the civil war, and had afterwards kept the new Russia at arms' length, treating her with a contempt and a suspicious hostility shown to no other Power. They might, for the time being, let her alone, but when they had recovered from the effects of the war and needed to distract their peoples from domestic troubles, might they not agree among themselves to set upon her—the one member of the European family who chose to be different and whose example was dangerous?

The behaviour of the western Powers towards Hitler did not reassure the Bolsheviks. Here was a man more dangerous to European peace than they had ever been, a man without honour or principle, who had proclaimed fantastic and horrid ambitions even before he became powerful, and who—if ever politician did—looked and spoke like a madman! Here was the most wicked

and nastiest creature that ever ruled a great country! How did the
western governments, so often and so easily shocked by Soviet
brutalities, treat him? With a deference rarely shown to a sane
ruler! Some of them at times even hoped he might lead a crusade
of 'civilized' Europe against the Communist barbarians. When
he broke his word, they hardly dared rebuke him, for fear he
should lose his temper and break it again. They treated this
appalling monster like gentle ladies sometimes treat a rude and
angry man at a tea party, hoping that, if they do not forget their
manners, he will at last remember his. Their disdain, their suspicion, their displays of moral superiority, they reserved for the
Bolsheviks, who never threatened them, nor broke their word,
nor killed anyone except each other. Stalin and his companions
were not men of delicate feelings; they were probably not shocked
either by Hitler's nastiness or by the favourable reactions to it of
so many educated and gentlemanly European politicians. They
did, however, take notice of it, and drew from it the conclusion
that the western governments were inveterate enemies of the
Bolshevik state. These governments had for a time—so thought
the Bolsheviks—hoped that Hitler would invade Russia, or at
least had not cared whether he did so or not. When the Russians
made their pact of non-aggression with Hitler, they believed that
they had served the western Powers as those Powers would have
been only too pleased to serve them.

The war against Hitler did not make real friends of Russia and
the western democracies. Even after the war had begun, Britain
and France appeared to resent the behaviour of the Soviet Government, with whom they were at peace, more than the aggressions
of the enemy. So at least thought the Russians. When the
German armies invaded Poland, Britain and France did nothing
to help their ally, and yet they took it badly when the Soviet
government, always mistrustful of Hitler, occupied the eastern
half of that country, and so prevented Hitler getting the whole of
it. When the Russians, who feared an eventual attack by Hitler
and looked upon Finland as Hitler's future ally, attacked that
country, the western Powers were more indignant than they had
been when first Austria and then Czechoslovakia were occupied;
and yet Russia's demands on Finland were modest, intended only
to increase her own security and not to reduce a free nation to

servitude. When Germany swallowed up Austria and then Bohemia, the whole balance of power in Europe was upset, but it was only slightly affected by the Russian annexation of the Baltic states and the pushing back of Finland's southern frontier a few miles. The Russian aggressions in Poland, the Baltic states and Finland were visibly precautions taken against a too-powerful and no longer sane Germany. But the western powers denounced them as crimes worse than those committed by Hitler. It was apparently intolerable to them that a proletarian state should make demands on anyone, even for the sake of strengthening its frontiers against Germany. All this, together with the inaction of the British and French for almost a year after they had declared war on Germany, seemed to the Russians to prove them hypocrites. It was perhaps even feared in Moscow that they might make peace with Hitler; and, with that prospect to frighten them, the Russians were more than ever anxious to take precautions. When all was said and done, what Great Power really cared about the independence of small states or the survival of democracy in the remoter parts of Europe? What Great Power would risk the life of a single soldier before it felt itself threatened? The Russians believed in the hypocrisy of the British and French. They were not surprised by it, but it did increase their hostility and mistrust.

When the Germans at last invaded Russia, almost the whole burden of the war weighed down upon the Russians. It seemed to them for three long years that no one was really fighting except the Germans and themselves, and that their allies' purpose was to let them exhaust themselves against the common enemy, until they were so much weakened that they could not press their claims strongly when victory came. The real victor in a modern war is not the country that expends itself most to win it, but the country that is fresh and strong when it ends. And later, when the Russians saw that their allies were disposed to be more generous than they had expected, they were not grateful to them; they felt that they were getting only their due. Their gigantic efforts had astonished themselves not less than their allies; they felt virtuous and deserving, and the adulation they now received from people accustomed to despise them, far from softening them, made them arrogant. They felt their superiority, and were determined that others should feel it too. No doubt, they took pleasure in the praise lavished on them, but they also felt the need to be rude to the people who praised them. This is a reaction not uncommon among persons who suddenly become objects of flattery instead of contempt. We have no cause to complain; it is not the moral duty of foreigners, whatever our previous treatment of them, to respond to our friendly advances whenever we choose to make them. We used to despise the Bolsheviks and never troubled to hide our contempt, even in the days of our meekness towards Hitler. For years we dealt with them as with inferiors; and then, all of a sudden, when our enemies became theirs, we decided to treat them as equals. Was this enough to win their friendship or to dispose them to trust us? It may be that they were as convinced of our inferiority as we of theirs, and that nothing has yet happened to make them change their minds.

I have no wish to defend the Bolsheviks, but only to explain what I believe to be their attitude to us. In spite of their stupendous achievements, I find it impossible to admire them; they are as arrogant and as near hypocrisy as anyone, and much more cruel than the western governments. All the enemies of freedom are repulsive, and few more so than those who destroy it for the sake of an ideal they have themselves distorted and debased. What abominable conceit it is to undertake to rule people for their own good, and to do it mercilessly, regardless of their wishes and most cherished beliefs, and in defiance of all common notions of humane and decent conduct! These new tyrannies are worse than anything the world has known before, for they cannot survive except by degrading their subjects, depriving them of self-respect and moral courage, and giving rewards to sycophants, cheats and bullies. The Bolsheviks are not to be defended, but are yet a part of mankind whose behaviour touches us nearly. It is more profitable to understand than to abuse or praise them. Why, indeed, should we abuse them? They, too, are victims of circumstance, and it happens to be easy for them to coerce millions in the service of a cause which to them seems important.

The Bolsheviks believe that we are their enemies. Their philosophy teaches them that it must be so, and our behaviour has ordinarily seemed to confirm what that philosophy teaches. Why did we engage so little with the enemy and husband our resources so carefully until almost the last year of the war, and then expend them lavishly at a time when Germany was already more than half beaten? Why did we, when Russian armies at last occupied most of the smaller countries of eastern Europe, countries whose docile friendship was necessary to Russia's security, show ourselves so anxious that democracy should flourish in regions where it had never existed? We had reasonable answers to these questions, but to the Bolsheviks they did not sound convincing. Not because the Bolsheviks are never amenable to reason, but because the habit of suspicion is so strongly upon them that it is almost out of their power to trust us.

What, then, must we do? Must we despair of peace, and make up our minds to a new war? Must we treat the Russians as enemies? That would be as foolish as to treat them as friends. We have no good reason to believe that they want another war. Everything they have done since 1938 is as easily explained on the assumption that they are seeking to be secure against us as that they mean to attack us. Having defeated Germany—and with much less assistance from their allies than they felt themselves entitled to expect—they are now determined to push the outer line of their defences as far westward as they can. The forces of their potential enemies are, they think, still much greater than their own. They must therefore, if they can, keep their enemies divided and occupied, and must use the Communist Parties of France and Italy to obstruct the western alliance directed against themselves. They no doubt welcome the triumph of Communism in China, but have done less to ensure it than the Americans did in the attempt to prevent it. Since the capitalist Powers are, they think, inevitably their enemies, and since they are still, when united, industrially and even militarily stronger than the Soviet Union and the satellite states, the Bolsheviks deem it mere prudence to make all kinds of trouble for them, domestic and foreign. The control of an international political movement that still claims to be revolutionary is the one great asset possessed by them and denied to their enemies, and they mean to take every advantage of it. That movement is their own peculiar weapon, but the use of it is not war; the more effectively it is used, the less likely—in their opinion—is war. Their hope and intention is, in any case, so to use it that they do not need to fight another great war.

The Bolsheviks are blinded by prejudice but are not without

shrewdness. They know that their control of international Communism makes them seem dangerous to the western Powers, and therefore that the use of their peculiar weapon may unite those Powers against them. On the other hand, they believe that the capitalist half of the world is exposed to recurrent and severe economic crises, causing widespread distress and disorder. The western governments, caught up in some such crisis, might seek relief from it by making war on the Soviet Union. Though the present intentions of these governments may be pacific, there is no relying that they will always be so. While the western nations enjoy as much prosperity as capitalism allows of, there is no need for their governments to contemplate war. Most peoples most of the time, whether their states are bourgeois or not, greatly prefer peace to war. But the crises to which capitalism is liable grow more severe as the years pass, and are therefore more likely than ever to drive bourgeois governments to desperate courses. Soviet Russia, while the larger and richer part of the world remains capitalist, must always be in danger, and therefore always mistrustful and on her guard. She must use the Communist Parties everywhere to weaken and divide her potential enemies, bringing them into war with one another rather than with her. She must, of course, be careful how she uses the Communists. She must not use them to threaten what they are too weak to perform; she must not exhort them to attempt revolution where there is, for the time being, no hope of success. She must not exasperate her potential enemies—who are potential enemies even when they seek to be friends[1]—into union against her; but she must look always to her own security and seek to strengthen Communism everywhere.

The rulers of the Soviet Union, whose empire was shaken to its foundations by Hitler, are probably more interested in security than in anything else. They are probably on the defensive; and yet that defensive is of a kind which can easily pass to offence. They still believe that the western world is capitalist in the old-fashioned Marxian sense of the word, and that it will eventually fall a victim

[1] We need not suppose that the Bolsheviks thought Franklin Roosevelt insincere when he offered America's friendship to them. It is more likely that they doubted his, or anyone else's, ability to establish an enduring alliance between a 'capitalist' and a 'socialist' Power. When the very course of history makes conflict 'inevitable' no well-meaning politician can avert it. Besides, the power of the American President—and his is the most important political office in the West—is short-lived and variable; he can never be sure of being able to carry out his own policies.

to proletarian revolutions; and they perhaps still think it their duty to lend assistance to revolutionaries everywhere, not only for their own security's sake, but to hasten the coming of socialism. Their first leader greatly qualified the historical materialism inherited from Marx and Engels, and they have not abandoned it. Indeed, Lenin's qualifications of it, which they still accept in principle, have served rather to multiply than to reduce the obligations imposed on them by their creed. They do not deny these obligations; and, no doubt, were they to see signs of the imminent collapse of the capitalist economy, they would work hard to hasten it. But at the moment they are probably more impressed by the immense power of their potential enemies than hopeful of their early downfall. They therefore use Communism more to defend themselves than to overthrow the 'bourgeois' states they choose to consider most hostile to them. The present business of Communist parties in the West (though not in Asia and Africa) is almost entirely to prevent an effective alliance against the Soviet Union, and hardly at all to prepare for proletarian revolution.

We must treat the Bolsheviks neither as friends nor as enemies. We cannot treat them as friends because they are still the victims of a creed teaching them that enduring friendship between us and them is impossible. But we need not assume that they mean to make war on us, nor yet that they will, in their endeavours to get security, use methods that make it difficult to avoid war. Lenin believed that the First World War would end with the collapse of capitalism, but Stalin lived to see it survive two such wars; and the Bolsheviks have now against them, in the United States, a country more prosperous and powerful by far than the Hitlerite Germany that nearly defeated them. Though they may still believe in the eventual downfall of capitalism, they have at least as much cause as the western Powers to fear war. Historical materialism does not guarantee that, if they fight, they must win. The final triumph of the proletarian cause is assured, but not the victory of every proletarian state in every war. Just as several abortive revolutions may precede the last and triumphant one, so the first proletarian state may be defeated, and even abolished, before the time has come for the final and decisive victory of the world proletariat. Ever since he defeated Trotsky, Stalin made it his first duty to preserve and strengthen the Soviet Union; he has done nothing to justify the belief that he would risk her destruction in a desperate attempt to make the world Communist by war. He neither preached war to the Russian people nor imposed on them a destiny not to be accomplished except by means of war. He may have thought himself the first servant of the proletariat, and therefore obliged to help them to victory everywhere; but he would not wantonly risk the destruction of the great society he so laboriously built up. He did not mind bloodshed; he did not officiously keep men alive when their living was no use to the cause he had made his own; but he did wish to preserve the new society whose structure is his monument. Like an Egyptian Pharaoh, he would sacrifice tens of thousands of lives to have his building, but his intention was that the building should endure.

The Bolsheviks are the dupes of a false philosophy, and are therefore blind and obstinate. They insist on using an inadequate and obsolete vocabulary to describe the world, and are therefore bound to misdescribe it. They are pedantic, wearisome and rude, almost past endurance. They are abominably cruel. But they are not mad. They make their calculations according to known principles, which, though mistaken, are not altogether unplausible. Because these principles are mistaken, when the Bolsheviks calculate, they ordinarily miscalculate. We cannot hope that they will, while they retain their present philosophy, understand either our society or their own. We must therefore expect to be misunderstood by them, and also mistrusted and disliked. To imagine that we can collaborate with them to establish a solid world order is mere illusion. They believe only in temporary accommodations with us, and while they hold to this belief, nothing more will be possible.

We can, however, since they have a philosophy and are also sane, so behave that it appears to them not worth while to attempt what does not suit our interest. If we avoid industrial crises and maintain a considerable prosperity, the Bolsheviks will not immediately conclude, either that capitalism will endure for ever, or that our society has ceased to be capitalist; they will long continue to expect our ruin and to hope for it; but they will, at least for the time being (having as much cause for fear as for hope), leave our domestic affairs more or less alone, lest a premature attempt to subvert our social order should unite us in war against them. If we contrive to give generous assistance to Asian and African peoples bent on making their economies more productive and their poor less wretched, the Bolsheviks will no doubt predict our failure; but they will also refrain from inciting men to revolution so long as what they have been taught to consider the 'objective conditions' of successful revolution are not sufficiently apparent. We must, in short, knowing how they see our world and interpret it, make it look the sort of place where it would be unprofitable and even dangerous for them to make trouble. We must look formidable to them and yet not seem to threaten their security. We cannot rely on their good will, but we can, if we act wisely, rely on their patience. Their false philosophy teaches them that time is their ally; and the more they can be persuaded to let time pass quietly the better for us and for them.

Let us at least thank God that Hitler is dead, and that the dictators we now have to deal with are sane.

INDEX

Address to the Communist League, The, 116, 127–35, 145, 164, 173, 217, 228, 237, 322

Alexander I, Tsar, 198

Alexander II, Tsar, 198–9, 202

Anti-Dühring, 5–6, 11, 50–1, 54, 56–7, 59–62, 71–2, 108–9, 111

Aquinas, St. Thomas, 306

Aristotle, xix, 14, 306, 311, 313

Attitude of Social-Democracy Towards the Peasant Movement, The, 234

Axelrod, Paul, 203–4

Bakunin, Michael, 119, 119 n., 121

Barrot, Odilon, 166

Bebel, August, 170, 171

Bentham, Jeremy, 315 n

Beria, L. P., 281

Bernstein, Edward, 171–2, 174–7, 184, 317–18

Bielinsky, Vissarion, 200

Bismarck, Otto, Prince von, 168, 317

Blanqui, Auguste, 119–21, 119 n., 126, 162

Bolsheviks, the: their variety of Marxism, 3–4, 7, 134, 163–4, 191, 252 n.; their conflict with the Mensheviks, 37, 192, 204; their attitude to German Social-Democrats, 165, 182–3; their struggle for power, 213–16, 252–61, 304; their party organization, 204–5, 259–60; how power and the struggle for it affected them, 250–61, 272–3, 319–29; their influence outside Russia, 270, 329–42; their present attitude to the West, 342–51; also, 181, 184, 185, 209, *et passim*

Bolshevik Revolution, The, 255, 260 n

Bonaparte, Louis (Napoleon III), 144–5, 160, 162, 168

Brest-Litovsk, Treaty of, 258

Büchner, Ludwig, 201

Burke, Edmund, xx, xxi, 14, 311

Cadets (Constitutional Democrats), the, 206–7, 255

Capital (Das Kapital), 30, 54, 63–5, 70–1, 92, 98–102, 106–8, 111–12, 168

Carr, E. H., 255, 260 n

Catherine II, Tsarina, 194–5, 197

Cheka, the, 260 n

Cicero, xxi

Charles I of England, 208

Civil War in France, The, 116, 156–64, 243, 246–8

Civil War in Russia, the, 256–61

Class Struggles in France, The, 116, 145–6, 164

Commune, the Paris, 156–64, 205, 243, 246–8

Communism in Asia, xiii, 337–42

Communism in Europe (outside Russia), xiii, 263–6, 329–37

Communism in Yugoslavia, 331–3

Communist Manifesto, The, 30, 32, 52–3, 65–6, 71, 91, 105–6, 116–17, 121–8, 131–5, 147–8, 156, 158, 173, 217–18, 312, 337

Communists, the (see Bolsheviks)

Communist International, the, 180, 262, 277 n

Communist League, the, 124–35

Comte, Auguste, 308, 310

Constituent Assembly, the (Russian), 255

Copperfield, David, 234

Critique of the Gotha Programme, The, 114, 156, 164, 247, 289

Critique of Political Economy, The Preface to the, 18–19, 27, 29, 32, 36, 42, 53, 65, 107, 134

Darwin, Charles, 44, 201

De l'Esprit des Lois, 306–7

Dialectical Materialism, 8–17, 18, 61

Dictatorship of the Proletariat, the, 121, 126, 155–6, 243–4, 246, 268–9, 284, 286, 299–300, 301, 322–4, 326–8

Discourse on the Origins of Inequality Among Men, The, 14, 309, 314

Dittmann, 179

Dresden SPD Convention, the, 171

Du Contrat Social, 250 n
Dühring, Eugen, 50-1, 61-2
Durkheim, Emile, xx

Eastman, Max, 16, 289
Ebert, Karl, 183
Eighteenth Brumaire of Louis Bonaparte, The, 116, 144-51, 159, 162, 243-4, 312
Emancipation of Labour Group, the, 204
Emancipation of the Serfs, the, 195-6, 197
Engels, Friedrich: his contribution to Marxism, 5-6, 55; his economic determinism, 56-63, 67 n., 71-3, 139 n,; his conception of classes and the class struggle, 56-9, 136-8, 140-3; his theory of morals, 46-51; his theory of property, 59-61, 108-11, 138-40, 143 n.; his views of capitalist economy, 108-11; his theory of the state, 57-9, 136-44, 151-5, 241-3; his conception of the communist society, 58-9; his views on slavery, 60-1, 139 n., 143; his inclination to 'reformism', 117, 121, 164-7; his inclination to anarchism, 151-5; his influence on German Marxists, 164-7, 169, 174-5, 211; his views on democracy, xv, 154-5, 158; mentioned with Marx as co-author of Marxism, *passim*; also 7, 8, 44, 185
Erfurt Programme, the, 170

Fascism, 330, 341
Federalist, The, xxi
Federn, Karl, 38
Feuerbach, Ludwig, 201
Foundations of Leninism, The, 238 n., 267-70, 275, 278
Fourier, Charles, 118, 119 n., 120, 158, 201
Francis, Emperor of Austria, xi n
Fundamental Problems of Marxism, 67 n

Gallacher, Will, 264
German Ideology, The, 11
German Social-Democratic Party (SPD), the, 3-4, 117, 169-87, 211, 238, 243, 246, 261, 303
Godwin, William, 124, 158
Guchkov, 207

Haase, 179
Hanover SPD Convention, the, 171
Harrington, James, xx
Hegel and Hegelianism, xix, 9-10, 12-17, 35, 44-5, 76, 200, 306, 309-11
Herzen, Alexander, 200

Hilferding, Rudolf, xxii
Historical Materialism, *passim*
Hitler, Adolf, 184, 296, 330, 336, 343-6, 348-9, 351
Hobbes, Thomas, xix, 14, 306, 309-10
Hobson, J. A., xxii n., 221 n
Holy Family, The, 11
Hook, Sidney, 67-70
Hume, David, xx

Imperialism, Marxist Conception of, xxii n., 111-12, 221 n., 239-40, 268-9
Imperialism (by J. A. Hobson), 221 n
Independent Social-Democratic Party, the German (USPD), 179-81, 183, 246
International, the Communist (see under Communist International)
International, the Second, 263 n., 268
Iskra, 204

Jacobins, the, 160, 232, 250 n., 293, 321 n., 339

Kant, Immanuel, 158, 306-7
Kautsky, Karl, 5 n., 171, 246-7
Kerensky, Alexander, 210, 214 n
Kienthal Congress, the, 180
Kronstadt Revolt, the, 260
Kugelmann, Ludwig, 243-4

Labour Party, the British, 324, 334
Lassalle, Ferdinand, 170
Left Opposition, the, 293
Left-Wing Communism, An Infantile Disorder, 263-6
Lenin, Nikolai: his qualities as a theorist, xxi-ii, 221, 221 n., 248-9, 250; his effect on Marxism, 5-7, 221-2, 320-6; his conception of his party's rôle in Russia, 213, 220-2, 224-7, 271-5; his conception of the 'party of the proletariat', 204-5, 222-7, 324-5, 336; his doctrine of 'uninterrupted revolution', 163-4, 228-38, 283-6, 304, 320-2; his conception of "imperialism", xxii n., 221 n., 239-40; his conception of the workers' state, 240-8; his conception of world revolution, 182, 213, 238-40, 253, 303, 325-6; his attitude to democracy, 225-7, 244; his attitude to the peasants, 214-5, 230-5, 253, 253 n.; his attitude to Mensheviks, 204-5, 240, 276 n.; his attitude to German Marxists, 3-4, 180-7, 224 n., 225, 239, 261-2, 323; his advice to western Communists, 263-6; his struggle for

power, 192, 213–16, 252–61; Marx's influence on him, 3–4, 126–8, 134–5, 147, 163–4, 228, 235–7, 241, 243–4, 246–9, 322; his influence on Stalin, 266–79; compared with Trotsky, xxii n., 221 n., 281–8; also, 12, 116, 148, 212, 267 ,291, 299, 301–4
Liebknecht, Karl, 181
Liebknecht, Wilhelm, 164–5, 170
Litvinov (in Turgenev's *Smoke*), 200 n
Locke, John, xiv, xvi, xx, 14, 309–10
Louis XV, 46
Louis XVI, 208
Luxemburg, Rosa, xxii, 181–5

Madison, James, xxi
Malenkov, G., 281
Majority Socialists, the (German), 181–2, 240, 243, 246
Malthus, T., 99, 112
Marashli Ali Pasha, xi
Martov, 204
Marx, Karl: his general philosophy, xix, 9–17, 61, 168; his variety of socialism, 3–6, 44, 48–50, 118–19, 169, 177, 182, 217–19, 241, 278, 306, 309–10, 317–9; his economic determinism, 17–35, 36–9, 55–6, 59, 61–73, 75, 81–7; his conception of classes and the class struggle, 28–35, 39–41, 46–54, 58–9, 90–1, 102–5, 107, 117, 121–35, 144–6, 148–51, 310–13, 326–7; his account of the capitalist economy, 90–108, 111–15; his conception of 'ideology', 41–6, 185, 313–15; his theory of the state, 135–6, 144–52, 241; his conception of the workers' state, 155–64, 243–4, 246–8; his theory of property, 20–8, 30–1, 67–8, 84–6, 108–9; his conception of society, 74–81, 89–90, 315–17; his conception of the communist society, 58–9; his views on 'imperialism', 111–12; his theory of morals, 46–51, 314–17; his conception of revolution, 129–35, 146–7, 174–6, 186–7, 243–4; his conception of class interests, 44, 47–8, 185, 242 n., 273–5, 274 n., 314–15; his views on democracy, xiv–xv, 125–7, 158–9; his inclination to anarchism, 136, 151–2, 155–6; Saint-Simon's influence on him, xvii, 37 n., 308; his influence on Lenin, xxii, 3–4, 126–8, 134–5, 147, 163–4, 228, 235–7, 241, 243–4, 246–9, 322; compared with Lenin, 6–7, 240 n.; compared with other socialists, xvii, 5, 74, 113–21, 308–9; also, 8, 282, 291

Marxism, Is It Science?, 16
Materialist Conception of History, The, 38
Mensheviks, the, their attitude to Bolsheviks, 204, 216, 238, 282–3; their conception of their party's rôle in Russia, 204–5, 210–3, 213 n., 215, 219–21, 254; also, 37, 214, 252, 255, 257, 262, 269, 281, 287, 304, 320
Molotov, V. M., 281
Montaigne, Michel de, 47
Montesquieu, Charles de Secondat, Baron de, xi, xiii–iv, xvi, 16, 306–7, 309–11, 315 n
More, Thomas, 319 n
Munich Agreement, the, 330
Murdstone, Mr. (from *David Copperfield*) 234

Napoleon I, 146–7, 208
Napoleon III (see Bonaparte, Louis)
Narodniki (see Populists)
National Socialists (Nazis), the, 184, 335 n
New Economic Policy, the, 261, 276, 286
New York Daily Tribune, The, 116–17
Nicholas II, Tsar, 205–10
Noske, 183

October Manifesto, the, 205–6
Octobrists, the, 206–7
One Step Forward, Two Steps Back, 226 n., 265
On the Road to October, 275
Origin of the Family, Private Property and the State, The, 61 n., 136–44
Orleanists, the, 130, 145
Organisateur, L', 308
Our Differences of Opinion, 203
Owen, Robert, 113, 117 n., 120, 158

Pankhurst, Sylvia, 264
Partisans, the Yugoslav, 332
Party of Order, the, 145
Paul, Tsar, 194
Persian Letters, The, xi
Peter the Great, Tsar, 153 n., 193–5, 198–9
Peter III, Tsar, 193
Petrograd Soviet, the, 210, 216
Plato, xix, 9, 12, 14, 306–7, 311, 319 n
Plekhanov, George, 5 n., 67 n., 203–4, 211, 217–19, 221 n., 227, 238
Populists, the, 201–3, 217, 219, 227
Potressov, 204
Potugin, S. I. (in Turgenev's *Smoke*), 200 n

Problems of Leninism, 267, 270–1, 275, 278
Proletarian Revolution and the Renegade Kautsky, The, 263
Proudhon, P. J., 119–21, 119 n., 160, 162, 201
Provisional Governments, the (Russian), 209–12 214–15, 253–4
Provisional Government, The (article by Lenin), 238 n
Pugachov, Emelyan, 195

Red Army, the, 258–60, 336–7
Revisionists and Revisionism, 171–2, 174–5, 174 n., 178, 184, 224 n
Revolution Betrayed, The, 289ff
Revolution and Counter-Revolution in Germany, 118, 145, 159
Ricardo, David, 90, 306
Robespierre, Maximilien de, 236, 250 n., 283, 293
Roosevelt, Franklin, 348 n
Roundheads, the, 339
Rousseau, Jean-Jacques, xiv–xvii, xx, 14–16, 76, 158, 250 n., 306–11, 314–15, 315 n
Russian Social-Democratic Party, the, 204, 206, 222, 282, 286–7, 320–2 (see also Bolsheviks and Mensheviks)

Saint-Just, Louis-Antoine, 283
Saint-Simon, Claude-Henri Comte de, his influence on Marx and Marxism, xvii, 16–17, 153–5, 308, 311, 313–14; also, xiv–v, xx, 5, 41 n., 66 n., 74–6, 79, 82, 89 n., 118–19, 119 n., 120, 124, 158, 309–11
Scheidemann, 183
Schelling, F. G. J., 200
Slavophiles, the, 200–2
Smith, Adam, xx
Smoke, 200 n
Socialist-Revolutionary Party, the (Russian), 202, 206, 210, 211 n., 214–16, 252–3, 269, 320, 323
Socialism, Scientific and Utopian, 6, 71
Socialism and the Political Struggle, 203
Spartacus League, the, 181, 183, 185–6, 261
Spencer, Herbert, 201
Staël, Madame de, 307 n
Stakhanovism, 295
Stalin, Joseph: his contribution to Marxism, 5, 7–8; as interpreter of Lenin, 266–79; his conception of the 'party of the proletariat', 270–5, 279; his views on 'socialism in one country', 275–9, 290; his views on

world revolution, 277; his quarrel with Trotsky, 275–8, 304; Trotsky's account of him and his policies, 289–90, 292–301; his foreign policy, 349–50; also 233, 238 n., 241, 250–1, 332
Stalin Constitution, the, 296, 300–1
Stalinism and Stalinists, 279–80, 289–90, 292–303
State and the Revolution, The, 240–8, 253 n., 261
Stolypin, 207–8

Tennyson, Alfred, 252 n
Thermidor, the 9th, 293
Theses on Feuerbach, 11
Tito, J. B., 331
Tocqueville, Alexis de, xx
Towards an Understanding of Karl Marx, 67
Trotsky, Leo: his contribution to Marxism, 5, 7–8; his place among Mensheviks, 205, 221 n., 281–3, 287; his place among Bolsheviks, 286–8; his conception of 'uninterrupted revolution', 233, 277 n., 283–6, 289, 304; his views on world revolution, 276–7, 290, 303–4; his views on 'socialism in one country', 276–7, 290; his views on democracy, 291–2, 296–301; his account of the Red Army, 295–6; his quarrel with Stalin, 275–8, 304; his account of Stalinism, 289–305; compared with Lenin, xxii, 221 n., 281–8; also, x, 241, 249
Trudoviki, the, 206
Two Tactics of Social Democracy in the Democratic Revolution, 228–31, 235, 284–5, 304

Ustashi, the, 331
Utopian Socialists, xviii, 44, 118–19, 123, 126

Versailles, Treaty of, 330
Vogt, Karl, 201
Vorwärts, 164–5

Westerners, the, 200–2
What Is To Be Done? 222–7, 265
White Guards, the (or the 'Whites'), 258–60, 291, 305
William II, Kaiser, 177
Witte, Count, 207

Zasulich, Vera, 203–4
Zimmerwald Congress, the, 180
Zinoviev, Gregory, 262